'The referendum was clear: the British people voted to leave the single market and to take back control of our borders.'

Nigel Farage

'There must be no attempts to remain inside the EU, no attempts to rejoin it through the back door, and no second referendum.'

Theresa May

'My role as the Labour prime minister would be to ensure that [another referendum] is carried out in a fair way, that the offers put are fair, and that I will carry out the result of that referendum.'

Jeremy Corbyn

'Every day we let this Brexit mess go on means less money being invested in the UK, fewer jobs being created and less tax revenue to pay for our public services.'

Jo Swinson

'We've got the deal. It's oven ready. Vote Conservative tomorrow to get Brexit done'.

Boris Johnson

'I think ... that we can turn the tide within the next 12 weeks and I'm absolutely confident that we can send the corona virus packing in this country.'

Boris Johnson

'The return of the virus and the return of restrictions were not an Act of God. They are a failure of government.'

Keir Starmer

Brexit Britain

In June 2016, more than 17 million people voted for Britain to leave the European Union. The fallout of this momentous referendum has been tumultuous and unpredictable. Now, from the authors of the highly acclaimed *Brexit: Why Britain Voted to Leave the European Union* (Cambridge University Press, 2017), comes the definitive guide to the transformation of British politics in the years following the Brexit vote. By charting the impact of Brexit on three major elections – the 2017 and 2019 general elections as well as the 2019 European Parliament elections – this book reveals the deeper currents reshaping modern Britain. The authors draw upon many years of unique and unprecedented data from their own surveys, giving key insights into how and why Brexit has changed British electoral politics. The book is written in a clear and accessible style, appealing to students, scholars and anyone interested in the impact of Brexit on Britain today.

Paul Whiteley's research interests include electoral behaviour, public opinion, political parties, political economy and methodology in the social sciences. He is a Fellow of the British Academy and a Fellow of the Academy of Social Sciences. He is the author or co-author of some twenty books and more than 100 articles in academic journals and a frequent blogger on British and comparative politics.

Harold D. Clarke was Ashbel Smith Professor in the School of Economic, Political, and Policy Sciences at the University of Texas at Dallas. His significant contributions to knowledge about people's political support and their valence (performance)-based evaluations informing electoral choice, and about research methodology applications were enabled by multiple research awards as well as numerous research publications. These include the Social Sciences and Humanities Research Council (Canada), the Economic and Social Research Council (UK), and the National Science Foundation (US), as well as Cambridge University Press, Oxford University Press and other major publishers and professional journals.

Matthew Goodwin is the author of several books including *Revolt on the Right*, which won the 2014 Political Book of the Year award, and *National Populism*, which was a *Financial Times* book of the year and a *Sunday Times* bestseller. He also won the PSA Richard Rose Prize and has a strong following on social media @GoodwinMJ

Marianne C. Stewart is a Professor in the School of Economic, Political and Policy Sciences at the University of Texas at Dallas. Her research contributions to knowledge about people's political attitudes and their political participation have been facilitated by multiple research awards and professional publications. These include the Economic and Social Research Council (UK) and the National Science Foundation (US), the university presses of Cambridge and Oxford, and the *American Journal of Political Science*, the *American Political Science Review* and the *British Journal of Political Science*.

Brexit Britain

The Consequences of the Vote to Leave the European Union

Paul Whiteley

University of Essex

Harold D. Clarke

University of Texas, Dallas

Matthew Goodwin

University of Kent, Canterbury

Marianne C. Stewart

University of Texas, Dallas

CAMBRIDGE
UNIVERSITY PRESS

Shaftesbury Road, Cambridge CB2 8EA, United Kingdom

One Liberty Plaza, 20th Floor, New York, NY 10006, USA

477 Williamstown Road, Port Melbourne, VIC 3207, Australia

314–321, 3rd Floor, Plot 3, Splendor Forum, Jasola District Centre,
New Delhi – 110025, India

103 Penang Road, #05–06/07, Visioncrest Commercial, Singapore 238467

Cambridge University Press is part of Cambridge University Press & Assessment,
a department of the University of Cambridge.

We share the University's mission to contribute to society through the pursuit of
education, learning and research at the highest international levels of excellence.

www.cambridge.org
Information on this title: www.cambridge.org/9781108496445

DOI: 10.1017/9781108677639

First published 2023

Printed in the United Kingdom by TJ Books Limited, Padstow Cornwall

A catalogue record for this publication is available from the British Library.

*A Cataloging-in-Publication data record for this book is available from the Library
of Congress.*

ISBN 978-1-108-49644-5 Hardback
ISBN 978-1-108-73379-3 Paperback

Contents

Figures

Tables

Foreword

Brexit Britain is a book is about the choices that people, parties and politicians make, and the consequences that follow from these in turbulent times. More precisely, the book is about the choices that people make as voters, and that parties and leaders make as vote seekers and policymakers in turbulent times. This book builds on the previously published book *Brexit: Why Britain Voted to Leave the European Union* by Clarke, Goodwin and Whiteley.[1]

In the *Brexit* book the authors explored what led more than 17 million people, in 2016, to vote to leave the European Union. It showed why many of the factors that led people to vote for Brexit, and that delivered the surprising success of the Leave campaign, had been 'baked in' long before the referendum campaign even began. It also showed how these Brexit voters had clear and coherent motives for voting to leave, including their concerns about national sovereignty and immigration.

However, at the time of its writing, neither the authors – nor anyone else for that matter – had the prescience to see what was to come. Leaving the EU would become a difficult and tortuous process that plunged the country into one of the most serious and protracted political and constitutional crises in modern history. Leaving the EU would also lead to the United Kingdom adopting a 'hard' version of Brexit that will continue to stoke controversies for years to come. These controversies include the potential independence of Scotland, where people voted overwhelmingly to remain in the European Union, and forging a new relationship between the United Kingdom and the EU with ongoing concerns over security and peace in Northern Ireland.

For these reasons, it became clear, in the time between the vote for Brexit in 2016 and Boris Johnson's electoral triumph in 2019, that a sequel to the *Brexit* book was in order. This sequel, *Brexit Britain*, has three principal and related objectives. First, it examines the long-running process of Brexit, particularly the years of turmoil which followed the

---

[1] Clarke, Goodwin and Whiteley (2017).

referendum vote and witnessed many twists and turns in the negotiations between the UK and the EU. Second, we study how the political turmoil that was unleashed by the Brexit vote shaped all three of the major nationwide elections in 2017, the spring of 2019 and the winter of 2019, producing major changes with significant consequences.

As we show in this book, this sequence of elections brought about the rise and fall of Jeremy Corbyn and the Labour Party, and the success of Boris Johnson and the pro-Brexit Conservative Party. As a result, they helped to produce what Members of Parliament had been unable to achieve – an outcome to the negotiations between the UK and the EU, with the final departure of the UK from the European Union on 31 January 2020. Thus, the country has been pushed in a fundamentally different direction, namely out of the European Union and into a so-called 'Global Britain'. In sum, the bases of electoral politics, political geography and political behaviour have changed in fundamental ways, while British politics has become increasingly polarized.

The third objective of *Brexit Britain* involves investigation of how the themes of change, choice, consequence and performance play in explanations of how short-term and longer-term forces have been at work during these tumultuous years. As we show, these choices have dynamic properties, that is, they change in the short – and longer-terms, as events and issues evolve, and as new information becomes available.

These choices are also influenced by, as we will see, what is known among political scientists as 'valence politics'.[2] Valence politics involves issues about which there is widespread agreement among people and parties about what the policy goals are, but disagreement about how to achieve them. Thus, people form evaluations of how well or badly an issue has developed and how the party-in-government has handled it, and these evaluations shape electoral choices. Typical examples of valence issues are economic growth combined with low inflation and unemployment, high-quality and accessible healthcare, protection from threats to physical security posed by rogue regimes, terrorists and criminals, and environmental quality. In the British case, several such issues have come to the fore in the time period covered by this book, that is, the period bracketed by the Brexit referendum in 2016 and the arrival of the Covid-19 pandemic in early 2020. In this book, we show how valence politics has had a profound impact on the country's politics.

We approach these three objectives by organizing the book in three parts. The first part focuses on short-term effects during the period from

---

[2] On valence politics theory, see Stokes (1992) and especially Clarke, Sanders, Stewart and Whiteley (2004) and Whiteley, Clarke, Sanders and Stewart (2013).

the referendum up to and including the 2019 European and general elections. The part consists of five chapters. Chapter 1 examines the political events which followed the shockwaves generated by the vote to leave the EU through to Theresa May's loss of her majority in the 2017 general election.

Chapter 2 continues the story by charting the major events during the Brexit negotiations from the aftermath of the 2017 general election through to the outcome of the 2019 general election. These propelled Boris Johnson into power and set the stage for the delivery of Brexit. Chapters 3, 4 and 5 then drill down into detail about each of the three elections that involved: the 2017 general election, the Spring 2019 European Parliament election and finally the December 2019 general election.

Part II takes a step back to examine three major and related developments involving longer-term changes and their effects, both across time and space, which have helped to produce the Brexit outcome. This has three chapters. Chapter 6 focuses on the decline of social class as a determinant of electoral choice and the rise of age-related politics. Ever since the path-breaking study by David Butler and Donald Stokes in 1969,[3] the 'class cleavage' has dominated much research on voting in Britain. This cleavage typically has been measured by support for Labour among voters in working-class occupations and support for the Conservatives in middle-class occupations. However, the influence of social class measured in this way was never as strong as Butler and Stokes claimed, something clearly revealed by their panel surveys which re-interviewed the same voters at multiple points in time. That said, there is a broader conception of class, described as the Human Development Index, which includes additional measures going beyond narrowly defined occupational status. This does have a considerable impact on electoral support at the constituency level. However, and as we show in this chapter, narrowly defined class politics has largely disappeared at the level of the individual voter. It has been replaced by the new age/education cleavage whose origins and effects are explored in Chapter 6.

Chapter 7 examines a second development of importance, the geographic fragmentation of electoral choice at the level of the different countries that form that the United Kingdom, and in particular the specific context of England. This fragmentation is well illustrated by the fact that Scotland and Northern Ireland voted to remain in the EU referendum whereas England and Wales voted to leave. Similar divisions also are apparent across the English regions. Since the referendum,

---

[3] Butler and Stokes (1969).

fragmentation and polarization have been sharply exacerbated by Brexit and the continuing controversies it has caused.

In Chapter 8, we take a look at how these two and other developments pose a threat to government accountability. Accountability means that voters form evaluations of how well or badly a government delivers the policies that people want, and these evaluations inform electoral choices. Accountability is a critical part of the process of democratic governance, and it is closely linked to the theory of valence politics. A number of developments in politics and the economy suggest that the ability of governments to deliver on key valence issues is now at risk. In an especially fragmented polity and society, accountability can be difficult to achieve. In addition to the two longer-term developments described above, there are other developments. There is a large number of people who feel left behind in the economy and society, and many of them voted to leave the EU in the referendum. The capacity of governments to satisfy voter expectations has also been challenged by the forces of globalization, European integration, the marketization of public services and growing social inequality. In Chapter 8, we look at government accountability for management of the economy, which is a key valence issue. Our finding that accountability is 'alive and well' in British politics challenges pessimistic views expressed by the critics of the processes associated with contemporary democracy.[4]

Part III looks to the future by exploring the economic and political fallout from the Brexit vote. Chapter 9 broadens the analysis by considering the impact of Brexit on the economy more generally. We address whether Brexit has the potential to reduce innovation and economic growth in the future. A key issue in evaluating this possibility is to try to untangle the effects of Brexit from the effects of the Covid pandemic, and this is done by looking at data over a long period of time. The conclusion is that the pandemic really overshadows the effects of Brexit, although this may change in the future.

In Chapter 10, we investigate the effect of Brexit, together with the pandemic on changes in support for the Conservative Party and for Prime Minister Boris Johnson. The chapter also looks more broadly at the effects of Brexit on the political system. This involves investigating citizen satisfaction with the performance of democracy, and also their trust in political institutions such as Parliament and the political parties. A third issue examined in the chapter is the threat to the unity of the United Kingdom posed by Scottish independence.

---

[4] See, e.g., Achen and Bartels (2016).

The Postscript at the end of the book summarizes our central conclusions. In brief, we show that, although Brexit has had and will continue to have disruptive consequences, it is not the disaster claimed by many commentators. The previously published *Brexit* book showed that, if Britain had not joined the European Union in the first place, it would have made little difference to the country's economic prosperity, its international influence, and the longer-term trends shaping electoral politics. This conclusion is largely reinforced by the findings in this book. And, although Brexit has been a highly divisive and occasionally traumatic experience for many, leaving the EU will not affect the reality that Britain's future continues to hinge on the choices made by its people, parties and politicians.

This is particularly true in a situation in which further European integration has stalled. The European Union currently faces a serious threat to its fundamental values, such as the rule of law, from its own member states in Eastern Europe, and an economic divide which is growing between northern and southern states. The EU is limited in what it can achieve, because of the heterogeneity of the countries that comprise it, and the fact that these countries are unlikely to cede significant sovereignty to Brussels in the foreseeable future. The EU's accomplishments in terms of economic prosperity and general security are also limited by the fact that it remains largely a regulatory entity, rather than a sovereign state.

Finally, for all readers, including those not familiar with the theories and methods used in this type of research, the book has been written with the general reader in mind. The figures and tables are presented in a very accessible way that allows readers to follow the arguments without having to know technical details. For those readers who want details about the survey methodology and the statistical methods used in the analyses, they can consult the two appendices.

Acknowledgements

We wish to take this opportunity to acknowledge the assistance of individuals and organizations that helped to make *Brexit Britain* a reality. The analyses in this book rely heavily on data from several representative national surveys of the British electorate that we have conducted since 2015. These data are crucial for understanding the attitudes and the behaviours of the British electorate during the tumultuous Brexit era – an era now overlaid by the Covid-19 pandemic. Funding provided by the British Academy of Social Sciences, the National Science Foundation, the University of Essex and the University of Texas at Dallas has made it possible for us to conduct these surveys. In addition, we have been very fortunate to have the assistance of Joe Twyman, formerly Head of Political and Social Research at YouGov and now Co-Founder and Director at Deltapoll. Since first working with us as part of the British Election Study, 2001–2010, Joe has continued to provide us with his valuable experience.

We also acknowledge colleagues and friends who have shared insights and knowledge with us throughout the years. In particular, we thank Janet Box-Steffensmeier, David Cutts, Russell Dalton, Roger Eatwell, Euel Elliott, Robert Ford, Jeff Gill, Jim Granato, Oliver Heath, Karl Ho, Jim Hollifield, Matt Lebo, Larry LeDuc, Michael Lewis-Beck, Caitlin Milazzo, Helmut Norpoth, Jon Pammett, Charles Pattie, David Sanders, Tom Scotto, Pat Seyd, Guy Whitten, and Stan Wong. A special tribute is due to the late Allan McCutcheon whose work on latent class models gave us the methodological leverage needed to understand the dynamics of party support in Britain and in other mature democracies.

Also deserving grateful recognition is Jennifer Holmes, Dean of the School of Economic, Political and Policy Sciences at the University of Texas at Dallas. She has consistently given strong support to Clarke and to Stewart. Also at UTD, Karl Ho and Russell Hoffman have provided valuable technical assistance, and John Eaton and Furkan Zengin have done excellent work as graduate research assistants. Colleagues in the

School of Politics and International Relations at the University of Kent also deserve our grateful recognition.

For their willingness to extend opportunities for Clarke to share our research results in presentations and seminars with others, we acknowledge Mebs Kanji, Director of the Workshops in Social Science Program at Concordia University, and Royce Carroll, Director of the Essex Summer School in Social Science Data at Essex University. Laura Hood, editor at *The Conversation*, and Chris Gilson, editor at the *LSE Politics and Policy* blog have expressed much-appreciated interest in articles written by Clarke, Stewart and Whiteley on British politics during the Brexit era and on related topics. And Sarah Baxter and Martin Ivens at the *Sunday Times* have provided Goodwin with occasions to share some of his research. Matt also extends much appreciation to his wife Fiona and their daughter Grace.

Finally, but not least, we are pleased to acknowledge the assistance, including valuable advice and continuing interest in our work, of John Haslam, Executive Publisher for Political Science at Cambridge University Press. John waited patiently while we continued our research as the 'battle of Brexit' extended much longer than anticipated. And, we also thank two anonymous reviewers for Cambridge University Press for their helpful comments on the manuscript.

Paul Whiteley
Harold D. Clarke
Matthew Goodwin
Marianne C. Stewart

Note to Readers: Harold made enormous contributions to this book in terms of its design, data collection and analysis, and writing, and he strongly wished its completion. We are very pleased to fulfil his wish and, since his death on 11 January 2022, we have much missed his humour, intellect and perseverance. Throughout his professional career, Harold, either individually or collaboratively, made significant contributions to knowledge and understanding of the contingent nature of public support in a representative democracy, and to the performance evaluations that many people bring to their electoral choices in Britain, Canada, Taiwan and the United States.

Paul, Matt, and Marianne

Part I

The Short Term

1   Welcome to Brexit Britain

On 23 June 2016, the United Kingdom held a referendum on its forty-three-year membership in the European Union (EU). People were asked whether they wanted to remain in or leave the EU. At twenty minutes to five on the morning of 24 June 2016, the BBC television presenter David Dimbleby turned to the millions of people watching the results at home: 'We can now say the decision taken in 1975 by this country to join the common market has been reversed by this referendum to leave the EU. We are absolutely clear now that there is no way that the Remain side can win.'

Contrary to virtually all forecasts, a majority of people had voted to leave the club. A few hours later, Conservative Prime Minister David Cameron, who had gambled his premiership and the future of the United Kingdom by calling the referendum, resigned. Standing in front of Number 10 Downing Street, Cameron looked directly into the camera and said:

I was absolutely clear about my belief that Britain is stronger, safer and better off inside the EU. I made clear the referendum was about this, and this alone, not the future of any single politician, including myself. But the British people made a different decision to take a different path. As such, I think the country requires fresh leadership to take it in this direction.

Some prime ministers are only remembered for one thing. Although Cameron was the youngest prime minister in nearly two centuries and a leader who had sought to 'modernize' the Conservative Party, none of that mattered now. In the history books, he would be remembered as the prime minister who had set the stage for Brexit, for the UK to become the first major power to leave the EU and for opening the door to a period of domestic political turbulence that is without precedent in recent history.

In the months and years that followed, the battle over Brexit would grip the country and much of the world. What began with that shock vote to leave in 2016 quickly spiralled into an intense, unpredictable, polarizing and protracted political battle that would rumble on for nearly five years;

3

through fierce debates in Parliament and Brussels, through three nation-wide elections that revived and replayed the Brexit debate. This involved an almost complete implosion of one of the world's most stable two-party systems, through a resurgence of public support for national populism, and through the formation of entirely new political parties, to the meteoric rise of Boris Johnson. It encompassed a dramatic collapse of Jeremy Corbyn's Labour Party and the arrival of an altogether different crisis in the form of the Covid-19 global pandemic, before, finally, culminating in January 2021, when the UK eventually exited the EU.

Yet even today, for reasons that we will explore, the battle over Brexit is still not over. While its impact still lingers in the realignment of electoral and party politics, both its causes and consequences will continue to be debated and dissected for decades to come. All of this raises a set of profound questions that we will explore in the pages ahead.

Why did so many people vote for Brexit? What factors determined the outcome of the various elections which shaped the battle over Brexit, including the 2017 and 2019 general elections and the 2019 elections to the European Parliament? How did these events reflect the changing political loyalties and behaviour of British voters? And what longer-term impacts might Brexit have on the country's political parties, political geography, voters and political system more widely?

In this chapter, we provide an introduction to the themes discussed in more detail in subsequent chapters, beginning by exploring what motivated the initial vote in 2016 and then considering how this vote affected three areas: political parties, public opinion and Parliament. This chapter sets the scene for the rest of the book, examining events from the referendum through to Theresa May's failure to win a parliamentary majority at the general election in 2017. The chapter that follows then discusses the events which gave rise to Boris Johnson's leadership of the Conservative Party, and his party's victory in the 2019 general election and the eventual delivery of Brexit. Along the way, we will take a step back to reflect on what we have learned about why so many people voted to leave the EU, the key events and negotiations that followed the result, and wider trends in public opinion, all of which provide the context for the elections to come.

Drawing on data gathered in a series of national surveys we conducted between 2015 and 2021, the chapters which follow examine in detail what shaped the outcome of these elections, which pushed the country toward Brexit, Boris Johnson and, finally, out of the EU. By the time our journey concludes, readers will have a detailed view of how the Brexit battle unfolded, the forces that shaped it and how it continues to impact the world around us.

Voting Brexit

In the shadow of the referendum, it was often heard that the people who voted to leave the EU 'had not known what they were voting for'. Yet in the years that followed, this claim was undermined by the findings of a large number of academic studies that examined in detail why 17.4 million people voted to overturn the status quo by pulling the country out of the European Union.

In the earlier book, *Brexit: Why Britain Voted to Leave the European Union*, which was published in the immediate aftermath of the vote in 2017, we drew on data from large-scale nationally representative surveys to examine the dynamics of the vote in detail.[1] Contrary to popular claims, we demonstrated how Brexit was not driven by one specific factor alone, or what took place during the referendum. Instead, the result reflected what we called 'a complex and cross-cutting mix of calculations, emotions and cues'.

Of particular importance for most Leavers were their intense concerns about the loss of national sovereignty as a result of EU membership, their desire to regain control over what they saw as a malfunctioning immigration system, and their frustration at being left behind by the economic transformation of the country, which they felt had become far too dependent upon the EU. In conclusion, we wrote that:

> it is important to recognize that a number of the forces that ultimately led to Brexit were operating for more than a decade before the referendum … there was no one single factor that shaped how people thought about EU membership. Rather, since at least 2004 the public's views about EU membership have been shaped by their assessment of how the governing parties were performing on key issues, especially immigration and, to a lesser extent, the economy and the NHS. People's anxieties about how immigration flows into the country had been managed alongside worries about a perceived loss of economic control to Brussels directly cultivated support for Brexit. While the 2016 campaign may have changed some people's minds and motivated them to cast a ballot, when it came to the fundamental question of whether to vote for Brexit, a number of key attitudes and beliefs were already in place.

In contrast to explanations that focus narrowly on things such as social media or who said what during the campaign, we demonstrated how the core motives for voting Brexit had been 'baked in' long before David Cameron called the referendum, in 2013. The belief that being a member of the EU was eroding sovereignty, that rapidly rising immigration from Central and Eastern Europe was damaging the economy and culture and that people were being left behind were all visible long before the referendum.

---

[1] Clarke, Goodwin and Whiteley (2017). See also Clarke, Goodwin and Whiteley (2019).

Furthermore, we showed how people's calculations of risk played a crucial background role in shaping their decision at the ballot box. If they believed being a member of the EU undermined sovereignty, that immigration was mainly having negative effects and they were being left behind, then they were much less likely to see Brexit as a major risk and more likely to roll the dice. None of this is to say that the events of the campaign did not matter. If people felt positively about the two most prominent Brexiteers, Boris Johnson and Nigel Farage, who provided them with powerful cues to vote Leave, then they were nudged toward Brexit. Yet, powerful drivers had been years if not decades in the making.

Since publishing our book, these findings have been confirmed by other studies. Most share a general consensus that the two key drivers flagged in our study, namely people's worries over a loss of sovereignty and uncontrolled immigration, were, by far, the most powerful drivers of the vote to leave.[2] John Curtice found that Leavers were driven strongly by a sense that EU membership and the large-scale immigration that accompanied it threatened Britain's distinctive identity. Sara Hobolt found that support was most heavily concentrated among less well educated and older voters who felt intensely concerned about the effects of immigration and multiculturalism. Matthew Goodwin and Caitlin Milazzo found that, even after accounting for other factors, concern over immigration was a major predictor of whether or not people voted Leave. And several other studies have also pointed to the role of deep-rooted value divides between liberal-minded and typically younger graduates who voted Remain and more culturally conservative and typically middle-aged or older non-graduates who feel more attached to their national identity, more opposed to the EU and more concerned about the ongoing impact of large-scale immigration, all of which led them to vote against the status quo and for Leave.[3]

It is also worth pointing out that this is what Leavers said themselves, when they were asked to explain their motivation in their own words. When YouGov asked Leavers why they had voted to leave the European Union, the most popular answer was 'to strike a better balance between Britain's right to act independently, and the appropriate level of co-operation with other countries', followed by 'to help us deal better with the issue of immigration'. When Lord Ashcroft asked them the same question, the most popular answers were: 'The principle that decisions about the UK should be taken in the UK', followed by 'A feeling that

---

[2] See e.g., Curtice (2017), p. 55; Goodwin and Milazzo (2017); Carl, Dennison and Evans (2019); Fieldhouse et al. (2021).
[3] See, e.g., Solobewska and Ford (2021).

voting to leave the EU offered the best chance for the UK to regain control over immigration and its own borders'. When the British Election Study investigators asked the same question, they found that sovereignty and immigration were again the two most frequently cited reasons. They pointed out that: 'These results show that while the single largest word that Leavers say is "immigration", they were actually more likely to mention sovereignty related issues overall.'

The clear picture portrayed by these analyses is that Leavers are concerned primarily about sovereignty and immigration. In fact, reading responses shows that many respondents mention both sovereignty and immigration together, showing that these two issues were closely linked in the minds of British voters.[4] And when the Centre for Social Investigation at the University of Oxford likewise asked Leavers to rank their motives, they selected: (1) to regain control over EU immigration; (2) 'I didn't want the EU to have any role in UK law-making'; (3) 'I didn't want the UK sending any more money to the EU'; and, in a distant fourth, 'I wanted to teach British politicians a lesson.'[5]

Much of the evidence on factors prompting the Leave vote that has been collected since the referendum, therefore, tells a consistent and coherent story. As our original analysis suggested, Leavers were mainly motivated by their desire to restore national sovereignty and acquire greater control over immigration.

Aftermath: Party Politics, Polls and Parliament

While the underlying cause of the Leave vote has attracted much attention, so too has its consequences. The outcome of the referendum soon had a major impact on three areas of the country's political life: on party politics, the polls and Parliament. The most immediate impact was visible in the world of partisan politics where the two major parties, the Conservatives and Labour, were thrown into turmoil.

David Cameron was promptly replaced as leader of the Conservative Party and, by extension, prime minister. His replacement was 60-year-old Theresa May, the former Home Secretary who, unlike 138 of her fellow Conservative MPs and 6 in 10 Conservative voters, had supported Remain, albeit while keeping a low profile throughout the referendum campaign. Indeed, May and her team even went out of their way to let it

---

[4] www.britishelectionstudy.com/bes-findings/what-mattered-most-to-you-when-deciding-how-to-vote-in-the-eu-referendum/#.Ybn6R73P39M
[5] CSE Brexit 4: 'People's Stated Reasons for Voting Leave or Remain', Centre for Social Investigation, Nuffield College.

be known that they did not believe the world would end if people voted to leave. While this reflected May's political pragmatism, it also owed much to the fact that she had never been especially animated by the Europe question, as one of her key advisors and speechwriters recalls.

'I think that she felt the whole thing was a bit of a distraction', said Chris Wilkins.

You know, she always pragmatically – not with a huge amount of enthusiasm, but pragmatically – felt that we had to be around the table. And that meant staying in … She was always on the pragmatic Remain side. In all the years I've known her – I started working for Theresa in 2000/2001 – I'd never really heard her express a view about Europe, particularly. It just wasn't high on her political agenda.[6]

In the end, Theresa May won her party's brief leadership contest after setting out a clear and direct position on Europe and while watching her main rivals, notably Boris Johnson and Michael Gove, implode on the leadership campaign trail. She was eventually crowned leader when her last remaining rival, Andrea Leadsom, withdrew from the race after making ill-advised comments about the benefits of being a mother (May had no children). For only the second time in history, the country had a female prime minister.

It also had a prime minister who was now committed to seeing through Brexit. Keenly aware that she would be leading a strongly pro-Brexit party that would be instinctively suspicious of a leader who had supported Remain, and in a country where a majority of the electorate had just voted to depart from the EU, May quickly doubled down on her pro-Brexit credentials. She pledged repeatedly that 'Brexit Means Brexit' and warned repeatedly against any attempt to undermine or re-run the referendum, as had happened following earlier referendums in Denmark in 1992–1993, Ireland in 2001–2002 and again in Ireland in 2008–2009.

There must be no attempts to remain inside the EU, no attempts to re-join it through the back door and no second referendum. The country voted to leave the European Union and it is the duty of the government and parliament to make sure that we do just that.[7]

She also categorically ruled out a fresh general election.

The Conservatives were not the only ones thrown into disarray. In the aftermath of the referendum, the Labour Party also imploded as the party was rocked by not one but two events. The first was the vote to

---

[6] Interview with Chris Wilkins. Special Advisor, Department of Education June 2014–June 2015 and Director of Strategy and Chief Speechwriter Number 10 Downing Street, July 2016–June 2017. Interview 22 June 2020. UK in a Changing Europe Brexit Witness Archives.
[7] www.bbc.co.uk/news/uk-46920529

leave the EU, which attracted considerable support across the Labour heartlands and posed a direct challenge to the dominant faction in the Labour movement. Whereas during the 1970s and 1980s, Labour had been strongly Eurosceptic, even campaigning in 1983 for an early Brexit, from then onwards the party had embraced a liberal cosmopolitanism which was far more supportive of EU membership, immigration and globalization. It peaked with Tony Blair's short-lived attempt to lead the country into the Euro single currency and Labour's complete embrace of freedom of movement. By the time of the Brexit referendum, it was reflected in the fact that only 10 of the 232 Labour MPs had campaigned for Brexit.

The second event to rock the party had arrived less than one year before the vote for Brexit when the radical left-wing activist Jeremy Corbyn had been elected leader of the Labour Party. Corbyn, who came from the more Eurosceptic wing of the Labour movement and was instinctively suspicious of the EU, proceeded to swing Labour sharply to the left. Such was his ambivalence on the Brexit question that some leading pro-EU Labour campaigners such as Will Straw worried during the referendum that Corbyn might even come out for Leave. 'There was an article in *The Guardian* or somewhere', said Straw, 'with some remarks that he had given at some hustings event. He basically gave a long-standing Jeremy Corbyn remark about his views on the EU. So, we were really worried about that, and what that would mean.'[8]

Corbyn's Euroscepticism was also reflected elsewhere. Throughout the referendum, Labour's pro-Remain campaigners had repeatedly struggled to build links with Corbyn's team, with members of the latter failing to attend meetings and publicly criticizing Remain efforts in the final weeks before the vote. Alan Johnson, who led Labour's campaign to stay in the EU, felt he did not have the backing of the Labour leadership. Meanwhile, both the Corbynistas and trade unions were critical of what they saw as a Conservative-led campaign to remain in the EU, which made it difficult to include more working-class voices. Corbyn himself repeatedly failed to set out a passionate and compelling case for Remain.

As a result, while New Labour grandees such as Gordon Brown and Tony Blair sought to fill the vacuum, there was no powerful pro-Remain cue for voters from the leader of the Labour Party. This fact was reflected in the finding, only three weeks before the referendum, that only half of Labour voters realized that their party wanted to remain in the EU.

---

[8] Interview with Will Straw, Executive Director, Britain Stronger in Europe, July 2015–September 2016. Interview date 12 February 2021. UK in a Changing Europe Brexit Witness Archives.

Focus groups commissioned by the Remain campaign suggested that many voters were 'uniformly uncertain' about Labour's position, did not know where Corbyn stood, or thought that while the Labour leader supported Remain 'his heart isn't in it.'[9]

This uncertainty also had been partly shaped by the fact that Corbyn's allies were often more focused on keeping their new leader in power, defending him against attempted internal coups and setting out a radical domestic policy agenda of their own than campaigning in the Brexit referendum. Some underestimated the scale of public support for Brexit: 'My own view then', recalled Shadow Chancellor John McDonnell, 'it shows you how we underestimated the whole thing, was that this [the referendum] was just party management by Cameron to shut up his Eurosceptics, win the referendum, move on, settle it for another number of years and just get on with the real world. I treated it very much like that.'[10]

When the shock result arrived, many Labour MPs not only felt disillusioned by the outcome but also with the direction of their party and what they saw as the failure of Corbynistas to make the case for Remain. Corbyn's critics saw the result as a much-needed opportunity to oust the leader and redirect Labour back toward its liberal cosmopolitan tradition. A wave of resignations by Labour MPs followed, including from a dozen shadow cabinet ministers. One of those ministers, Hilary Benn, recalled: 'It was a culmination of, I suppose, frustration at the referendum result and what was perceived as having not been a very energetic effort on his [Corbyn's] part during the campaign, where we were in the polls and the fact that while Jeremy has many qualities, leading the main opposition party was not one of them.'[11]

Yet Corbyn and his allies dug in. In a leadership election three months later, in September 2016, Corbyn was comfortably re-elected with almost 62 per cent of the vote, a larger share than what he received when he was first elected leader of the Labour Party in 2015.[12] Reflecting similar arguments being made about Brexit, Corbyn urged Labour MPs and members to 'respect the democratic choice that has been made.'

---

[9] 'Labour Voters in the Dark about Party's Stance on Brexit, research says', *The Guardian*, 30 May 2016.

[10] Interview with John McDonnell, Shadow Chancellor of the Exchequer, September 2015–April 2020. 19 February 2021.

[11] Interview with Hilary Benn, Chair of the Select Committee on Exiting the European Union, October 2016–January 2021. UK in a Changing Europe Brexit Witness Archives.

[12] In the leadership election of September 2016, Jeremy Corbyn polled 62 per cent and Owen Smith 38 per cent. Corbyn had received just short of 60 per cent of the vote in the initial leadership election in 2015. On Labour membership and leadership see Whiteley, Poletti, Webb and Bale (2019).

Yet while the question of leadership in the major parties appeared to have been settled, at least for the time being, the deeper divides that had found their expression through the referendum vote had most certainly not. Polls soon indicated that Brexit had completely changed the issue agenda in British politics. Whereas during 2014 and 2015, the most important issues for voters had been the economy, immigration and the National Health Service, in the immediate aftermath of the referendum Brexit surged to the forefront of the agenda and remained at or near the top for much of the next three years.[13]

Crucially, Brexit did not sit comfortably in the existing 'left versus right' divide in British politics. Support for leaving the EU cut directly across traditional party lines, clearing the way for entirely new political identities and loyalties and pushing the country toward a far more polarized, volatile and unpredictable politics. This was reflected in the nature of the Leave vote. Our 2015–2016 national panel survey indicates Brexit had been supported by 61 per cent of people who had cast ballots for the Conservatives in 2015, 26 per cent of 2015 Labour voters and 36 per cent of 2015 Liberal Democrat voters. Attitudes towards Brexit not only cut across traditional political lines but, as we will see in the chapters to come, would soon reshape the nature of support for the major parties, reconfiguring them around the new fault line.

Aside from cutting across party lines, the new Brexit divide would prove to be remarkably durable. Contrary to the idea, fashionable in the aftermath of the referendum, that Leavers would change their minds, between the vote for Brexit in 2016 and the eventual delivery of Brexit, public support for exiting the EU remained remarkably stable. As shown in Figure 1.1, between 2016 and late 2021 the percentage of voters who felt that the decision to Leave the EU had been 'wrong' remained generally consistent, falling by a modest amount from 47 to 40 per cent over the entire five-year period. Meanwhile, the percentage who felt that the country had been 'right to Leave' also remained stable, rising by a similar margin from 44 to 48 per cent.

There was also considerable polarization among Leavers and Remainers; while typically more than 80 per cent of Leavers felt that the vote to Leave had been the 'right decision', more than 80 per cent of Remainers felt it was the 'wrong decision'. These divides would remain clearly visible as the Brexit struggle continued, with young, graduates and liberal left voters being far more likely than their older, non-graduate and conservative counterparts to express Bregret about the events of 2016.

---

[13] We draw here on issue salience data compiled by the Ipsos-MORI Issues Index. Available online: Ipsos.com/Ipsos-mori/en-uk/issues-index-2007-onwards

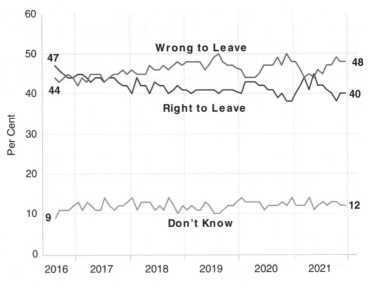

Figure 1.1 Percentages Thinking Britain Was Right or Wrong to
Leave European Union in Sixty-Five National Polls, August 2016–
December 2021.
Source: https://whatukthinks.org; YouGov polls.

To some extent, this polarization was reflected in public opinion
concerning a potential second referendum on Brexit, which quickly
became a talking point in the post-referendum climate. By 2018, polls
suggested that while only 8 per cent of 2016 Leave voters had switched
to Remain a similar 7 per cent of 2016 Remain voters had switched to
Leave. While Remain appeared to take a lead in some of these polls, it
was more because of undecided non-voters switching to Remain than
actual 2016 voters changing sides.

The Brexit fault line also gave rise to something else that would contribute to the profound political and electoral changes to come: the rise
of entirely new political identities. In the aftermath of the referendum,
large numbers of voters not only embraced their new Brexit identities as
Remainers or Leavers but often became more strongly attached to these
identities than their traditional party-political identities as Conservative,
Labour, Liberal Democrat or UKIP supporters. When asked whether
they thought of themselves as Leavers, Remainers or neither, consistently
35 per cent identified as Leavers and 40 per cent identified as Remainers.[14] Even in late 2021, almost one year after Brexit had been finally
delivered and more than five years after the referendum, these identities

---

[14] Hobolt, Leeper and Tilley (2018).

remained both visible and strong. Still 86 per cent of people identified with one of the two Brexit tribes ('Remainers' or 'Leavers'), which was only slightly below the 89 per cent who did so when the National Centre for Social Research had first asked about these identities in 2018.[15]

The extent to which the British people now identified as Remainers or Leavers underpinned the rise of a more fractious and polarized politics, which was further reflected in evidence of what researchers call 'affective polarization', namely a tendency among people on either side of the Brexit divide to dislike and distrust their opponents while liking and trusting their own side. In the aftermath of the shock vote, as debates over the direction of Brexit intensified, significant numbers of Remainers and Leavers saw people on the other side of the debate as hypocritical, selfish and closed-minded while describing those on their own side as honest, intelligent and open-minded.[16] This polarization also was reflected in the finding that while 9 per cent of Leavers said they would mind if one of their close relatives married a Remainer, a significantly higher 37 per cent of Remainers said they would mind if one of their relatives married a committed Brexiteer.[17] This was another sign of how fierce the battle over Brexit was becoming.

These divisions were exacerbated by the very different visions of what Brexit should, or should not, entail. Given that a majority of voters had voted to leave, much of the debate turned to what Brexit would actually involve. This prompted a new divide between those who supported a 'soft' Brexit, which referred to a close relationship between the UK and the EU, and those who supported a 'hard' Brexit, which referred to a looser relationship where the UK exits both the single market and the customs union, potentially without a trade deal. Between the referendum and the country's eventual departure from the EU there also was a fairly consistent 25–30 per cent of the public who wanted to stop Brexit completely, while about the same percentage favoured the idea of holding a second referendum which they designated 'A People's Vote'.[18]

Opinion polls and academic surveys suggested that these competing visions of a hard or soft Brexit tended to align with the underlying divide between Remainers and Leavers. Whereas Leavers tended to support a hard Brexit, which included prioritizing the control of immigration, Remainers tended to support softer forms of Brexit, which prioritized the country's continuing access to the single market and customs union.[19]

[15] Sivathasan (2021).
[16] Hobolt, Leeper, and Tilley (2020).
[17] YouGov, 13–14 January 2019.
[18] For a useful summary of the polls on Brexit options, see Carl (2017).
[19] Lord Ashcroft (2016).

One academic study which presented voters with different hypothetical Brexit deals and then used statistical analyses to infer their underlying preferences found that Leavers were far more likely than Remainers to prefer Brexit deals where the UK regained control over EU immigration, was no longer subjected to rulings from the European Court of Justice (ECJ) and where the country only paid a small exit fee. Remainers, in sharp contrast, were far more likely to choose deals in which the EU nationals who were already in the country were granted the right to stay and where the country faced fewer barriers to trade with the EU.[20] While much of this work painted a complex and often contradictory picture, most studies stressed the point that a large majority saw free movement as incompatible with the referendum result.

Detailed analyses of public opinion by the National Centre for Social Research found that many voters subscribed to a vision of Brexit that was unlikely to correspond with the EU's statement that being inside the single market requires the acceptance of freedom of movement. Large numbers simultaneously said they were in favour of retaining free trade with the EU while no longer granting freedom of movement to EU nationals. While 70 per cent of Remainers said they were willing to allow the free movement of EU nationals into the UK in return for securing ongoing free trade with the EU, an equal percentage of Leavers were unwilling to make such a compromise, reflecting the new battle lines among voters that would continue to influence both party politics and the negotiations.[21]

Many of the same surveys also threw light on other aspects of public opinion that provided important context for the forthcoming negotiations with the EU. There was, for example, widespread public support for allowing existing EU nationals who were already living and working in the UK to remain in the UK. Contrary to fashionable claims that the British people were deeply intolerant of migrants and wanted to remove EU nationals from the country altogether, large majorities found that most people were entirely comfortable with the idea of granting EU nationals the right to stay in the UK. However, at the same time, large majorities did not view either the continuation of freedom of movement or continuing financial contributions to the EU budget as being compatible with the result of the referendum. For example, in the aftermath of the referendum Lord Ashcroft found that 77 per cent of people felt that allowing EU nationals who were already in the country to stay in the country was entirely consistent with Brexit while only 19 per cent and

---

[20] Hobolt and Leeper (2017).
[21] National Centre for Social Research (2016).

21 per cent felt the same way about continuing to pay into the EU budget and giving new EU nationals the right to live and work in the UK, respectively.[22]

In Parliament, meanwhile, the divisions unleashed by Brexit were quickly spiralling into a full-blown crisis. One reason why the outcome of the referendum appeared destined to propel Parliament into crisis was because it was the first occasion in recent history when a majority of people outside the institution formally asked for something that a majority of people inside it had not supported. While 52 per cent of the electorate supported Leave, only 25 per cent of Members of Parliament (MPs) felt the same way.[23] Of the 650 MPs in the House of Commons, 479 were estimated to have backed Remain, including more than half of all Conservative MPs and twenty-four of the thirty members of Cameron's cabinet.[24]

The disconnect between the rulers and the ruled was especially visible on the Labour benches. Although not even a dozen Labour MPs supported Brexit, Leave had won a majority in no less than 148 Labour-held seats. And in many of these solidly working-class seats – such as Kingston-upon-Hull East, Stoke-on-Trent North, Doncaster North and Walsall North – the scale of support for leaving the EU had been enormous. When the dust had settled, 142 Labour MPs who had campaigned to Remain in the EU found themselves representing seats where a majority of people had voted to leave the EU and chart a new direction.[25]

While some Labour MPs represented some of the most strongly pro-Remain seats in the country, such as London-based Hornsey and Wood Green, or Hampstead and Kilburn, most were now representing Brexit country. Contrary to those who argue that Labour's woes were specifically caused by Brexit, the growing rebellion in the Labour heartlands had been visible for some time. Only one year before the referendum, at the 2015 general election, forty-four Labour MPs had found that their main rival, in second place, was not the Conservatives or Liberal Democrats but the national populist UK Independence Party (UKIP), a movement popular among blue-collar and self-employed workers who had often voted Labour in the past.[26] The growing disconnect between

[22] Lord Ashcroft (2016).
[23] BBC News. 'EU vote: Where the cabinet and other MPs stand', 22 June 2016. Available online: www.bbc.co.uk/news/uk-politics-eu-referendum-35616946 (accessed 2 April 2020).
[24] BBC News. 'EU vote: Where the cabinet and other MPs stand', 22 June 2016.
[25] Only in four cases did Labour MPs vote Leave and a majority of people in their constituencies voted to Remain. On these numbers see Whitaker (2019).
[26] On the 2015 campaign and UKIP threat to Labour, see Goodwin and Milazzo (2016).

Labour and its heartlands would soon play a major role in the electoral decline of the Labour Party, as we will see in the pages to come. The Liberal Democrats now hoped to prosper from this tension by appealing loudly and directly to Remainers on an anti-Brexit ticket.

Brexit piled further pressure on an already strained United Kingdom. Although the UK, overall, voted to exit the EU, Scotland and Northern Ireland had supported Remain and so were now on course to be pulled out of the EU against the wishes of 62 and 56 per cent of their voters, respectively. The Scottish National Party (SNP) hoped that the result would help drive support for a second referendum on Scotland's independence. Much of this reflected the fact that the Brexit vote had been mainly, though not exclusively, delivered by residents of England and Wales, and in those areas by people who tended to live outside of big cities and university towns, in communities filled with workers, non-graduates and middle-aged or elderly voters, reflecting the growing importance of education and age as key drivers of politics.

In their study of the Brexit vote, Matthew Goodwin and Oliver Heath found that support for Leave had consistently been strongest in England's Midlands, North East, Yorkshire and Eastern regions, in areas such as Boston, South Holland, Castle Point, Thurrock and Bolsover, and in communities that tended to be more economically disadvantaged than average, where average levels of education were low, the local population was heavily white British and which had often experienced a sudden and sharp increase in immigration in only a short period of time. In contrast, support for Remain had been strongest in Scotland, London and Northern Ireland, in the big cities, university towns and in communities filled with middle-class professionals, young voters and graduates. Much of this reflected the growing geographical polarization of the country, whereby big cities and university towns are becoming steadily more socially liberal over time while smaller and industrial towns are becoming more conservative.[27]

This was the scene that met the country's new Conservative Prime Minister, Theresa May, when she entered Number 10 Downing Street on 13 July 2016. May, the Remainer, was now in charge of designing and delivering the most complex political and policy challenge that the country had faced since the Second World War. No major power had ever exited the EU before.[28] Article 50, the official process whereby a member state leaves the EU, remained theoretical, since it had never before been triggered. Across the country, people and politicians remained deeply divided, while most of the MPs who were about to oversee the Brexit process had voted

[27] Heath and Goodwin (2016).
[28] Although Greenland left in 1985, with negotiations focused heavily on fishing rights.

against it. To make matters worse, in the House of Commons, May and her government had inherited a slender majority from David Cameron, which stood at just seventeen.[29] The battle for Brexit had begun.

Enter May – Brexit Begins

Theresa May, the country's new prime minister, was a largely unknown political figure. Although she had been on the frontline of politics since the early 2000s, as Chair of the Conservative Party (2002–2003) before becoming Minister for Women and Equalities (2010–2012) and then Home Secretary (2010–2016), throughout much of this time she avoided media and the limelight. As a result, when it came to Brexit it was not really clear what she believed or where she wanted to take the UK's relationship with the EU. Unlike other members of the cabinet, May had been deliberately quiet during the referendum campaign.

But had voters been watching closely then they would have noticed that their new prime minister and her advisors subscribed to a different conservatism than their predecessors, David Cameron and George Osborne. Even before entering Number 10 Downing Street, May, who had been raised by a Church of England clergyman, talked about the need to tackle the 'burning injustice' facing millions of people. 'As we leave the European Union', said May, 'we will forge a bold new positive role for ourselves in the world, and we will make Britain a country that works not for a privileged few, but for every one of us.' Much of this was shaped by how she and her team saw Brexit, which in their eyes was about far more than the country's relationship with the European Union, as one of her key advisors recalls:

And the view we came to [in late summer 2016] was that it was a vote for change in the country and a whole host of other social and economic policies, not just our relationship with Europe. If you look at the language she used in her main conference speech that year, she talked about this quiet revolution .... That it was people who had – after so long being ignored and not listened to – used this as an opportunity to hit back. Europe was part of it, but it was more what Europe represented and the way Britain had conducted itself in Europe and what that signified about their relationship with the Government. So, it was seen as that broader vote for change amongst the top team in Number 10, and that was a view that Theresa certainly shared.[30]

[29] House of Commons (2017).
[30] Interview with Chris Wilkins, Special Advisor, Department of Education, June 2014–June 2015 and Director of Strategy and Chief Speechwriter, Number 10 Downing Street, July 2016–June 2017. Interview 22 June 2020. UK in a Changing Europe Brexit Witness Archives.

This vision was clarified in October 2016, when May addressed the party faithful at the annual conference of the Conservative Party. Rather than view Brexit solely through the lens of Europe, May presented it as nothing short of 'a revolution in which millions of our fellow citizens stood up and said they were not prepared to be ignored anymore'. Much of this reflected the thinking of her advisors, Nick Timothy and Fiona Hill, who advocated a more communitarian conservatism which sought to appeal to not just middle-class True-Blue Tories in the southern shires but to a wider coalition of voters scattered across Brexit country, including working-class, non-graduates and cultural conservatives in the Labour heartlands.[31]

In both Conservative and Labour areas, Brexit exposed the fact that millions of people felt left behind not just by the elite consensus on EU membership but by the arrival and acceleration of globalization, immigration and social liberalism. With Brexit now cutting directly across traditional party lines, Theresa May and Nick Timothy cultivated a position they hoped would resonate strongly among this audience, including in the more than six in ten Labour-held seats which had voted to leave. Even Maurice Glasman, a Labour peer and architect of Blue Labour, was invited into Number 10 Downing Street to discuss how Conservatives might appeal to 'ordinary working families' or the 'just managing'.

Much of this rhetoric was infused with a more populist style, with the homogeneous people contrasted with distant, self-serving and suspicious elites. Influenced by her time in the Home Office, May saw immigration as a particularly important symbol of how Westminster elites had decoupled from the people. '[Today]', May told conference, 'too many people in positions of power behave as though they have more in common with international elites than with the people down the road, the people they employ, the people they pass in the street. But if you believe you're a citizen of a world, you're a citizen of nowhere.'

It was not long, however, until May herself was mingling with the people of nowhere. The Prime Minister used a speech at a meeting of international elites in Davos to flesh out her vision of Brexit Britain. The country, she declared, would 'step up to a new leadership role as the strongest and most forceful advocate for business, free markets and free trade anywhere in the world'. Britain would be 'even more global and internationalist' and pursue 'genuine free trade' while ensuring businesses behaved responsibly and a 'shared society' respected the obligations of citizenship.

In the same week, on 17 January, May used a speech at Lancaster House to set out her twelve priorities for Brexit ahead of the looming

---

[31] See Ford and Goodwin (2014).

and difficult exit negotiations with the EU. Overall, she committed both her premiership and government to the pursuit of a hard Brexit, talking about the need for 'a new, comprehensive, bold and ambitious free trade agreement' while also ruling out membership of the single market and full membership of the customs union, ending the jurisdiction of the European Court of Justice, ending the free movement of EU nationals and 'the days of Britain making vast contributions to the European Union every year'.[32] May anticipated that all of this could be achieved within two years, a time frame that Brexit experts considered ambitious, naïve or 'absurdly short'.[33]

May's plan soon collided with political reality, however. Initially, the government had insisted it could trigger Article 50 without the consent of MPs. It would rely on the use of prerogative power, which it argued authorized ministers to conduct foreign affairs, including decisions relating to international treaties, such as the power to notify the EU of the country's intention to withdraw. Yet in January 2017 the Supreme Court ruled that parliamentary approval would be required before triggering Article 50. The ruling reinforced the role of Parliament in Brexit and was widely seen as a direct rebuke to May for trying to exclude MPs from the Brexit process. Reflecting the febrile atmosphere, the *Daily Mail* ran with an infamous and what many people saw as a divisive headline: 'Enemies of the People'.

Two days after the ruling, the government published the European Union (Notification of Withdrawal) Act which subsequently passed through Parliament. Yet while the margin in the House of Commons was large, 498 votes to 114, it had required a significant amount of work behind the scenes by the party whips, a fact that would feed a growing appetite in Number 10 Downing Street for a fresh general election and, it was hoped, a larger majority for the far more complex battles to come.

The events in the House had thrown light on the underlying divides that would continue to play out in Parliament for the next three years. Despite Jeremy Corbyn urging Labour MPs not to vote against the bill, and despite Labour having voted for the referendum on EU membership to take place, nearly fifty Labour rebels alongside the SNP, the Liberal Democrats, Plaid Cymru, the SDLP, one Green and one Conservative rebel, Kenneth Clarke, voted against it. Labour's Shadow Home Secretary, Diane Abbott MP, was accused of having Brexit Flu after failing to show up to the historic vote.

---

[32] www.gov.uk/government/speeches/the-governments-negotiating-objectives-for-exiting-the-eu-pm-speech
[33] Menon and Wager (2021), p. 30.

Nonetheless, the bill passed and, on 29 March 2017, Prime Minister May sent a letter to the President of the European Council, Donald Tusk, formally triggering Article 50, the process of withdrawal. 'We are leaving the European Union, but we are not leaving Europe', wrote May. 'I hereby notify the European Council in accordance with Article 50(2) of the Treaty on European Union of the United Kingdom's intention to withdraw from the European Union.' Nine months after a majority of people had voted to leave the EU their new prime minister had passed the first hurdle. Theresa May was leading the country out. Or so she thought.

Majority Lost – The 2017 General Election

Ever since coming to power, Theresa May and her advisors had become increasingly frustrated with their small majority in Parliament and the sheer scale of opposition to Brexit among MPs, which they worried would weaken their hand during forthcoming negotiations with the EU. They also knew that their plan to use Brexit to bring about more sweeping and fundamental change in British society extended well beyond the contents of David Cameron's manifesto, in 2015. All of this led them to the same conclusion: they would require a fresh mandate from the British people.

'At this moment of enormous national significance', said May, standing in front of Number 10 Downing Street, 'there should be unity here in Westminster, but instead there is division. The country is coming together, but Westminster is not.' Influenced by research that had been undertaken by Sir Lynton Crosby, and which advocated a different approach from what had been proposed by some of her own advisors, May fleshed out the core themes of her general election campaign: the need for 'strong and stable' leadership, to push back against anti-Brexit forces in Parliament and to avoid the weakness, instability and chaos of a government led by Jeremy Corbyn.

Coming in the shadow of the 2014 elections to the European Parliament, the 2015 general election and the 2016 Brexit referendum, the 2017 general election would be the country's fourth nationwide vote in as many years and would test a visibly exhausted, divided and volatile electorate.[34] 'You're joking!' said Brenda from Bristol, when she was told of the plan for yet another election in a vox-pop that quickly went viral. 'Not another one! Oh, for God's sake I can't stand this! There's too much politics going on at the moment. Why does she need to do it?'

---

[34] It was even worse for the Scots, who after navigating the general elections in 2010 and 2015, Scottish Parliament elections in 2011 and 2016, European Parliament elections in 2014 and two referendums in 2014 and 2016 would now head to the polls for the eighth time in only seven years.

The answer to Brenda's question was that May and her team not only hoped to strengthen their Brexit hand while securing their own mandate but also capitalize on the wider trends in the opinion polls, which looked incredibly favourable. Ever since coming to power, in the summer of 2016, May and her team had watched their support, rather surprisingly, rocket in the polls. In the days after May's election as leader, the Conservative Party averaged an 11-point lead over Jeremy Corbyn's Labour Party; by the time May finally called the election she had promised not to hold, the lead had rocketed to 17 percentage points. The polls suggested an overwhelming majority that would leave May unassailable in Parliament and send a powerful display of strength to the European Union.

Other things also seemed to be moving in her direction. Shortly before calling the election, in February 2017, the Conservative Party captured the pro-Brexit seat of Copeland at a parliamentary by-election. It was the first time since the 1930s that the Labour Party had failed to win the seat, the first time since the early 1980s that an incumbent party had captured a seat in a by-election and represented the biggest increase in the share of the vote for a governing party at a by-election since 1966. Aside from throwing yet more light on growing unrest in the Labour heartlands, it was another sign that British politics had entered a deeper state of realignment and that a huge, potentially historic majority awaited May and her team.

And when it came to the big issues of the day, the Conservatives held commanding leads over the Labour Party. When the British people were asked which party was 'best' able to manage the crunch issues of Brexit and managing the economy, the Conservatives held commanding leads.[35] And while some had started to voice criticism of May, whose robotic communication earned her the name 'May-bot', her leadership ratings were still far stronger than Jeremy Corbyn's. When people were asked who would make the best prime minister, 54 per cent said May, while only 14 per cent favoured Corbyn.[36] While Corbyn remained popular among Labour activists, in the wider country he went into the election as one of the most unpopular opposition party leaders on record.[37]

Nonetheless, in the end the 2017 general election became a gamble that May and her team lost. After a Conservative campaign that was widely considered a shambles, including a major U-turn on an unpopular

[35] The exceptions were housing and the National Health Service. But the Conservatives led on law and order, the economy, Britain's exit from the EU, immigration, taxation, unemployment and education. YouGov data.

[36] YouGov polling data 18–19 April 2017.

[37] A majority of the Labour Parliamentary Party wanted to oust Corbyn, as the vote of no confidence in his leadership in June 2016 demonstrated, but he was protected by party members who by this time had increased to more than half a million. However, the party infighting meant that it lost ground in the polls. See Whiteley, Seyd and Clarke (2021).

social care policy labelled the 'dementia tax' by opponents, and a surprisingly strong and passionate campaign by Jeremy Corbyn and the Labour Party, the election delivered another shock in a country that was quickly becoming used to shocks.

Contrary to widespread expectations of a huge Conservative majority, when the exit poll was revealed it pointed to a hung Parliament: 'We cannot see any way at all that the Conservatives can get to the 326 mark [the number of seats required for a majority]', said John Curtice, 'and we think it's pretty clear that there is going to be a hung parliament.' 'Well', said David Dimbleby, 'the prime minister called this election because she wanted certainty and stability and this doesn't seem, at this stage, to look like certainty and stability.'

When all ballots had been tallied, Theresa May and the Conservative Party had won 42.3 per cent of the vote, an increase of more than 5 percentage points on what David Cameron had managed in 2015. It was the party's highest share of the vote since Thatcher's landslide victory in 1983. But it was a pyrrhic victory. The Conservatives captured only 317 seats, 13 fewer than David Cameron had managed in his surprise majority of 2015 and the party's lowest number of seats since 2010. The result was not a big majority but a minority government which would soon be dependent upon the Northern Irish Democratic Unionist Party (DUP). Had Theresa May and her party not gained a surprising twelve seats north of the border, in Scotland, then things would have been even worse.

Like Harold Wilson in 1970 and Ted Heath in 1974, both of whom called early elections and then lost, May was humiliated. She left the election weaker, not stronger. While the polls and academic forecasts had suggested Corbyn and Labour were heading for disaster, in the end they enjoyed a surprisingly strong result, although they still lost the election. Labour went into the campaign offering a radical manifesto that included the renationalization of key industries and the scrapping of university tuition fees, all of which was wrapped in the populist promise to campaign 'for the many, not the few'. And, crucially, when it came to Brexit, Corbyn said he accepted the vote to leave the EU and the need to reform the widely unpopular free movement of EU nationals into Britain. Yet he also opposed what he argued would be a costly 'No Deal' Brexit and called for the country to retain what he argued was its economically beneficial access to Europe's single market and customs union.

In the end, Labour attracted a broader coalition of support than most commentators thought possible. With 40 per cent of the vote, Labour won its highest vote share since Tony Blair's second landslide in 2001 and a higher share than Blair and New Labour managed at their final victory four years later. Although Corbyn had been widely criticized by commentators and members of his own party, he could now claim to have brought the Labour Party its largest number of seats since 2005. Labour outperformed the final polls by an average of 5 percentage points and, compared to 2015, increased its vote share by nearly 10 percentage points; the strongest election-on-election increase since Clement Attlee led Labour in 1945.

Theresa May and her team had gambled that their path to winning a big majority ran not only through the Conservative Party's existing 330 seats but also by capturing a large number of the almost 150 Labour seats that had voted for Brexit. The plan had been to retain support in more economically prosperous, highly educated and middle-class Remainia while simultaneously making big inroads into the more economically disadvantaged, less well-educated and working-class parts of Brexit country, thereby expanding the Conservative electorate. In some ways, as we will see, the strategy was a success.

More than five years later, we can now see how the Conservative Party campaign in 2017 set the stage for the subsequent rise of Boris Johnson and a new Conservative electorate. But in the immediate context of 2017, Theresa May's plan had been thwarted by the fact that support for the Labour Party had also held up in many seats, thereby depriving her of the much anticipated larger majority.[38]

This would also have profound consequences for the Brexit negotiations. Rather than holding a stronger hand, Theresa May was now a weakened prime minister with a minority government in a Parliament that was bitterly divided over Brexit. Opponents of the decision to depart from the EU now saw opportunities to thwart Brexit, while supporters worried that their project might be finished before it had even begun.

The battle for Brexit was about to enter an entirely new and historic next stage. This is the subject of Chapter 2.

---

[38] Heath and Goodwin (2017).

2 Getting Brexit Done

The outcome of the 2017 election was a personal humiliation for Theresa May and a severe blow to her political authority. In the aftermath, her advisors, Nick Timothy and Fiona Hill, resigned. While May stayed on as leader of the Conservative Party and prime minister, her political capital and stature among the Conservative Parliamentary Party, Parliament and the European Union were diminished.

The government was confronted with the most complex constitutional and public policy challenge since the Second World War, with no majority in the House of Commons. To retain power, Theresa May was forced to establish a confidence and supply arrangement with the DUP, which introduced a new 'veto player' in the Brexit negotiations. They wanted to maintain Northern Ireland as an equal partner in the United Kingdom. As a result of the new arithmetic in Parliament, onlookers in both the UK and the EU were now sceptical that May would be able to get a Brexit deal through Parliament, and this influenced the negotiations. In short, a prime minister who had repeatedly promised both her party and the country that 'Brexit Means Brexit' now appeared to lack the political capital to see it through.

This political reality was reflected in the mood in Parliament. On the Leave side of the debate, the outcome of the 2017 general election, combined with renewed enthusiasm among pro-Remain campaigners, stoked growing fears that Brexit might be softened or overturned altogether. In response, over the next two years, a loose alliance of strongly Eurosceptic Conservative MPs along with national populists outside Parliament, became increasingly opposed to Theresa May's vision of Brexit and more supportive of a No Deal hard Brexit.

Meanwhile, on the Remain side of the debate, Jeremy Corbyn and the Labour Party were triumphant in defeat. They celebrated their surprisingly strong performance in the 2017 election and now set their sights on finally winning power by exploiting a weaker prime minister, a visibly divided Conservative Party and pushing for yet another general election. While the Corbynistas sensed that the pendulum was swinging in their direction, pro-Remain campaigners were also buoyed by the result of the 2017 election, pointing to strong turnout in pro-Remain districts as evidence of a serious opportunity to soften Brexit, hold a second referendum or even to stop it altogether.[1] Increasingly, MPs steadily drifted further apart from one another over the course of the negotiations, with some rallying around a No Deal Brexit and others pushing for a soft Brexit or a second referendum.

What followed was a prolonged period of political chaos that will be debated by social scientists and others for decades to come. Amid a deeply polarized and rapidly fragmenting politics, one of the world's most stable two-party systems would implode into a multi-party race, Parliament would be plunged into total gridlock, the government's proposed Withdrawal Agreement would be defeated on no less than three occasions and the Brexit process enshrined in Article 50 would be extended three times. In addition, the governing Conservative Party would become even more bitterly divided over the Europe question and the electorate would become visibly angry, restless and hungry for change.

In the end, all of this not only paved the way for historic losses for the Labour Party and the left and the resignation of Prime Minister Theresa May, but also for the rise of Boris Johnson and what turned out to be a very popular promise indeed: 'Get Brexit Done'.

Aftermath: 2017–2018

Brexit defined Theresa May's premiership. It completely dominated her time in Number 10 Downing Street and it was the reason for her ascent to power as well as her downfall. One of her closest advisors divides May's quest to resolve the Brexit issue into three distinct phases.

The first, between her appointment as leader and the 2017 general election, was devoted to preparing for the Brexit negotiations with the EU. The second, from the 2017 general election through to November 2018, concentrated on negotiating. The third, from November 2018 until May confirmed her decision to resign in May 2019, was preoccupied with trying, unsuccessfully, to get Parliament to approve a Brexit deal, or some version of it. Her failure to do so would set the stage for the ascent of Boris Johnson.

The second phase of formal negotiations between the UK and the EU began only eleven days after May lost her election gamble. The EU had already laid out guidelines for the Brexit negotiations, making clear its

---

[1] On turnout, Remain and the 2017 general election see Heath and Goodwin (2017). See also Cowley and Kavanagh (2018).

view that both sides had to follow a sequenced approach which prioritized an orderly withdrawal before any discussion of their future relationship could begin. Whereas the UK saw the issues of withdrawal and the
future relationship as intimately entwined, the EU saw this as a violation
of the Article 50 process – the only legal mechanism for a member state
of the EU to leave.[2] Contrary to early claims in the UK about this difference sparking 'the row of the summer', Prime Minister May agreed
to the sequencing laid out by the EU, a decision that was at least partly
shaped by her earlier decision to trigger the Article. The clock was tick-
ing, piling pressure on May, her advisors and the government to keep
moving.

As a result, both sides focused on resolving outstanding issues relating
to the UK's forty-four-year membership of the EU, including money the
UK owed to the EU, the rights of EU nationals who were already living and working in the UK and solutions for the island of Ireland which
reflected its unique situation. The vote for Brexit and subsequent call to
leave the EU single market and the customs union meant that the UK
would become a 'third country' as far as the EU were concerned. If the
UK and EU failed to find a new arrangement, then the Irish land border
would become a customs and regulatory border involving the standard
checks that the EU has at its border with any third country. Only once
these issues had been resolved and sufficient progress had been made
could the two sides progress onto the next phase of the negotiations to
discuss their future relationship.

While payments to Brussels have long been a source of tension in
UK politics, the UK's commitment to settle outstanding obligations
was soon underlined by Prime Minister May in a speech in Florence in
September 2017. In this speech, May restated her desire for the UK to
leave both the single market and the customs union and to pursue a new
and bespoke relationship with the EU (though some advisors suggest
she made this decision during the 2017 election campaign). She also
requested a time-limited implementation period that would cover the
end of the withdrawal period and the start of the new trading relationship
between the two sides.

Yet while some outstanding issues were quickly resolved, there
emerged significant tension between May's vision of Brexit and the vision
being pursued by her more strongly Eurosceptic MPs, many of whom
had campaigned for a complete break with the EU. As May's Chief of
Staff, Gavin Barwell, who was brought in after the 2017 general election

---

[2] Brexit Brief: Article 50, Institute for Government. Available online: www.institutefor
government.org.uk/brexit/brexit-brief-article-50

to improve relations between May's operation in Number 10 and the Conservative Parliamentary Party, later recalled, at the root of this disagreement was a philosophical difference concerning compromise:

Theresa's view was that the referendum result was clear but close and that two of the four nations of the UK had voted to remain, so while we should leave, we should have a close relationship with the EU after we had left. Boris rejected any idea of compromise – if you didn't break completely free of the EU, he said, there was no point leaving.[3]

Whereas Johnson and other Eurosceptics were instinctively supportive of the idea of a No Deal Brexit, May and her team had always been of the view that such an outcome would not only be economically damaging but could lead to the break-up of the UK. The outcome of the 2017 election, May's weakened position and the fact that most MPs opposed a No Deal Brexit also dampened the threat of a No Deal in the eyes of the EU, which also influenced the dynamics of the negotiations.

There also remained strong disagreement in the Conservative Party over issues relating to governance, the transition period and the Irish border, all of which would continue to influence the direction of the negotiations. Nor were these tensions cooled when May later made a series of concessions to the EU and reneged on her commitment to keep a No Deal Brexit as a plausible option.[4] Increasingly, the two sides of the debate would drift apart and become more polarized.

From the outset, May's negotiation was complicated by the fact that she was pursuing what some saw as three mutually incompatible objectives: an exit from the single market and the customs union; no hard border on the island of Ireland; and an all-UK approach to Brexit. The difficulty in resolving the tension between these objectives became known as the 'Irish trilemma'.[5]

While the Irish border had not been a prominent issue during the referendum campaign or the early phase of the Brexit negotiations, in the months that followed it became a major point of friction. The Irish government would not agree to any deal without a firm guarantee that a physical border would not be placed between Ireland and Northern Ireland. Meanwhile, Eurosceptics on the Conservative benches, organized around the European Research Group (ERG), feared that any agreement by the UK and the EU negotiation teams not to impose a hard border might be used to keep the UK aligned to the EU single market and customs union. At the same time, the DUP feared that any bespoke solution

---

[3] Barwell (2021), p. 12.
[4] Timothy (2020).
[5] Menon and Wager (2021).

would threaten their overriding goal of keeping Northern Ireland as an equal partner in the United Kingdom. These concerns would gradually converge and bolster opposition to Theresa May.

In July 2018, May had sought to resolve these issues at a meeting of ministers at Chequers, where the prime minister laid out her plans for the future relationship between the UK and the EU while also reminding them about the very difficult arithmetic in Parliament. It was a major turning point in the Brexit process, which confirmed in the minds of Conservative Eurosceptics that May's vision of Brexit was fundamentally different from their own.[6] Within two days, May's Brexit and Foreign Secretaries, among others, resigned, plunging the government into chaos.

David Davis, the Brexit Secretary, attributed his resignation to his belief that the UK was 'giving away too much and too easily' in the Brexit negotiations. He was replaced by Dominic Raab, although he too would resign in the months ahead. Boris Johnson, the Foreign Secretary, resigned while complaining that May was leading the UK into a 'semi-Brexit', that the Brexit 'dream is dying, suffocated by needless self-doubt' and unless it changed course the UK would be reduced to the 'status of a colony'.[7] From here on, Johnson became the rallying point for opponents of May's deal.

The departure of Davis and Johnson symbolized the growing opposition to May's deal among Conservative Eurosceptic MPs. Increasingly, MPs and others who had campaigned to leave the European Union now feared they were heading toward a soft Brexit or BRINO (Brexit In Name Only), or even that Brexit might be thwarted entirely. The European Research Group (ERG), consisting of Eurosceptic Conservative MPs, became more vocal in its criticism of May, and Conservative MPs in general became more supportive of a No Deal Brexit. Increasingly, after Chequers, a growing number of Conservatives rallied round the idea of a No Deal, which by early 2019 had become a major narrative in the Leave camp.[8]

These voices were also joined by another influential figure who had played a key role in the delivery of both the Brexit referendum and the Brexit vote. In the shadow of the Chequers summit, the national populist Nigel Farage, previously leader of UKIP, announced his return to front-line politics. Disillusioned with the direction of the Brexit negotiations, Farage threw his weight behind Leave Means Leave, a grass-roots campaign that was run by businessmen Richard Tice and John Longworth and brought together both left and right Leavers.

[6] Shipman (2017), p. 96.
[7] 'Boris Johnson tells PM she is suffocating Brexit "dream"', *BBC News*, 9 July 2018.
[8] Kettell and Kerr (2020).

'Over the last few months, and particularly since the Chequers betrayal', wrote Farage in August 2018, 'scores of people have stopped me in the street to ask: "When are you coming back?" Well now you have your answer: I'm back.'[9] A few months later, in March 2019, Farage would take over the Brexit Party and launch a new electoral assault on the Conservative Party.[10] There was no doubt about the scale of the disillusionment. Both Conservative and Leave voters strongly disapproved of May's Chequers proposals and her vision of Brexit, which was too soft for many. In the aftermath of Chequers, just 33 per cent of Conservative voters and 24 per cent of Leavers, respectively, felt that the deal would 'respect the result of the referendum' while just 22 per cent and 18 per cent felt it 'would be good for Britain'.[11]

Many Leavers felt the proposals were not faithful to what they had voted for at the 2016 Brexit referendum. As one academic summary of the polling in the shadow of Chequers pointed out:

the problem for the government is that many Leave voters appear to have decided that the agreement fails to meet their expectations. As a result, it is in effect being disowned by some of the very voters whose electoral institutions the government is meant to be implementing. Moreover, those voters do not just think that the Prime Minister has been incompetent in developing her Brexit stance but rather they are also having doubts about whether the government is in favour of the kind of Brexit they want in the first place.[12]

Such feelings contributed to a wider deterioration of public confidence in the perceived ability of May's government to manage Brexit. Ever since the referendum in 2016, many voters had been willing to give May the benefit of the doubt. A year before the Chequers proposals, only 25 per cent of all voters had felt that the government was doing 'well' at the negotiations while 55 per cent felt it was doing 'badly'.[13] Leavers were more divided, with 40 per cent approving of the negotiations and 42 per cent disapproving. Yet in the aftermath of the Chequers proposals, the picture changed dramatically.

Large majorities of Leavers and all voters now agreed that the Brexit negotiations were being handled 'badly' (70 per cent of Leavers felt this way).[14] For a prime minister and a Conservative Party which had

---

[9] Nigel Farage, 'The time has come to teach the political class a lesson: I'm back fighting for a real Brexit', The *Daily Telegraph*, 17 August 2018.
[10] Cutts, Goodwin, Heath and Milazzo (2019).
[11] Curtice (2018).
[12] Curtice (2018).
[13] Curtice (2018).
[14] YouGov polling 16–17 July 2018 (post-Chequers) and 31 July–1 August 2017 (a year earlier). For a more detailed discussion of the polling around Chequers, see Curtice (2018).

realigned their entire electorate around the Leave vote, this was a dangerous development which left the party vulnerable to attack on its right-wing flank, which is exactly what happened.

The growing domestic pressure on May was further exacerbated when the EU also rejected the Chequers proposals. While some EU officials wanted to recognize new momentum after months of limited progress, the EU was ultimately unable to support proposals that allowed UK businesses free access to the single market without being legally bound to follow EU rules.[15] In Salzburg, in September 2018, Donald Tusk, President of the European Council, made it clear that the EU would not accept a deal where the UK had free movement in goods without accepting the other core freedoms. He also took to Instagram with a picture of May looking at cakes: 'A piece of cake, perhaps? Sorry, no cherries.' At the same time, at Labour's conference in Liverpool, Jeremy Corbyn confirmed that Labour would vote against the Chequers plan and any attempt to leave the EU with no deal and would continue to push for a fresh general election which, he hoped, would propel him to power.

Inside the House of Commons, tensions over Brexit were escalating as pro-Brexit MPs on the Conservative benches and pro-Remain MPs went into another proxy war over the issue. While Eurosceptics used a Customs Bill to add amendments that were designed to undermine May's Chequers proposals, advocates of a soft Brexit adopted a similar approach, adding amendments to a Trade Bill which called for a customs union with the EU. In the end, the government appeased the Eurosceptics while staring down supporters of a soft Brexit, though in the end they were only saved by a group of five rebel pro-Brexit Labour MPs (the bill was seen off by only six votes). The government only narrowly survived. It was a reminder of May's weakness in Parliament.

Outside Parliament, meanwhile, the campaign for a second referendum was gathering pace. People's Vote, an organization which had partly emerged from the earlier 'Open Britain' campaign, was formally launched in April 2018 at an event in the strongly pro-Remain area of Camden. Drawing together nine different pro-EU groups, and fronted by MPs Chuka Umunna, Anna Soubry, Layla Moran and Caroline Lucas (former New Labour communications chief Alastair Campbell also played a key role), it called for a 'people's vote' on any final Brexit deal. It deliberately avoided the phrase 'second referendum'.

More specifically, People's Vote sought to win the case for a second referendum among Labour MPs by pointing out that while a majority of Labour seats had backed Brexit, a majority of Labour *voters* had backed

[15] Jensen and Kelstrup (2019).

Remain. Initially, in 2018, People's Vote claimed to have support from an estimated twenty to thirty MPs, but would later claim to have support from an estimated 300 MPs. Aside from lobbying MPs and commissioning polls, the group also organized high-profile marches, including what it claimed was the 'second most attended demonstration this century' after an estimated 700,000 Remainers turned out in central London in October 2018.[16]

'If we ever had a strategy', reflected Tom Baldwin, its Director of Communications and Strategy, 'it was to persuade people that a People's Vote was the democratic solution for this gigantic Brexit mess – whether you are a Remainer, a Leaver or not sure – a vehicle to solve the problem.'[17] Increasingly, it framed the idea of a second referendum as a necessary move to block what it saw as the looming threat of a No Deal Brexit, a fear that was stoked by the government appearing to make plans for this during the summer of 2018 to try and appease Conservative Eurosceptics.

Efforts to derail Brexit, if not to stop it altogether, were also helped by events at the Labour Party conference in 2018 when delegates voted overwhelmingly to accept the principle of a second referendum if the party could not secure a general election. The motion was passed only hours after Sir Keir Starmer, Labour's shadow Brexit Secretary and future leader, told Labour delegates: 'It is right for Parliament to have the first say but if we need to break the impasse, our options must include campaigning for a public vote and nobody is ruling out Remain as an option.'[18] Jeremy Corbyn said that he would respect the result of the vote, although senior trade unionists opposed the move, warning Labour was reopening the Brexit wound which had cut across the Labour heartlands.

Growing internal opposition to May was underlined on 11 October 2018, when Graham Brady, chairman of the 1922 Committee, warned the prime minister that the number of Conservative MPs who were submitting letters of no confidence in her leadership was approaching 15 per cent of the parliamentary party – the level required to trigger a vote of confidence.

On 14 November 2018, the UK government and EU negotiators managed to bridge some of their divides and released the draft Withdrawal

[16] 'Almost 700,000 March to Demand "People's Vote" on Brexit Deal', *The Guardian*, 20 October 2018.
[17] Interview with Tom Baldwin, 5 July 2021. UK in a Changing Europe Brexit Witness Archives.
[18] https://news.sky.com/story/labour-conference-sir-keir-starmer-insists-nobody-is-ruling-out-remain-as-an-option-11508213

Agreement. It set out the principles of how the UK would depart from the EU on 29 March 2019 and was accompanied by a political declaration on the future relationship. The two sides now had four and a half months to ratify the agreement.

At the core of this agreement, however, was the highly controversial idea of the 'backstop', an arrangement for the Irish border that would come into effect if no other solutions to maintain the current open border could be found once the UK had exited the EU. It was, in essence, an insurance policy designed to protect the Good Friday/Belfast Agreement and ensure that an open border between Northern Ireland and Ireland remained after Brexit. After much negotiation about its precise format, the draft Withdrawal Agreement in November 2018 included a protocol on Northern Ireland which set out the details of the backstop.

Yet the backstop was highly unpopular. Theresa May's governing partner, the Democratic Unionist Party, opposed it because it would have introduced differences in regulation between Northern Ireland and the rest of the UK, while Eurosceptics opposed it because they feared it would mean the UK remaining in a customs territory with the EU, thereby removing the UK's ability to vary its tariffs, which is a key aspect of trade deals, and that the UK might not be able to leave it.

Partly for these reasons, in the aftermath of the release of the Withdrawal Agreement, internal opposition to May's deal soon spiralled into a fresh rebellion. Dominic Raab, the new Brexit secretary, alongside cabinet minister Esther McVey and junior ministers Suella Braverman and Shailesh Vara resigned from government, piling further pressure on May. Like others, Raab pointed to what he felt were two fatal flaws in the deal: that the terms offered by the EU threatened the integrity of the UK and would lead to a situation where the UK was locked into a regime with no say over the rules and laws applied and that this, in turn, would undermine public trust in democracy.

Amid growing rumours of a leadership challenge to May, Eurosceptic Conservatives also hit the airwaves to complain that the government had made too many concessions to the EU and that Brexit risked becoming BRINO. 'The deal risks Brexit because it is not a proper Brexit', complained Jacob Rees-Mogg.[19] Speaking for Leavers, *The Spectator*, which had campaigned for a more economically liberal version of Brexit, branded the Withdrawal Agreement 'Remain minus'.[20]

While EU member states provided support for the Withdrawal Agreement, it was the UK that appeared visibly divided. Fears that May might

[19] www.bbc.co.uk/news/uk-politics-46219495
[20] 'Remain Minus', *The Spectator Magazine*, 1 December 2018.

seek to 'run down the clock' in order to pressure MPs to endorse her proposed deal or face a No Deal Brexit were stoked by her decision to withdraw a vote on the deal, originally scheduled for 11 December 2018. Instead, May and her team sought to obtain further reassurances on the question of the backstop from the EU. At the same time, she also stared down a vote of no confidence among Conservative MPs, winning by 200 to 117 votes. Yet May was also forced to pacify her critics by ruling out the possibility of her leading the Conservative Party into the next election. In theory, she was at least safe for twelve months, but as it turned out, she would not last that long.

No Deal had essentially been taken off the table at this point. Around Christmas, senior Conservatives such as Philip Hammond, Amber Rudd, David Gauke and others had made it clear to May that they would not support a No Deal, while May's advisors were continually being lobbied by junior ministers and parliamentary private secretaries to take No Deal off the table.[21] The EU had also concluded that this was not a realistic option. Strong opposition to a No Deal Brexit was then further underlined in early January 2019 when MPs amended a finance bill to prevent the Treasury implementing No Deal measures unless Parliament sanctioned a No Deal exit from the EU.

Controversially, when Parliament returned from recess, Speaker John Bercow also broke with convention by allowing arch Remainer Dominic Grieve to bring an amendment to a motion that was in theory unamendable. Supported by Conservative and Labour MPs, it stated that in the event of Theresa May losing the vote on her proposed deal, the government would have to return to the House of Commons within three days of her deal being defeated. The amendment, passed by 308 votes to 297, prevented the government from running down the clock and was widely interpreted as not just Parliament pushing back against the executive but Remainers pushing back against Brexit. It also flew in the face of the convention that the Speaker of the House should remain neutral. The controversial amendment also followed a previous amendment by Grieve which meant that any statement after a defeat of May's Brexit deal was itself amendable, thereby allowing MPs to table their own alternatives to the Brexit process. Many of these alternatives would soon appear after MPs, as widely anticipated, comprehensively rejected May's Brexit deal on 15 January 2019. Overall, it was defeated by 432 votes to 202; the largest defeat for any government for at least a century.

In total, 118 Conservative MPs from the Leave and Remain wings joined with opposition parties to vote down the deal. Most Conservative

[21] Barwell (2021), p. 355.

rebels either opposed the backstop or had come round to the idea of a more distant relationship, or both. In the aftermath, Jeremy Corbyn tabled a vote of no confidence in the government: 'She cannot seriously believe that after two years' failure she's capable of negotiating a good deal for the people of this country.'[22] While May won that vote, by 325 votes to 306, it was abundantly clear to everybody that something would have to change.

May's weakness was reflected in other developments. In the aftermath of the vote, she was forced to reach out to parliamentarians from across the political divide, meeting with the SNP, Plaid Cymru, the Liberal Democrats and senior Labour MPs (Jeremy Corbyn refused to meet unless May categorically ruled out No Deal). Most either wanted a second referendum or a much closer relationship that involved remaining in the customs union and the single market, while a small number said the government should revoke Article 50 and cancel Brexit altogether. Nonetheless, given that there was no majority for these outcomes, and the deal was unlikely to pass, there was little incentive for Labour MPs who wanted a fresh general election to rally around a deal.[23]

Further amendments, notably the Brady Amendment which required May to return to Brussels to try and renegotiate the backstop, led to further negotiations. Yet there was little progress, as both sides continued to accuse May of running down the clock; while Conservative Eurosceptics had lost faith in her entire approach, others feared that May was merely playing for time and would still return to Parliament to try and force her deal through.

Failure to modify the backstop, combined with the lack of any clear incentive for Labour MPs to support the deal, meant that when another vote was held on 12 March the result was another big defeat for May, by 391 to 242 votes. Although thirty-nine Conservatives who had previously opposed the deal now swung behind it, support for the deal was still nowhere near strong enough. In the aftermath, Theresa May requested an extension to Article 50, and one was granted until 22 May should her deal pass Parliament, or until 12 April should it not.

Over the next few weeks, May and her team continued to fail to cobble together a viable coalition to pass the deal. A third vote on the Withdrawal Agreement, on 29 March, when the UK should have officially exited the EU, also ended in defeat, with 344 votes against 286.

While Brexit was having a clear impact on the internal discipline of the Conservative Party, it was also having other effects on the workings of British government and the electoral system more generally.

---

[22] 'Labour tables no-confidence vote as Theresa May's Brexit deal suffers worst Commons defeat in a century', ITV News, 15 January 2019.
[23] Pogrund and Maguire (2020).

Implementing Brexit had been a largely unprecedented test for the government, not least because it overturned the status quo, challenged convention and forced observers to rethink how government worked. The issue had also cut directly across the traditional left–right divide and did not sit comfortably on the existing political map.

Against this backdrop, three key changes became especially visible as the country continued to grapple with the Brexit wars. First, throughout the entire process there was a general breakdown in the traditional discipline of collective responsibility. The weakness of May's government was reflected in the continual willingness of cabinet ministers and others to voice dissent and criticize her government's approach without being asked to resign.[24] The loss of Prime Minister May's authority after the disastrous election in 2017 was continually put on display, reflected in public disagreements over Brexit policy, regular incursions by Boris Johnson and the refusal of her ministers to accept offers of various positions during a reshuffle in early 2018.[25]

The second was the sheer regularity of resignations that now rocked British politics. While a first wave of resignations had followed the Chequers plan in the summer of 2018, a second wave followed the publication of the draft Withdrawal Agreement. Overall, between the general election of 2017 and the eventual resignation of Theresa May in July 2019, her government suffered nearly twenty resignations because of Brexit. In the first six months of 2019, May lost more ministers than any other recent prime minister had lost in a single year (with the exception of herself in 2018). It was a symbol of just how fractious and divided British politics had become.

Third, in electoral behaviour British politics was also experiencing a much higher degree of fragmentation. In February 2019, seven Labour MPs suddenly left the Labour Party to launch a new rival party, the Independent Group, which would later morph into Change UK. In the days that followed, they were joined by three (pro-Remain) Conservative MPs. The rebel politicians talked of challenging Brexit and offering a home to voters who felt completely fed-up with extremes on both sides; with Jeremy Corbyn and Labour's failure to tackle charges of anti-Semitism and with what they saw as the Conservative Party's sharp turn to the hard right.

---

[24] Institute for Fiscal Government (2019).

[25] Jeremy Hunt turned down a move from his job as Health Secretary, Greg Clark resisted attempts to move him from his role as Business Secretary and Justine Greening, who refused to move from Education, quit the cabinet and then became a leading Conservative advocate of a second referendum.

All three of these changes remained visible as the country hurtled through 2019. Though originally the UK had been scheduled to exit the EU on 29 March 2019, both sides had failed to reach an agreement that was acceptable to a divided Parliament. In late March, a large majority of MPs rejected May's proposed agreement, producing heavy and embarrassing defeats for May. The House of Commons rejected the deal that May had negotiated on three separate occasions, and so she was forced to delay the date of departure twice. On 14 March 2019, Parliament voted to extend the Article 50 process for the first time.

In another vote against a No Deal Brexit, the prime minister was forced to accept that she was unable to force her government into one lobby or another. Initially, the prime minister allowed a free vote, but when the motion was amended to rule out a 'No Deal' for good, the government imposed a three-line whip against the amended motion. Five cabinet ministers, eight ministers and five parliamentary private secretaries (PPSs) abstained on that vote, without handing in their resignations or facing dismissal.

With no Brexit deal in sight, on 5 April 2019, Theresa May requested a second extension until 30 June 2019. Forty ministers voted against the government's own motion to extend Article 50, including five cabinet ministers and Brexit Secretary Stephen Barclay, who only minutes earlier had commended the motion to the House. An extension was granted, but only until 22 May, and provided that, in the meantime, the Withdrawal Agreement was passed. Eurosceptics compared the national humiliation to the occasion when Labour's Denis Healey was forced to ask the International Monetary Fund for an emergency loan in 1976. 'Lord North is one of the few beneficiaries of the May premiership', quipped one magazine. '[H]e is no longer the worst prime minister in our history.'[26]

At an emergency EU summit held on 10 April 2019, the EU agreed to a further Brexit extension until 31 October 2019. By this time, it had become abundantly clear that many voters, regardless of whether they had voted Leave or Remain, were distinctly unimpressed. After the failure to leave the EU on 29 March 2019, a large majority of voters disagreed with the statement, 'I trust MPs to do the right thing for the country over Brexit' while also agreeing that 'Parliament seems determined not to implement the will of the electorate on Brexit.'[27]

Conservative voters were especially disillusioned and soon made this known to the party. At local elections in May 2019, the Conservative

---

[26] 'Agony prolonged', *The Spectator Magazine*, 23 March 2019.
[27] Curtice (2019).

Party suffered massive losses, with more than forty councils and 1,300 seats lost. It was the party's worst performance at a set of local elections for a quarter of a century. The last comparable defeat had taken place in 1995, when the party had been heavily defeated by New Labour under the leadership of Tony Blair. But whereas Blair and Labour had surged to nearly 50 per cent of the vote, this time around, Corbyn's Labour Party did not fare much better than their Conservative rivals; Labour lost more than eighty seats and half-a-dozen councils. Furthermore, Labour's loss of control of northern pro-Brexit areas such as Ashfield, Bolsover, Bolton, Darlington, Derbyshire, Hartlepool, Middlesbrough and Stockton-on-Tees was yet another sign of a more profound change in the country's political geography.

The local elections also underlined how a once stable and secure two-party system was coming unstuck. The Conservative and Labour parties were now visibly in retreat, and challengers were on the rise. This was also reflected in the polls, where support for the two major parties crashed; shortly before the local elections their combined share of the national vote was just 58 per cent. One irony of the Brexit vote is that in its aftermath British politics looked increasingly European, with the traditional two-party system making way for a far more fragmented and volatile multi-party race.

Britain's majoritarian system was witnessing many of the same winds that had been sweeping through other democracies: a resurgent national populism in the form of Nigel Farage's new Brexit Party, increased support for the Liberal Democrats and the Greens, and higher rates of volatility, whereby larger numbers of people were now switching their vote from one election to the next. While many commentators drew a straight line from this fragmentation to Brexit, the reality is that the two-party system had been under strain for some time.[28]

Whereas until the mid-1970s, nine in ten voters had been locked into the system, voting Conservative or Labour, by 2005 it had fallen below seven in ten. The British had also become much less tribally loyal to the main parties and more willing to support alternatives. By 2010, more than one in three were already supporting other parties, whether Nick Clegg's Liberal Democrats, the Scottish National Party, the UK Independence Party or, to a lesser extent, the Greens. In short, the fragmentation of the system had been underway for a while, even if Brexit had put it on steroids.

The weakening grip of the main parties was then powerfully displayed at elections to the European Parliament, held only a few weeks after

---

[28] Sanders (2017).

the local elections in late May 2019. Because the country was still a member of the EU it was required to hold a fresh set of elections to the European Parliament, an institution a majority of voters had decided to leave nearly three years earlier. With no resolution to the escalating crisis in sight, and much of the electorate exasperated, ahead of the contest pollsters put combined support for Labour and the Conservatives at just 52 per cent – their lowest share in forty years of polling.[29] Increasingly, the brief return to dominance of the main parties at the 2017 general election looked like an outlier amid a wider trend of dwindling support.

For reasons that we outline in Chapter 4, the big winners at the European elections were the two challengers to the mainstream parties who had articulated the most polarizing positions on Brexit.[30] Nigel Farage's new national populist Brexit Party, which demanded a hard Brexit on World Trade Organization lines, topped the polls with 32 per cent of the vote, while the anti-Brexit Liberal Democrats, who had urged voters to say 'bollocks to Brexit', finished second with almost 20 per cent.[31] The election was widely seen as a proxy second referendum between Leave and Remain. While Farage entered the history books as the only politician to win two different national elections with two different political parties, the Liberal Democrats had enjoyed their highest share of the vote at any election since Cleggmania had erupted ahead of the 2010 general election.

The two major parties, in sharp contrast, suffered a disastrous night. While Labour finished in third place with just 13.6 per cent of the vote – the party's lowest share of the vote at any nationwide election since 1910 – the Conservatives slumped into fifth place with just 8.8 per cent, their lowest share of the vote in their entire history. Many Conservative activists had simply refused to campaign. Between them, the two parties attracted just 23 per cent of the vote, their lowest combined share since the emergence of the modern two-party system. It underlined both

[29] Ipsos-MORI May 2019 Political Monitor put the Conservatives on 25 per cent, Labour on 27 per cent, the Brexit Party on 16 per cent, the Liberal Democrats on 15 per cent, the Greens on 7 per cent and a lingering UKIP on 3 per cent. The previous low – of 54 per cent – had been recorded in 1981. Available online: www.ipsos.com/ipsos-mori/en-uk/support-conservatives-and-labour-falls-sharply (accessed 2 April 2020).
[30] Cutts, Goodwin, Heath and Milazzo (2019).
[31] The Brexit Party was founded in November 2018. Farage officially left UKIP the next month and was appointed leader of the Brexit Party on 22 March 2019, seven days before Britain was supposed to be officially leaving the EU under Article 50. Farage launched the new party in Coventry on 12 April 2019. The party's 2019 European Parliament election campaign was overseen by some of the same figures who had orchestrated the rise of UKIP. The party soon claimed to have recruited more than 100,000 registered supporters.

the scale and speed at which politics was becoming more polarized and the wider system was fragmenting.

The next day, amid the electoral ruins, a visibly emotional Theresa May resigned and cleared the way for a new leader of the Conservative Party and a new Prime Minister. 'I will shortly leave the job that it has been the honour of my life to hold. The second female prime minister, but certainly not the last. I do so with no ill will, but with enormous and enduring gratitude to have had the opportunity to serve the country I love.'[32] After Margaret Thatcher, John Major and David Cameron, Theresa May became the fourth successive Conservative prime minister to have been brought down, at least partly or fully, by the Europe question. The issue on everybody's minds now was whether the question of Britain's relationship with Europe was about to devour another leader who had been waiting in the wings for some time.

Enter Boris

Ever since the Brexit referendum, Boris Johnson had deliberately cultivated an image of himself as a populist outsider. He was one of only a few senior Conservatives to break with the consensus in Westminster by campaigning for Brexit and had then campaigned more strongly than most against Theresa May's soft Brexit. Now, through his campaign for the Conservative Party leadership and, by extension, the office of prime minister, he sought to reap the dividend and realign his party and its electorate around Brexit.

'Deliver Brexit, unite the country and defeat Jeremy Corbyn. And that is what we are going to do!' This was the claim by Boris Johnson when he finally became leader of the Conservative Party and the country's new prime minister, in July 2019. With support from two-thirds of the Conservative Party's membership, and much of his support within the Conservative Parliamentary Party coming from the pro-Brexit wing, he became the fifty-fifth person to hold the office of prime minister.

Yet when it came to the defining issue of Brexit, Boris Johnson swiftly departed from past practice. He adopted a more combative and direct approach, telling both his party and the country that his priority would be to 'Get Brexit Done'. He also talked of renegotiating Theresa May's unpopular Brexit deal, though remained vague on the detail. Sensing the exasperation among Leave voters and across the wider country, he also pledged that the country would finally exit the EU 'do or die'.

---

[32] 'Theresa May quits: UK set for new PM by end of July', BBC News, 24 May 2019. Available online: www.bbc.co.uk/news/uk-politics-48395905

'The doubters, the doomsters, the gloomsters – they are going to get it wrong again', he said, after accepting the Queen's invitation to form a government. 'The people who bet against Britain are going to lose their shirts because we are going to restore trust in our democracy and we are going to fulfil the repeated promises of Parliament to the people and come out of the EU on October 31, no ifs or buts.'[33]

Fearing that MPs could once again act to prevent the country from exiting the EU by the new deadline of 31 October, in the last week of August, Prime Minister Johnson sought to 'prorogue' or suspend Parliament from sitting for an unusually long period of five weeks. After another case that was brought by Gina Miller – and much talk about a 'coup' – the Supreme Court subsequently ruled that the move was 'unlawful' and that the common law placed limits on the scope of the government's power of prorogation and that these limits had been breached. The ruling marked another reassertion of the role of the judiciary and Parliament in the Brexit process, although some saw it as yet another worrying example of the misuse of judicial power in politics.[34]

Two weeks later, Boris Johnson sought to regain momentum by proposing an alternative to the backstop. On 17 October 2019, he agreed a new Withdrawal Agreement with the EU. After Parliament voted for more time to scrutinize the agreement, Johnson was forced to renege on his 'do or die' pledge and request an extension. This was granted with the new date being 31 January 2020.

None of this hurt the Conservative Party in the polls, however. Ever since Johnson took over, the party's position had steadily improved. Along with his advisor, Dominic Cummings, who had also overseen the Leave campaign at the 2016 referendum, Johnson had deliberately set out to lure back disillusioned Leavers who had been defecting to Farage's Brexit Party. The strategy was successful. Between the start of Johnson's campaign for the leadership of the Conservative Party in mid-May 2019 and the supposed Brexit deadline on 31 October, the percentage of Leave voters who planned to vote Conservative rocketed from 36 to 66 per cent. Meanwhile, the percentage of Conservatives who were loyal to Farage crashed from 29 to 10 per cent.[35]

The picture on the other side of the Brexit divide, however, looked different. Whereas two-thirds of Leavers were falling into line behind the Conservatives, at the end of October, Remainers were far more divided; 41 per cent were with Labour, 28 per cent the Liberal Democrats, 17 per

---

[33] www.news.com.au/world/new-british-pm-johnson-says-the-brexit-doomsters-are-going-to-get-it-wrong-again/video/af34a892582751b0826f1a935f979e6d

[34] Finnis (2019).

[35] YouGov polling data 13–14 May 2019 and 31 October–1 November 2019.

cent the Conservatives, 7 per cent the SNP and 6 per cent the Greens.[36]
If Johnson's aim was to consolidate the Leave vote and engineer a Brexit
election then the pieces appeared to be falling into place.

These shifts helped the Conservatives establish a strong lead in the polls.
When Johnson had won the party leadership in the summer, the Conservatives had been trailing Labour and sometimes even Nigel Farage's Brexit
Party. But then, over the next three months, his unequivocal pro-Brexit
message and pledge to meet the Brexit deadline 'do or die' resonated. By
the time that the 31 October deadline came and went, the Conservative
Party was averaging a 12-point lead over Labour in the polls.[37]

While Labour had not led in the opinion polls since the summer, the
main opposition party was suffering from other weaknesses. An already
unpopular Corbyn had become even more unpopular. In February 2019,
public satisfaction with the leader of the Labour Party had fallen to its
lowest level ever; fewer than one in five voters, just 17 per cent, felt satisfied with how the Labour leader was doing his job.[38] It was the lowest
figure for any Labour leader since Michael Foot in 1982. Nearly three
in four voters, 72 per cent, felt dissatisfied with Corbyn's performance,
putting his net satisfaction at –55.

As the summer of 2019 rolled by, Corbyn's already weak position in
the polls deteriorated further. Some 63 per cent of all voters rejected the
idea that Corbyn was 'ready to be Prime Minister'; 62 per cent felt that
Labour should change its leader before the next election; less than half of
all Labour voters felt satisfied with how Corbyn was doing his job; when
asked to choose whether Boris Johnson or Jeremy Corbyn would make the
most capable prime minister, 50 per cent said Johnson while only 29 per
cent said Corbyn; and only 20 per cent felt that Corbyn 'has what it takes
to be a good Prime Minister'.[39] A few months later, in October 2019, Corbyn's net satisfaction score among all voters plunged to a new low. With
75 per cent of all voters dissatisfied and just 15 per cent satisfied, this put
Corbyn's popularity even lower than that of Michael Foot. He was now,
officially, the most unpopular opposition leader in the history of polling.[40]

Once he became prime minister, Boris Johnson's strategy focused on
securing an early election as the only way to break the impasse created

---

[36] YouGov polling data 13–14 May 2019 and 31 October–1 November 2019.
[37] Taken from polling trends ahead of the UK 2019 general election. To view these polls
see polling for the 2019 general election. Available online: https://en.wikipedia.org/wiki/
Opinion_polling_for_the_2019_United_Kingdom_general_election
[38] www.ipsos.com/en-uk/jeremy-corbyns-satisfaction-ratings-fall-historic-low
[39] Data taken from YouGov polls.
[40] www.ipsos.com/en-uk/jeremy-corbyn-has-lowest-leadership-satisfaction-rating-any-
opposition-leader-1977

Table 2.1 *The Sequence of Events Leading Up to the 2019 General Election*

4 September 2019	Parliament votes against Johnson's motion to call an October general election by 298 votes to 56 (Labour abstained)
9 September 2019	Speaker John Bercow announces he will resign. The Benn Act comes into place requiring the prime minister to seek an extension in the case of a No Deal scenario. Parliament is prorogued until 14 October
24 September 2019	The Supreme Court rules that the decision to prorogue Parliament was unlawful and Parliament is recalled on 25 September
14 October 2019	Queen's Speech
17 October 2019	Revised Withdrawal Agreement agreed by UK and European Commission and endorsed by the European Council
19 October 2019	Withdrawal Agreement debated, Letwin amendment (to withhold approval of deal until the legislation to enact it is passed) passes by 322 votes to 306. Benn Act activated, requiring Johnson to request an extension
19 October 2019	Johnson requests an extension until 31 January (through an unsigned letter). He also writes a signed letter saying he believes a delay would be a mistake
22 October 2019	Withdrawal Agreement bill (second reading) approved by 329 votes to 299
24 October 2019	Johnson asks Corbyn to support a motion for a December general election – Corbyn insists No Deal be off the table
28 October 2019	European Council agrees to extend the deadline until 31 January
28 October 2019	Motion for a 12 December election defeated by 299 votes to 70. Government withdraws the Withdrawal Agreement bill
29 October 2019	Parliament votes to call an early election by 438 to 20

by the lack of a parliamentary majority bequeathed by his predecessor. Table 2.1 charts the convoluted sequence of events leading up to the calling of the 2019 general election. Johnson actually asked Parliament for an election on four different occasions. Finally, the Liberal Democrat leader Jo Swinson supported the call for an election, arguing that her party could win it (she subsequently lost her seat to the SNP). This meant that Corbyn could no longer oppose an election without appearing to run away from voters. MPs finally approved an early general election in a parliamentary vote on 29 October by a margin of 438 to 20.

British voters were heading to the polls again, for their third general election in just four years and their seventh nationwide election in nine years.[41] Scheduled for 12 December, the 2019 general election would

---

[41] After the 2010 general election, 2014 European Parliament election, 2015 general election, 2016 EU membership referendum, 2017 general election and the 2019 European Parliament election. For the Scots, the 2019 general election would be the tenth major electoral contest in only nine years after also holding the 2014 independence referendum and the 2011 and 2016 Scottish Parliament elections.

also be Britain's first December election since 1923. As we explain more fully in Chapter 5, the general election produced the largest Conservative Party majority since Margaret Thatcher's third and final majority in 1987 and the largest for any party since New Labour's second victory in 2001.

Despite the Conservatives having been in government for nearly a decade, and the 'costs of government' problem that incumbent parties tend to lose rather than gain votes, Boris Johnson and the Conservatives attracted 44 per cent of the vote, an increase of 1.2 points on their result in 2017. The Conservative Party had now increased its share of the vote at every general election since 1997, including at every one of the four general elections that were held from 2010 onwards, when the party was in power.

For Labour, in sharp contrast, the election produced the historic defeat that some of the party's MPs had feared. Under the leadership of Corbyn, the main opposition party was reduced to just 203 seats, a loss of 59 seats on 2017 and its lowest number of seats since 1935. Most notably, however, was the severe damage that was inflicted across Labour's traditional 'Red Wall'. A Conservative Party that was led by an Old Etonian Oxford graduate captured more than fifty seats from Labour, including many heartland, working-class seats which had either not elected Conservatives for decades or had never done so before in history.[42] It had also been a dismal night for the challenger parties, which less than seven months earlier had dominated elections to the European Parliament. Sensing the changing winds, ahead of the election Nigel Farage announced that he would stand down Brexit Party candidates in 317 seats the Conservative Party had won at the 2017 election, aiming to help pro-Brexit candidates win.[43] The Brexit Party, much like UKIP before it, in 2017, witnessed a sharp decline in support, winning only 2 per cent of the vote and averaging 5.1 per cent in seats where they stood candidates.

The election also had other effects. When the 2016 referendum was held, a clear majority of Conservative MPs (57 percent) had supported Remain. They had easily outnumbered their Leave counterparts. After the 2017 general election, this figure fell slightly but only to 54 per cent, and so Remain supporters were still dominant in the parliamentary party. But after the 2019 general election this was no longer the case; 55 per

---

[42] These included Great Grimsby (Labour's since 1945), Bishop Auckland (1935), Bassetlaw (1935), Wakefield (1932), Leigh (1922), Don Valley (1922) and Bolsover, a seat that Labour had never lost.
[43] 'General election 2019: Nigel Farage defends decision not to contest Tory seats', *BBC News*, 5 December 2019.

cent of all Conservative MPs had voted to leave the EU, reflecting the realignment of the Conservative Party.[44]

Boris Johnson had thus achieved what Theresa May could not, a majority – and had reshaped the Conservative Party around a strong pro-Brexit message. Whereas history will remember her gamble as a reckless one, it will remember Johnson's as one that paid off handsomely. The riddle of the Brexit withdrawal process could now be solved. Within days of the general election, MPs approved the Second Reading of the European Union (Withdrawal Agreement Bill) by 358 votes to 234. Diehard Eurosceptics who had strongly opposed May's deal three times now endorsed Boris Johnson's deal, believing that it had removed the Northern Irish backstop, would allow more divergence with the EU and contained new protections during a future transition period. And so, on 31 January 2020, the United Kingdom officially and finally left the European Union.

'Tonight, we are leaving the European Union', said Boris Johnson, in an address to the country, on 31 January 2020. 'The most important thing to say tonight is that this is not an end but a beginning. This is the moment when the dawn breaks and the curtain goes up on a new act in our great national drama.'[45]

The vote for Brexit pushed the United Kingdom in a new and fundamentally different direction. As we have seen in this chapter, aside from changing the country's relationship with its closest trading partner, the referendum result has also had a profound impact on both the workings of British government and electoral politics. But many questions remain unanswered. What factors shaped electoral politics throughout this period? Why was Theresa May unable to win a majority in 2017 while Boris Johnson managed to win a very large one only two years later? Why has the Labour Party and the left suffered a series of defeats? And what do all of these elections and voting decisions reveal about the deeper changes that are sweeping through British politics? These are the questions that we will explore in the chapters that follow.

---

[44] Lynch (2019). Furthermore, and as Lynch notes, of the 106 new Conservative MPs elected in 2019, 67 stated that they had voted Leave. Leavers form a majority of both MPs elected in seats gained and those replacing incumbent Conservatives.

[45] 'PM Address to the nation: 31 January 2020'. Available online: www.gov.uk/government/speeches/pm-address-to-the-nation-31-january-2020

3 Political Paralysis
The 2017 General Election

Held just two years after the 2015 general election and only one year after the shock vote for Brexit, the 2017 election amplified the political stalemate that had been building ever since the referendum. Brexit was a dominant but certainly not the only issue on the minds of the British people. In particular, Jeremy Corbyn, the leader of the Labour Party, found a receptive audience among millions of young voters who were attracted by his radical socialist agenda. The end result was an unexpected 'Youthquake' which gave Labour a share of the vote only slightly lower than the Conservative Party's share, while Theresa May and her team were denied their much anticipated big majority in the House of Commons.

The outcome of the 2017 election, as we have seen, had a profound impact on British politics. By delivering a hung Parliament rather than the 'strong and stable' majority that May and her team desired and required for the Brexit negotiations, the outcome of the election directly contributed to the tightening gridlock in Parliament. In the aftermath, Theresa May's Brexit deal would fail to command majority support and so, as we saw in the last chapter, the quest to secure and deliver Brexit ground to a halt amidst a storm of increasing bitterness and acrimony. And this, in turn, would ultimately pave the way for the rise of Boris Johnson.

But what actually shaped the outcome of the 2017 general election? What factors pushed people into the Conservative or Labour camps? And what did the election reveal about the deeper currents blowing through British politics? Drawing on our unique surveys, these are the questions we explore and answer in this chapter.

2017: The Context of Choice

As we saw in Chapter 1, in the aftermath of the Brexit referendum the two main parties were plunged into leadership elections, giving rise to Theresa May on the right and an emboldened Jeremy Corbyn on the left. As Figure 3.1 shows, this new political context was soon reflected in the polls. After the referendum and the abortive attempt to oust Jeremy

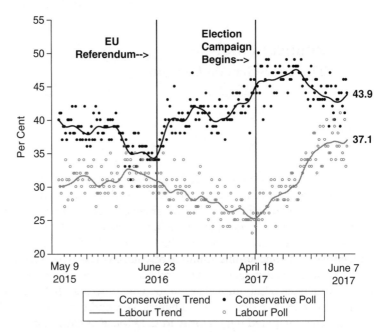

Figure 3.1 Trends in Conservative and Labour Vote Intentions in 257 Polls, 9 May 2015–7 June 2017.
Source: https://en.wikipedia.org/wiki/Opinion_polling_for_the_2017_United_Kingdom_general_election

Corbyn, the Labour Party trended almost steadily downward, under the new leadership of Theresa May, the Conservatives saw their poll numbers surge upwards, with the favourable trend continuing into the early spring of 2017. This trend contributed to the decision by May and her team to renege on an earlier promise and call a fresh general election, and on 19 April 2017 she secured the necessary two-thirds majority in Parliament needed to hold a new election. Contrary to May's promise not to hold an early election, voters would now go to the polls on 8 June.

May's decision to change her mind and request a mandate to provide what she called 'strong and stable government' was understandable. Forecasting models that translated the polls into parliamentary seats indicated that a huge Conservative majority – perhaps upwards of 100 seats – was in the offing.[1] If correct, such an outcome would immediately free the prime minister from the very real prospect that small groups of

---

[1] See, e.g., https://en.wikipedia.org/wiki/2017_United_Kingdom_general_election#Opinion_polling_and_seat_projections

ardently pro-Remain or pro–hard Brexit 'veto players'[2] would hold her government hostage and defeat the legislation that was needed to secure agreement with any deal she might negotiate with the EU. For its part, the EU would also be forced to recognize that May had solid backing, both in Parliament and across the country. This would lessen the possibility that Brussels would 'slow walk' the Brexit negotiations in the hope that her government would eventually implode. If the latter occurred, the whole Brexit project might be scuttled.

Corbyn's calculus was different. Faced with the poll numbers displayed in Figure 3.1, it might be assumed he would run and hide from the prospect of an election. However, as a committed left-wing socialist who had improbably captured the leadership of his party after years of New Labour control and then seen off a serious internal coup to oust him, Corbyn could view a general election campaign as an opportunity – perhaps a once in a lifetime one – to extol the progressive politics that were his passion before a national audience. And, as the recent defeat of his internal critics had demonstrated, he could wage that campaign with the enthusiastic and vocal backing of thousands of new Labour members.

Many of these Corbynistas were young people who had flooded into Labour's ranks when Corbyn had first become a candidate for the party leadership in 2015. Many more had joined since then. If these people could secure Corbyn's position as Labour leader, they also could propel him to victory in a general election campaign, or so he hoped. Principled politics could be a winner at the ballot box. At the very least, he could use the campaign to deliver his message that politics should be 'for the many, not the few' to millions of people.

To The Polls

The Conservatives' theme of 'strong and stable government' was quickly undercut by negative reactions to specific policies May and her colleagues advanced when the campaign began. Perhaps most damaging was a widely publicized U-turn on their proposal to limit expenditures on care for the elderly. Labelled a 'dementia tax' by her opponents, May quickly backtracked on the ill-considered proposal while claiming nothing had changed. It did not look good for someone promising strong and stable governance.

As the campaign progressed, it became evident that May was an inept campaigner with a wooden personal style. Refusing to participate in party leader debates, she was ill at ease with the media. Illustrating the problem, when asked during an interview if she had ever done anything

---

[2] Tsebelis (2002).

ill-toward as a child, May hesitated and then replied that she had 'run through farmers' wheat fields'.[3] An electronic game 'Come Wheat May' poking fun at this curious, comical response soon appeared. Reacting to May's robotic style, critics labelled her the 'Maybot', and this became a viral meme on social media.

The contrast with Jeremy Corbyn was stark. Confident in his strongly held beliefs, he was a committed socialist, as Labour's manifesto forcefully testified. A Corbyn-led Labour government would retake the 'commanding heights' of the UK economy. To do this, Labour's policy proposals included public ownership of the railways, water and energy utilities as well as the Royal Mail. On the distribution side, Labour advocated, inter alia, elimination of university tuition fees, enhanced childcare support, large increases in public spending on the NHS and a massive investment in new social housing.

Although voters of a certain age might view Labour's 2017 manifesto as a rerun of leftist 'ideological totems' from a bygone age, millions of young people saw things differently. For youth, the politics and economics of the Cold War era were things they might have read about in history books, not the stuff of personal experience. For them, the policies the Corbyn-led Labour Party were putting on offer were a novel, much-needed relief package that promised to redress a decade of harsh Tory austerity.

As the campaign progressed, the public opinion polls signalled that support for Labour was on an upward trajectory. As illustrated in Figure 3.1, the public's increasingly pro-Labour mood continued until election day. Labour's surge over the course of the campaign was accompanied by a modest decrease in Conservative support. The net result was that Labour closed most of the gap in the polls. On 7 June, the day before the election, the Conservatives stood at 43.9 per cent on trend, with Labour at 37.1 per cent.[4] In the event, many polls substantially underestimated the Labour vote. When the ballots were counted, Labour had 40.0 per cent, up almost 10 percentage points compared to 2015 (see Figure 3.2). It was the party's highest vote percentage since 2001.

This is not to say that the Conservatives fared poorly in the popular vote. Their share was 42.4 per cent – up nearly 6 percentage points over 2015 and the largest since Margaret Thatcher led the party to victory in 1987. In contrast, the Liberal Democrat vote was a dismal 7.4 per cent, almost the same as in 2015, and far below the 23 per cent the party had achieved in 2010. For its part, the SNP's vote fell from 4.7 per cent

---

[3] https://en.wikipedia.org/wiki/Running_through_fields_of_wheat
[4] The trend line in Figure 3.1 is calculated using the Hodrick-Prescott filter. See Hodrick and Prescott (1997).

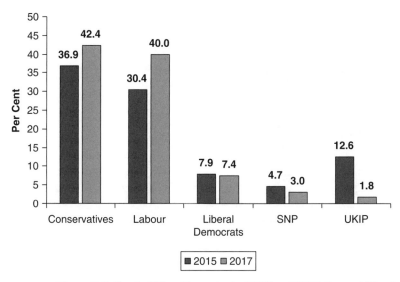

Figure 3.2 Parties' Vote Shares in the 2015 and 2017 General Elections. Source: https://commonslibrary.parliament.uk/research-briefings/cbp-7979/

to only 3.0 per cent (from 50.0 per cent to 36.9 per cent in Scotland). UKIP suffered even larger losses, with its vote collapsing from 12.6 per cent to 1.8 per cent. And, as is usual in Westminster elections, other minor parties such as the Greens and Plaid Cymru were competitive in only a handful of constituencies. Overall, the vote distribution was reminiscent of the two-party politics of the 1950s when the Conservatives and Labour were effectively the 'only game in town'.

Although the Conservatives had a larger popular vote than in 2015, they won only 317 seats in Parliament, nine fewer than they needed for a majority government (see Figure 3.3). This was exactly the opposite of what Prime Minister May required to have a strong hand in Brexit negotiations. The ability of small groups of rebels to derail any Brexit deal she might strike with the EU had been magnified, not eliminated. To stay in power, the Conservatives struck a deal with the small Northern Ireland DUP party that had won ten seats. Mrs May's government was on a knife edge.

In sharp contrast, Labour captured 262 seats, 30 more than it had won in 2015. Included in Labour's victory column were many pro-Brexit 'Red Wall' seats in the Midlands and North that the Conservatives had targeted.[5] Labour's ability to hold these seats and add

---

[5] See Allen (2018).

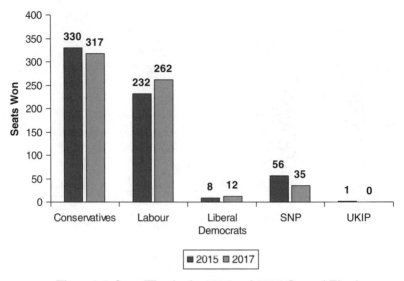

Figure 3.3 Seats Won in the 2015 and 2017 General Elections.
Source: https://commonslibrary.parliament.uk/research-briefings/cbp-7979/

substantially to its overall total seemingly demonstrated to Corbyn's supporters that advocacy of a full-throated socialist agenda was far from a recipe for electoral disaster. What Corbyn and his followers failed to acknowledge was that they were still very far from a parliamentary majority, something that would be very difficult to achieve as long as the SNP held the lion's share of seats in Scotland. Although the SNP's seat total had fallen from fifty-six to thirty-five, the party continued to be a dominant force in Scottish politics – something that was not about to change any time soon. Furthermore, any attempt to form a coalition government with the SNP would be political poison for Labour in England.

Nor could Labour contemplate forming a coalition with the Liberal Democrats. The fifty-seven seats that the Liberal Democrats had captured in the 'I agree with Nick' election of 2010 were long gone.[6] In 2015, the party had won only eight seats and in 2017, it managed only twelve. Other parties also failed to harvest more than a handful of seats. UKIP had precisely zero, while Plaid Cymru and the Greens had four and one, respectively. The 2017 election had produced a Parliament that would be hugely deadlocked, as Prime Minister May

[6] See, e.g., Whiteley, Clarke, Sanders and Stewart (2013).

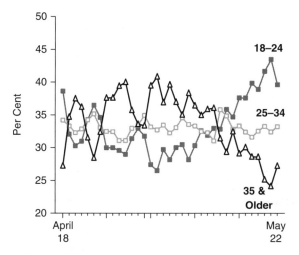

Figure 3.4 Percentages of People in Various Age Groups Joining the Electoral Register by Day during the 2017 General Election Campaign. Source: www.ons.gov.uk/peoplepopulationandcommunity/elections/electoralregistration/datasets/electoralstatisticsforuk
Note: 22 May was the last day to register to vote in the 2017 general election.

repeatedly struggled to make a Brexit deal a reality. In the next section, we examine the forces that led voters to behave as they did in the 2017 general election.

Corbyn's Youthquake

As discussed above, one of the most striking aspects of the 2017 election was the strong appeal of Jeremy Corbyn's Labour Party among youth. Although election surveys almost always overestimate turnout,[7] there is evidence that large numbers of young people joined the active electorate in the spring of 2017. First, Figure 3.4 shows trends for people in various age groups joining the electoral register over the period when Parliament was dissolved on 18 April and the end of the registration period on 2 May. As illustrated, the percentages of 18–24- and 25–34-year-olds were substantial throughout this period, with the former surging upward as the end of the registration period approached. Altogether, over 1 million in the 18–24 age bracket registered during the campaign and upwards of 2 million under the age of 35 did so. As we will see

[7] DeBell et al. (2018).

Table 3.1 *Binomial Logit Analysis of Factors Associated with Conservative and Labour Constituency Victories in Great Britain in the 2017 General Election*

	Conservative	Labour
Constituency Characteristics		
Per Cent Blue Collar Occupations	−0.51***	0.52***
Per Cent University Education	0.28***	−0.23***
Per Cent Vote Leave EU Referendum	**0.34*****	**−0.27*****
Per Cent White	0.05**	−0.060***
Per Cent Age 18–29	**−0.24*****	**0.15*****
Per Cent Age 65 and older	−0.03	−0.09
Region/Country[†]:		
North/Yorkshire	−0.06	0.09*
Midlands	1.94***	−1.77***
South East	2.48***	−2.67***
South West	3.27***	−2.70***
Scotland	4.45***	−0.90***
Wales	−0.13	0.11*
Constant	−21.29***	19.42***
McKelvey R^2 =	0.83	0.82
Percentage Correctly Classified =	89.5	89.5

Note: [†] London is region/country reference category. Note that the asterisks indicate the statistical significance of the coefficients. This enables us to rule out chance as an explanation of the effect. *** means that the chances of this effect being due to a chance outcome is less than 0.001.

below, large majorities of these people held positive views of Jeremy Corbyn and cast their votes for Labour.

To provide an initial view of the electoral impact of the youth vote, we analyse factors associated with Conservative and Labour victories at the constituency level.[8] Census data on the percentages of people aged 18–29 and 65 and over in each to the 632 constituencies in Great Britain are used as predictor variables. Other predictors include the percentage voting Leave in the 2016 EU referendum, social class as indexed by the percentage engaged in blue-collar occupations, the percentage with university education, ethnicity/race (percentage white) and county/region of residence. The aim here is to model the relationship between various demographics along with age and voting behaviour at the constituency level. The results (see Table 3.1) show

---

[8] Constituency-level electoral and socio-demographic data are available at Pippa Norris's website: www.pippanorris.com/data

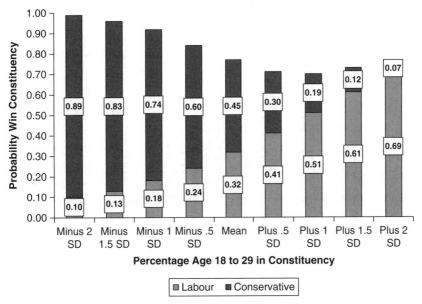

Figure 3.5 Probabilities of Conservatives or Labour Winning Seats by Percentage of 18–29-Year-Olds in Constituencies.
Note: Constituency age categories on horizontal axis vary from −2 standard deviations below average to +2 standard deviations above average.

that social class and education have expected relationships with party vote shares – the probability that the Conservatives would win a constituency is negatively related to the percentage of blue-collar workers and is positively associated with the percentage of university graduates.

The pattern for Labour is exactly the opposite. In addition, the Conservatives do relatively better in areas outside of London and the North and Labour does worse, especially in the South. Beyond these well-established patterns, attitudes towards Brexit matter too. The likelihood that the Conservatives would win a constituency is significantly and positively related to the percentage voting Leave in the EU referendum ($p \leq 0.001$), and the likelihood of a Labour victory has a significant and negative relationship with the size of the Leave vote ($p \leq 0.001$).

Finally, consistent with the attractiveness of the Corbyn-led Labour Party to young people, the percentage of young people in a constituency is significantly related to the election outcome. As the percentage of people under 30 years of age grows, the probability of a Labour victory increases and, in contrast, the probability of a Conservative victory declines. Figure 3.5 illustrates the strength of these relationships. With all

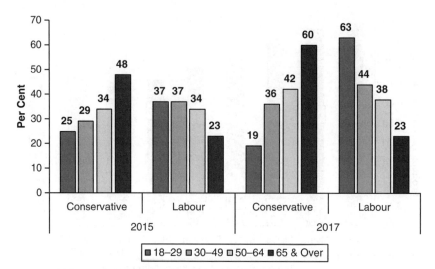

Figure 3.6 Conservative and Labour Vote by Age Group in the 2015 and 2017 General Elections.
Source: 2015 and 2017 Essex–UTD pre- and post-election panel surveys.

other factors held as their average values, the probability of a Labour constituency victory moves sharply upward from 0.10 to 0.69 (on a 0–1 scale) as the percentage of people in the 18–29 age bracket in that constituency increases.[9] The Conservative pattern is the opposite and even stronger, with the likelihood of a Tory win decreasing from fully 0.89 to only 0.07 as the percentage of young people in a constituency grows.

These constituency-level patterns foreshadow what we see in individual-level national survey data. Figure 3.6 compares the relationship between age and voting in the 2015 and 2017 Essex–UTD election surveys.[10] There is a sizeable relationship between age and Conservative support in both years. In 2015, the percentage voting Conservative climbs steadily from 25 per cent among 18–29-year-olds to 48 per cent among people aged 65 and over. The pattern is exaggerated in 2017 when the equivalent percentages move from 19 per cent among the 18–29-year-olds to 60 per cent among the 65 and older group.

The Labour patterns are even more striking. Figure 3.6 shows that in 2015 the relationship between age and Labour support was relatively

---

[9] Note that the horizontal axis is measured in standard deviation units of the age distribution. The standard deviation is a measure of the average dispersion of a distribution rather than a simple range of scores.

[10] For a description of the surveys, see Appendix A.

weak with the percentage of Labour voters being 37 per cent among the 18–29- and 30–49-year-olds to 34 per cent among the 50–64-year-olds and then falling to 23 per cent among those 65 or older. The pattern changes dramatically in 2017. As illustrated, the percentage of Labour voters is fully 83 per cent in the youngest age group and then falls sharply and steadily to merely 23 per cent in the oldest group. In the next section, we investigate the relationship between age and voting in greater detail as part of a larger analysis of factors driving the 2017 vote.

Issues, Leaders, Partisanship

For many years, scholars maintained that social class was the driving factor shaping the choices British voters made in successive elections.[11] However, analyses of data gathered in British election surveys conducted since the 1960s show that the relationship between class and voting has long been in decline and was never as strong as many researchers had assumed.[12] Studies conducted over the past two decades have repeatedly documented that what is often termed the *valence politics* model provides a much better account of how people in Britain and elsewhere make their electoral choices at particular points in time.[13]

The valence politics model was originally developed by Donald Stokes, a pioneering figure in voting behaviour research in Great Britain, the United States and other mature democracies. In a path-breaking article written in the early 1960s, Stokes argued that the electoral issues of principal concern to voters are typically those upon which virtually everyone is agreed on the goals of public policy.[14] Although 'pro–con' issues ('position' issues as political scientists call them) such as Brexit that deeply divide electorates occasionally gain prominence, valence issues are often dominant in electoral politics. Accordingly, much debate during election campaigns and in the interims between them focuses not on 'what to do' but rather on 'how to do it' and 'who is best able?'

The classic valence issue is the economy – overwhelming majorities consistently want robust and sustainable economic growth coupled with low rates of inflation and unemployment. Healthcare, education and crime are other prominent valence issues. Voters are virtually unanimous in their preferences for high quality, accessible and affordable healthcare and education, as well as protection for their lives and property.

[11] See, e.g., Butler and Stokes (1969).
[12] Clarke, Sanders, Stewart and Whiteley (2004).
[13] See, e.g., Clarke, Sanders, Stewart and Whiteley (2004, 2009); Clarke, Kornberg and Scotto (2009).
[14] Stokes (1963).

Similarly, they place a premium on government efforts to safeguard citizens from terrorists and rogue regimes that threaten to endanger national and personal security. In recent years, calls to heed the 'existential threat' of climate change are convincing an increasing number of people that environmental protection should join this list of perennially high-salience valence issues. However, as we shall see, environmental concerns have yet to have a major impact on electoral choice in Britain.

According to the valence politics theory, voters make their decisions primarily by evaluating the demonstrated and anticipated performance of parties and politicians on the valence issues they consider to be most important. When voters make these performance judgements, they rely heavily on 'heuristics' or simple 'rules of thumb' provided by party leader images and partisan affiliations. Buttressed by abundant research in experimental economics and cognitive psychology,[15] the idea is that voters are 'smart enough' to recognize that they often do not understand or cannot accurately evaluate the consequences of many of the specific policy proposals that politicians advance. To make sensible decisions in a world of radical uncertainty,[16] people depend on their impressions of politicians and parties' reputations for dealing with prominent valence issues. These performance-grounded impressions and reputations are periodically updated over time and can prompt voters to revise their views of leaders and change their partisan affiliations.[17]

Issues That Mattered

Given its enormous impact and continuing salience in the press, it might be anticipated that Brexit would dominate the issue agenda in the run-up to the 2017 general election. Indeed, Figure 3.7 shows that Brexit was the single most important election issue, according to respondents in our pre-election survey. One-third of those participating in the survey said that Brexit was their most important issue and, altogether, 60 per cent said it was one of their 'top three' issues. However, slightly more (61 per cent) designated the National Health Service as a top three issue, and 21 per cent said it was most important.

Several other issues attracted substantial attention. Some, such as immigration and the economy, played large roles in shaping voters' decisions in the 2016 EU referendum. As discussed above, the economy is a

---

[15] See, e.g., Gigerenzer (2008); Gigerenzer, Hertwig and Pachur (2015); Kahneman (2011).
[16] Kay and King (2020).
[17] Clarke and McCutcheon (2009).

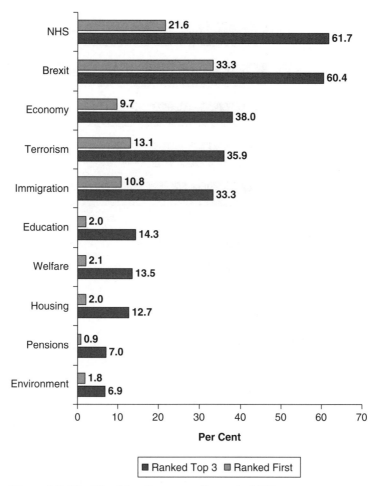

Figure 3.7 The Ten Most Important Issues in 2017.
Source: 2017 Essex–UTD pre-election survey.

perennially important valence issue and, in 2017, nearly four people in ten designated it as a top three issue, but just one in ten said it was the single most important one. The pattern for immigration is quite similar. Terrorism was yet another issue with 'intermediate' salience in 2017 – very likely a consequence of the horrific terrorist attacks in Manchester and London that occurred during the election campaign. Just over a third of those in our pre-election survey chose terrorism as a top three issue, and one in ten said it was number one.

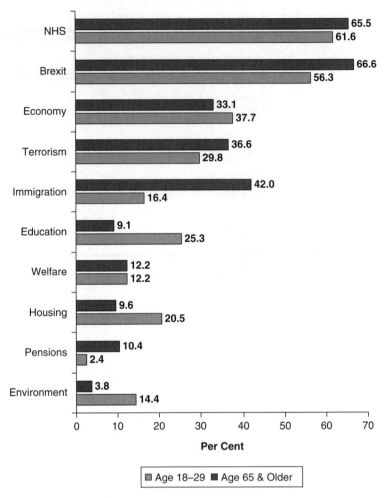

NHS 65.5 / 61.6
Brexit 66.6 / 56.3
Economy 33.1 / 37.7
Terrorism 36.6 / 29.8
Immigration 42.0 / 16.4
Education 9.1 / 25.3
Welfare 12.2 / 12.2
Housing 9.6 / 20.5
Pensions 10.4 / 2.4
Environment 3.8 / 14.4

Per Cent

■ Age 18–29 ■ Age 65 & Older

Figure 3.8 Top Three Important Issues for Younger and Older People in 2017.
Source: 2017 Essex–UTD pre-election survey.

All other issues were less salient. Topics such as education, welfare, housing and pensions were all mentioned by fewer than one person in five, and in every case fewer than one person in twenty said one of these issues was most important. Still further down the list, the environment was chosen as a top three issue by less than 7 per cent and less than 2 per cent designated it as most important. Despite the large differences in party support between younger and older people documented above, for the most part, differences in issue concerns across age groups were muted. Figure 3.8, which compares the issue emphases of people of less than 30 years of age with those 65 and older, illustrates this point. As the figure shows, Brexit was chosen as a top three issue by two-thirds of the 65 pluses but well over half (56 per cent) of the 18–29-year-olds chose it as well. Differences between the two groups in terms of emphasis on the NHS were even smaller, with over three-fifths selecting the health service as a top three issue in both groups. Similarly, small differences also obtain for several other issues, such as the economy, terrorism and welfare.

There were some issues for which the age gap is greater. Perhaps not unexpectedly given the huge increase in university tuition fees imposed by former Prime Minster Cameron's austerity-minded government, slightly over 25 per cent of the 18–29-year-olds cited education as an important issue. Less than 10 per cent of the 65 pluses did so. Similarly, young people were more concerned about housing and the environment. In contrast, not surprisingly the 65 and over group were more likely to cite pensions as a topic, and this was of lesser salience for young people far from retirement age. More generally, although differences on issues like pensions, housing and the environment are evident, the data indicate that levels of concern did not vary much by age.

The dominance of Brexit and the NHS on the issue agendas of all age groups does not imply that party preferences on these or other issues were similar. Consonant with the sharp age gradient in party support discussed above, there were large differences in judgements regarding how people in various age brackets evaluated the issue competence of the major parties. When asked to indicate which party was best on the issue they considered most important, only 15 per cent of the 18–29-year-olds selected the Conservatives (see Figure 3.9). The equivalent percentages for those in the 30–49, 50–64 and 65 and older age groups are 24 per cent, 37 per cent and 52 per cent, respectively. The pattern of preferences for Labour is the opposite, with the percentage thinking the party was best on the most important issue falling steadily from 38 per cent among people under 30 years of age to merely 14 per cent among those aged 65 and older. The implication of these findings is that partisan attachments have a big influence on the issues which people think are important.

These age differences aside, the overall distribution of party preferences on important issues clearly favoured the Conservatives. Among all of our 2017 pre-election survey respondents, 33 per cent chose the Conservatives and 22 per cent chose Labour. Only 4 per cent selected the Liberal Democrats, with another 10 per cent picking one of the minor parties. An additional 31 per cent said none of the parties was best on important issues or replied that they 'didn't know'. Broken down by age, we see that one-third and nearly two-fifths of those in the 18–29 and

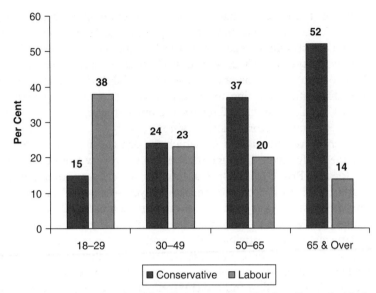

Figure 3.9 Party Best on Most Important Issue by Age Group in 2017.
Source: 2017 Essex–UTD pre-election survey.

30–49 age groups, respectively, declined to say that any of the parties would be best on the issue they believed was most important. Just over one-fifth of those in the 65 and older group also failed to pick any party. These percentages are sizeable and testify to widespread uncertainty about the parties' issue competence. Overall, the Conservatives had a clear edge, but still two-thirds of the electorate was not convinced that Prime Minister May and her colleagues would be able to address important issues facing the country.

Leader Images

Images of the party leaders do much to influence electoral choice. Voters rely heavily on their impressions of the leaders' character and competence for cues about how various parties would perform in office. Affective reactions to the leaders provide a convenient summary of their overall images in the public mind.[18] Our survey evidence indicates that in 2017 none of the leaders were enthusiastically received by the electorate as a whole. Theresa May and Jeremy Corbyn both had reasonably solid but hardly outstanding scores on a 0 (strongly dislike) to 10 (strongly like) scale. May's average score was 4.6 and Corbyn's was a

---

[18] Clarke, Sanders, Stewart and Whiteley (2009).

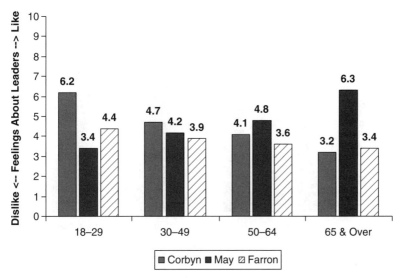

Figure 3.10 Feelings about Theresa May, Jeremy Corbyn and Tim Farron on 0 to 10 Scale by Age Group in 2017.
Source: 2017 Essex–UTD pre-election survey.

nearly identical 4.5 (see Figure 3.10). Other leaders fared considerably worse; Liberal Democrat Leader Tim Farron's average score was 3.8 and UKIP chieftain Paul Nuttall, who was heartily disliked by much of the electorate, recorded a dismal 2.5. Similarly, Nicola Sturgeon's UK-wide score was only 3.3 points. However, in Scotland where feeling about Sturgeon mattered for her party's electoral fortunes, her average score was somewhat better, if unspectacular, at 4.3.

Although Theresa May's and Jeremy Corbyn's likeability scores were very similar across the entire electorate, they varied sharply across age groups. As could be anticipated by how they voted, young people were much more enthusiastic about Corbyn, whereas those in older age categories were much more positively disposed towards May. Figure 3.10 shows that Corbyn's like–dislike score was a very healthy 6.2 among 18–29-year-olds, but it fell steadily across older age cohorts to only 3.2 among the 65 and older group. May's scores took the opposite trajectory, moving steadily upward from a low of 3.4 among people under 30 to 6.3 among those 65 and older. In keeping with his mediocre overall score, Liberal Democrat Leader Tim Farron's average scores were under 4 for all age groups except the under 30s, where his average was 4.4.

The large differences in feelings about May and Corbyn across various age groups anticipate striking age-related differences in perceptions

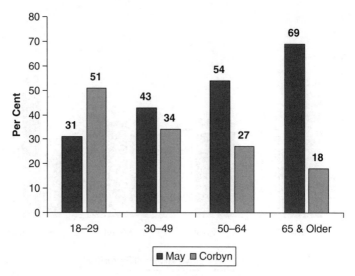

Figure 3.11 Percentages Rating Theresa May and Jeremy Corbyn 'Very' or 'Fairly' Competent by Age Group in 2017.
Source: 2017 Essex–UTD pre-election survey.

of specific leadership traits. For example, Figure 3.11 presents data on how people judged the competence of the two leaders. The age cohort differences are striking. For May, only 31 per cent of those younger than 30 years of age said that the word 'competent' described her 'very' or 'fairly' well. The number doing so climbs sharply and steadily to fully 69 per cent of those in the 65 and older age group. All of the comparable competence numbers are somewhat smaller for Corbyn, and the pattern is reversed. Among the under 30s, over half (51 per cent) rated him very or fairly competent, but fewer than one in five (18 per cent) of the 65 and over group did so.

These patterns are replicated for other leader traits such as caring, trustworthiness and strong leadership. The latter numbers are illustrative. For May, the percentages agreeing that the words 'strong leader' described her well climb from 33 per cent in the 18–29 age group to 72 per cent among the 65s and over. Once more, the pattern for Corbyn is a muted mirror image, with 45 per cent in the youngest group but only 14 per cent in the oldest one seeing him as a strong leader. Overall, the leadership image data emphasize the huge differences in how voters evaluated the Conservative and Labour leaders as the 2017 general election approached. As we will see, these differences did much to account for why people in various age groups voted as they did in that contest.

Partisanship

Partisan attachments constitute a second major heuristic after leadership that guides voters' behaviour at the polls. Building on the results of early national election studies conducted in the 1960s, subsequent generations of British psephologists have recognized that party identifications have direct effects on electoral choices as well as indirect effects by influencing how voters react to party leaders and political issues. Although it was originally assumed that psychological links with parties were very durable and grew in strength over the life cycle, panel surveys that monitor the psychology of individual voters over time have demonstrated that sizeable minorities change their partisan attachments from one election to the next. This has been true since at least the 1960s when the first national election studies with panel components were conducted.[19] This ongoing flexibility in partisanship is a product of changing evaluations of the performance of parties and their leaders. At any point in time, voters' partisan attachments provide powerful, easily accessible cues that facilitate electoral choice.

In our 2017 pre-election survey, the incidence of identification with one of the major parties was quite even, with 29 per cent saying they generally thought of themselves as Conservatives and 26 per cent reporting that they considered themselves to be Labour. Identifications with other parties were much less common – only 6 per cent claimed they were Liberal Democrats and a total of only 10 per cent identified with any of the other parties. Indicative of the potential volatility of political psychology at the time, the largest group (29 per cent) was composed of people who said that they did not identify with any of the parties or simply 'didn't know'.

There were sharp differences among party identifiers in their views about Brexit. In our pre-election survey fully 69 per cent of Conservative identifiers said that they disapproved of EU membership and only 25 per cent approved (see Figure 3.12). In contrast, 63 per cent of Labour identifiers approved and 27 per cent disapproved. Although these differences are large, it is clear that both major parties had substantial minorities of identifiers whose positions on Brexit were at odds with majority opinion in their parties. Clearly, both parties were split on the issue. The Liberal Democrats were more united on the issue – over three-quarters of Liberal Democrat identifiers were against leaving the EU and fewer than one in five were in favour.

---

[19] Clarke and McCutcheon (2009).

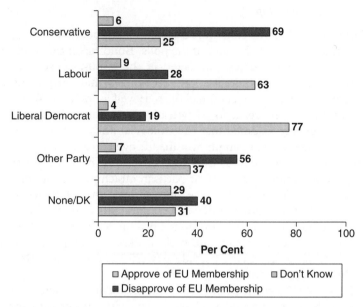

Figure 3.12 Attitudes Towards Brexit by Party Identification in 2017.
Source: 2017 Essex–UTD pre-election survey.

Figure 3.13 presents the distribution of partisanship across demographic groups. Looking first at country/region, consistent with parties' electoral strength in various geographic locales, the Conservatives had the largest percentages of identifiers in East Anglia (39 per cent) and the South East (39 per cent), whereas Labour was strongest in the North (36 per cent) and London (31 per cent). Consonant with their weak showing nationally, the Liberal Democrats lacked large numbers of identifiers in any region. Even in the South West, where the party traditionally has performed relatively well, fewer than one person in ten reported being a Liberal Democrat in 2017.

Reflecting the weak relationship between social class and voting in recent general elections, class differences in partisanship were similarly unimpressive. As Figure 3.13 illustrates, Conservative identification was most prevalent (38 per cent) in the upper and upper-middle classes (group A/B) and declined to 22 per cent in the lowest class (group D/E). However, Labour identification varies only slightly (from 26 per cent to 22 per cent) across the class hierarchy. And, although some researchers argue that educational qualifications constitute the new dividing line demarcating social class location,[20] educational differences in partisanship were very small. In addition, gender differences were virtually non-existent.

[20] See, e.g., Evans and Tilley (2017).

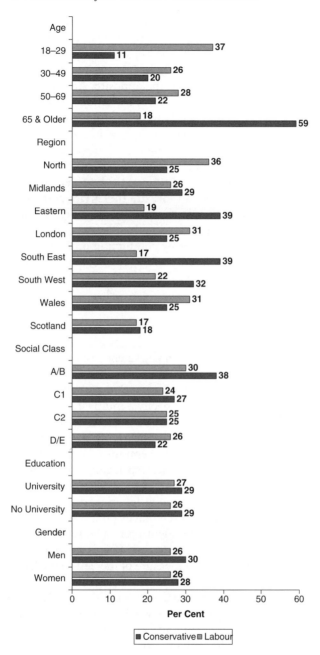

Figure 3.13 Party Identification by Socio-Demographic Characteristics in 2017.
Source: 2017 Essex–UTD pre-election survey.

The relationship between age and partisanship was very different. Consistent with the large age gap in voting in 2017 discussed above, the percentage of Conservative identifiers among 18–29-year-olds was only 11 per cent, but this climbed steeply to fully 59 per cent among those 65 and older. The Labour pattern is the opposite. Among the 18–29 age cohort, 37 per cent identified themselves as Labour, but among the 65 and older group the percentage of Labour partisans was only one-half as large. Liberal Democrat partisans were sparse in all age categories, the maximum being only 7 per cent among the 18–29-year-olds.

Age thus was a major dividing line in political psychology at the time of the 2017 general election. Young people had very different party preferences than their elders on Brexit, the NHS and other salient issues. Younger and older people also had sharply varying images of the party leaders and typically identified with different parties. In the next section, we bring this all together by conducting multivariate statistical analyses to determine how issue preferences, leader images, partisanship and various other predictor variables influenced electoral choice in that contest.

Making Choices

Evaluations of party performance on key valence issues such as the economy and healthcare, along with the cues provided by leader images and partisan identifications, do much to drive electoral choice in successive British elections. Accordingly, we specify a multivariate model of voting in 2017 that includes predictor variables measuring voters' evaluations of the state of the economy and healthcare, as well as their positions regarding Brexit, immigration and perceptions of being left behind economically.[21] Other predictor variables tap feelings about party leaders and partisan identifications.

In addition, to proxy voters' general left–right ideological positions, we include a measure of voters' preferences on a 0–10 tax–spend scale, where a score of 0 means a respondent prefers large tax cuts and lower spending, and a score of 10 the opposite. This is a perennially divisive issue in British politics and so is a measure of the 'left–right' dimension in public attitudes. We also specify a 'tactical voting' variable that indexes if voters chose a particular party because the party they really preferred was uncompetitive in their constituency. Several socio-demographic variables (age, education, gender, income and country/region) also are included in the model. Since the dependent variables in the voting analyses are

---

[21] For descriptions of how various predictor variables were constructed, see Appendix A.

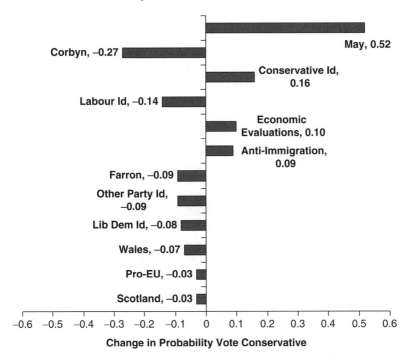

Figure 3.14 Factors Affecting Probability of Voting Conservative in the 2017 General Election.
Note: Results of binomial logit analysis.

dichotomies (e.g., vote Conservative = 1, vote for another party = 0), we use binomial logit analyses to estimate model parameters.[22] This model can be used to determine the effects of different variables on the probability that an individual will vote Conservative in the election. It allows us to identify the effect of each variable while at the same time taking into account other variables in the modelling.

Results of the Conservative voting analysis are summarized in Figure 3.14. This table contains only statistically significant predictors that influence the probability of voting for the Conservatives in comparison with the other parties.[23] The most powerful predictors are feelings about party leaders Theresa May and Jeremy Corbyn. With all other predictors held at their average values, as feelings about May move from

---

[22] Long and Freese (2014).
[23] Informally speaking, a statistically significant effect rules out chance as an explanation for the size of the effect. This means that it is not only found in the survey, but also in the population were we to (hypothetically) interview the entire electorate.

highly negative to highly positive, the probability of voting Conservative increases by 0.52 points (on a 0–1 scale).[24]

The effect of feelings about Corbyn work in the opposite direction, with the likelihood of voting Conservative dropping by 0.27 points as feelings about Corbyn move from very negative to very positive. As the figure also shows, the impact of party identification is somewhat weaker; for example, the likelihood of casting a Conservative ballot goes up 0.16 points if a voter identifies with that party and falls by 0.14 points if a voter is a Labour identifier. The effects of being a Liberal Democrat or an 'other' party identifier are smaller, but statistically significant.

Issue effects are present as well. As expected, voters who evaluate the economy positively and those who espouse negative attitudes towards immigration are more likely to support the governing Conservatives. In the case of economic evaluations, the change in probability is 0.10, and in the case of anti-immigration attitudes, the change is 0.09. It is also noteworthy that the impact of attitudes towards Brexit, although statistically significant, are small – all else equal, the probability of voting Conservative drops by 0.03 points if someone favours EU membership instead of Brexit. In addition people in Wales and Scotland are also somewhat less likely to support the Conservatives. Finally, when other factors are taken into account in the modelling, age does not have a significant *direct* effect on the probability of casting a ballot for the party. The latter is an interesting finding because it shows that the 'Youthquake' mentioned earlier operates through attitudes rather than simply through age. Young people have different attitudes than their older counterparts, and this is why they vote differently.

The multivariate analyses of Labour voting are summarized in Figure 3.15. Similar to the Conservative analyses, feelings about the party leaders are the dominant predictors of Labour voting. Specifically, the probability of voting Labour climbs by 0.45 points as feelings about Jeremy Corbyn move from very negative to very positive. And, as anticipated, the effects of feelings about Conservative leader Theresa May and Liberal Democrat leader Tim Farron work in the opposite direction. Increasingly positive feelings about May lessen the likelihood of voting Labour by 0.21 points and increasingly positive feelings about Farron do so by 0.16 points.

Party identifications have significant effects as well. With all other predictors set at their average values, Labour partisanship boosts the likelihood

---

[24] A probability scale varies from 0, meaning that something will never happen, to 1, meaning that it is certain to happen. So a coefficient of 0.52 in Figure 3.14 for Theresa May means that moving from disliking her to liking her increases the chances of voting Conservative by just over 50 per cent.

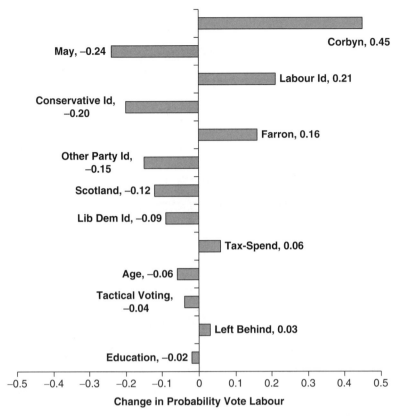

Figure 3.15 Factors Affecting Probability of Voting Labour in the 2017 General Election.
Note: Results of binomial logit analysis.

of a Labour vote by 0.21 points and Conservative, Liberal Democrat and 'other party' identifications reduce it by 0.20, 0.16 and 0.15 points respectively. Positions on the tax–spend scale and feelings of being left behind matter too, as does tactical voting, education and residence in Scotland. People who prefer a combination of higher taxes and more government spending on welfare programmes and those who sense they have been left behind economically were slightly more likely to vote Labour. Those with university education, residents of Scotland and tactical voters were less likely to do so. And, unlike in the Conservative case, older people were significantly less likely to vote Labour. However, the effect is modest – the probability of supporting the party differs by 0.06 points on the 0–1 scale for the oldest as compared to the youngest voters. In addition, attitudes towards Brexit do not have significant direct effects on Labour voting.

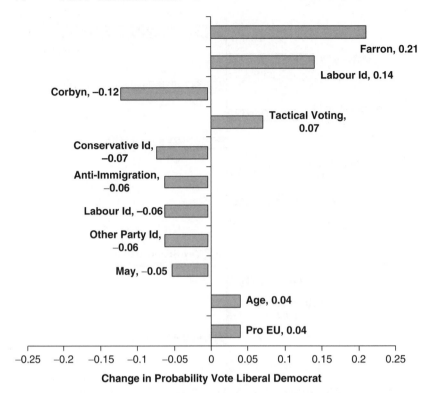

Figure 3.16 Factors Affecting Probability of Voting Liberal Democrat in the 2017 General Election.
Note: Results of binomial logit analysis.

The multivariate analysis of Liberal Democrat voting echoes many of the results just described. Once more, the strongest predictors are leader images and partisanship. Positive feelings about Tim Farron boost the probability of a Liberal Democrat vote by 0.21 points and positive feelings about Jeremy Corbyn and Theresa May reduce that probability by 0.12 and 0.06 points, respectively (see Figure 3.16). Partisanship works as expected as well, with Liberal Democrat identifications raising the likelihood of voting for the party, and identification with the Conservative, Labour or another party lowering it. Also, as expected given the party's strong pro-Remain stance, positive attitudes towards EU membership increase the likelihood of supporting the Liberal Democrats, but the direct effect is quite small, only 0.04 points. And, as might be anticipated given the Liberal Democrats' advocacy of tactical voting, casting one's ballot tactically increases the likelihood of voting for the party by

0.07 points. Finally, controlling for all other factors, older people are marginally more likely to vote Liberal Democrat.

Corbyn's Dual Effect

As we have seen, younger people were much more favourably disposed towards Jeremy Corbyn than were older voters in 2017, and feelings about him were the most important single predictor of the probability of voting Labour. But is it also the case that the impact of feelings towards Corbyn on Labour support was stronger among young people? To answer this question, we return to the analysis of Labour voting, this time using what statisticians call a two-group finite-mixture model.[25] In statistics this model identifies the presence of subpopulations or groups in an overall population, without requiring that observed data identifies the subpopulation to which an individual belongs. It is a test of how strongly feelings about Corbyn and other variables can be used to distinguish between groups of voters.

The analysis also allows researchers to compute the probabilities that a voter belongs to a particular group and to see how voters' characteristics are associated with the probabilities of group membership. In effect, it turns the earlier analysis on its head by focusing on whether support for Corbyn distinguishes between groups of voters, whereas earlier we were predicting support for Corbyn from knowledge of a voter's age and their other characteristics. In addition to looking at age, we examine level of political interest and political knowledge as well as feelings of being left behind to look for effects.

Viewed generally, the two-group finite mixture model of Labour voting fits the data better than the simple one-group model described earlier. In other words, there is a clear difference between the members of one group and another when it comes to their attitudes to the Labour leader. Although many of the predictor variables in the two-group model have statistically significant effects for both groups, as Figure 3.17 shows, the impact of feelings about Corbyn on the likelihood of voting Labour is considerably stronger for one of the groups.

For Group One, with all other predictors set at their average values, the probability of voting Labour increases from 0.22 to 0.46 (on a 0–1 scale) as feelings about Corbyn vary from highly negative to highly positive. Although this change in the probability of casting a Labour ballot is both statistically significant and sizeable, it is dwarfed by the equivalent for Group Two voters. For people in Group Two, the move from

---

[25] McLachlan, Lee and Rathnayake (2019).

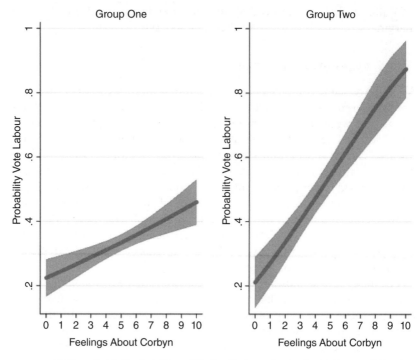

Figure 3.17 Probability of Voting Labour in the 2017 General Election by Feelings about Jeremy Corbyn, Two-Group Binomial Logit Finite Mixture Model.
Note: 52 per cent of voters have highest probability of being in Group One and 48 per cent have highest probability of being in Group Two. Probability of Group Two membership is negatively related to age, political interest and political knowledge.

negative to positive feelings about Corbyn increases their probability of voting Labour from 0.21 to fully 0.87, – a 66-point change. In other words, the Group Two voters feel much more strongly about him than the Group One voters.

The finite mixture model results also indicate that there are large numbers of voters in both groups. Fifty-two per cent of them have the highest probability of being in Group One, and the remaining 48 per cent has the highest probability of being in Group Two. Furthermore, as anticipated, group membership is related to age. Younger people are significantly more likely (p < 0.001) to be in the high-impact Group Two, with feelings about Corbyn on Labour voting being much stronger than in Group One. This relationship between group membership and age holds with statistical controls for levels of political interest and political knowledge and feelings of being left behind economically. In a nutshell, there was a fundamental difference between the young and the old in this election when it came to judging the Labour leader: young people liked him a lot more than the old.

It is also noteworthy that political interest and political knowledge (but not feeling left behind economically) help to predict group membership. The overall picture is that people in Group Two where the impact of feelings about Corbyn on Labour voting was very strong tended to be younger as well as less interested in and knowledgeable about politics. Many of them became members of the active electorate for the first time in 2017 and were very enthusiastic about the Labour leader, and they expressed these positive feelings by voting Labour.

Conclusion: Stalemating Brexit

On 25 June 2017, thousands of attendees at the Glastonbury Music Festival burst into song, repeatedly chanting 'Oh Jeremy Corbyn!' During the 2017 election campaign, Corbyn had become a political 'rock star' for millions of young people and would later be seen by many other young social democrats across Europe as one potential answer to the strange decline of centre-left politics. In Britain, many of these young people had registered to vote shortly before the election to demonstrate their support for Corbyn and his more radical platform. For his young fans, the 68-year-old Corbyn did not appear to be a proponent of left-wing ideological nostalgia; rather, he was offering a new politics that would serve the interests of 'the many, not the few'. Promising free university education, greater support for the NHS, affordable housing and much more, Corbyn's proposals found a receptive audience of young voters who had had come of age amid Tory austerity.

Across the electorate as a whole, although Brexit was a major concern for many voters, it did not dominate the agenda to the extent that might have been anticipated. Rather, other issues such as the NHS, the economy, immigration and terrorism were also on people's minds. As is typical in British elections, judgements about parties' issue performance, images of leaders and partisan attachments did much to determine the choices voters made. The end result was that the Corbyn-led Labour Party fared much better than most pundits had predicted before the campaign. Labour did not win but came within just over 2 per cent of the Conservatives' popular vote. Labour's unexpectedly strong performance denied Mrs May the solid majority she desperately needed to make Brexit a reality.

By producing a hung Parliament, the 2017 general election set the stage for a total stalemate in British politics on Brexit. Both major parties were divided by the issue and small groups of anti- and pro-EU MPs repeatedly blocked Prime Minister May's efforts to pass legislation needed to make any deal with the EU a reality. As the deadlock dragged on throughout all of 2018 and into 2019, frustration on both sides of the Brexit divide mounted. For those wishing to leave the EU, Brexit was not being delivered, and for those wishing to remain, the country was not preventing Brexit. Since the UK was still an EU member, it would participate in the May 2019 EU Parliament elections. This provided millions of disgruntled voters with an opportunity to express their frustration with the political nightmare that had gripped Brexit Britain. What happened at those elections is the story we tell in the next chapter.

4   The Collapsing Party System
The 2019 European Parliament Election

On 23 May 2019, British voters went to the polls in an election that was never supposed to happen. Taking place nearly three years after the public vote to leave the European Union, European Parliament elections determined who would represent voters in an institution most of them had already decided to leave. The fact that the election was going ahead reflected the failure of the country to find a resolution to its Brexit crisis. The main story was the surprising success of an entirely new party in British politics: the Brexit Party. Formed only a few months before the European elections, the Brexit Party held its roots in the older UKIP, which had now veered off to the far right, and the grass-roots network 'Leave Means Leave', which had been founded to ensure that Brexit was delivered. Between the vote for Brexit and the arrival of the Brexit Party, 'Leave Means Leave' had played an important role in British politics by holding a series of rallies across the country, featuring Farage and frontline pro-Brexit politicians from both the Conservative and Labour parties, such as Jacob Rees-Mogg, Kate Hoey, Iain Duncan Smith and prominent business leaders.

The Brexit Party built on this, emerging in response to Prime Minister Theresa May agreeing to another delay to Brexit, and the general failure of the country's leaders to deliver on the vote to leave the EU nearly three years earlier. Many of the party's leading donors and activists had previously been involved with UKIP, even if it sought to present a 'fresh face' by appointing candidates who were less affiliated with the past. The party soon claimed to have more than 100,000 registered supporters.

Led by Nigel Farage, at the European election campaign launch the former UKIP leader pledged that the new Brexit Party would lead a 'democratic revolution' in British politics. 'This party is not here just to fight the European elections', he boomed at the launch event, 'this party is not just to express our anger – 23 May is the first step of the Brexit Party. We will change politics for good!'[1]

---

[1] www.bbc.co.uk/news/uk-politics-47907350

The Brexit Party immediately surged in the polls. Farage campaigned on a classic populist platform, arguing that Parliament's failure to agree on a Withdrawal Agreement had clearly demonstrated that 'politics are broken.' He claimed that the over 17 million people who had voted for Brexit in 2016 had been betrayed by an alliance of pro-EU political, cultural and media elites. To break the impasse and ensure that the people's will was honoured, he argued that the country should stage a 'Hard Brexit' and leave the EU immediately on World Trade Organization (WTO) terms.

It was classic, unadulterated populism. Like other national populists around the globe, Farage promised to prioritize the interests of the majority against what he argued was a distant, self-serving, neglectful and even corrupt elite.[2] He targeted everybody who was disappointed by the inability of Prime Minister Theresa May and her Conservative government to deliver Brexit, as well as the significant numbers of MPs who had sought to dilute, delay or simply block Brexit altogether in the House of Commons.

The Brexit Party pursued a core vote strategy, targeting areas that had previously given strong support to UKIP and which were overseen by campaigners who had orchestrated UKIP's by-election triumphs in Clacton and Rochester and Strood five years earlier. Of the Brexit Party's twenty-three rallies that were held in the final weeks of the campaign, only three took place in areas where a majority of people had not voted for Brexit.

Farage was not the only game in town, however. In sharp contrast, at the other end of the spectrum, stood the established minor party challengers, the Liberal Democrats and the Greens, who in the aftermath of the 2016 referendum had both adopted strongly pro-Remain positions. Under its leader Vince Cable, the Liberal Democrats appealed directly to millions of disillusioned Remainers, organizing their entire campaign around a simple message – 'stop Brexit' – and calling for a 'People's Vote' to end the Brexit 'paralysis'. Somewhat more controversially, they urged the British public to say 'Bollocks to Brexit'.

The smaller Green movement similarly urged the British people to say 'Yes to Europe', while claiming to be the strongest pro-EU party in the country. 'Our message to the people is very simple', said the party's co-leader Sian Berry.

It's time to say Yes to Europe, Yes to investing in communities and No to climate chaos. It's also about saying a very loud No to the failed Brexit project … The Brexit project led by Nigel Farage has capitalized on the neglect of our

---

[2] On national populism, see Goodwin and Eatwell (2018).

communities and unleashed the darkest elements onto our nation, bringing them dangerously close to the mainstream.[3]

As we will see, the appeals of both the Liberal Democrats and the Greens resonated strongly with Remainers, who were deeply unhappy with the prospect of a looming Brexit and frustrated that it had not been thwarted. Concluding that neither the governing Conservatives nor the main opposition Labour Party were able to resolve the Brexit crisis, large numbers of Leavers and Remainers were primed to support radical alternatives in the EU Parliament election. In the event, many of them did so. And along the way, British politics was to be polarized to an unprecedented degree, while the two-party system would almost implode into a far more chaotic multi-party race.

In this chapter, we look at how this happened. We first consider the wider mood of the country as the 2019 EU Parliament elections approached. We then discuss the forces that produced the highly consequential outcome of the election and which in many respects set the stage for the general election to follow a few months later. Once again, throughout the chapter we draw on analyses of data that were gathered in polls and representative national surveys throughout 2017, 2018, and before and after the 2019 European elections.[4] It is one of the most comprehensive pictures that has been taken to date.

A Protracted and Unresolved Struggle

The UK's 2019 European Parliament election occurred in a context of deep division and simmering discontent. Brexit dominated the country; two-thirds of people who replied to our surveys before the 2019 European election said that Brexit was one of the three most important issues, and more than two-fifths said it was their single most important concern. Brexit Britain was exactly that, a country consumed by one issue.

In the hotly and closely contested 2016 EU referendum, 72.2 per cent had gone to the polls and 51.9 per cent had voted to leave, while 48.1 per cent had voted to remain. Contrary to hopes of a return to national unity, three years later the country remained deeply divided. As shown in Figure 4.1, just before the 2017 general election, the percentages of Leavers and Remainers in nationwide polls were virtually identical, but afterwards there had been a gradual downward trend in public support for Leave which continued into early 2019. Then, Prime Minister May's inability

---

[3] www.greenparty.org.uk/news/2019/05/08/eu-election-launch-greens-are-the-strongest-pro-eu-party/
[4] For details about these surveys, see Appendix A.

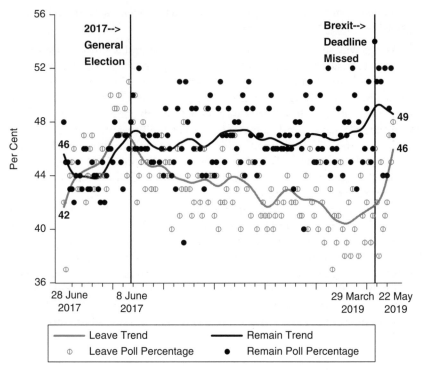

Figure 4.1 Trends in Leave and Remain Support, 2016–2019.
Source: 163 polls conducted between 28 June 2016 and 22 May 2019.

to secure passage of her ill-fated Brexit deal through Parliament and the
ensuing failure to meet the 29 March 2019 deadline to exit the EU re-
energized the Leave side of the debate. Large numbers of them once
again began to rally around their cause. After the deadline was missed,
support for Leave in the polls trended upwards, reaching 46 per cent on
22 May, the day before the European election. Although Remain stayed
ahead, the gap in the trend had narrowed to only 3 per cent, revealing just
how polarized the country had become over the Europe question.

This was echoed in our national survey, conducted in the week before
the European elections. When asked, 44.4 per cent of the survey respondents reported that they approved of EU membership and an almost
identical number, 44.1 per cent, said that they disapproved. All of the
arguments that had been made for and against Brexit after the referendum made almost no difference to public opinion. Both sides had dug in,
remaining strongly committed to their position. Similarly, when asked
about what they would do if there were to be another referendum on the

subject, 45.6 per cent said they would cast a ballot to stay and 46.0 per cent said that they would choose to leave. The balance of public opinion on Brexit was as close as – if not closer than – it had been at the time of the fractious referendum three years earlier.

This also carried through to questions about the likely consequences of Brexit, where once again public opinion appeared largely unchanged.[5] Ahead of the 2016 referendum, Remain strategists had chosen to focus almost exclusively on the alleged negative economic effects that would follow Brexit. Rehearsing the 'Project Fear' strategy that had been successfully employed during the 2014 Scottish independence referendum, Prime Minister David Cameron and his advisors recruited an 'A list' of prominent politicians and high-ranking bureaucrats to make the case, from US President Barack Obama to IMF Chief Christine Lagarde and Head of the Bank of England Mark Carney.

Leading economists, journalists and media personalities joined the chorus, making gloomy forecasts of the adverse trends in growth and painful job losses that would follow in the wake of Britain's departure from the EU. In addition to portraying dismal economic scenarios, pro-Remain commentators lectured their audiences about the adverse global implications of Brexit. It was argued that the country's influence in international affairs would be eroded and the long peace that Europe had enjoyed since the end of the Second World War would be jeopardized. David Cameron, notably, attracted a wave of headlines after suggesting that peace in Europe would be threatened, a view that was later endorsed by five former secretary generals of NATO.

For its part, the Leave campaign's 'Take Back Control' message had focused heavily on protecting Britain's sovereignty and democracy, which, it claimed, were being subverted by the post-Maastricht march towards a European superstate run by an unelected and unaccountable Brussels bureaucracy. In addition, ending the 'free movement of peoples' – a core EU principle and sacrosanct requirement for membership – would enable Britain to stem the rising tide of immigration which Leave campaigners argued was threatening the country's culture, language, traditions and distinctive identity, while enhancing the risks of terrorism and violent crime.

The economic and immigration threats emphasized by the Remain and Leave campaigns, respectively, resonated strongly with the electorate in 2016, as we have shown in our earlier book. But they also continued to resonate three years later. Large pluralities of people who participated in our survey before the European elections accepted the idea that leaving the EU would impose economic penalties – 45 per cent

---

[5] See Clarke, Goodwin and Whiteley (2017), ch. 7.

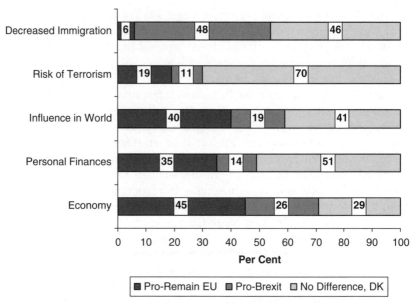

Figure 4.2 Forecast Effects of Leaving the European Union.
Source: 2019 pre-EU Parliament election survey.

believed that leaving the EU would hurt the British economy, whereas
only 26 per cent thought that leaving would help it (see Figure 4.2).
Comparable numbers for the impact on personal finances were 35 per
cent and 24 per cent, respectively. Similarly, just over one-third thought
that continued EU membership would boost Britain's standard of living,
while one-quarter disagreed (see Figure 4.3). Slightly over 50 per cent
also saw the EU as a source of cheap labour to do the kinds of jobs that
native British people eschewed, while only one in five disagreed. And, as
in 2016, immigration was seen very differently – 48 per cent of people
believed that quitting the EU would reduce the flow of immigrants into
the UK while only 6 per cent thought otherwise.

Opinions about other arguments for and against EU membership were
also similar to those that had characterized the electorate three years earlier. For example, 40 per cent judged that the UK's international influence would be diminished by leaving the EU and 42 per cent thought that
EU membership had helped to preserve the peace in Europe. Only 19 per
cent and 20 per cent respectively disagreed with these ideas. In contrast,
many people continued to express reservations about the consequences of
EU membership for British democracy. Specifically, 47 per cent believed
that continued membership would erode Britain's ability to make its own

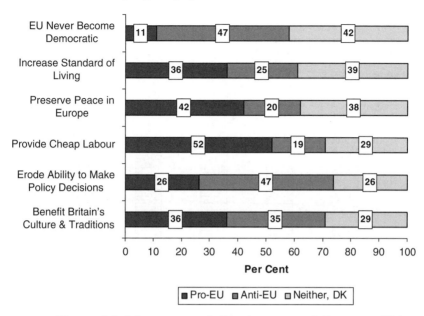

Figure 4.3 Advantages and Disadvantages of European Union Membership.
Source: 2019 pre-EU Parliament election survey.

policy decisions and an equal number concluded that the EU would never become democratic. Only 26 per cent and 11 per cent, respectively, disagreed with these propositions. Forecasts for Britain's culture and traditions were more evenly balanced, with just over one-third judging the consequences of leaving to be negative and a slightly larger number saying they would be positive. Finally, there was huge uncertainly about the implications for terrorism; nearly three-quarters said they 'didn't know' if it would increase or decrease if Britain left the EU.

Statistical analyses reveal these evaluations of the benefits and costs of EU membership were organized in two interrelated 'summary factors' which we label 'economy-influence' and 'immigration-terrorism'. The first of these factors was dominated by economic evaluations and judgements about Britain's international influence should it leave the EU, whereas the second concerned the perceived consequences of continuing membership for immigration and terrorism. These two factors are essentially the same as those that structured public thinking at the 2016 referendum. Below we employ survey respondents' scores on these summary factors in an analysis of the strength of forces shaping voters' attitudes towards Brexit as they prepared to cast their ballots in the 2019 EU Parliament election.

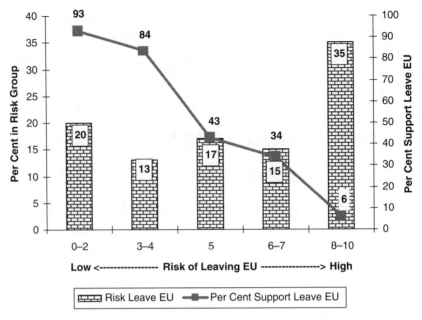

Figure 4.4 Perceived Risks and Support for Leaving the European Union.
Source: 2019 pre-EU Parliament election survey.

A Risky and Emotionally Fraught Business

The prospect of finally exiting the EU also generated a variety of cognitive and emotional reactions. When asked to use a scale ranging from 0 (low) to 10 (high) to summarize their overall risk assessments of Brexit, large numbers of our respondents said that it entailed substantial risks. As displayed in Figure 4.4, exactly half of them had scores greater than 5 on the scale and more than one-third had scores of 8 or greater. In contrast, one-third offered scores less than 5, indicating that they did not think that leaving was a particularly risky proposition. As Figure 4.4 also shows, risk assessments were strongly and predictably related to attitudes to EU membership. Only 6 per cent of those viewing Brexit as very risky said they favoured leaving, but this number climbed steadily to fully 93 per cent among those who judged that the risk of leaving was minimal.

Emotions about continued EU membership varied widely as well. When asked to choose among four positive and four negative words to describe their feelings about leaving the EU, slightly over one-third reported that they felt 'uneasy', a quarter said they were 'afraid', and an equal number said they were 'angry'. Just over one in five claimed to be 'disgusted' (see Figure 4.5A). The distribution of positive emotions was quite similar, with one-third stating they were 'hopeful', one-quarter saying they were 'happy', one-fifth 'proud' and one-fifth 'confident'. Calculating the total numbers of positive and negative answers reveals that 48 per cent chose one or more negative words to describe their feelings, but almost exactly as many (47 per cent) designated one or more positive words. Brexit was an emotional stand-off across the electorate.

These emotional reactions were strongly correlated with attitudes to whether the UK should leave or remain. As Figure 4.5B shows, fully 80 per cent of those whose emotions about Brexit were on balance negative wanted to stay and 11 per cent wanted to go. In contrast, 84 per cent of people whose emotions tilted in a positive direction wanted to deliver on the Brexit vote and only 11 per cent wanted to remain in the EU. As had been the case three years earlier, Brexit was a matter of 'heart' as well as 'head' in the spring of 2019, polarizing Leavers and Remainers along the lines of emotion, not just public policy.

To investigate in greater depth the idea that attitudes towards EU membership were shaped by a variety of cognitive and emotional considerations, we specify a statistical model of these attitudes. We use evaluations of the benefits and costs of membership, perceived risks and emotional reactions as predictor variables. Other predictors include evaluations of the country's and individual economic conditions, general attitudes to immigration and several socio-demographic characteristics that often influence people's voting behaviour, including their age, level of education, gender, income and country of residence, i.e., whether they live in England, Scotland or Wales.[6]

We estimate two versions of the model. The first, which we call a one-class model, specifies that everyone was influenced the same way by the variables identified above.[7] In contrast, the specification of a second, two-class finite mixture version of the model is guided by the idea that attitudes towards Brexit were products of both 'heart and mind' but in different proportions for different people. To implement this idea, the second version allows for heterogeneity – specifically, for the possibility that some people made their Brexit choice primarily based on their assessments of the risks involved and a second group discounted these risk assessments and were motivated more strongly by emotional considerations.[8]

[6] Details on the measurement of the variables used in this and other analyses presented in this chapter are presented in Appendix A.
[7] Parameters are estimated using a standard ordered logit model. See, e.g., Long and Freese (2014).
[8] This is an ordered logit finite mixture model. See, e.g., Mclachan and Peel (2000).

A. Emotional Reaction

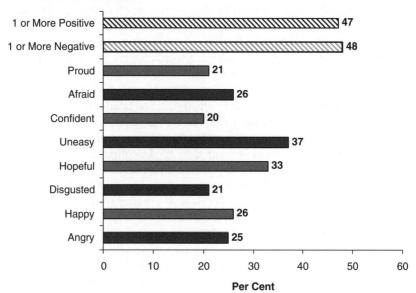

B. Leave and Remain Support by Balance of Emotional Reactions to Leaving EU

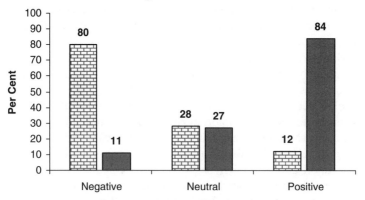

Figure 4.5 Emotional Reactions to Prospect of Leaving the European Union and Support for Leaving or Remaining (A) Emotional Reaction (B) Leave and Remain Support by Balance of Emotional Reactions to Leaving EU.

Source: 2019 EU Parliament pre-election survey.

Table 4.1 *Models of Factors Influencing Attitudes Towards Leaving the European Union*

Predictors	One Class Model	Two Class Model	
		Class 1	Class 2
Benefits & Costs of Leaving EU:			
Economy-Influence	1.259***	1.013***	2.435***
Immigration-Terrorism	1.259***	1.389***	1.202***
Risks of Leaving EU	−0.224***	−0.315***	0.029
Emotional Reactions to Leaving EU	0.409***	−0.069	1.129***
Economic Evaluations	−0.324***	−0.172*	−0.614***
Attitudes Towards Immigration	0.252***	0.111	0.468**
Age	0.009**	0.006	0.028**
Education	0.032	−0.006	0.245
Gender	−0.093	0.443*	−0.855**
Income	−0.123**	−0.257***	−0.197*
Country:			
Scotland	−0.202	−0.218	−0.393
Wales	0.330	0.982	
McKelvey R^2 = 0.80 per cent Correctly Classified = 81.5			
N =	2525	2525	
AIC	2447.18	2307.86	
BIC	2528.86	2494.55	
Predicted Class Membership per cent		39.8	60.2

Class 2 Membership	Predictors
Age	0.176***
Education	−1.050**
Left Behind	−1.331***
Constant	−6.198***

*** – p < 0.001; ** – p < 0.01; * – p < 0.05; one-tailed test.
Note: Ordered-logit estimates; dependent variable is scored +1 = favour leaving EU, 0 = not sure, DK, −1 = favour remaining in EU; AIC and BIC model selection criteria: smaller numbers indicate better model performance.

The results of estimating these models using data that were collected before the European Parliament elections are displayed in Table 4.1. Considering the one-class model first, we see that the two benefit–cost factors operate as anticipated – people who minimized the possibility that Brexit would entail economic costs and erode Britain's international influence were more likely to support leaving the EU, as were those who believed that leaving would reduce immigration and the threat of terrorism. As also anticipated, those who emphasized Brexit's risks and those for whom it stimulated negative emotions were more likely to support remaining. There were other significant effects as well; people who were generally negatively disposed towards immigration were more likely to support Brexit, as were those who judged that economic conditions were not good even though Britain was still an EU member. All else being equal, older persons and those in lower income brackets also were more inclined to support leaving.

These relationships are in line with our expectations, and they echo the results of our analyses conducted at the time of the 2016 referendum.[9] However, findings from the two-class model indicate that people varied in how their risk calculations and emotional reactions influenced their attitudes towards Brexit. Table 4.1 shows that for people in class one, risks had a significant effect, whereas for people in class two, emotions rather than risks really mattered. Both of these groups are large, with 39.8 per cent in class one and 60.2 per cent in class two. These numbers underline that, while a sizeable minority of people were led by their assessments of risk, for a larger number of people their emotions had a more significant influence on how they were reacting to the Europe question. This helps to make sense of why Remainers struggled and eventually failed to win the debate: a large number of people were not thinking about the contest through the prism of risk but rather through their emotions, which wielded a powerful influence. In other words, 'project fear', which overwhelmingly emphasized the risks, was a poor strategy.

The conclusion that voters were characterized by substantial variety in the factors driving reactions to Brexit is bolstered by the model selection criteria (Akaike Information Criterion (AIC) and Bayesian Information Criterion (BIC)) statistics.[10] These show that the two-class model fits the data better than its simple one-class rival. But who was most likely to be in the 'risk assessment' or the 'emotional reaction' groups? As Table 4.1 reveals, when it came to forming their views of the EU, it was mainly older and less well-educated people who tended to be in the group that relied on emotions rather than risk assessments. In contrast, people who judged that they had been left behind economically were more likely to emphasize risk assessments.

Dual Discontents

Britain's protracted Brexit impasse generated widespread public discontent. Although Prime Minister Theresa May finally negotiated an agreement with the EU in November 2018, the status of the border between the Irish Republic and Northern Ireland and various other provisions of the deal had precipitated resignations by major cabinet ministers such as Boris Johnson and David Davis and fuelled ongoing

---

[9] Clarke, Goodwin and Whiteley (2017).
[10] See, e.g., Burnham and Anderson (2011).

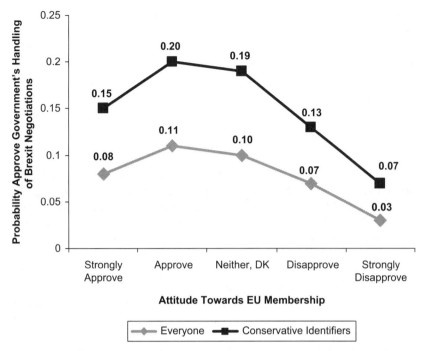

Figure 4.6 Probability of Approving the Government's Handling of Brexit Negotiations by Attitudes Towards European Union Membership.

controversy. The Brexit vote and its aftermath revived serious tensions in the Conservative Party over the country's relationship with the EU. A large number of Conservative MPs refused to ratify the proposed With-drawal Agreement, and it was defeated in Parliament on three separate occasions. As a result, the UK failed to meet the 29 March 2019 dead-line for exiting the EU and so a new deadline of 31 October was set.

Consistent with polls documenting widespread public discontent with the protracted stalemate, over 70 per cent of our survey respondents judged the Brexit negotiating process unfavourably. Analysing these answers with statistical controls for partisan identification and socio-demographic characteristics (age, education, gender, income, country of residence) indicates that positive judgements were least likely among those who either strongly approved or strongly disapproved of EU membership. The government had managed to alienate both sides by its negotiating tactics, particularly polarized individuals. Across all survey respondents the probability of a positive reaction was only 0.08 (on a 0–1 scale) among the approvers and merely 0.03 among the disapprovers (see Figure 4.6).

Low approval for the conduct of the negotiations were not just a product of negative appraisals by people who identified with parties other than the governing Conservatives. Although Conservative identifiers were somewhat more likely to endorse the Government's conduct of the negotiations, the probabilities of doing so remained very low (no more than 0.20) regardless of how they felt about the EU. And, like other people, Conservative identifiers were least likely to view the negotiations favourably if they either strongly approved or strongly disapproved of staying in the EU (see Figure 4.6).

With assistance from large numbers of stubborn MPs on both sides of the aisle, unhelpful rulings by the pro-Remain Speaker of the House John Bercow, and the EU's continued 'slow-walking' of the negotiations, Prime Minister May and her government succeeded in making much of the electorate unhappy with the Brexit process. Remainers were dismayed that Prime Minister May had continued to insist that 'Brexit means Brexit' and refused to entertain the possibility of holding another referendum on the topic. Leavers, meanwhile, were deeply frustrated that the May government appeared unable to extricate the UK from the European Union, let alone deliver the 'No Deal Brexit' departure that many of them (55 per cent in our May 2019 pre-election survey) desired.

The British public did not restrict its discontents to how the government handled Brexit negotiations per se. Summary judgements about the prime minister and her government's overall performance also became very sour. Although evaluations of May's discharge of her prime ministerial duties had never been brilliant, they deteriorated markedly as the Brexit process dragged on. When interviewed just before the June 2017 general election, 43 per cent had stated that they were dissatisfied with her performance and a slightly larger number, 48 per cent, were satisfied (see Figure 4.7). The ranks of the dissatisfied then soared to reach 65 per cent in 2018 and, in 2019, 73 per cent. At this point, only 23 per cent of people said they approved of how Theresa May was handling her job.

To underscore the point, when answering a question on their images of party leaders, two-thirds of our 2019 survey respondents responded that May was incompetent. The prime minister was not alone – unfavourable ratings extended to the Conservative government – 71 per cent declared that they were dissatisfied with the government's record and an equal number judged that it was dishonest and untrustworthy. These highly adverse reactions signalled a negative and fractious climate of public opinion that created a receptive audience for the populist messages of the Brexit Party and the opposing anti-Brexit challengers, the Liberal Democrats and the Greens.

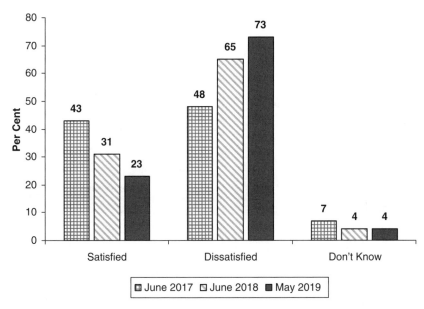

Figure 4.7 Evaluations of Theresa May's Performance as Prime Minister, 2017, 2018, 2019.
Source: 2017, 2018, 2019 Essex–UTD surveys.

The Brexit Party's formation was announced in January 2019, only four months before the European elections. Nigel Farage became leader on 22 March, a week before the UK failed to meet the date for its scheduled departure from the EU. Farage was the former leader of UKIP which had played a major role in mobilizing public support for Brexit in the 2016 EU referendum. Stridently opposed to large-scale immigration and EU membership, and disdainful of what he characterized as a decidedly out-of-touch establishment, Farage was a classic and experienced populist politician who was adept at leveraging his high profile. His presence as leader of the Brexit Party was exactly what the party needed to quickly attract widespread media attention and harvest large numbers of Leave voters dismayed by the failure of Prime Minister May and her government to deliver Brexit.

With Farage at the helm, the Brexit Party surged in the polls, especially after the 29 March deadline for leaving the EU passed (see Figure 4.8). With less than 7 per cent support at that time, Farage's party skyrocketed into first place over the next two months, recording nearly 34 per cent on 22 May, the day before the election. Much of this support arrived from disgruntled Conservative voters who had become dismayed at the

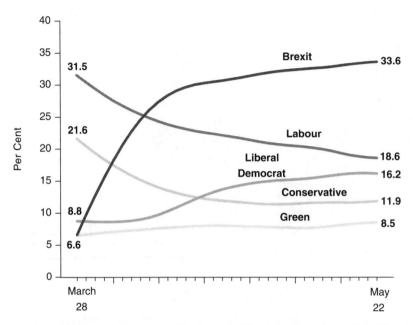

Figure 4.8 European Parliament Election Vote Intention Trends, 28 March–22 May 2019.
Source: Thirty-four national polls, 28 March–22 May 2019.

handling of Brexit. National opinion polls suggested that the percentage of 2017 Conservative voters who switched to the Brexit Party jumped from 3 per cent when the new party was formed to 30 per cent on the eve of the European elections, while the percentage of Leavers backing the insurgent party similarly rocketed from just 4 to 37 per cent. The rise of the party was an important episode that re-energized and reunified the Leave side of the debate.[11]

The Brexit Party was not alone in attracting growing support from a passionate and increasingly angry electorate. The Liberal Democrats and the Greens also attracted large numbers of votes. Although the Greens remained a minor player with 8.5 per cent of the vote, support for the Liberal Democrats increased to over 16 per cent. This was almost double what the Liberal Democrats had registered in the polls just two months earlier and more than twice what they had achieved in the 2017 general election. Much of this support came from Remainers, whose support for the Liberal Democrats between February and May 2019 increased from 16 to 30 per cent. Remainers and Leavers were looking for new and

[11] Data taken from YouGov polling February and March 2019.

more radical alternatives that would articulate their very different positions on the Brexit issue.

The big losers were the two established mainstream parties. Their support plummeted as Britain's historically stable two-party party system rapidly fragmented into a multi-party contest. Reflecting the widespread public dissatisfaction, in the aftermath of the 29 March with the Brexit deadline being missed, support for the Conservatives dropped by nearly 10 percentage points, from 21.6 per cent to 11.9 per cent (see Figure 4.8). Support for Jeremy Corbyn's Labour Party also crashed, with its vote intention share down nearly 13 points (from 31.5 per cent to 18.6 per cent). Under Corbyn, whose hard-left socialist ideology encouraged him to view the EU as an institutional embodiment of the interests of global capitalism, Labour's position on Brexit was ambiguous. Corbyn's resistance to commit unequivocally to Remain frustrated many Labour MPs who passionately supported staying in the EU and holding a second referendum to ratify that decision. Most Labour voters, particularly in London and the South, also harboured pro-Remain feelings, as did most Labour members and activists who were drawn mainly from the more pro-EU liberal middle class. In our May 2019 pre-election survey, nearly two-thirds of Labour identifiers said that they favoured staying in the EU, while only one-quarter wanted to get out.

Signalling that both the Conservative and Labour parties were about to be punished by the widespread disaffection, polls conducted just before the election showed that millions of Leavers and Remainers were now marching in new directions. Britain's party system appeared to be imploding as insurgents on both sides of the aisle were on the march.

Brexit at the Polls

When the EU Parliament election results were announced, Britain's Brexiteers had reason to celebrate. On a turnout of 37.0 per cent, Nigel Farage and the new Brexit Party captured 31.6 per cent of the vote in Great Britain and finished comfortably in first place (see Figure 4.9).[12] The former UKIP leader became the only politician in British history to win two national elections with two different political parties, having previously won the 2014 European Parliament elections with UKIP. He had reasserted his mainstream credentials.

---

[12] In the wake of the election, some commentators tried to use the party's vote shares to infer that, despite the Brexit Party's success, a majority of voters would opt for Remain if a second EU referendum were held. This enterprise was error prone since turnout in the election was only 37 per cent. As discussed above, our pre-election surveys showed that the percentages of people reporting that they would vote to Leave or Remain was a virtual dead heat.

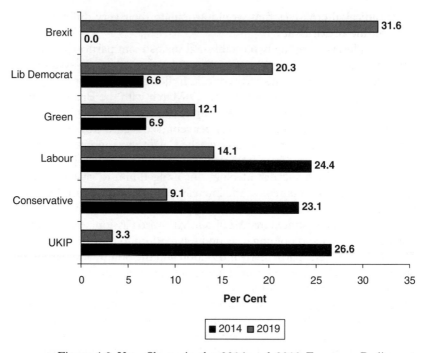

Figure 4.9 Vote Shares in the 2014 and 2019 European Parliament Elections (Percentages Voting for Party in 2014 and 2019).
Source: Electoral Commission.

The Brexit Party received its strongest support in the two Midlands regions and the North East, where it averaged more than 40 per cent of the vote. It also surpassed the performance of its predecessor, UKIP, five years earlier. Whereas UKIP had only won an outright majority in the local government district of Boston on England's east coast, in 2019 the Brexit Party won an outright majority in nearly twenty districts, with its strongest result arriving in the eastern areas of Castle Point and Boston and South Holland. Other studies find a very strong and positive relationship between support for the Brexit Party in 2019 and support for UKIP five years earlier, in 2014, underlining how Nigel Farage essentially cannibalized his former party's vote. Individual-level data from Lord Ashcroft's surveys similarly suggests that more than two-thirds of people who had voted for UKIP at the 2017 general election voted for the Brexit Party two years later.[13]

[13] See Lord Ashcroft polling data: https://lordashcroftpolls.com/2019/05/my-euro-election-post-vote-poll-most-tory-switchers-say-they-will-stay-with-their-new-party/#more-15953

The Brexit Party also finished ahead of Labour in almost every local authority area in Wales, which has been completely dominated by the party since the 1920s. Farage and his party were, unsurprisingly, weakest in the strongly pro-Remain London and Scotland. The Liberal Democrats and the Greens also performed well. The Liberal Democrats saw their share of the vote climb from 6.6 per cent in the 2014 EU Parliament Election to 20.3 per cent in 2019, their highest share of the vote at any European election and their strongest result at any election since 'Cleggmania' had followed Nick Clegg and the party in 2010.

Vince Cable and the Liberal Democrats received their strongest vote in London and the South East, averaging more than 25 per cent of the vote and performed especially well in areas such as leafy Richmond-upon-Thames, where nearly seven in ten people had voted to Remain in the European Union.

The Greens' showing was not quite as impressive, but the party nearly doubled its vote, moving up to 12.1 per cent after getting 6.9 per cent five years earlier. It was their best performance since 1989 and underlined the increasing fragmentation of British politics. The Greens polled noticeably well in parts of the South West, including Bristol, Exeter and Stroud, as well as Brighton and Hove, where more than 60 per cent of people had backed Remain.

Taken together, the results revealed how Leavers and Remainers were now quickly and dramatically abandoning the two main parties in favour of smaller and more radical ones that offered diametrically opposing and unambiguous positions on Brexit. It was in many respects a sequel to the 2016 referendum and one that was pushing British politics and the country more generally down a far more polarized path.

It also reflected how, over a much longer period, public support for the two main parties at European elections has declined. At the first ever set of elections in 1979 the combined share of the vote for the Conservative and Labour parties had been on par with their support at the general election that was held in the same year. But since then, their combined share of the vote at European elections declined, while the difference between their support at general and European elections has steadily increased. By 2004, fewer than half of all voters supported the Conservative or Labour parties at these elections, while challengers flourished, revealing not only how the party system had been experiencing significant changes long before Brexit but also how the European elections were an ideal breeding ground for anti-establishment parties.

This not only continued but accelerated in 2019. The Brexit Party attracted a large number of Leavers who were profoundly disillusioned with the inability of Prime Minister May's Conservative government to

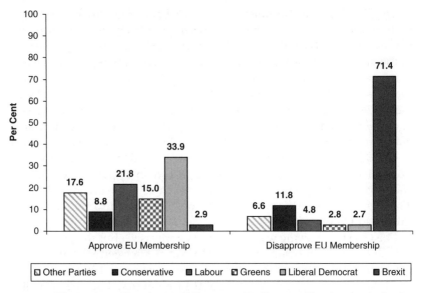

Figure 4.10 Vote in 2019 European Parliament Election by Attitudes Towards European Union Membership.
Source: 2019 pre-post EU election panel survey.

secure passage out of the EU. Equally, the Liberal Democrats and the Greens appealed to Remainers by offering strongly pro-EU platforms. This polarization was accompanied by a sharp erosion of public support for the Conservative and the Labour parties who together – and remarkably – attracted only 23 per cent of the total vote. It was their lowest combined vote share since they became the two main representatives of the country's historically strong and stable party system.

The Labour Party's share of the vote collapsed by more than 10 points (from 24.4 per cent in 2014 to 14.1 per cent in 2019), while the Conservatives did even worse, crashing from 23.1 per cent to a dismal 9.1 per cent. It was the worst result for the Conservatives in their 185-year history. Reacting quickly to the disaster, Prime Minister May appeared in front of Number 10 Downing Street on the morning of 24 May and announced her resignation. After Margaret Thatcher, John Major and David Cameron, she became the fourth Conservative Party leader to have been brought down by the Europe question. While claiming that she had done 'everything I can' to try and convince MPs to support her Brexit withdrawal deal, May now conceded that it was in the 'best interests of the country for a new prime minister to lead that effort'.

The powerful appeal of the Brexit Party to voters wishing to get the UK out of the EU can be seen in our survey data. Figure 4.10 shows that fully 71 per cent of those who disapproved of the country's EU membership voted for the Brexit Party, and less than 12 per cent opted for the Conservatives. Labour attracted fewer than one in twenty voters in the pro-Brexit group and the Liberal Democrats and Greens did even worse. Voting patterns among those who approved of EU membership were considerably more diffuse. The Liberal Democrats garnered the support of slightly over one-third of those wishing to stay in the EU and the Greens received 15 per cent of their votes. Labour fared badly with just over 20 per cent and the Conservatives were virtual non-starters – fewer than one in ten voters with pro-EU views supported them. While the major parties were unattractive options for Leavers and Remainers, it was also a portent of what was to come at the general election a few months later, namely that the Remain vote was far more fragmented than the Leave vote.

Farage's Brexit Party had demonstrated its attractiveness to a large segment of the electorate and had also underlined the benefits of consolidating the Leave vote, something that Boris Johnson and Dominic Cummings had no doubt noticed. But who had voted for Farage and the Brexit Party, exactly? Our survey data can answer this question. Support for the Brexit Party varied widely. Age was a major line of demarcation – Brexit Party voting rose from 17 per cent among people under 30 years of age to fully 50 per cent among Britain's pensioners, aged 65 or older (see Figure 4.11). These age differences were similar to the ones between Leave and Remain voters in the 2016 EU referendum, as well as in polls on attitudes towards the EU.[14]

Though Brexit Party support did not vary by gender, it was stronger among people with lower levels of education with the share of Brexit Party voters being 42 per cent among people, with secondary school educations or less to only 29 per cent among those with postgraduate degrees. Support for the new party was also greater among those in lower income brackets and, to a lesser extent, among those in lower social class categories. It was also concentrated heavily in England and Wales, where nearly two in every five voters backed the Brexit Party compared to only one in four in Scotland. Overall, the patterns of Brexit Party support closely resemble the patterns of support for the earlier UKIP.[15]

---

[14] As discussed in Chapter 3, there also were strong age differences in party support in the 2017 general election, with Labour doing very well among younger voters and the Conservatives gathering the support of many older voters.

[15] See, e.g., Ford and Goodwin (2014); Goodwin and Milazzo (2016). Brexit Party support, was also broadly similar to that for national populist parties in other EU member states, albeit Brexit Party voters tended to be slightly older than their populist counterparts in several European countries. See Eatwell and Goodwin (2018); Norris and Inglehart (2019).

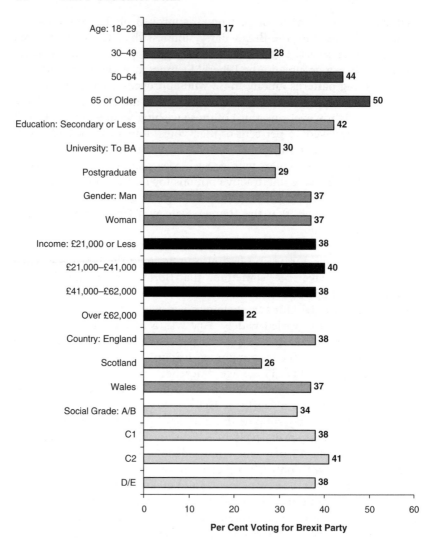

Figure 4.11 Brexit Party Vote in the 2019 European Parliament Election by Socio-Demographic Characteristics.
Source: 2019 pre-post EU Parliament election survey.

Shortly after the first ever EU Parliament elections were held in 1979, analysts had designated these contests 'second-order' events. By this, they meant that the forces driving party support were largely domestic, with voters rewarding or, more likely, punishing, incumbent governments for their performance on important valence issues, such as the economy.[16] However, recent research indicates that concerns about the EU and how it is exercising its power have become increasingly influential.[17] The 2019 UK European Parliament election exemplifies this latter point. The debate about Britain's future relationship with the EU completely dominated the issue agenda and reshaped the contours of political competition in profound ways.

But Europe was not the only factor that mattered. As we noted in Chapter 3, research in Britain and other democracies has repeatedly demonstrated that attitudes towards party leaders and feelings of attachment to political parties can also have strong effects on how people vote. In the context of studying factors influencing support for the Brexit Party, the literature on populist parties documents that anti-establishment attitudes, feelings of being neglected or 'left behind' economically and where people place themselves on the 'left–right' scale can have significant effects.[18] And, as noted, studies of the demographic bases of these parties indicate that their adherents tend to be concentrated among working class and self-employed people with lower than average levels of education. In fact, their support among the working class is often so strong that some academics refer to them as the 'new working-class parties'.

Our national survey data allows us to study the drivers of Brexit Party support by gauging the impact of several predictor variables. We specify a statistical model that includes predictors measuring attitudes toward the EU, assessments of risks associated with leaving the EU and evaluations of the Brexit negotiating process. The model also includes variables that capture how people feel about party leaders, whether they identify with parties and where they place themselves on the left–right scale.

Populist sentiments are indexed by variables that tap anti-establishment feelings and judgements about being left behind economically. Sociodemographic predictors include people's age, level of education, gender, income and country of residence. Since the dependent variable is scored 1 (voted Brexit Party) or 0 (voted for another party), model parameters are estimated using a binomial legit analysis.[19]

Several of the predictors have statistically significant effects. As expected, negative attitudes towards the country's EU membership increased the likelihood of Brexit Party voting. Leader images and partisan identifications mattered too, with positive feelings about the party's

---

[16] See. Valence issues typically dominate the issue agenda in British general elections but, as the 2019 EU election illustrates, this is not inevitable.

[17] DeVries (2018); Hobolt and Tilley (2014).

[18] See, e.g., Arzheimer (2018. See also Mudde and Kaltwasser (2017); Eatwell and Goodwin (2018).

[19] Long and Freese (2014).

leader, Nigel Farage, and identifying with the Brexit Party boosting support for the party. In contrast, but as also expected, positive impressions of the Labour Party leader, Jeremy Corbyn, and the Conservative Party leader, Theresa May, lessened the likelihood of voting for the Brexit Party. Populist attitudes were also in play. Consistent with other studies of support for national populist parties, anti-establishment attitudes increased the probability of Brexit Party voting. There were significant age differences too – as was the case for its predecessor party UKIP. All else equal, older people were more likely to cast their ballots for Farage's new party.

Although there were a number of significant predictors of the Brexit Party, they were not all equally important. To determine which factors mattered most, we calculated how the probability of voting for the party changed as scores on various predictor variables moved from their lowest to their highest values while other predictors were held at their average values. Figure 4.12, Panel A shows the results. Not surprisingly, responses to a question about the desirability of the UK leaving the EU altered the likelihood of voting for the Brexit Party by a large amount –0.49 points on a 0 to 1 probability scale.

Although this effect is impressive, attitudes toward the European Union were not the only consequential predictor. Changing feelings about party leader Nigel Farage from their lowest to their highest level increased the probability of a Brexit Party ballot by 0.38 points. This result underscores the point that feelings about Farage were a major factor in the Brexit Party's success, just as they had been three years earlier when he played a key role in Leave's successful referendum campaign. This underlines the importance of party leadership to national populist mobilization.

Farage's leadership was crucial for the rapid rise of the Brexit Party. Although detested by Remainers, he was a political 'rock star' for Britain's Brexiteers and, as shown above (see Figure 4.8), Brexit Party support increased markedly after he became its leader. In our pre-election survey, respondents who strongly approved of EU membership gave Farage an abysmal average score of only 1.4 on a 0 to 10 dislike–like scale, whereas his average among those who strongly disapproved of staying in the EU was a strong 6.9. Overall, Farage's average score on the 0–10 scale was 4.1 points, and half of the survey respondents (47 per cent) rated him at 5 or higher. His overall rating was significantly better than for the Labour Leader Jeremy Corbyn, and quite similar to those for Liberal Democrat and Conservative leaders Vince Cable and Theresa May. Corbyn's average score was only 3.6 on the 0–10 dislike–like scale. Cable and May's ratings were 4.5 and 4.2 respectively. In a context in which

A. Brexit Party Voting

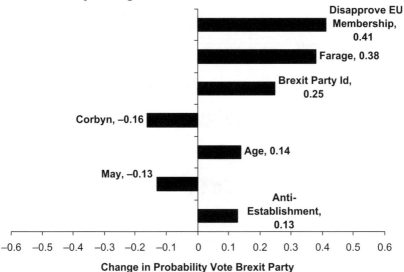

Change in Probability Vote Brexit Party

B. Conservative Voting

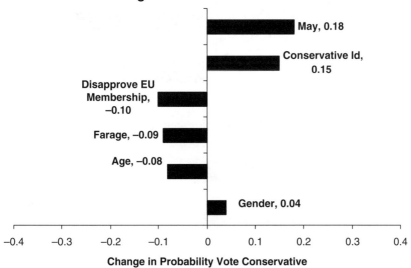

Change in Probability Vote Conservative

Figure 4.12 Significant Predictors of Voting in the 2019 European Union Parliament Election (A) Brexit Party Voting (B) Conservative Voting (C) Labour Voting (D) Liberal Democrat Voting.

C. Labour Voting

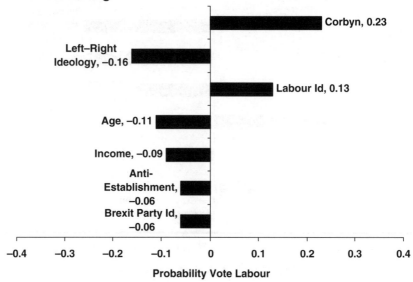

D. Liberal Democrat Voting

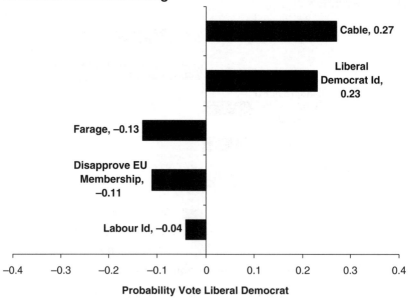

Figure 4.12 (cont.)

none of his rivals was held in especially high regard, Farage's strong appeal among Britain's Brexit voters worked to his advantage.

Impressions of other leaders mattered less for Brexit Party support, with increasingly positive feelings about Labour leader Jeremy Corbyn and Conservative leader Theresa May lessening the likelihood of a voting for Farage's party by 0.16 and 0.13 points, respectively.

As discussed above, Brexit Party partisanship mattered too, but its effects were limited by the fact that the new party lacked many identifiers – only 8 per cent of the electorate identified with the Brexit Party when the EU Parliament election was held. However, when it existed, identification with the new party was important, boosting the probability of voting for the party by 0.25 points over what would be expected for someone who did not identify with any party. General anti-establishment attitudes were operative too, and as anticipated, they boosted the likelihood of a Brexit Party vote (by 0.13 points). Age differences were evident as well – with all other factors controlled, the probability of voting for the party was 0.14 greater for the oldest as compared to the youngest voters.

Several factors had significant influences on voting for other parties. As Figure 4.12 (Panels B, C and D) indicate, positive attitudes towards Brexit lessened the probability of voting for the Liberal Democrats and the Conservatives. Reflecting the party's ambiguity on EU membership, Brexit attitudes were not a significant predictor of Labour voting. Consistent with previous research, feelings about party leaders mattered as well. Predictably, increasing positive feelings about Theresa May boosted the likelihood of a Conservative vote, while positive feelings about Jeremy Corbyn and Vince Cable enhanced the probability of voting for Labour and the Liberal Democrats, respectively.

Similarly, and not surprisingly, the more people liked Nigel Farage, the less likely they were to vote for the Conservatives or the Liberal Democrats. Also, as expected, identifying with the Conservative, Labour or Liberal Democrat parties increased the likelihood of casting a ballot for them, and right-of-centre ideological orientations decreased the probability of voting Labour. Reflecting the Brexit Party's populist appeal, people with anti-establishment attitudes were less likely to support Labour. Finally, men were slightly more likely to vote Conservative and older people were less likely to vote for the two major parties. As observed above, a sizeable number of more senior members of the electorate had responded favourably to Farage's message and decamped temporarily to his Brexit Party. In the subsequent 2019 general election, a great many of them would return to the Conservatives.

Conclusion: Redrawing the Battle Lines

Britain's 2019 European Parliament election was unexpected and produced a surprising outcome. If the 29 March 2019 deadline for Britain's exit from the EU had been met, then Britain would have been out of the EU before these elections took place. However, with Prime Minister May's Brexit deal rejected three times by Parliament, the UK was still in the EU and the election was held. It would prove highly consequential.

As our survey evidence documents, the public mood was very sour and many voters – Leavers and Remainers alike – were inclined to give the major parties a 'good kicking'. The arrival of the new anti-EU Brexit Party, led by arch-Eurosceptic Nigel Farage, gave Britain's disillusioned Brexiteers an opportunity to do exactly that – and one that they grabbed with both hands. The Liberal Democrats, the Greens and other minor parties countered with strong pro-EU platforms that appealed to large numbers of disgruntled Remainers. When the ballots were tallied, the Conservatives and Labour collectively had been reduced to less than one-quarter of the total vote. By itself, the new Brexit Party eclipsed that number, attracting the support of nearly one-third of those casting a ballot.

The 2019 European elections testified to the corrosive impact Brexit was exerting on Britain's traditional two-party system. Only two years beforehand, the Conservatives and Labour had dominated the political landscape, collectively capturing over 80 per cent of the vote in the June 2017 general election. Reduced to less than one-third of that figure less than two years later, the two major parties found themselves victims of an electorate that was sorely vexed by the protracted and polarizing battle over Brexit.

The election result precipitated the immediate departure of Conservative Leader Theresa May, whose failure to successfully prosecute the Brexit process had seriously eroded her image among a large swathe of the electorate. But the election outcome did not have a similar consequence for Labour leader Jeremy Corbyn, who remained at the helm of his party despite also being very unpopular across the electorate. His ambiguity on Brexit continued to alienate Leavers and Remainers alike. As we will see in Chapter 5, Corbyn's presence as Labour leader would have major consequences for his party's fortunes in the ensuing 2019 general election. Equally consequential was May's replacement by Boris Johnson. Johnson's message that it was time to 'Get Brexit Done' helped him to win the Conservative leadership race and boosted his appeal among pro-Leave voters in the electorate. But it was a slogan guaranteed to alienate the millions of voters who continued to hope that the country would remain in the EU.

Whether either leader could help propel their parties to victory in a forthcoming general election was debatable. It appeared that the continuing salience of the pro-/anti-EU cleavage would make it difficult for either the Conservatives or Labour to win a parliamentary majority. As discussed in this chapter, the cleavage had created a highly polarized and corrosive climate of opinion that paved the way for the success of Farage's Brexit Party as well as strong showings by avowedly the pro-EU Liberal Democrats and the Greens. The 2019 EU election demonstrated the ability of the several minor parties to profit from the 'leave or remain' issue agenda that dominated British politics for over three years. Whether these parties could continue to do so as the 'Battle for Brexit' renewed in the summer and autumn of 2019 remained to be seen. Chapter 5 tells that story.

5   The Johnson Breakthrough
The 2019 General Election

'It is time, frankly, that the opposition summon up the nerve to submit themselves to the judgement of our collective boss, which is the people of the UK.' Those were the words of Boris Johnson, the new leader of the Conservative Party, when in October 2019 he tried for a third time to secure an early general election.

The election would be one of the most consequential since the Second World War. Aside from handing the Conservative Party their fourth consecutive victory, it would also deliver what MPs had so far proven themselves unable to deliver: a resolution to Brexit. Since the vote for Brexit in 2016 Parliament and politics had been plunged into total gridlock. By pushing through an election, Johnson hoped that the people would endorse his 'oven ready' Brexit deal and, once and for all, 'Get Brexit Done'.

All of this led observers to view the election as a proxy referendum on Brexit, as another opportunity for the British people to have their say on the Europe question. But while the 2019 election is commonly seen as the 'Brexit election', was this really the case? The evidence that we present in this chapter testifies that the answer to that question is 'no'. It obviously played a very important part in the election, but Brexit was not the only important issue, nor was it the only factor that shaped voters' decisions. Rather, data gathered in our national pre- and post-election surveys[1] reveal that the choices voters made in 2019 were shaped by the same kinds of forces that had driven voting in many earlier general elections. Brexit was certainly a significant part of the story, but it was ultimately only one part.

After the EU Parliament Elections: Trending Back to the Polls

It is impossible to make sense of the 2019 election without examining the events that preceded it. Because of the failure to deliver Brexit more

---

[1] For details about these surveys, see Appendix A.

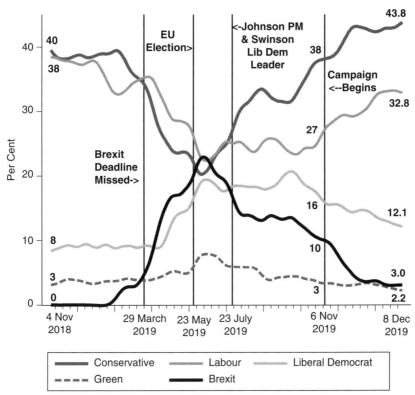

Figure 5.1 Trends in Vote Intentions in 236 Polls, 4 November 2018–8 December 2019.
Source: https://en.wikipedia.org/wiki/Opinion_polling_for_the_2019_United_Kingdom_general_election

than three years after the referendum, the country remained a member of the EU. This meant that during the spring of 2019 it was also obliged to hold elections to the European Parliament. As discussed in Chapter 4, both of the major parties suffered significant losses in that election. The governing Conservatives, with 42.6 per cent of the vote in the preceding 2017 general election, saw their share of the vote plummet to merely 8.8 per cent. Labour did slightly better, at 13.3 per cent, but this was far below the 40.0 per cent they had captured in 2017.

These poor performances were reflected in the polls in 2019 which asked people how they planned to vote at a forthcoming general election. As Figure 5.1 shows, in the aftermath of the European elections the combined share of the vote for the Conservative and Labour parties was just above 20 per cent. Had these numbers continued, they would have spelled disaster for both parties with the political system completely fragmenting.

Reacting to her party's crushing defeat in 2017 and under intense pressure because of her continuing inability to secure Parliament's support for a Brexit deal, Prime Minister May immediately resigned as Conservative Party leader. This precipitated a leadership election that culminated on 23 July with a convincing first-ballot victory for the former mayor of London and renegade Brexiteer Boris Johnson. Both Boris Johnson and the then-UKIP leader Nigel Farage had played a major role in driving the Brexit victory at the 2016 referendum.[2] Breaking the Brexit deadlock and extricating the UK from the EU as quickly as possible were key themes in Johnson's leadership campaign.

The message resonated strongly with many Conservative members. While Johnson might not have fulfilled his boyhood dream of becoming 'world king', he was now at least leader of the incumbent Conservative Party and prime minister. While the Conservatives were choosing their new leader, both major parties saw their support in the polls move modestly upwards to the mid-20s, far below what they would need to win a general election (see Figure 5.1). During this period, the Liberal Democrats also chose a new leader, Jo Swinson, and continued to record poll numbers close to what they had secured at the European elections (19.6 per cent). This level of support was considerably greater than the dismal 7.4 per cent that the party had won at the 2017 election. For the Liberal Democrats, the good times were back – or so it seemed.

After Boris Johnson became their new leader, the Conservative Party's fortunes continued to revive in the polls. Not surprisingly, Johnson expressed enthusiasm for an early general election, arguing that this was the only way to dispatch a deadlocked Parliament and replace it with one that would pass the legislation that was needed to deliver Brexit. Reacting to her party's strong showing in the EU Parliament elections and encouraging poll numbers, the new Liberal Democrat Leader Jo Swinson enthusiastically agreed. An ardent Remainer, Swinson argued that a general election would provide an opportunity to oust the Conservatives and prevent their efforts to secure Brexit. By campaigning on a strong pro-Remain platform, symbolized by the Liberal Democrat slogan 'Bollocks to Brexit', Swinson and her Liberal Democrat colleagues hoped to attract large numbers of Labour supporters who wanted to remain in the EU.

If the Liberal Democrats could do this, it seemed possible that they might even replace Labour as the official opposition. In a burst of

---

[2] See Clarke, Goodwin and Whiteley (2017).

unbridled optimism Swinson stated: 'I am ready to take my party into a general election and win it.'[3] Her growing ambitions were fuelled by Labour's mediocre performance in the polls and Jeremy Corbyn continuing to sit on the fence by refusing to commit himself to a clear 'pro' or 'con' position on Brexit. Although survey data presented in the last chapter indicated that a majority of Labour supporters were Remainers, Corbyn would not accede to their wishes on Brexit. Rather, he repeatedly stated that any future Labour government would negotiate a new deal with the EU and hold a second referendum on Brexit, where, presumably, the entire Brexit project could be voted down. With this 'neither fish nor fowl' policy on Brexit, Labour languished in the mid-20 per cent range in the polls through much of October, as Corbyn rejected calls for an early election. Without support from Labour, an early election bill could not secure the necessary two-thirds support in Parliament.

This only arrived when Corbyn changed his mind. Under intense pressure to take action to resolve the Brexit impasse, he called on his MPs to get behind the early election bill. They did so and the bill became law on 31 October. The election campaign officially began on 6 November and the vote was scheduled for 12 December. When the campaign began, the Conservatives stood at 38 per cent in the polls, with Labour and the Liberal Democrats on 27 per cent and 16 per cent respectively (see Figure 5.1). Nigel Farage's new Brexit Party, which had captured over 30 per cent of the vote at the European elections, had fallen back to 10 per cent, but the ongoing revolt on the right was still enough to make it difficult for the Conservatives to win a majority. Statistical analyses of the polls suggested that Brexit Party voters could have a major impact on the election outcome.[4]

The polls made disappointing reading for Labour and Liberal Democrat supporters and their friends in the media. In reaction, some commentators speculated that since the polls had been quite wide of the mark in previous general elections such as 1992 and 2015, perhaps they would get it wrong again.[5] Others implored people to vote tactically and support whichever party had the best chance of defeating the Conservatives in their constituency.[6] All this proved to be largely wishful thinking.

---

[3] www.telegraph.co.uk/politics/0/jo-swinson-mp-liberal-democrats-leader/
[4] These analyses are based on a 'uniform national swing' model where the vote in each constituency in 2017 is adjusted in terms of parties' current vote intention percentages. The party with the largest adjusted percentage is forecast as the winner of that constituency.
[5] www.theguardian.com/commentisfree/2019/nov/12/polls-2019-election
[6] See, e.g., www.theguardian.com/politics/2019/dec/08/tactical-voting-guide-2019-keep-tories-out-remain-voter-general-election

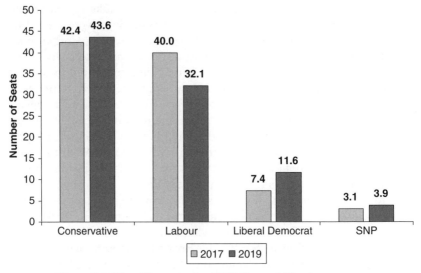

Figure 5.2 Vote Shares in the 2019 General Election.
Source: House of Commons Library Report https://commonslibrary
.parliament.uk/research-briefings/cbp-8749/

On the evening of 12 December, the national exit poll proclaimed that
the Conservatives were on track for a huge victory – they were set to
capture fully 368 seats, compared to 191 for Labour and only 13 for the
Liberal Democrats.[7] These projected numbers proved very accurate.

As Figure 5.2 shows, when all votes had been counted, the Conservatives emerged with 43.6 per cent of the vote, compared to only
32.1 per cent for Labour and 11.6 per cent for the Liberal Democrats.
Although the Conservative tally was up only 1.2 percentage points from
2017, Labour's share was down by 7.9 points to 32.1 per cent. This
was Labour's third worst vote share in any election since the end of the
Second World War.[8] For their part, the Liberal Democrats saw their
vote go up, but only to 11.6 per cent. This was a disappointing result for
Jo Swinson, who only a few months earlier had proclaimed her party's
readiness to govern. Adding insult to injury, Swinson lost her own seat
(Dunbartonshire West) and promptly resigned as party leader.

The vote totals enabled the Conservatives to win 365 seats. This was
48 more than in 2017 (see Figure 5.3) and sufficient to give Boris Johnson

[7] www.theguardian.com/commentisfree/2019/dec/12/exit-poll-election-boris-johnson-
jeremy-corbyn-labour
[8] https://commonslibrary.parliament.uk/research-briefings/cbp-7529/

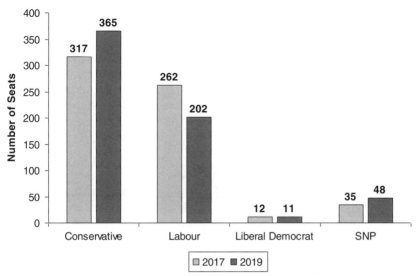

Figure 5.3 Seats Won in the 2019 General Election.
Source: House of Commons Library Report https://commonslibrary
.parliament.uk/research-briefings/cbp-8749/

and his colleagues a solid majority. Although Labour did slightly better than the exit poll had predicted, its total of 202 seats was down by 60 from 2017 and was the lowest total since 1935. A number of Labour's losses occurred in the Midlands and the North – seats like Bishop Auckland, Blyth Valley, Bolsover, Don Valley, Sedgefield, Workington and Wrexham that had been Labour strongholds for decades. Now, they returned Conservative MPs. Labour's 'Red Wall', as it was described in the media, had collapsed.[9]

Unlike Swinson, Jeremy Corbyn did not resign in the immediate aftermath of his party's debacle. Rather, he declared that would not stand as Labour's leader in the next election. There would now be a leadership contest in spring 2020, which Corbyn wanted to influence to the advantage of a successor who shared his ideological views. Here, we focus on the factors that affected the outcome of the crunch 2019 election.

Explaining the Vote

Historically, British psephologists have argued that people's social class and their political behaviour are very closely intertwined. One analyst,

[9] For views on the Red Wall collapse, see, e.g., Mattison (2020) and Rayson 2020).

Peter Pulzer, famously put it: 'in British party politics, social class is everything, all else is embellishment and detail.'[10] Although this may have been true at one time, the strength of the relationship between social class and voting has trended downward over time. Today, explanations that focus heavily on class have only modest explanatory power.[11] Extending this well-established pattern, the correlation between social class and voting was very weak in 2019. Using the Market Research Society's standard social class categorization, our survey evidence shows that whereas 47 per cent of those in the upper and upper-middle classes (A/B) voted Conservative, 23 per cent voted Labour and 15 per cent voted Liberal Democrat. The comparable percentages for the working and lower classes (D/E) were 46 per cent, 31 per cent and 11 per cent respectively. Thus, the difference between middle-class and working-class support for the Conservatives was negligible. Although there were somewhat larger differences with regard to income with higher earners being more likely to vote Conservative or Liberal Democrat and less likely to vote Labour, that aspect of class location was offset by the tendency by less well-educated people to support the Conservatives (see Table 5.1).

As for other demographics, the pattern for age and party support is striking. Similar to what had occurred two years earlier, younger people were much more likely to vote Labour in 2019, with 55 per cent of those 29 or younger supporting the party as compared to only 13 per cent of those 65 or older (see Table 5.1). The Conservative pattern was the opposite; only 23 per cent of those 29 or younger cast a Conservative ballot as compared to fully 59 per cent of the 65 and older group. There were gender differences in the vote as well, but the relationship was much weaker. Men were more likely to support the Conservatives than women (by a 51 per cent to 42 per cent margin) and women were slightly more likely to vote Labour. Finally, as expected given the SNP's strength in the pre-election polls, the Conservatives and Labour were much weaker in Scotland than in England or Wales. Labour's representation in Scotland had collapsed to only one seat in the 2015 election and this increased to seven seats in 2019. But this was well below the forty-one seats the party achieved in the 2010 election.

In their election post-mortems, commentators focused on polls showing the weakness of the relationship between class and voting.[12]

---

[10] Pulzer (1967), p. 98.
[11] See, e.g., Clarke, Sanders, Stewart and Whiteley (2004), ch. 3.
[12] See, e.g., www.theguardian.com/politics/2019/dec/13/five-reasons-why-labour-lost-the-election

Table 5.1 *Voting in the 2019 General Election by Socio-Demographic Characteristics*

	Vote			
	Conservative (%)	Labour (%)	Liberal Democrat (%)	Other Party (%)
Age				
18–29	23	55	9	14
30–49	42	33	12	14
50–64	50	27	12	11
65 and over	59	13	10	18
Education				
Primary or Less	54	17	4	25
Secondary	51	28	10	11
University BA	44	32	13	11
Postgraduate	28	22	14	36
Gender				
Man	51	26	11	12
Woman	42	31	11	16
Income				
Under £21,000	37	41	9	13
£21,000–£40,999	48	25	9	18
£41,000–£54,999	50	22	16	12
£55,000–£76,000	47	31	15	7
Over £76,000	57	20	18	5
Social Class				
A/B	47	23	15	16
C1	48	26	14	12
C2	47	33	6	15
D/E	46	31	11	12
Country				
England	47	34	12	7
Scotland	25	19	9	47
Wales	36	41	6	17

Source: 2019 Essex–UTD pre-/post-election panel survey; country figures from House of Commons Library Report, https://commonslibrary.parliament.uk/research-briefings/cbp-8749/

This finding fit well with Labour's loss of Red Wall seats in the Midlands and the North noted above. Together with its demise in Scotland, Labour's inability to maintain its working-class base in its traditional heartlands was certainly a factor in the party's defeat. But, as just discussed, young people aside, Labour's support was at best mediocre in most other demographic groups. Why was this?

Three explanations quickly gained broad currency. The first was that the election was effectively a second Brexit referendum. Attitudes towards EU membership had divided the electorate in half at the time of the 2016 referendum. Acrimonious debates between Leavers and Remainers and seemingly endless political manoeuvring between the two groups had dominated public life since then. Two factors gave the Brexit issue its potency in the 2019 general election. The first was that the issue was unresolved – three and a half years after the referendum, the UK had still not left the European Union, nor had it abandoned efforts to do so. Recognizing widespread frustration with the situation, the new Conservative Leader, Boris Johnson, made the straightforward slogan 'Get Brexit Done!' the centrepiece of his campaign. With Nigel Farage's Brexit Party not siphoning off significant numbers of pro-Leave voters, Johnson's message rallied those people as well as others who were both anxious that the debilitating impasse be resolved and keen to get on and deliver Brexit.

Commentators also claimed that Labour's failure to take a clear stand on the Brexit issue was a major mistake. Jeremy Corbyn's position that he would negotiate a new and better deal with the EU and then hold a referendum on it was widely seen by many voters as a fudge on the key issue confronting the country. Perhaps Corbyn was motivated by recognition that while there were many Remainers in Labour's ranks, there were sizeable numbers of Leavers as well – especially in the party's northern Red Wall heartlands. But it was argued that he also should have recognized that it was time to declare one way or another.

Labour's ambiguity on Brexit was contrasted with the strong pro-Remain positions adopted by the Liberal Democrats, the Scottish Nationalists and smaller parties such as the Greens and Plaid Cymru. These parties cost Labour Remain supporters while Leavers flocked to the Conservatives. In short, the claim was that the electorate was deeply concerned about Brexit and Labour failed to address the issue in a politically successful way.

A second, related, explanation for why many voters behaved as they did focused on the growing role of populism in British politics. The Leave majority in the 2016 EU referendum was an obvious manifestation of the rise of populist sentiment in the electorate, but there were a number of related factors as well. Widespread perceptions that immigration was excessive and uncontrolled had played a key role in producing the Leave majority.[13] These perceptions continued and were accompanied by feelings of being left behind economically and threatened by rising crime and the erosion of traditional British values. The image was that political and economic elites were failing to protect the interests of

[13] Clarke, Goodwin and Whiteley (2017), ch. 7.

ordinary people, while at the same time holding them in contempt, not least by trying to overturn the vote for Brexit.

This combustible complex of populist attitudes was part of the context of electoral choice in 2019. Labour was hurt not only by its failure to take a stand on Brexit, but also by perceptions that its leadership had abandoned the party's core working-class voters to seek support from a coalition of young, highly educated cosmopolitans living in London and other affluent urban areas. Expressing solidarity with a currently fashionable menu of radical causes, most of Labour's candidates and party operatives were university educated and decidedly middle class – a counter-elite that was as alien to the party's traditional working-class base as the bankers and 'True Blue' Tories in the southern shires.[14] A continuing failure to express sympathy with the concerns and values of 'ordinary' working-class people damaged Labour's prospects around the country.

A third explanation focused squarely on Jeremy Corbyn's leadership – or lack thereof. This argument accords well with the valence politics theory of voting. As the earlier discussion indicates, this theory emphasizes the importance of party leaders' images as cues that people use to inform their choices at the ballot box. Observers emphasizing Labour's 'Corbyn problem' argued that his ambiguity on Brexit was just the most obvious example of a broader leadership deficit that had prompted negative reactions in much of the public. Claims that Corbyn was an antiquated 1970s radical who was sympathetic to terrorist groups such as the IRA and Hamas as well as Russia were coupled with charges that, if ever given the keys to Number 10, he would be a distinct threat to national security and public safety.

Further damage to Corbyn's image had been done by a stream of widely publicized media reports that he had continually downplayed disturbing charges of anti-Semitism in his party. In addition, Labour's 2019 election manifesto promising huge spending increases in many policy areas lacked credibility and was politically counterproductive. Although a number of individual promises Corbyn put on offer proved popular, some analysts contended that the package as a whole struck the British public as an over-ambitious exercise. The bottom line was that much of the electorate did not like Corbyn and believed that he could not be trusted to manage Britain's affairs responsibly. By the time of the 2019 election, polling suggested that he was the most unpopular opposition party leader since records began, in the early 1970s. But which of these explanations is the most convincing?

[14] Evans and Tilley (2017), ch. 6.

The Issue Agenda

Were the observers who claimed that the 2019 general election was all about Brexit correct? We answer this question using national survey data gathered in the two weeks prior to the election.[15] Respondents were presented with a list of twelve issues and asked to select their top three. The results (see Figure 5.4) show that Brexit was indeed the most frequently mentioned issue, with 61 per cent selecting it. That is a solid majority, but not an overwhelming one. In fact, almost as many (58 per cent) chose the NHS and healthcare, and close to two in five (39 per cent) picked the economy. Other prominent issues included immigration (23 per cent), the environment (21 per cent), crime (21.0 per cent) and terrorism (19 per cent). Issues like housing, welfare and education were further down the list, but still attracted the attention of at least 10 per cent of the people who we surveyed.

The 2019 issue agenda, then, was multifaceted. Brexit certainly topped the list but just barely, and nearly two people in five did not mention it as one of their top three issues. This indicates that claims that the election was simply a second Brexit referendum were incorrect. Instead, widespread concern with two perennially salient valence issues, the economy and health, underscore the resemblance of 2019 with other earlier general elections.

When asked which party would do the best job handling various 'top three' issues, 33 per cent of our survey respondents chose the Conservatives, 23 per cent selected Labour, 8 per cent said the Liberal Democrats and 12 per cent opted for various other parties. Nearly a quarter answered, 'none of the above' or that they 'didn't know'. What is striking in these numbers is not Conservative strength but Labour weakness. With fewer than one person in four thinking that Labour was the best party on Brexit or other issues emphasized by voters, the party needed other ways, including a large partisan base and an appealing leader, to construct a winning coalition. In the event, that need went unfulfilled.

First, however, we examine the relationships between key issues and how the electorate voted. We start with Brexit. Brexit as a classic position or 'pro–con' issue and how voters felt about it was strongly correlated with party support. As Figure 5.5 shows, nearly three-quarters (73 per cent) of the participants in our national election survey who reported that they would vote Leave if there were to be a second EU referendum voted Conservative in the 2019 election. The Conservative vote fell to

---

[15] For descriptions of how variables discussed in this chapter were constructed see Appendix A.

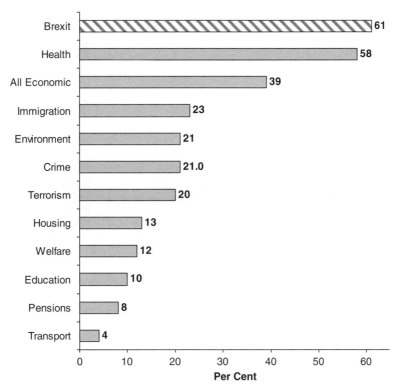

Figure 5.4 Top Three Important Issues Facing the Country.
Source: Essex–UTD pre-election panel survey.

44 per cent among those who were unsure or said they would not vote in a second referendum and to 18 per cent among those who would vote Remain. The Labour pattern is a muted mirror image of this – the percentage of Labour voters dropped from 44 per cent among Remainers to 15 per cent among Leavers. Similarly, the Liberal Democrat vote share decreased from 23 per cent among Remainers to merely 2 per cent among Leavers. While the Leave vote was much more strongly organized around the Conservative Party, the Remain vote was much more fragmented and divided between several competing parties.

These data testify that a large majority of voters favouring Brexit in December 2019 believed that the Conservatives were the 'only game in town'. But, as just discussed, many voters expressed concern with other issues, such as the NHS and the economy. These are classic valence issues – public demand for vigorous economic growth coupled with low rates of inflation and unemployment is overwhelming. The same is true

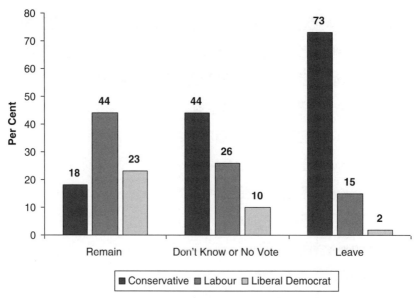

Figure 5.5 Vote in the 2019 General Election by How Would Vote If Another European Union Referendum.
Source: Essex–UTD pre-/post-election panel survey.

for affordable, accessible and effective healthcare. What matters politically for these issues are people's judgements about how the economy and the health service are performing. Studies in Britain and elsewhere repeatedly document that voters who evaluate the economy and the health system positively are more likely to support governing parties, while those who have negative evaluations oppose them. This familiar reward–punishment pattern was clearly evident in the 2019 election.

In the run-up to the vote, 36 per cent of our respondents said that they believed the Conservatives would do the best job on the economy, 25 per cent chose Labour, 9 per cent picked the Liberal Democrats, 3 per cent chose one of the minor parties and 28 per cent were uncertain. Although the Conservatives were favoured by a plurality to manage the economy effectively, the data also testify that the balance of economic evaluations was not especially favourable to a governing party seeking re-election. Specifically, only 15 per cent judged that the economy had improved over the past year and fully 50 per cent thought it had deteriorated. The remainder said things had stayed the same or they 'didn't know'. Similarly, only 19 per cent reported that their personal financial situation had gotten better and 31 per cent said it had gotten worse. Similarly,

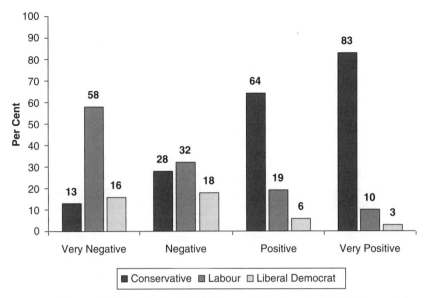

Figure 5.6 Vote in the 2019 General Election by Evaluations of the Economy.
Source: Essex–UTD pre-/post-election panel survey.

optimism about the economy's future prospects was not widespread; only 22 per cent thought things would improve over the next year and 43 per cent believed they would get worse. Expectations about personal economic prospects were less than stellar as well.

Figure 5.6 shows predictable patterns between economic judgements and party support. The percentage of Conservative voters in our election survey increased sharply from a low of 13 per cent among those evaluating economic conditions very negatively to a high of 83 per cent among those offering very positive evaluations. The Labour pattern is the opposite, with the percentage of Labour voters falling steadily from 58 per cent among those offering negative economic evaluations to 10 per cent among those offering positive ones.

Similar patterns obtain for healthcare. Labour was fond of reminding voters that it was the party that had founded the NHS and the party's 2019 election manifesto placed heavy emphasis on the issue.[16] Focusing on the NHS seemed to be a smart thing for Jeremy Corbyn

---

[16] https://labour.org.uk/wp-content/uploads/2019/11/Real-Change-Labour-Manifesto-2019.pdf

and his party to do. A majority of voters identified healthcare as one of their most important issues and, historically, Labour had laid claim to being the champion of the NHS. In the language of political science, when it comes to healthcare, Labour traditionally has enjoyed 'issue ownership' – it has owned the NHS issue[17]

Labour's advantage on the issue, however, was not evident in the run-up to the 2019 election. When respondents in our pre-election survey who identified healthcare as an important issue were asked which party was best able to deal with it, only about one person in every four chose Labour, slightly fewer than the number who selected the Conservatives. Labour's emphasis on the NHS – one of its historic strengths – clearly was not 'cutting through' to the party's benefit in 2019. This was potentially important because our pre-election survey indicated that many people were dissatisfied with how the health system was functioning – only 12 per cent stated the NHS had performed better over the past year, whereas 60 per cent said it had done worse. Similarly, when asked about how the government was handling the NHS, fewer than one person in five replied 'very' or 'fairly' well and over half said 'fairly' or 'very' badly.

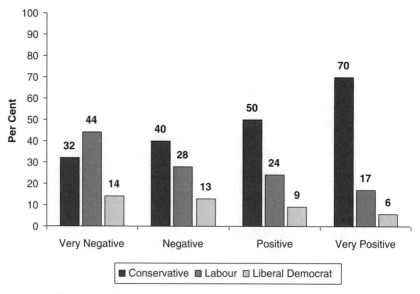

Figure 5.7 Vote in the 2019 General Election by Evaluations of the NHS. Source: Essex–UTD pre-/post-election panel survey.

[17] See, e.g., Petrocik (1996).

Moreover, judgements about the state of the healthcare system were correlated with how people voted. Figure 5.7 illustrates that among those judging the NHS's performance very negatively, 32 per cent voted Conservative and 44 per cent voted Labour but, among those assessing the health service's performance very positively, the percentages are 70 per cent Conservative but only 17 per cent Labour. Below we examine if these strong relationships held up once we take into account other factors that may have influenced the vote.

Political-Economic Beliefs and Values

In earlier chapters, we discussed the rise of populism and its effects on voting and British politics over the past decade. And, as noted earlier in this chapter, after the election a number of pundits pointed to populist sentiments as an important factor that 'turned off' many traditional Labour voters. Our survey data reveal that some, but not all, aspects of populism worked the way this narrative suggests.

There has been considerable discussion of the political consequences of voters' feelings of being 'left behind' economically and by the values that have come to dominate the new mainstream.[18] We address this theme using survey questions that asked respondents about their expectations for Britain's economy and their personal financial situation over the year ahead. Comparing responses to these questions shows that nearly two persons in five thought that they would do better than the country as a whole, whereas about one in five thought that they would be left behind. Table 5.2 reports that 58 per cent of those in the left behind group voted Conservative and 17 per cent voted Labour. In contrast, among those in getting ahead group, 17 per cent opted for the Conservatives but 35 per cent chose Labour. These numbers testify that feelings of being left behind economically were far from pervasive at the time of the election and they did not work to the advantage of Labour, despite the party's historic image as the champion of working people and other disadvantaged groups. If anything, Boris Johnson, the Old Etonian and Oxford graduate, became the main representative of people who felt they were being left behind.

Populist sentiments are not animated solely by economic discontents. Rather, they are linked to more general perceptions that British society is beset by inequality and social injustice or political values.[19] These perceptions were quite widespread in 2019: 61 per cent of our survey respondents agreed that 'economic inequality is a major problem',

[18] See, e.g., Ford and Goodwin (2014).
[19] Eatwell and Goodwin (2018).

Table 5.2 *Voting in the 2019 General Election by Political-Economic Beliefs and Values*

	Vote			
	Conservative (%)	Labour (%)	Liberal Democrat (%)	Other Party (%)
Left behind Economically				
Yes	58	17	6	19
Keeping Up	54	27	7	12
Moving Ahead	34	35	17	13
Pro-/Anti-Establishment				
Very Pro	83	5	5	7
Pro	52	19	12	16
Anti	42	34	10	13
Very Anti	21	50	13	15
Social Values				
Very Conservative	80	12	2	5
Conservative	59	22	9	10
Liberal	33	35	16	16
Very Liberal	11	44	9	35
Left–right Ideology				
Extreme Right	79	12	3	6
Moderate Right	56	17	11	17
Centre	45	25	14	17
Moderate Left	13	52	19	16
Extreme Left	9	72	8	12

Source: 2019 Essex–UTD pre-/post-election panel survey.

57 per cent felt that 'social injustice is a major problem', 55 per cent said the same about 'corporate greed' and 56 per cent said the same about 'excessive profiteering' by banks. In every case, less than 10 per cent disagreed that these were major problems.

Combining these responses into an overall 'pro-/anti-establishment' scale, we see that there is a strong correlation between positions on this scale and the choices people made in the 2019 election. With Nigel Farage's populist Brexit Party largely sidelined when people went to the polls, Labour, rather than the Conservatives, was the principal beneficiary of those harbouring anti-establishment views. Specifically, 50 per cent of those with strong anti-establishment views voted Labour and only 21 per cent supported the Conservatives (see Table 5.2). Liberal Democrat support, although a modest 13 per cent, also was at its greatest among the strongly anti-establishment group. In contrast, Conservative voting was greatest (83 per cent) among people with strong pro-establishment views and declined steadily to 21 per cent among those in the strongly anti-establishment group.

The Brexit Party's effective absence also meant that the Conservatives were the only viable option for voters who wished to express their small 'c' conservative values. A sizeable number of people indicated that they agreed with such values, but there was considerable disagreement as well. For example, three-fifths of those interviewed in our survey agreed that 'young people did not have enough respect for traditional British values' and over half thought that 'convicted criminals should be given longer prison sentences'. In contrast, less than two in five did not want to legalize marijuana and disagreed with the idea of banning the death penalty for serious crimes. Only about one in ten disagreed with the idea of being more tolerant of those who lead unconventional lifestyles.

Combining these answers into a summary scale shows a very strong relationship between conservative values and Conservative voting. Specifically, fully 80 per cent of those with very conservative values in Table 5.2 supported the Conservatives, and the percentage doing so fell steadily to merely 11 per cent among those with very liberal values. The Labour pattern is the opposite – Labour voting falls from 44 per cent among persons with very liberal values to 12 per cent among those with very conservative ones. Liberal Democrat support is also greater among those espousing liberal values, but, once more, the party was not successful in harvesting many votes from any of the value groups.

Finally, we examine relationships between 'left–right' ideological orientations and vote choice. The concepts of 'left' and 'right' long have been staples of elite and mass political discourse in Britain and they help to summarize thinking about where parties and voters stand on various issues[20]. When asked to place themselves on an 11-point scale ranging from 0 (right) to 10 (left), 36 per cent of our survey respondents chose a score of 0 to 4, 23 per cent picked the midpoint (5) and 21 per cent gave a score between 6 and 10. The remaining 20 per cent said that they 'didn't know'. These numbers indicate that slightly over half of the 2019 electorate was neither on the left nor on the right. Of the remainder, the number to the right of centre exceeded that to the left by a ratio of about 1.7 to one. Thus small 'c' conservative values exceed small 'l' liberal values in Britain by a considerable margin.

Left–right orientations were strongly correlated with the choices voters made. Again, as Table 5.2 shows, the percentage of voters supporting the Conservatives declined steadily from 79 per cent among those at the extreme right end of the scale (scores 0 to 2) to only 9 per cent among those on the extreme left (scores 8 to 10). The Labour pattern is the opposite, with voting support moving sharply upwards from 12 per cent

---

[20] Dalton, Farrell and McAllister (2011).

of those on the extreme right to 72 per cent among those on the extreme left. Once more, the Liberal Democrats failed to do well among any ideological group, with their maximum being 19 per cent among those placing themselves on the moderate right.

To summarize, there are several strong statistical relationships between people's political-economic beliefs and the choices they made in the 2019 election. The results resemble those found in studies of earlier elections – people with pro-establishment viewpoints, conservative social values and those on the right ideologically strongly favoured the Conservatives, while those holding the opposite positions opted for Labour. The only departure from this familiar pattern concerns Conservative strength among those who judged that they were falling behind economically.

In the next section, we consider the nature of voters' partisan attachments and their images of the party leaders. Traditionally, these are key factors driving the vote.

Two Heuristics: Partisanship and Leader Images

The Role of Partisanship at the 2019 Election

People's psychological attachments to political parties are accorded a prominent place in valence politics and earlier social psychological theories of electoral choice.[21] As discussed earlier, in the original analysis these 'party identifications' were thought to be initially formed in adolescence or early adulthood, and they affect voting directly as well as indirectly by influencing the acquisition and processing of information relevant to the choices that people make. The emphasis in the original literature was on the stability of partisanship over time, but research conducted over the past two decades indicates that sizeable numbers of British voters are willing to update their partisanship in light of new evidence about parties' actual and anticipated performance.[22] At any point in time, partisan attachments constitute an important shortcut or 'heuristic' that people employ to help them make political decisions. Other things being equal, parties with larger groups of partisans than their rivals enjoy a distinct electoral advantage.

Figure 5.8 shows that there was substantial aggregate volatility in partisanship over the three and a half years separating the 2016 EU

---

[21] The concept of party identification was originally developed by electoral researchers at the University of Michigan in the early 1950s and later in Britain in the 1960s. See Campbell, Converse, Miller and Stokes (1960); Butler and Stokes (1969).

[22] Clarke, Sanders, Stewart, Whiteley (2004), ch. 6; Clarke and McCutcheon (2009).

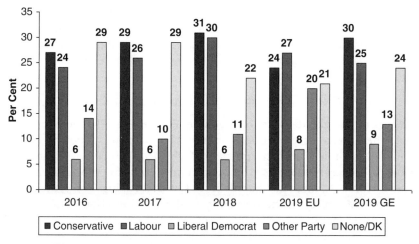

Figure 5.8 Party Identification, 2016–2019.
Source: 2017 and 2019 Essex–UTD pre-election surveys.

referendum and the 2019 general election. At the time of the referendum, 27 per cent of the electorate identified with the Conservatives, and 24 per cent and 6 per cent identified with Labour or the Liberal Democrats, respectively. The Conservative share then climbed to 29 per cent in 2017 and to 31 per cent in 2018, before falling back to only 24 per cent at the time of the May 2019 EU Parliament elections. Labour's pattern was broadly similar, except that its decline between 2018 and May 2019 was smaller. As a result, Labour held an edge over the Conservatives in partisanship (27 per cent v 24 per cent) when Theresa May stepped down as Conservative Leader.

Throughout this period, the number of Liberal Democrat identifiers remained meagre, varying from 6 per cent to 8 per cent. Although the Liberal Democrats made a strong showing in the EU Parliament elections, the failure to increase their share of partisans extended a longstanding pattern and did not bode well for the party. Party leader Jo Swinson may have claimed she was ready to govern, but the very anaemic number of Liberal Democrat identifiers in the electorate rendered that prospect highly unlikely.

Trends in party identification were not kind to Labour either. As Figure 5.8 shows, after the 2019 EU Parliament elections, Conservative identifications recovered such that in late November, 30 per cent said that they identified with the party. This was an increase of 6 per cent over this period. In contrast, Labour's partisan share decreased by 2 per cent over the same period. In May of 2019 the Conservatives had 3 per cent fewer identifiers than Labour, but shortly before the general election of that year the Conservatives had 5 per cent more. This turnaround in the balance of partisanship in favour of Prime Minister Johnson and his colleagues was a harbinger of what was to come on election day.

The Role of Leaders at the 2019 Election

Images of party leaders are the second major heuristic that voters use to help them make up their minds about which party to support.[23] Faced with policy choices the consequences of which are difficult, if not impossible, to forecast, voters rely on their impressions of competing parties' leaders for assistance. In Chapter 3, we saw that feelings about the party leaders had strong effects on voting in the 2017 election. This would prove true again in the general election of 2019.

Figure 5.9 summarizes data from our pre-election survey concerning the electorate's affective reactions to Boris Johnson, Jeremy Corbyn, Jo Swinson and Nigel Farage. Survey respondents were asked to use a 0 (strongly dislike) to 10 (strongly like) scale to indicate their feelings about each of these leaders. Figure 5.9 records the average score for each leader, and it indicates that none of them were held in especially high regard. Boris Johnson was the most popular leader with an average score of 4.5, and all of the others have average scores below 4.0. Corbyn's average score was only 3.6, the lowest of any of the four leaders in 2019 and lower than the 'like–dislike' average scores recorded by his three most recent predecessors, Tony Blair, Gordon Brown and Ed Miliband.

A comparison of individual survey respondents' feelings about Johnson and Corbyn shows that 52 per cent liked Johnson better than Corbyn, whereas 36 per cent favoured Corbyn over Johnson, and the rest of them (dis)liked the two leaders equally. All of this was bad news for Jeremy Corbyn and his party. Studies conducted over the past two decades reveal that no party has won a British general election when feelings about its leader are less than 4.0 on the like–dislike scale, and leaders of winning parties always have higher scores than their rivals. Party leaders' images matter.

There is more to the story of leader images. Survey respondents were asked if various descriptors such as 'trustworthy' and 'caring' well described each of the leaders. As Figure 5.10 shows, many voters expressed doubts about whether either Johnson or Corbyn possessed the qualities needed for effective leadership. Specifically, only 33 per cent thought Johnson was trustworthy and only 32 per cent thought he cared

---

[23] Clarke, Sanders, Stewart and Whiteley (2009), ch. 2.

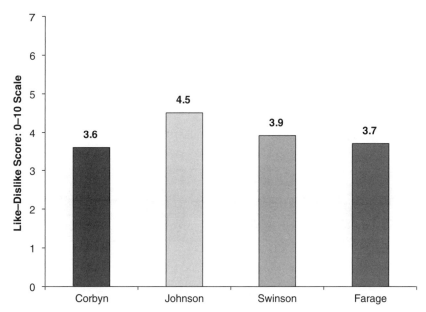

Figure 5.9 Feelings about Party Leaders.
Source: Essex–UTD pre-post-election panel survey.

about ordinary people's problems. Somewhat larger minorities thought he was competent (40 per cent) and would provide strong leadership (45 per cent). These numbers are hardly brilliant, but, in some respects, Corbyn's were worse. While Corbyn basically matched Johnson on trustworthiness (30 per cent) and responsiveness (34 per cent), his ratings on strength of leadership (25 per cent) and competence (27 per cent) lagged well behind the already less than stellar numbers recorded by his Conservative rival. Perhaps most telling, when asked who would make the best prime minister, only 21 per cent chose Corbyn, while 36 per cent selected Johnson. The rest either picked Jo Swinson (13 per cent) or Nigel Farage (6 per cent) or said they 'didn't know'.

Dissatisfaction with Corbyn's leadership was hardly new. Hundreds of polls conducted since he first became Labour leader in September 2015 had documented widespread reservations about him. A set of monthly IPSOS-MORI surveys shown in Figure 5.11 illustrates the point. When Corbyn initially became leader 33 per cent said they were satisfied with his performance and about as many (36 per cent) were dissatisfied. His job dissatisfaction numbers then quickly climbed upwards reaching highs of 65 per cent in July 2016 and 64 per cent in March 2017. However, as discussed in Chapter 3, positive judgements about

A. Boris Johnson

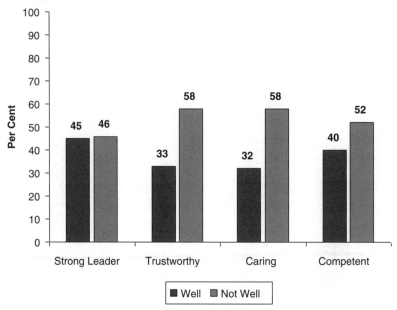

B. Jeremy Corbyn

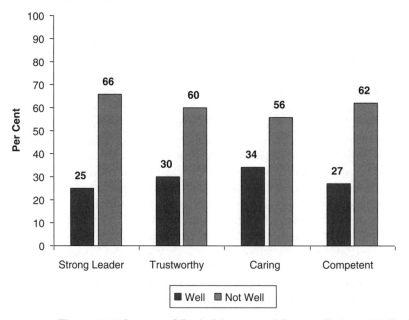

Figure 5.10 Images of Boris Johnson and Jeremy Corbyn (A) Boris Johnson (B) Jeremy Corbyn.
Source: Essex–UTD pre-/post-election panel survey.

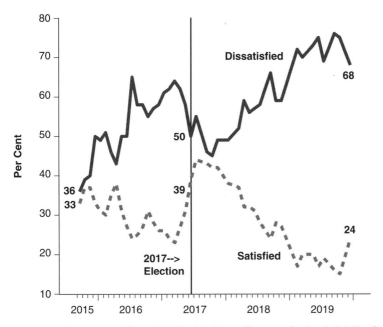

Figure 5.11 Trends in Evaluations of Jeremy Corbyn's Job Performance in Fifty-Two Polls, September 2015–December 2019.
Source: IPSOS-MORI www.ipsos.com/ipsos-mori/en-uk/political-monitor-satisfaction-ratings-1997-present.

Corbyn picked up considerably during the 2017 general election campaign. His vigorous campaign performance surprised many observers and, although Labour did not win, his job satisfaction ratings climbed to 44 per cent shortly after that election. This surge proved short-lived, however, and was eroded by charges of radicalism and anti-Semitism and ensuing intra-party disputes, so that Corbyn's approval ratings slid badly. In June 2019, shortly after Labour's poor performance in the EU Parliament elections, only 17 per cent stated they were satisfied with Corbyn's performance as party leader and fully 75 per cent said they were dissatisfied.

Unlike 2017, Corbyn's standing with the public did not improve substantially as the 2019 general election approached. In October, just before the campaign began, only 15 per cent of the participants in a monthly IPSOS-MORI survey said they were satisfied with his job performance and fully 75 per cent stated they were dissatisfied. These numbers moved only modestly in a pro-Corbyn direction as the campaign progressed and, shortly before the ballots were counted on 12 December, polls conducted by several major survey houses testified that the electorate remained deeply unenthusiastic about the Labour leader.[24] Corbyn's dismal approval numbers portended an electoral disaster for his party.

At the Polls: What Mattered Most

We have looked at relationships between several factors influencing the vote in the 2019 election. But what was the relative importance of these factors? We answer this question using multivariate models of voting for the Conservatives, Labour and the Liberal Democrats. These analyses enable us to see if a particular explanatory variable has a statistically significant effect, controlling for the effects of all the other factors. The explanatory variables employed in these models include attitudes towards Brexit, judgements about the performance of the economy and the NHS, feelings of being left behind economically, attitudes towards immigration, anti-establishment attitudes, social values, leader images, partisan attachments, and the general left–right ideological orientations of respondents. We also include several socio-demographics variables: age, education, gender, income and residence in England, Scotland or Wales. As in Chapter 3, since the dependent variables in these models are dichotomies, we conduct binomial logit analyses,[25] with the dependent variables scoring 1 if a person voted for a particular party and 0 if they did not.

The results of these analyses for the three major parties are summarized in Figure 5.12. This figure charts the effects of a given predictor on the probability of voting for the party in question. For brevity, we restrict attention to the five strongest predictors in each case, so all the effects are highly statistically significant. The one exception to this is the measure of the respondent approving of Britain leaving the EU, which was not always in the top five but was always statistically significant. We isolate the importance of a specific predictor by calculating what would happen to the probability of voting for a party, by comparing the difference between minimum and maximum scores on that variable. We control for the effects of other predictors by holding all their scores at the mean values. When this is done rival predictors have no effect on the probability of voting for a party, allowing us to identify the unique contribution of a particular variable to the overall vote.

Starting with the Conservatives, we see that feelings about Boris Johnson had by far the strongest effect of any of the predictor variables. With

---

[24] https://en.wikipedia.org/wiki/Leadership_approval_opinion_polling_for_the_2019_United_Kingdom_general_election

[25] Long and Freese (2014).

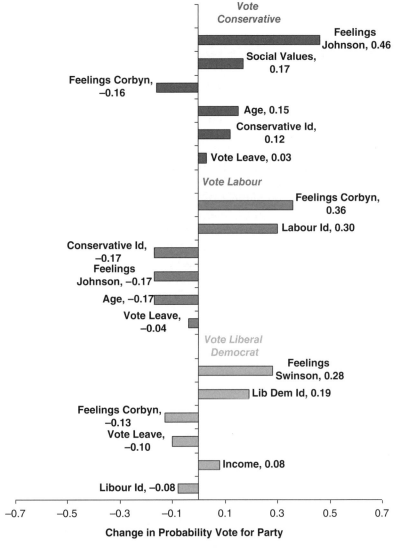

Figure 5.12 Most Important Predictors of Vote in the 2019 General Election.

statistical controls for all other factors in place, as feelings about Johnson moved from extremely negative to extremely positive, the probability of voting Conservative increased by 0.46 points (on a 0 to 1 scale), a massive effect. Two other variables in the valence politics model were also in the top five predictors of Conservative voting. A change from negative to positive feelings about the Labour Leader Jeremy Corbyn reduced the probability of voting Conservative by 0.16 points. In addition, Conservative Party identification increased it by 0.12 points. Other top five significant predictors included social values and also age. Holding conservative as opposed to liberal values enhanced the likelihood of voting Conservative by 0.17 points and being old rather than young did so by 0.15 points.

Figure 5.12 shows that support for Brexit did have an impact on the Conservative vote, but it was very modest once the other factors were taken into account. All else being equal, the direct effect of wanting to leave rather than remain in the EU increased the probability of voting Conservative by only 0.03 points. This reinforces the earlier point that a lot more was going on in the 2019 general election than merely voting in a second referendum on EU membership.

The story for Labour voting is quite similar. The two most important predictors of Labour voting were feelings about Jeremy Corbyn and Labour partisanship. As feelings about Corbyn increased from very negative to very positive, the likelihood of voting Labour increased by 0.36 points. The effect of being a Labour identifier as opposed to a non-identifier was almost as large, at 0.30 points. Feelings about Boris Johnson and Conservative partisanship also were top five predictors of Labour voting. Increasingly positive feelings about the Conservative leader decreased the likelihood of casting a Labour ballot by 0.17 points and Conservative partisanship did so by the same amount. Age also had an equally strong effect and in line with the earlier discussion younger voters were more likely to vote Labour than were older ones. As in the case of Conservative voting, Brexit attitudes had a statistically significant, but lesser impact on the Labour vote. With other factors controlled, being a Leave as opposed to a Remain supporter lessened the probability of voting Labour by 0.04 points.

Once again, support for the Liberal Democrats had a similar profile to support for the two major parties. As Figure 5.12 shows, the two most important predictors were feelings about party leader Jo Swinson and Liberal Democratic partisanship. Increasingly positive feelings about Swinson enhanced the probability of voting for her party by 0.28 points and being a Liberal Democratic party identifier (as opposed to a non-identifier) did so by 0.19 points. In contrast, positive feelings about the Labour leader and Labour partisanship worked in the opposite direction to reduce the likelihood of a Liberal Democrat vote, by 0.13 and 0.07 points respectively. Unlike in the Conservative and Labour models, attitudes towards EU membership were one of the top five predictors of Liberal Democrat voting.

Not surprisingly, being a Leaver rather than a Remainer decreased the probability of a Liberal Democratic ballot by 0.10 points. So attitudes to Brexit were a more important driver of Liberal Democrat voting than was true either for Labour or the Conservatives. Income also was relatively influential in the Liberal Democrat case; moving from the lowest to the highest income category boosted the probability of voting for the party by 0.08 points.

Viewed generally, these multivariate models of voting testify to the importance of valence politics variables. Feelings about their party leaders were the strongest predictors of voting for all three parties, and in all three cases feelings about opposition leaders were top five predictors as well. Partisanship, another key valence politics variable, also exerted relatively strong effects on voting for the three parties. In sum, leader images and partisan attachments accounted for eleven of the fifteen strongest predictors of Conservative, Labour and Liberal Democratic voting.

The conclusion that valence politics considerations were very important is bolstered by the analyses summarized in Table 5.3. In this table, we summarize the explanatory power of five different sets of explanatory variables. As mentioned earlier values of the McKelvey R^2 statistic[26] indicate the overall explanatory power of a model on a 0–1 scale, while the AIC values discount the explanatory power of a model by the number of explanatory variables it contains.[27] Larger values of R^2 and smaller values of AIC indicate that a model is doing a better explanatory job than a competitor.

Table 5.3 shows that a basic socio-demographic model has relatively little purchase for explaining voting for any of the three parties, a finding that echoes the results of similar analyses of voting in 2017 in Chapter 3 and other recent British general elections. Echoing the results reported above, a 'pure Brexit' model also has only modest explanatory power, particularly in the case of Labour voting where the R^2 is only 0.17, which is only marginally greater than the R^2 for the socio-demographic model. Similarly, a pure left–right ideology provides only moderate explanatory power for Conservative and Labour voting, and it fails almost entirely in the Liberal Democrat case.

A populism model does considerably better. This model uses Brexit, immigration and anti-establishment attitudes, as well as feelings of being left behind economically and social values as predictors. As discussed above, Nigel Farage's decision to stand down his Brexit Party candidates

[26] Long and Freese (2014), p. 98.
[27] Burnham and Anderson (2011).

Table 5.3 *Rival Models of Voting in the 2019 General Election*

	Vote					
	Conservative		Labour		Liberal Democrat	
Rival Models	R^2	AIC	R^2	AIC	R^2	AIC
Demographics	0.15	1984.27	0.14	1715.90	0.07	1066.63
Left–right	0.33	1774.58	0.26	1580.54	0.01	1083.37
Brexit	0.33	1660.27	0.17	1677.29	0.36	911.11
Populism	0.55	1409.67	0.29	1555.99	0.38	902.71
Valence Politics	0.80	762.47	0.76	812.68	0.51	638.29
Composite	0.83	722.85	.81	743.63	0.63	528.81

Models
Demographics: age, education, gender, income, country of residence (Scotland, Wales, England)
Left–right: Left–right ideological position
Brexit Only: Vote if second EU referendum
Populism: Vote if second EU referendum, anti-immigration, left behind economically, anti-establishment attitudes, social values
Valence Politics: Feelings about party leaders, partisanship, economic evaluations, NHS
Composite: All predictor variables in various models
R^2: McKelvey pseudo R^2 – larger values indicate better model performance
AIC: Akaike Information Criterion – smaller values indicate better model performance

in 317 constituencies won by the Conservatives deprived a large segment of the electorate of the clear populist choice his party presented. But this did not reduce the power of populist sentiments to affect the vote. The populist model's R^2 values are greater than the socio-demographic, left–right and Brexit models for voting for all three parties and its AIC values are smaller in the Conservative and Labour cases.

The valence politics model provides even greater explanatory purchase. This model has only four explanatory variables – evaluations of the performance of the economy and the NHS, feelings about party leaders and partisan attachments. As Table 5.3 shows, this model has considerably better goodness of fit (larger R^2 values) than any of the competing models in the analyses. It also has smaller (better) AIC values. Similar to the results of comparable analyses of voting in other general elections, the valence politics model does much to account for the choices that the British people made in 2019.

Finally, although the valence politics model does much of the 'heavy lifting', a composite model that includes all of the several explanatory variables performs slightly better. The R^2 values for the composite model are larger for Conservative, Labour and Liberal Democrat voting. Also, despite the fact that the composite model contains several more explanatory variables than the valence politics model, it has lower AIC values in the voting analyses for all three parties. Again, this result echoes findings on what drives voting at several earlier British general elections.

Follow the Leaders

The preceding analyses clearly show that the images of party leaders were major drivers of Conservative, Labour and Liberal Democrat support in 2019. Given this, it is important to see what factors were shaping how people thought about the leaders. We do this by estimating multivariate models of like–dislike feelings about the leaders using the several other predictor variables in the voting analyses described above. The results, presented in Figure 5.13, reveal that in the case of Boris Johnson, Conservative identifiers and those judging the state of the economy positively were especially likely to have favourable views of him.[28] Other 'top-five' predictors of feelings about Johnson included left–right ideological orientations, readiness to vote Leave if a second EU referendum were held, evaluating the performance of the NHS positively and holding conservative social values.

The analysis of feelings about Jeremy Corbyn shows that being a Labour identifier mattered most, followed by being a Conservative identifier, the latter having a negative impact. The third most important predictor was age; controlling for all everything else, younger people were significantly more favourably disposed towards Corbyn. Other top five predictors included immigration and anti-establishment attitudes. People favouring increased immigration and those with anti-establishment views held the Labour leader in higher regard than did others. Although attitudes towards Brexit were not one of the strongest predictors of feelings about Corbyn, they were statistically significant. Other things being equal, people who wished to remain in the European Union tended give Corbyn higher scores than did those who wanting to Leave, although the effect was rather weak.

Although attitudes towards Brexit are not the most important influence on feelings about Johnson or Corbyn, they do rank first in the analysis of factors affecting reactions to Jo Swinson. As discussed above, throughout the election campaign, Swinson stressed her strong support for remaining in the EU and voters' attitudes towards the Liberal Democrat leader reflected their positions on the issue. Additional high-ranking predictors of feelings towards her included: being a Liberal Democrat identifier,

---

[28] Lewis-Beck and Lewis-Beck (2015), pp. 83–86.

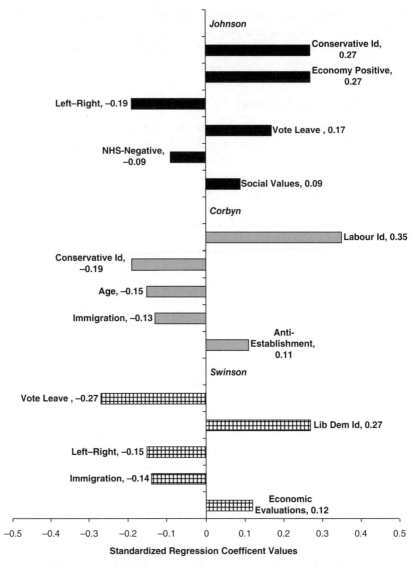

Figure 5.13 Most Important Predictors of Feelings about Party Leaders in the 2019 General Election.

being to the right-of-centre ideologically, holding pro-immigration attitudes and evaluating the economy favourably. Similar to other leaders, attitudes towards Swinson reflected a variety of considerations. Unlike Johnson or Corbyn, positions on Brexit were the most important predictor in her case, but other factors were in the mix as well.

Valence Politics Plus

The 2019 general election was a highly consequential contest. Recognizing its significance, over 32 million people went to the polls – the second highest number of participants in the history of general elections. In this chapter we have analysed the forces that drove the choices that voters made. Although some commentators were quick to characterize the election as a second Brexit referendum and concluded that attitudes towards the EU dominated the picture, the evidence does not support this claim. The forces that shaped the outcome of the 2019 election were rather similar to the forces that influenced electoral choice in earlier general elections. To be sure, many voters were exercised about Brexit, and the issue exerted direct and indirect effects on the choices people made, shaping for example how they felt about party leaders. However, many voters were also concerned with other issues, especially the state of the economy and the condition of the NHS. The economy and health are classic valence issues and judgements about parties' ability to deliver 'good outcomes' on them typically do much to shape voters' decisions.

Voters rely heavily on their partisan attachments and their images of leaders to help them make up their minds about who can do the best job on such issues. Like earlier elections, this was true in 2019 – partisanship and feelings about leaders did much to determine the choices that people made at the ballot box. Reactions to Conservative leader Boris Johnson and Labour leader Jeremy Corbyn were especially important. Although neither of these figures was warmly welcomed across the electorate, Corbyn's reception was especially chilly. The Labour leader was widely disliked in all parts of the country, and many of our survey respondents judged him to be incompetent, untrustworthy and incapable of strong leadership. None of this should have come as a surprise because, except for a brief period during the 2017 election, Corbyn's poll numbers had been consistently bad since he first became Labour leader in autumn 2015.

His persistent unwillingness to take a stand one way or another on Brexit only added to Labour's 'Corbyn problem' and made it difficult for his party to capitalize on populist sentiments that were widespread in the electorate. Corbyn's presence as party leader was a key reason why so many people decided not to vote Labour and why the party experienced one of its worst election performances since the 1930s. Valence politics brought Labour down in 2019, reducing the party to historic losses, paving the way for the rise of Boris Johnson and for the country to finally exit the European Union.

Having reviewed the results of all the national elections since the EU referendum in the last three chapters, in the next section of the book we look at changes in British electoral politics over a much longer period of time. It is time to step back and take a look at much longer-term trends in electoral politics, to see how much they have influenced the short-term events examined up to this point. So we turn to the task of evaluating how electoral politics has changed over a period of more than fifty years.

Part II

The Long Term

6   Time and the Fragmenting Party System

The fragmentation of the UK party system was dramatically illustrated in the discussion of the 2019 European Parliament Elections in Chapter 4, but this process has been going on over a much longer period of time. In the first fully peacetime general election in 1950, Labour and the Conservatives received 89 per cent of the popular vote on a turnout of 84 per cent. In contrast, in the general election of 2019 these parties obtained 76 per cent of the vote on a turnout of 67 per cent.[1] So fewer eligible people are voting, and when they do so, they are less likely to support the two major parties. The share of the vote for the two main parties recovered to some extent in the 2017 and 2019 elections compared with 2015, as previous chapters have shown. But the growth in support for minor parties has substantially reduced their share of the vote compared with fifty years ago.

As we have seen, a major contributor to this development has been differences in age-related electoral turnout and support for the major parties, trends which have been growing over time. We have known for a long time that young people are less likely to turn out than the middle-aged and elderly in British elections.[2] Moreover, as discussed earlier, age was not only significantly related voting to Leave in the 2016 referendum on the country's EU membership but was also a strong predictor of voting Labour in the 2017 and 2019 general elections.[3] Young people were very likely to vote Remain in the referendum and then to vote Labour. After the 2017 election, this surprisingly strong age effect was described as a 'Youthquake'.

This chapter investigates why the process of party fragmentation has occurred over a long period of time with a particular focus on the role of age. We will explain why electoral participation among different age groups is so varied, why this variation has grown over time and how this

---

[1] House of Commons (2020).
[2] Franklin (2004); Grasso (2016).
[3] Clarke, Goodwin and Whiteley (2017), p. 155; Allen and Bartle (2018), p. 166.

has contributed to the fragmentation of the party system. We begin by focusing on turnout, and then subsequently look at voting for parties over a period of fifty-five years using British Election Study (BES) surveys as well as our own more recent national surveys. This exercise uses every BES survey from 1964 through 2017.[4]

At first sight, it appears easy to analyse if young people participated in greater numbers in recent elections compared with the past simply by looking at turnout and party support by different age groups over time. But it is a more complicated exercise than it first appears, since there are three different aspects to the relationship between age and voting behaviour that we need to examine. These are what are known as life-cycle, period and cohort effects, each of which makes a separate contribution to the relationship between age and voting.[5]

To consider each of these in turn, *life-cycle* effects are associated with individuals getting older and therefore having a variety of life experiences which can affect their attitudes, beliefs and rates of political participation. For example, 18-year-olds are unlikely to have full-time careers, or high incomes; few will own properties and have mortgages and they are less likely to be in a stable relationship with a partner or to have children than are older people. All these experiences are likely to influence the way they look at politics and the world more generally in comparison with the middle-aged or elderly, most of whom will have had a number of politically relevant experiences over the course of their lives.[6]

One way of explaining lower turnout among the young is to note that they have less of a 'stake in the system'. If they do not pay taxes, have full-time jobs, own property, are relatively healthy and do not have children, they are less likely to be concerned about politics because, while issues related to these characteristics are central to policy, they are peripheral to young people's concerns. Youth are less focused on issues such as taxes, employment, health and housing, in comparison with older groups because their experiences in the labour market and in society differ from their older counterparts. On the other hand, when young people get into the world of work, acquire a partner, a mortgage and have children, their circumstances change. The more they acquire a stake in the system the more they will pay attention to government, politics and voting.

---

[4] The first BES survey was conducted in 1963, but the 1964 survey was the first to follow a general election, a procedure which has continued ever since. The data for the 2017 and 2019 elections come from surveys commissioned by the authors.

[5] Yang and Land (2013).

[6] Verba, Schlozman and Brady (1995).

Period effects, in contrast, arise from the state of society and the political context at the time when an election takes place. Each election is to an extent unique and so the specific context in which it takes place can influence participation. For example, the 2015 election occurred at the end of the Conservative–Liberal Democrat coalition government during which the worst effects of the Great Recession had eased. This allowed the government to claim success in managing the economy, while at the same time blaming New Labour for 'crashing the economy' prior to the Great Recession. Circa 2015, the ideological distance between the parties was not especially large and the date of the election was known well in advance, such that the parties were well prepared for the campaign.[7]

Things were very different in the 2017 general election, which came as a surprise to everyone, had a longer than usual campaign and was dominated by the Brexit debate, as we discussed in Chapter 3.[8] In addition, the ideological divisions between Theresa May's Conservatives and Jeremy Corbyn's Labour Party were much wider than two years earlier. Equally, the effect of the campaign was much larger in 2017 than it had been in 2015, with significant increases in public support for Labour occurring as polling day approached, something which had not happened in the previous election. Clearly, period effects were quite different in the two elections. A similar point can be made about the 2019 general election as the analysis in Chapter 5 makes clear.

The third aspect of the relationship between age and participation involves *cohort effects*, an idea originally introduced by the social scientist Karl Mannheim.[9] Cohort effects are based on the idea that the values, attitudes and beliefs that determine people's voting behaviour are formed in late adolescence and early adulthood. As this process happens it is influenced by the economic, social and political circumstances of the time. Once formed, the evidence suggests that, unlike life-cycle effects, cohort effects remain relatively stable over time as people grow older, even if their social and economic circumstances change.[10] In this respect higher education is an important socializing agency. For example, consider an 18-year-old student who became politically aware in 2003 and joined in several protests against the UK's participation in the war in Iraq. There is evidence suggesting that these experiences are likely to stay with this person for many years after graduation, working to shape their subsequent political attitudes and behaviour.

---

[7] Cowley and Kavanagh (2016).
[8] Allen and Bartle (2018).
[9] Mannheim (1928).
[10] Inglehart (1977); Alwin and Krosnick (1991).

At a collective level, these early-life socialization processes can produce 'generational' or *cohort effects* among voters. This means, for example, that individuals who 'came of age' politically during the Second World War and who faced physical dangers and wartime deprivation are likely to look at the world differently from those brought up in the relatively peaceful and affluent 1960s. Moreover, this will continue to be true for the wartime generation even when they live comfortably in the changed circumstances of later decades. The claim is that early experiences can mark a generation of people for life, and this is also true of their politics and voting behaviour.

One prominent researcher, Ronald Inglehart, developed these ideas in a series of publications about changing cultural values across the world.[11] In a series of widely cited studies, Inglehart argued that successive cohorts of people coming of age in affluent post–Second World War societies increasingly have 'post-materialist' values focusing on 'self-realization' and 'personal development'. In contrast, older cohorts who reached maturity during periods of economic hardship and war were much more likely to have 'materialist' values that prioritize 'economic successes' and 'personal security'. Inglehart's central argument is that the evolution of political orientations is primarily driven by the successive replacement of cohorts with different socialization experiences rather than by age or period effects.

Taken together, the preceding discussion implies that if we wish to understand the relationship between age and political participation, we need to identify age, period and cohort effects using a longitudinal study. However, there is a serious problem in doing this because the following relationship holds between the three effects.

$$\text{Period} - \text{Age} = \text{Cohort}$$

If we know the age and period effects, then the cohort effects are fixed and cannot be independently estimated. To illustrate this, consider an 18-year-old student who was a first-time voter in the 2019 general election. We know her age and the period or election in which she participated, so she must be a member of the cohort who became politically aware at some point between the 2016 EU referendum and the 2019 election. This assumes that she had to be at least 15 years of age before she started to take an interest in politics just prior to the referendum. Clearly, she cannot be part of a cohort who came of age politically in the 1960s or 1970s, so age and periods perfectly predict her cohort

---

[11] Inglehart (2018).

membership. Technically this is referred to by statisticians as an 'identification problem'. This means that it is impossible to estimate the three effects in a linear regression model of electoral turnout.[12]

Recent debates have divided the methodological community on the issue of overcoming this problem and estimating trends in turnout among age groups over time. All are agreed that it cannot be done with a survey conducted at a single point of time, but it is argued that the availability of longitudinal data collected over time may make this possible.[13] We will begin the data analyses in this chapter by examining turnout before going on to look at support for the parties, utilizing these three age-related measures to examine how voting behaviour has changed over time. Each of these aspects plays an important role in explaining electoral participation and voting for the major parties, and they help to explain the observed fragmentation of the British party system.

Periods, Cohorts and Turnout in Britain 1964–2019

We begin our investigation of age-related influences on electoral participation by looking at the effects of periods and cohorts on turnout in surveys conducted between 1964 and 2019. This is the longest period over which national survey data on voting behaviour in Britain are available. We first examine trends in periods and cohorts without separating them out in order to provide an overall picture of what happened across this fifty-five-year time interval. Subsequently, we distinguish between the different age-related effects after introducing *hierarchical age-period-cohort* modelling. Altogether, there were sixteen different election studies conducted between 1964 and 2019, and so we start by examining them. The cohort and life-cycle effects are discussed more fully below.

The analysis of turnout utilizes self-reported voting by the survey respondents. This presents a potential problem, since there is abundant evidence indicating that individuals tend to exaggerate their electoral participation when they are questioned in surveys.[14] However, we can examine the extent to which this is a problem by calculating an average figure for self-reported turnout in each of the sixteen surveys and then compare these figures with official turnout statistics from the actual elections. The relationship between the two appears in Figure 6.1, where each dot is an election, and the regression line summarizes the association

---

[12] This is an extreme example of what is referred to as a multicollinearity problem in multiple regression analysis. See Kennedy (2008).

[13] See Yang and Land (2013).

[14] Clausen (1968–1969); Traugott and Katosh (1979); Bernstein, Chadha and Montjoy (2001).

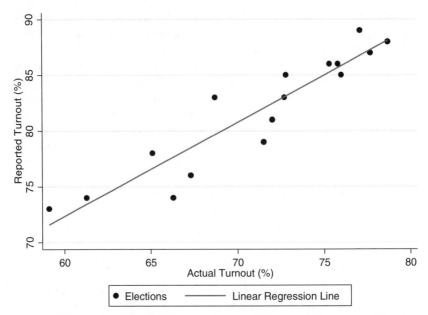

Figure 6.1 The Relationship between Reported Turnout in Election Surveys and Actual Turnout in General Elections, 1964–2019.

between the two measures over time. The correlation between them in these 16 elections is very strong (r = +0.93). Thus, self-reported turnout is an excellent guide to what actually happened in an election.

Having established that self-reported turnout is a suitable proxy measure of actual turnout, Figure 6.2 shows levels of electoral participation by age groups in all sixteen general elections. The figure confirms the point that younger age groups have always voted at lower rates than their older counterparts. It is also evident that the differences in turnout among age groups have grown significantly over time. These age-related differences reached an all-time high in the 2005 election, after remaining fairly stable between the 1964 and 1992 elections. The years when Tony Blair was prime minister were associated with the largest changes in age-related turnout over the entire period. Electoral participation in the Labour landslide victory in 1997 declined rather sharply among those below the age of 40 compared with 1992 and subsequently fell even more in the 2001 election. The latter was undoubtedly influenced by the fact that the Conservatives had little chance of eliminating Labour's massive majority, and this clearly had an impact on participation by all age groups, except for the very old. If people think elections are a 'done deal' then they are less likely to participate.

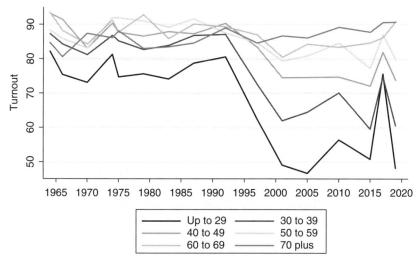

Figure 6.2 Turnout in General Elections by Age Groups (Periods), 1964–2019.

One of the most striking observations in Figure 6.2 is the rather dramatic rise in turnout during the 2017 general election among young voters, something which amply justifies the description 'Youthquake'. This change had a lot to do with the referendum on EU membership which took place a year earlier and which mobilized many young people to vote.[15] In addition, as we pointed out in Chapter 3, in 2017 Jeremy Corbyn ran a very successful barnstorming campaign in comparison with Theresa May, whose campaign was largely ineffective.[16]

Corbyn was a new face at the time and held a series of very successful open-air rallies attended by many young people, including at the Glastonbury festival. In addition, much of Labour's campaign was conducted online and this was also very effective.[17] However, Figure 6.2 also shows that this surge in turnout among the young did not continue through to the 2019 general election. Many young people failed to vote on this later occasion when their counterparts over the age of 60 turned out in even greater numbers. This helped to produce a very different result, helping to clear the way for the rise of Boris Johnson.[18]

[15] Clarke, Goodwin and Whiteley (2017), ch. 7.
[16] Cowley and Kavanagh (2016), pp. 1–20.
[17] Cowley and Kavanagh (2016), p. 308.
[18] Allen and Bartle (2021).

Figure 6.2 shows the relationship between elections and turnout when these occur at well-defined periods of time, but what about cohort effects? While period effects are relatively easy to identify the same cannot be said for cohorts. Becker was one of the earliest political scientists to examine cohort effects, and he defined them as 'a grouping of a number of cohorts characterized by a specific historical setting and by common characteristics'.[19] The important point about defining cohorts is to locate them in a political and historical context. If they are defined too broadly this will bundle together rather different political eras, and so we will not be able to distinguish between them. On the other hand, if they are defined too narrowly this will treat rather similar political contexts as if they were uniquely different from each other and give a misleading picture.

Researchers often have defined cohorts more or less arbitrarily as time intervals of five- or ten-years' duration. This may be acceptable in some contexts, for example in medical research where it is difficult to pin down when a problem like obesity started to be a serious issue. In this case it makes sense to divide the time into equal periods.[20] But in electoral politics there are clear differences between political eras, and they are not all of the same duration. For example, there are good reasons to expect that individuals who reached political maturity during the years of consensus politics in the 1950s are likely to look at the political world differently from those who came of age in the divisive Thatcher era of the 1980s.

In our earlier book, *Political Choice in Britain*, we identified five different age cohorts in an analysis which looked only at age and cohort effects in the 2001 election.[21] We assumed that individuals would reach political maturity by the age of 21 in that analysis, although it is now more common to assume that this happens by the age of 25.[22] Our original classification of the different cohorts was:

(1) 'Post–Second World War' cohort who achieved political maturity before 1950;
(2) 'Macmillan' cohort who achieved it between 1951 and 1964;
(3) 'Wilson-Callaghan' cohort who achieved it between 1964 and 1979;
(4) 'Thatcher' cohort who achieved it between 1979 and 1992;
(5) 'Blair' cohort who achieved it after 1992.

That analysis focused only on one election and so did not consider period effects, and therefore did not encounter the statistical

---

[19] Becker (1990), p. 2.
[20] See, e.g., Reither et al. (2015).
[21] Clarke, Sanders, Stewart and Whiteley (2004), pp. 270–271.
[22] Grasso (2016), p. 40.

identification problem discussed earlier. There may have been period effects, but they could not be identified using data from a single survey. The findings suggested that both the 'Thatcher' and 'Blair' generations were less civically minded than their earlier counterparts, and this was manifested by their lower participation.

More recently, Maria Grasso has suggested that different researchers working on age-related effects in politics have identified rather similar political cohorts in Britain, indicating that there is something of a consensus about them in practice.[23] Her focus was on studying age-related political participation across several European democracies and for this reason her definition of cohorts is rather broad. She identified five cohorts in her study: 'Pre–Second World War', 'Post–Second World War', 'Baby-Boomers', '80s generation' and '90s generation'.

Since the present focus is solely on Britain, we can be somewhat more specific about the definition of cohorts, linking them to periods of post-war political history which are clearly different from each other. Accordingly, we use the original cohorts introduced in the 2001 analysis but add another four to bring it up to date. Specifically, we define members of a cohort as people between the ages of 15 and 25 living during a given political era, at which point they are assumed to have reached political maturity.[24] The nine cohorts are defined as follows:

(1) 'First World War' cohort who achieved political maturity before 1919;
(2) 'Post–First World War' cohort from 1919 to 1929;
(3) 'Great Depression' cohort from 1930 to 1939;
(4) 'Second World War' cohort from 1940 to 1949;
(5) 'Macmillan' cohort from 1950 to 1963;
(6) 'Wilson/Callaghan' cohort from 1964 to 1979;
(7) 'Thatcher' cohort from 1980 to 1997;
(8) 'Blair' cohort from 1998 to 2010;
(9) 'Austerity' cohort from 2011.

These cohorts are not equal in duration, but rather reflect the circumstances of different periods of British political history. It is useful to sketch out some of the key differences. The First World War radically changed the country not merely because of the large number of deaths and wartime shortages, but also because the existing Conservative–Liberal

---

[23] Grasso (2016), pp. 42–43.
[24] To illustrate, a respondent interviewed in 1964 who was 25 years of age in 1918 and therefore a member of the First World War generation, would be 71 years of age at the time of the interview.

two-party system was shattered in the 1918 general election.[25] This meant that the wartime cohort faced a different political landscape from the post-war cohort. The latter came of age in a period of turbulent party politics and conflicts over public spending and industrial relations, the latter exemplified by the general strike of 1926. This era ended with the election of the first minority Labour government in 1929.

The Great Depression cohort went through the severe economic disruption in which the unemployment rate exceeded 15 per cent in 1932, at a time when welfare benefits were meagre.[26] This was followed by a period of recovery that was largely associated with rearmament and increased defence spending in the face of the growing threat from Nazi Germany. It was also a period when the National Government was formed by Labour leader Ramsey Macdonald. The Labour Party split and was subsequently heavily defeated in the 1931 general election.[27] This was a turbulent period in British politics.

The Second World War cohort experienced physical dangers, civilian and military losses, and major shortages as the country was placed on a wartime footing. Children were evacuated from cities and thousands of adults were drafted into the armed forces, many of whom did not see their families for years. However, victory in 1945 did not bring an end to austerity, since rationing continued up to the end of the decade and beyond. Elected in 1945, Clement Atlee's post-war Labour government started the huge task of reconstruction, while at the same time laying the foundations of the modern welfare state and creating the National Health Service.[28]

Conservative governments, in power in the 1950s, were exemplified by that of Prime Minister Harold Macmillan, who presided over a period of growing prosperity as post-war reconstruction and full employment finally brought an end to wartime deprivation. It was an era of broad consensus politics described at the time by the epithet 'Butskellism', i.e., a combination of 'One Nation' Conservatism associated with prominent Conservative R.A. Butler, and the centre-left politics of Labour leader Hugh Gaitskell.[29] Macmillan captured the mood of the era in a 1957 speech in which he claimed: 'Our people have never had it so good.'[30]

---

[25] Butler and Butler (1994).
[26] See www.bankofengland.co.uk/statistics/research-datasets
[27] Marquand (1997).
[28] Harris (1982).
[29] Horne (1989).
[30] www.telegraph.co.uk/news/politics/8145390/Harold-Macmillans-never-had-it-so-good-speech-followed-the-1950s-boom.html

The Macmillan era came to an end when Labour leader Harold Wilson won a narrow victory in the 1964 general election. Wilson captured the desire for change in the country at that time with a speech in 1963 in which he talked about using the 'white heat of technology' to invigorate the British economy.[31] He won a large majority in the subsequent 1966 election, but then lost power in 1970 following an economic crisis, the devaluation of the pound and a recession. Edward Heath's Conservative Party won that election, but his administration was largely a political failure beset by industrial relations problems and the emergence of rising inflation. Labour subsequently returned to power in the February 1974 election and stayed in office until 1979 under James Callaghan who took over from Wilson as prime minister in 1976. By then the government's majority was precarious and the loss of a vote of no confidence in the House of Commons precipitated the 1979 election, won by Margaret Thatcher.

The Thatcher government marked a new era in British politics, following a policy characterized by Andrew Gamble as 'The Free Economy and the Strong State'.[32] Initially it created a period of austerity with the aim of quelling rampant inflation and became involved in serious industrial conflicts exemplified by the miners' strike of 1984. Austerity proved unpopular, but the victory in the Falklands War and a split in Labour in 1981 enabled the Conservatives to win a large majority in the 1983 election. Mrs Thatcher's government then embarked on a policy of extensive privatization of state assets and deregulation of the City of London. In turn, these actions helped to produce a stock market rally and consumer boom in the economy. However, the seeds of divisions over Brexit were sown in the Conservative Party at this time by a growing conflict between the prime minister and the European Union over Britain's budgetary contributions, reflected in her phrase: 'I want my money back!'

In November 1990, Mrs Thatcher was ousted as prime minister, largely as a result of her determination to push through a highly unpopular poll tax to finance local government.[33] She was replaced by John Major, who won a surprise victory in the 1992 general election, but his term in office was very much an extension of the Thatcher era. The 'Black Wednesday' currency crisis in September 1992 blighted his administration from the start and intra-party divisions over the European Union grew stronger among Conservatives, symbolized by the political rebellion over the signing of the Maastricht Treaty. The Thatcher era finally

---

[31] Pimlott (1992).
[32] Gamble (1994).
[33] Moore (2020).

came to an end with Tony Blair and New Labour's landslide victory in the 1997 general election.

Tony Blair served as prime minister for ten years, during a period of growing prosperity and rapid increases in public expenditure on health, education and welfare described as the 'New Labour' era.[34] But Blair's popularity was blighted by his support for the Iraq War of 2003 and infighting with the Chancellor of the Exchequer, Gordon Brown, who took over as prime minister in June 2007. Brown's premiership was undermined by the financial crash which started with a run on the Northern Rock bank in October 2007. The crash precipitated a deep recession that had major effects on the economy and the course of British politics.[35]

As a result, Labour lost the 2010 general election and was replaced by David Cameron's Conservative–Liberal Democrat coalition government which chose to respond to the crisis with a long period of austerity. Voters who came of age in this period also experienced increasingly fractious politics associated with the debate about whether or not to continue membership of the European Union, which served to exacerbate age-based political divisions and had also been reflected in the rise of the new populist UK Independence Party. The latter drew most of its votes from older Britons. As discussed in Chapter 4, in the 2016 referendum on EU membership many young people voted to remain while their older counterparts largely supported Brexit, with these divides over age among the largest reported at the referendum.[36]

Using the nine distinct political cohorts defined above, Figure 6.3 displays the relationship between electoral turnout and cohort membership over time. The figure differs from Figure 6.2 because older cohorts die out and younger ones take their place, so cohorts appear and disappear at different points in time. Turnout in the various cohorts remained similar up to the start of the Wilson/Callaghan era in the 1970s. At that point electoral participation among the youngest cohort started to decline and fell precipitously during the Thatcher era. To a lesser extent turnout also decreased among the under-40s making electoral participation among cohorts much more variable. Participation by the youngest cohort then increased during the austerity years, reflecting the rise in youth voting culminating in the 2017 election.

These are interesting findings which we explore more fully below, but it is important to remember that they do not separate age, period and

[34] Gould (1998).
[35] Tett (2009).
[36] Clarke, Goodwin and Whiteley (2017).

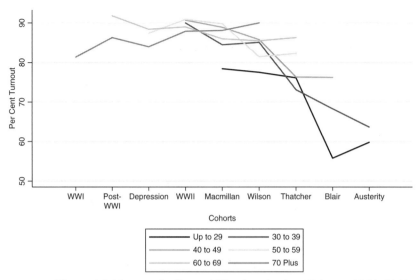

Figure 6.3 Turnout in General Elections by Age Cohorts, 1964–2019.

cohort effects, which are all mixed together. Table 6.1 shows the inter-action in turnout between the sixteen general elections and nine cohorts over the 1964 and 2019 election surveys. If we read the table by rows, we can see that people in the 'Blair cohort' who first appeared in the 1992 election were less likely to vote in all subsequent elections in comparison with their predecessors. In Labour's landslide, for example, only 60.7 per cent of the Blair cohort voted in comparison with 72.3 per cent of the Thatcher cohort. In the 2001 election, which had the lowest turnout of any election in the post–Second World War period, the equivalent figures were 48.4 per cent and 66.8 per cent.

This decline in electoral participation continued into the era when the Austerity cohort began. The members of that group who first appeared in 2001 were less likely to vote than members of the Blair cohort in every single subsequent election after 2001. For the Austerity cohort, the low point of participation was reached in the 2005 election when only 44.3 per cent of them cast a ballot. It is not an exaggeration to say that these two cohorts are increasingly abandoning electoral participation in a way not observed in the past. The only exception to this trend occurred in the 2017 general election when young people turned out in numbers equivalent to that of their older counterparts. But as mentioned earlier, the 2019 election showed that this was an exception.

If one reads Table 6.1 by columns this shows how particular cohorts behaved in different elections over time. For example, 84.3 per cent of

Table 6.1 *Turnout by Periods and Cohorts, 1964–2019*

Percentage within cohorts

Period Effects (16)	First World War	Post-First Word War	Depression	Second World War	Macmillan	Wilson/Callaghan	Thatcher	Blair	Austerity	Total
1964	84.3	92.5	88.9	93.0	83.7	88.6				88.6
1966	77.5	90.3	85.8	89.5	84.8	71.0				85.6
1970	83.8	89.6	83.8	85.2	82.6	71.0				81.0
Feb1974	76.9	88.8	90.9	91.9	88.7	84.1	70.0			87.8
Oct1974	84.2	91.4	86.8	91.5	87.0	77.8	75.0			85.0
1979	70.6	81.4	90.3	91.6	88.4	81.2	70.1			84.8
1983		82.0	84.2	87.7	87.9	84.2	73.8			83.4
1987		68.6	86.1	90.4	91.3	86.0	80.4			86.1
1992		76.9	87.7	90.7	88.3	89.5	84.4	74.5		87.0
1997			75.5	88.8	88.0	83.6	72.3	60.7		78.8
2001			79.4	85.9	84.4	77.8	66.8	48.4	58.6	72.6
2005			77.1	86.0	86.3	82.1	72.1	53.2	44.3	74.0
2010				93.2	89.3	83.9	77.8	68.8	54.4	77.8
2015				65.4	89.5	86.1	75.4	66.0	51.8	73.6
2017					86.9	88.8	85.5	79.3	74.2	82.8
2019					88.2	90.9	83.2	70.0	53.3	75.9
Total	81.5	88.1	86.5	89.5	87.5	84.1	77.3	66.4	61.0	81.1

Source: BES and Essex–UTD Surveys.

the First World War cohort turned out in the 1964 general election but by 1979, the last survey to include enough of them for meaningful analysis, their turnout was down to 70.6 per cent. Turnout among the really elderly tends to be lower than among their younger counterparts, but electoral participation by the elderly in 1964 stands in stark contrast to the figure of 53.3 per cent for the Austerity cohort in the 2019 election. Again, the biggest contrast in the columns of Table 6.1 is between the average turnout of 89.5 per cent among the Second World War cohort in fourteen separate elections and 61.0 per cent among the Austerity cohort in six elections.

A third way of reading Table 6.1 is to look at it diagonally from left to right. Unlike the row figures which classify voting in each election by successive cohorts, or the column figures which look at each cohort in different elections, the diagonal identifies the interaction between cohorts and elections. For example, it shows that voting by the First World War cohort was still at 81.2 per cent during the Wilson/Callaghan era and fell to 73.8 per cent in the last (1979) election in which enough of them could be counted.[37] Generally, diagonal comparisons show that the pattern of declining turnout began in the Thatcher years and continued until the present era.

In this section we have focused on the relationship between periods and cohorts and electoral participation over time. But it is equally interesting to look at the relationship between these variables and party support. We examine this next.

Periods, Cohort and Party Support 1964–2019

Table 6.2 shows vote shares for the Conservative, Labour and Liberal/Liberal Democrat parties in each of the sixteen elections.[38] These figures are consistent with the story sketched earlier that Labour won the 1964 and 1966 elections, but narrowly lost the 1970 election. Labour then regained power in February 1974, but with only four seats more than the Conservatives. This subsequently led Harold Wilson to call the second election in October of that year. In that election, Labour increased its majority by eighteen seats, producing a lead over the Conservatives of forty-two seats, but with a narrow overall majority.

---

[37] Note that if the election studies were panels, with the same individuals being re-interviewed over time rather than independent cross-section surveys, then the diagonals would reveal the extent to which the same people changed their participation in different elections.

[38] These data differ slightly from official election turnout statistics in Figure 6.1 due to sampling error in the surveys, but these are all well within the margin of error.

Table 6.2 *Party Vote Shares by Periods, 1964–2019*

Percentage within period effects (16)

		Conservatives	Labour	Liberals/LibDems	Others
Period Effects (16)	1964	42.3	46.6	10.7	0.4
	1966	39.4	51.7	8.3	0.7
	1970	45.3	45.2	7.2	2.3
	Feb 1974	38.0	40.6	19.1	2.3
	Oct 1974	36.0	42.5	18.0	3.5
	1979	47.0	37.6	13.8	1.6
	1983	44.9	29.4	13.0	12.7
	1987	43.8	31.2	23.5	1.4
	1992	41.9	35.0	15.9	7.2
	1997	26.4	49.1	16.5	8.0
	2001	25.3	48.2	18.0	8.5
	2005	28.7	39.6	21.3	10.4
	2010	35.7	32.1	21.9	10.3
	2015	39.9	32.3	7.5	20.3
	2017	39.2	41.8	9.6	9.4
	2019	49.3	26.4	13.5	10.7
Total		38.5	38.5	15.4	7.6

Source: BES and Essex–UTD Surveys.

Mrs Thatcher's victory in 1979 set the stage for nearly two decades of Conservative dominance. As the previous discussion indicated, this dominance continued through to1997, the start of the 'New Labour' era. After winning in 2001 and again in 2005, Blair stepped down as Labour leader in 2007 and Gordon Brown took over only to be engulfed in the financial crisis and the subsequent Great Recession. This was followed by the coalition government of 2010–2015, at which point David Cameron's Conservative Party won a narrow majority. This subsequently disappeared in the 2017 election called by Theresa May in the middle of the Brexit negotiations. Finally, May's successor, Boris Johnson, won a decisive majority of eighty seats in 2019. Overall, the table illustrates the well-known story of the two major parties alternating in office, a pattern interrupted by the Coalition government interlude from 2010 to 2015.

Less familiar is Table 6.3 which shows the parties' support for nine different cohorts over time. It is striking how support for the Conservatives has declined markedly across the cohorts. Almost 60 per cent of the First World War cohort voted Conservatives and only about a third of them supported Labour. In contrast, nearly 55 per cent of the Austerity cohort voted Labour, with only just over a fifth of them supporting the

Table 6.3 *Party Vote Shares by Cohorts, 1964–2019 (Percentages within Cohorts)*

	Conservatives	Labour	Liberals /LibDems	Others
First World War cohort	59.6	32.8	7.6	0.0
Post–First World War cohort	47.8	40.1	10.0	2.1
Depression cohort	48.3	37.1	11.5	3.1
Second World War cohort	41.1	41.1	14.3	3.5
Macmillan cohort	39.5	39.0	15.2	6.3
Wilson/Callaghan cohort	41.0	33.1	16.8	8.7
Thatcher cohort	34.0	39.0	17.1	9.9
Blair cohort	30.6	42.6	16.1	10.7
Austerity cohort	21.3	54.4	12.3	12.0
Total	38.6	38.5	15.4	7.6

Source: BES and Essex–UTD Surveys

Conservatives. Liberal support in the First World War cohort was below 8 per cent and it reached a high point in the Thatcher cohort at 17 per cent, before falling to 12 per cent in the Austerity group. Interestingly, there were no respondents to be found in the First World War cohort who voted for minor parties, compared with 12 per cent who did this in the Austerity cohort.

This long-run perspective on generational change shows that the Conservatives had a consistent advantage over the other parties among the pre–Second World War cohort, but Labour caught up by the time of the Second World War and thereafter moved ahead of its main rival – this gap widening to a chasm by the time of the Austerity cohort. Having presented this overview of the relationship between voting and cohort membership since 1964, we next discuss how we can separate age, period and cohort effects on turnout and party support.

A Hierarchical Age-Period-Cohort Analysis of Turnout

As discussed above, the problem of trying to separate age, period and cohort effects is that, when we know the person's age and the elections in which they voted, that automatically fixes their cohort membership. This 'identification problem' is analogous to trying to solve a single equation which contains two unknown variables. The problem has been known about for many years and some researchers have argued that it is impossible to separate the three effects.[39] However, other analysts contend that

[39] Glenn (1976), pp. 900–904; Goldstein (1979); Bell and Jones (2014, 2018).

the problem arises from a *linear* relationship between the variables and if the model can be recast in a non-linear form, then the difficulty can be circumvented.[40]

A number of political scientists have attempted to identify separate age, period and cohort effects using various approaches.[41] Clearly, cohort and period effects have very different implications for electoral behaviour. If cohort effects predominate then it means that change will be quite slow, since it relies on younger groups replacing older ones over a relatively long period of time. This is also true but to a lesser extent for life-cycle effects. On the other hand, if period effects dominate, then change is likely to be much faster but at the same time voting behaviour will be more volatile. Since any given election can be held in very different circumstances from the previous one, period effects can produce large short-term changes.

The Hierarchical Age-Period-Cohort (HAPC) approach divides the estimation procedure into two parts which are examined at different levels of analysis. One equation is estimated at the level of individual survey participants, and it delineates the relationship between age and turnout. This is known as a 'fixed' effects model, and it is used to examine life-cycle effects. The second or aggregate level of analysis examines cohorts and periods as the cases rather than individuals and is known as the 'random' part of the model. This looks at cohort and period effects by predicting changes in the intercept of the individual-level model. This intercept represents what is left over after accounting for various factors such as a respondent's age, educational level, occupational status and gender. If the second level equation contains variables that significantly influence the intercept of the first-level equation, it means that contextual factors such as an individual's cohort membership are influencing turnout.

This approach enables us to determine how age influences turnout over time while controlling for cohorts and periods. We also can identify if individuals who became politically aware at particular points in time, e.g., the Blair cohort were less likely to vote in the 2015 election than individuals who came of age in the 1980s during the Thatcher cohort. If true, this would mean that there are cohort effects that operate independently of age or life-cycle effects when they are included in the analysis.

---

[40] A linear relationship means that the association between two variables can be represented by a straight line in a graph, and the correlation coefficient provides a reliable measure of the strength of the association between them. If, however, the relationship is non-linear, the correlation coefficient is weaker and no longer accurate, and so the problem of multicollinearity, that is a very high correlation between variables, is reduced. This is often referred to as 'breaking' the linearity between variables. See e.g., Reither et al. (2015).

[41] Tilley (2002); Dassonville (2013); Neundorf and Niemi (2014); Grasso (2016).

Yang and Land are leading advocates of the HAPC approach, and they explain why they think this works in the following terms: 'An HAPC framework does not incur the identification problem because the three effects are not assumed to be linear and additive at the same level of analysis.'[42] In their view, this solves the identification problem.[43] However, their approach has been challenged, particularly by Bell and Jones in a series of papers based on simulating the results of HAPC modelling.[44] They create a model with known parameters and then try to estimate it using the HAPC procedure. They conclude: 'For us, the key critique of the HAPC model lies in its inability to accurately represent data generating processes (DGPs) in simulations.'[45] In other words, their statistical analyses are unable to accurately delineate the model they constructed to produce the data. In addition, they find that period effects tend to dominate the cohort effects, although the reason for this is unclear.

This suggests that it may be unwise to try and estimate all age, period and cohort effects at the same time. One solution to this problem is to focus just on estimating life-cycle effects at the individual level and cohort effects at the aggregate level and ignore period effects. It is important to know the extent to which individuals change their party support as they get older (life-cycle effects) as opposed to remaining loyal to the parties they supported when first becoming aware of politics in their teens and early adulthood (cohort effects). However, if period effects are important, then the life-cycle and cohort effects alone will produce inaccurate estimates which fail to take into account differences between elections.

We respond to the Bell and Jones critique not by ignoring the period effects but by changing their definition in the modelling. In a full HAPC analysis, the period effects would represent all sixteen elections between 1964 and 2019, but this is what gives rise to the identification problem. An alternative is to look only at a limited number of elections which are chosen on theoretical grounds as being important turning points in electoral politics. In the subsequent modelling we do not attempt to assess the impact of all elections or periods, but only those which meet a specific criterion which we expect to be important. This is done by focusing only on 'turnover' elections that produced a change in government and ignoring the others.

A 'turnover' election is defined as one in which an incumbent party or coalition government was removed from office by a challenger party.

---

[42] Yang and Land (2013), p. 191.
[43] For how the HAPC model is technically written, see Appendix B.
[44] See Bell and Jones (2014, 2018).
[45] Bell and Jones (2014, 2018).

There were seven elections between 1964 and 2019 when this happened. Labour replaced the Conservatives in power after the 1964, February 1974 and in the 1997 elections, and the Conservatives replaced Labour after the 1970 and 1979 elections. In addition, the Conservative–Liberal Democrat Coalition government replaced Labour after the 2010 election and the Conservatives replaced the coalition government in 2015.

When incorporating these period effects as controls in the statistical analysis, they are treated as significant political 'shocks' to the system, rather than as recurring events covering all elections from 1964 to 2019. This approach removes the identification problem referred to earlier, since the periods are no longer systematically linked to changes in the respondent's age defined by their cohort membership and life-cycle experiences. Rather they are defined by political events which we have good reason to expect will influence voting because they have a major political consequence.

Turnout 1964–2019

We begin by examining turnout in the individual-level model. We use a logistic regression specification which is appropriate when the dependent variable is a dummy variable scoring one if people voted and zero if they did not.[46] We have met this model already in Chapters 3 and 5. The Austerity cohort is treated as the reference category with which to compare the others, and therefore is omitted from the model specification. This means we are evaluating how turnout has changed over time in the different cohorts in comparison with the most recent one.

Figure 6.4 depicts the impact of both the individual and aggregate variables on turnout over the 1964–2019 period. The individual-level or fixed effects appear in the bottom of the table in a lighter shade than the aggregate-level random effects which appear further up in the figure. The middle dot shows the size of the effect of the variable on the probability of voting.[47] The left-hand and right-hand bars linked by a horizontal line measure the uncertainty associated with the estimate, i.e., the confidence interval.[48] When the confidence interval crosses the vertical

---

[46] See Hox, Moerbeek and Van de Schoot (2018) for an explanation of the logistic model in the context of multilevel modelling.

[47] The logistic regression model is a non-linear model which means that the coefficients or effects vary along the range of observations. The figure captures the mean effect averaged over the range of outcomes on the probability of voting.

[48] The confidence intervals measure the uncertainty surrounding the estimates which arises from the fact that we are using sample data to measure what happened in the entire electorate. Inevitably, the use of samples means that estimates of turnout differ from the actual turnout and the confidence intervals are wider when that uncertainty is larger.

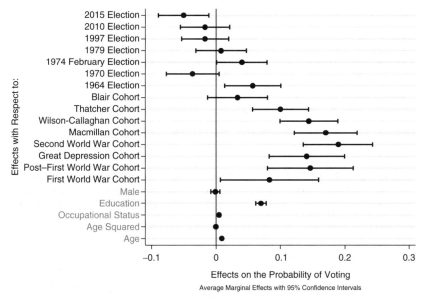

Figure 6.4 Hierarchical Age Cohort Model of Turnout with Period Controls, 1964–2019.
Note: Aggregate random effects are first followed by individual fixed effects.

line at zero, it means we do not have a statistically significant effect, since the true coefficient may be zero rather than positive or negative. This happened in the case of the Blair cohort, for example, which means we cannot be sure that this cohort differs from the Austerity cohort when it comes to voting.

Unlike the Blair cohort, all the other cohorts had significantly higher turnout than the Austerity cohort, since they all show statistically significant positive effects compared with this most recent cohort. In these cases, the uncertainty bars do not cross the zero line, so we infer that they voted in greater numbers than the Austerity and Blair cohorts. This suggests that there was a significant 'break point' in socialization processes that encourage young people to vote after the Labour government won the 1997 general election. Cohorts that became politically aware prior to that period consistently voted in greater numbers than cohorts emerging after that election.

The implication of this finding is that the Blair era was a key turning point for electoral participation over this lengthy sixty-year period. Those who became politically aware during and after the Blair years

were less likely to vote even when their occupational status, age, education and the controls for turnover elections are considered in the analysis. This is particularly true of the Second World War and Macmillan
cohorts, who were much more likely to vote than their Austerity counterparts. Those years represented something of a golden age in electoral
participation in Britain. This is illustrated by the fact mentioned earlier
that the highest turnout in any post-war election was 84 per cent in
1950, at a time when the post–Second World War cohort was coming
of age politically. That compares with a turnout of only 67 per cent in
the 2019 election.

The age or life-cycle effects in the individual-level model reinforce
this conclusion, since age is a strong predictor of turnout throughout
the entire period,[49] with older people voting in greater numbers than the
young. But as Figures 6.2 and 6.3 show, the gap between the old and the
young has grown significantly wider over time, and the modelling confirms this point. However, the quadratic specification of the age variable
in the analysis shows that the effect of age on turnout tends to decline
as individuals get really old, which is not surprising given the physical
infirmities that accompany ageing.[50]

The election 'shocks' in the figure should be compared with the average
turnout in those elections which did not lead to a change in government.
In general, these period effects are weak, with two clear exceptions. The
February 1974 election saw an upsurge in turnout following the troubled
Conservative government of Edward Heath which had come to power in
1970. The second exception was the turnout in the 2015 election, when
David Cameron's Conservative Party almost wiped out their coalition
partners, the Liberal Democrats. Participation in this election was below
average. Apart from these exceptions, the long-term decline in turnout
is clearly driven by cohort replacement and persistent age effects rather
than by specific period shocks.

This finding carries a disturbing implication, namely that decline in
electoral participation over time is unlikely to be easily reversed in the
future.[51] The growing gap between the young and the old apparent in
Figure 6.2 is being 'baked in' to the system in the long run, as the

---

[49] The age effects appear to be small in the individual level model, but this is because they
show the average impact of an extra year's age on turnout, which is much more limited
than the cohort effects which last over many years.

[50] The coefficient of the age squared variable associated with the quadratic specification is
statistically significant, although the sizes of the coefficients are very small in the figure.

[51] There have been small increases in electoral participation since the 66 per cent turnout
achieved in the 2015 election, but these are not politically significant except for young
voters in 2017.

low participation age cohorts are subsequently joined by new cohorts as the future unfolds. Unless something unforeseen happens, these new cohorts are likely to continue voting in lesser numbers than their older counterparts, leading to a continuing decline in overall electoral participation.

Party Choice, 1964–2019

We turn next to support for the two major parties. The results of applying the HAPC analysis to the Labour share of the vote are presented in Figure 6.5. Starting with the fixed effects or individual-level part of the analysis, age, occupation and education are all statistically significant predictors of Labour voting. The confidence intervals around age are very narrow, indicating that we are estimating effects with little uncertainty. Unfortunately, this means that the effects are hard to see in the figure, but suffice it to say that they are very strong.[52] As expected, the coefficients indicate that older working-class people have been more likely to support the party and the highly educated professionals have been less likely to do so. Of course, these relationships are very familiar to students of British party politics. In addition, and similar to the turnout model, the analysis does not indicate any significant gender effects on party support.

Figure 6.5 shows that cohort effects on Labour voting have been rather different from those on turnout in Figure 6.4. None of the cohorts were significantly different from the Austerity cohort, with the sole exception of the Second World War cohort, members of which were more likely to support Labour in successive elections. That said, the post–First World War and the Macmillan cohorts are both close to being statistically significant, implying that they contain more Labour supporters than the Austerity cohort. But these effects are rather weak evidence of a preference for Labour. Just as the Second World War cohort have been more likely to vote in elections, they are more likely to vote Labour, suggesting that wartime experiences provided a turning point in support for the party.

The turnover election effects for Labour also are rather sparse. Clearly, the 1964 election under leader Harold Wilson mobilized additional support for the party after thirteen years of Conservative rule. Equally, and not surprisingly, the 1997 election victory produced considerable additional support for Labour reflecting the fact that it was

---

[52] The coefficient on the age variable is 0.08 and the t statistic is 10.5, indicating a highly statistically significant effect.

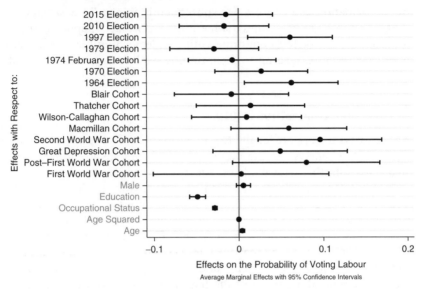

Figure 6.5 Hierarchical Age Cohort Model of Labour Voting with Period Controls, 1964–2019.

such a landslide win for the party. But in other respects, the impact of election-related shocks on Labour support has been rather modest.[53] The general conclusion from this analysis is that neither cohorts nor electoral shocks have had large effects on support for the party over this long period of time.

There has been a recurring argument which surfaces every time Labour loses an election ever since Mark Abrams and Richard Rose first raised it over a half-century ago.[54] It is the proposition that Labour can never win again because of a lost generation or cohort which was very supportive of the party in the past but is not being renewed. However, there is little statistical evidence to support this idea. Rather the analysis suggests that the party fights each election as it comes and, depending on the circumstances, it will do well if the context is favourable and badly if it is not. Examples of this are the 2017 general election discussed earlier, in which the party did very well, although it did not win.

[53] If Labour had won the 2017 election, it would have been counted as a realigning election and included in the modelling and would have shown additional support for the party.

[54] The first publication on this theme was over sixty years ago by Abrams and Rose (1969), and it has recurred every time the party loses an election.

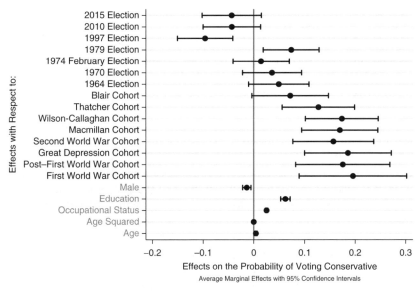

Figure 6.6 Hierarchical Age Cohort Model of Conservative Voting with Period Controls, 1964–2019.

Similarly, the 2019 election produced the worst result for Labour since its 1935 election defeat. These are very different outcomes in elections held only two years apart.

Results of the Conservative HAPC analysis displayed in Figure 6.6 are very different from those for the Labour model. Once again, in the individual-level model, age has a highly significant impact on party support, with older people more likely to vote Conservative than the young.[55] The occupational status and education effects are the opposite of Labour's, with highly educated individuals in professional occupations being more likely to vote Conservative than the rest of the electorate. Again, these effects have been known about for many years. Also, unlike Labour, gender has a significant effect, with women being more likely to vote Conservative than men.

The really striking feature of the Conservative vote model is the importance of the cohort effects. They show that all cohorts, with the sole exception of the Blair cohort, are more likely to vote for the party than the Austerity cohort. These strong cohort effects for Conservative support mirror what we observed in Figure 6.4 in relation to turnout.

[55] In this case there is no evidence to suggest that this effect declines as people get really old since the quadratic age effect is not significant.

In a reflection of the results depicted in that figure, there has been a significant decline in support for the Conservatives among young people who came of age politically during and after the Blair years. These most recent cohorts in British politics have abandoned the party in a way not seen before. The effect associated with the Blair cohort is strikingly different from the previous Thatcher cohort, whose members support the Conservatives to a much greater extent.

We will examine this further below, but a clue to the causes of this loss of support lies in the period effects. The first significant period effect occurred in the 1979 election, when Mrs Thatcher won a comfortable majority and achieved a significant boost in Conservative support. However, it is evident that the negative impact of the loss of support for the party in the 1997 election was considerably greater than the positive effect of winning the election in 1979.[56] Again, this suggests that the election which brought Tony Blair to power was a turning point in the Conservative Party's history. In effect, the party has never fully recovered from Labour's 1997 victory, since the socialization processes which renewed Conservative support in the years prior to that election were wiped out during and after the Blair era.

To summarize, cohort effects are strong for the Conservative Party and point in the direction of it losing support among younger voters. As regards period shocks, the Conservatives did well in 1979 and badly in 1997, and since then, specific elections have had no impact on Conservative support, despite winning in 2010 and again in 2015 and 2019. This shows that electoral success for the party is now dependent on the context of each election, much as it is for Labour. Labour lost the 2010 general election in the context of the aftermath of a serious financial crisis and subsequent Great Recession. But as analyses in Chapter 9 will show, although their effects are still playing out, the large-scale economic and social disruptions caused by Brexit and the Covid-19 pandemic have the potential to be more serious than those associated with the financial crisis of a decade ago. If so, as new voters join the electorate and old voters fade away, the Conservatives may find it increasingly difficult to win majorities in general elections. That said, the population in Britain is ageing and this could offset these trends to some extent, with the party retaining strong support among the elderly via life-cycle effects. Overall though, the results show that electoral politics is becoming more volatile and unpredictable over time.

---

[56] The coefficient for the 1979 election in the logistic regression model was 0.37 (t = 2.6) compared with a coefficient of –0.50 (t = 3.4) in the 1997 election.

Explaining the Dynamics of Turnout and Party Voting

Up to this point we have examined HAPC effects on turnout and party support for the two main parties and established that there are important differences between them with respect to the age-related voting. But we have not fully explained these differences except in rather general terms. In this section we probe the reasons for these differences in more depth. To do this, it is useful to draw on the three prominent theoretical explanations of electoral participation and party choice. These are the social class, valence and spatial models of voting behaviour, which we introduced in earlier chapters. We begin by briefly summarizing all three.

The Social Class Model

The social class explanation of electoral participation was discussed in the earlier chapters and is rooted in Butler and Stokes' seminal analysis of voting behaviour in Britain.[57] To repeat an earlier quote, their starting point, in the words of their contemporary, Peter Pulzer, was that 'class is the basis of British party politics: all else is embellishment and detail.'[58] At that time, working-class people by and large supported Labour at the ballot box, while the middle and upper classes opted for the Conservatives, although there were always exceptions to this.

The contribution of Butler and Stokes to this analysis was to introduce the concept of partisanship. This idea originated in studies of US elections conducted at the University of Michigan in the 1950s and Butler and Stokes imported it into the study of British politics. They defined partisanship in the following terms: 'most electors think of themselves as supporters of a given party in a lasting sense, developing what might be called a "partisan self-image".'[59] Partisanship is seen as an emotional attachment to a political party rooted in an individual's identity, much like football fans identify with their favourite club. Butler and Stokes' key argument was that such partisan attachments in Britain had their origins in social class. They wrote: '[t]here is, in fact, evidence that partisanship has followed class lines more strongly in Britain than anywhere else in the English-speaking world.'[60] How exactly does social class give rise to partisan attachments?

---

[57] Butler and Stokes (1969).
[58] Pulzer (1967), p. 98.
[59] See Butler and Stokes (1969), p. 39.
[60] Butler and Stokes (1969), p. 67.

In Butler and Stokes' analysis, the social class environment in which people are socialized in terms of the family and community creates and subsequently reinforces their partisan attachments. Blue-collar workers who are employed in large factories, live in council houses and are trade union members, are very likely to identify with and vote Labour. All these different characteristics reinforce their support for the party. On the other hand, highly educated, middle-class professionals, who own their homes and have well-paid jobs identify with and vote Conservative. Minor parties such as the Liberals were not accommodated in this theoretical scheme because, in the middle of the twentieth century they had a small and apparently declining vote share and so were considered irrelevant to the main story.

Butler and Stokes focused on partisanship and party support, so they had little to say about the links between social class and turnout, largely because participation in elections was high and thus taken for granted.[61] However, the resources model of political participation developed by Verba and Nie[62] shortly after Butler and Stokes were writing, fills this gap in the analysis. Verba and Nie explained their model in the following terms: 'According to this model, the social status of an individual – his job, education, and income – determines to a large extent how much he participates.'[63] Since the middle and upper class have higher social status than the working class, and therefore greater resources, they are more likely to vote in elections and, more generally, to participate in politics in various ways. Subsequent work by Verba and his colleagues defined resources as 'time, money and civic skills'.[64] This implied that Labour had more of a challenge to turn out its supporters than did the Conservatives.

A decade after Butler and Stokes published their study, it became increasingly apparent that party politics in Britain was 'de-aligning', i.e., the relationships between social class, partisanship and voting were weakening.[65] According to the framework they laid down for explaining partisanship these developments originated in long-run changes in British society, with class distinctions beginning to blur over time. In the 1960s, 'blue-collar' industrial workers were easily distinguishable from 'white-collar' professionals.[66] But if we look at contemporary Britain,

---

[61] For example, turnout in the first fully peacetime election following the Second World War in 1950 was 84 per cent. See Butler and Butler (1994), p. 216.
[62] Verba and Nie (1972).
[63] See Verba and Nie (1972), p. 13.
[64] Verba, Schlozman and Brady (1995), p. 271.
[65] Sarlvik and Crewe (1983).
[66] Goldthorpe (1968).

these distinctions are much less clear-cut, since massive changes have taken place in the composition of the labour force, not to mention in social values and attitudes of the population.

There has been a decline in skilled and semi-skilled industrial employment and a rise in service sector employment. The latter involves many white-collar occupations, but they are often insecure and lowly paid. Call centre workers are not traditional manual workers like miners, since they require social skills not physical strength, and the former are unlikely to be members of a trade union or to live in council accommodation. At the same time, they are low-paid and relatively insecure. As a result, they will look at the world differently from a miner. These developments imply that the relationship between occupational status, partisanship and voting behaviour will change over time.

To understand some of these trends, we can examine demographic data from the earliest and the most recent election surveys. In 1964, some 61 per cent of respondents in the BES survey were either skilled or unskilled manual workers, but by the time of the 2019 Essex–UTD survey this had fallen to 26 per cent.[67] In the intermediate occupational groups, lower non-manual workers made up 9 per cent of the workforce in the 1964 survey, but by 2019 this had risen to 29 per cent.[68] This is the insecure white-collar group we referred to above. At the other end of the scale, some 15 per cent of respondents in 1964 were in the management or professional categories, but by 2019 this had risen to 25 per cent.[69] Occupational status may predict partisanship, but the effects will weaken if the status of jobs changes over time and other factors like housing tenancy and union membership no longer reinforce it. Another important demographic change has been the rapid growth in higher education which itself serves to socialize participants into a new set of values and attitudes.[70]

In the 1964 BES survey, only 43 per cent of respondents reported receiving an education beyond the minimum school leaving age, but by 2019 this figure had risen to 58 per cent, most of them going on to higher education. That said, if education is an important resource, then its expansion creates something of a paradox for explaining the long-run decline in turnout. If tertiary education has grown rapidly over this period and participation is driven by resources, this should produce a rise in turnout rather than a decline. However, this interpretation assumes

---

[67] These are respondents in the D and E categories in the Market Research Society social grade variable.
[68] These are respondents in the C1 category of the social grade variable.
[69] These are respondents in the A and B categories of the social grade variable.
[70] See, inter alia, Inglehart (1977, 1990).

that there is no distinction between absolute and relative educational status, a topic which has been discussed extensively in the literature on political education.[71]

Absolute status refers to an individual's location in the status hierarchy at any one point of time, for example, if their income is in the top 10 per cent of the income distribution. In contrast, relative status refers to their position in the social structure relative to everyone else. If large numbers of people become more highly educated, this will not necessarily increase the relative status of individuals possessing such qualifications. This is because many others are acquiring similar qualifications at the same time. It follows that their relative position in the social structure will not change very much and so more education will not necessarily increase their participation.

In fact, these changes will serve to decrease participation overall since those left behind by a general improvement in educational standards will experience a loss of status which serves to discourage their participation. Some of the 'Left Behind' have shifted to radical right parties like UKIP, so it does not always inhibit participation, but this can be a problem in general. Other demographic factors such as the increase in female participation in the workforce have also brought about significant changes, which collectively have served to weaken the traditional relationship between class, partisanship and voting.

Overall, the links between social class and partisanship have changed over time, but the class model is nonetheless part of the mix in explaining electoral choice in the long run, as we have observed in the HAPC analysis. We have investigated its effect already by including occupational status and education as predictors in the individual-level models. To develop this further, we include two additional variables in the analysis, treating them as contextual effects. These are the percentage of professionals and higher managers and the percentage of skilled and unskilled manual workers in the workforce. These are included as additional period effects in the analysis.[72]

The Valence Model

As discussed in the Foreword and in Chapter 3, the valence model is based on the idea that the most important issues in politics involve policies over which there is widespread agreement about what should

---

[71] Nie, Junn and Stehlik-Barry (1996).

[72] We cannot investigate the cohort effects of the social class variables since data are not available to identify the various class measures prior to the Second World War.

be done. Voters prefer prosperity to recession, secure streets to crime-ridden ones, protection from terrorism and external aggression, efficient and effective public services in areas such as healthcare, education and transport. As a result, elections typically are about which party will do the best job at delivering on these widely accepted, high priority policy objectives. A party which is thought to be effective at delivery will win votes and a party which is thought to be ineffective will lose them. To examine the impact of valence issues we use data on levels of unemployment and inflation found during the periods defined earlier. If election-related effects linked to these variables are significant it suggests that short-term economic performance is a key to understanding valence effects.

At the same time, if cohort effects remain significant in the modelling it means that economic performance and other factors relating to the performance of governments have a longer-term impact on electoral behaviour. To illustrate this point, it may be that declining electoral participation among the Blair and Austerity cohorts is explained by the economic insecurity they have experienced since the Great Recession and the slow recovery from that made worse by the Coalition Government's austerity policies after 2010.

Partisanship is also part of the valence model, but it has a rather different interpretation from the class model. In an analysis introduced by Morris Fiorina, an American political scientist, partisanship is a major heuristic or cue that voters use when making their electoral choices. However, according to his account, partisanship is both dynamic and performance-based rather than being solely the product of early-life socialization experiences.[73] It is a 'running tally' of public evaluations of the past performance of rival political parties which cumulates over time. Thus, a poor performance by an incumbent party in delivering on highly salient issues like the economy and public services will cumulatively weaken support for the party. As a result, fewer voters will feel an attachment to that party over time which undermines its support. In contrast, a strong performance by an incumbent party will have the opposite effect, with more voters identifying themselves as supporters of that party. This dynamic conception of partisanship replaces early socialization processes in the family and community, although they may still play a role in the initial formation of partisanship.

There is a lot of evidence to suggest that this dynamic version of partisanship is more accurate than the static socialization story espoused by Butler and Stokes.[74] These differing interpretations have implications

---

[73] Fiorina (1981).
[74] Clarke and McCutcheon (2009).

for what we are likely to observe in statistical analyses. If partisanship is largely a matter of early-life socialization, then its effects are likely to be observed among cohorts. On the other hand, if it is dynamic, then life-cycle and period effects will be important. Partisanship is included in the extended modelling as a contextual variable to capture its dynamics over time.[75] This has been described as 'macropartisanship' in research on this topic in the United States, where it exhibits considerable change over time that is more consistent with a valence interpretation than a class interpretation of the effects.[76]

The Spatial Model

The third major theoretical account of electoral choice – the one which Stokes criticized[77] – is the spatial model of party competition. It is based on the early work of the economist Harold Hotelling, subsequently pop-ularized by Anthony Downs, and has generated an enormous body of research[78] involving extensive theoretical elaboration and testing.[79] As our previous discussion of the Brexit issue showed, the spatial model's key assumption is that *position or spatial issues* are the dominant factors governing electoral choice. Unlike the valence model in which consensus policy goals are centre stage, the spatial model focuses on policy goals over which there is widespread *disagreement* among voters about what governments should do.

Britain's decision to leave the European Union following the 2016 referendum is very much a spatial issue, with 'Leavers' outnumbering 'Remainers' by a small margin in the referendum. And as we discuss in Chapter 5, the division of opinion between the two groups has remained quite closely balanced since then. There are many other spatial issues which divide the parties and voters, such as the relationship between taxation and spending, the trade-offs between national security and civil liberties, and the conflict between economic growth and environmental concerns.

A key assumption in the spatial model is that the major divisive issues in electoral politics can be bundled together into an overall 'left–right' ideological scale. Parties on the left generally support public spending, even if this involves higher taxes, and parties of the right favour lower

---

[75] Macropartisanship is measured using a seven-point scale with 1=very strong Labour; 2= fairly strong Labour; 3=not very strong Labour; 4 =no partisanship; 5 = not very strong Conservative; 6=fairly strong Conservative; 7=very strong Conservative.

[76] Mackuen, Erikson and Stimson (1989). See also Erikson, Mackuen and Stimson (2002).

[77] Stokes (1963).

[78] Hotelling (1929); Downs (1957).

[79] Adams, Merrill and Grofman (2005).

taxes and less spending. Similarly, left-wing parties such as the Greens are more concerned about environmental protection than delivering cheap but non-renewable energy, the latter being more of a priority of parties of the right. The assumption is that voters will choose the bundle of issue positions which is closest to their own views on this overarching left–right ideological scale.

A weakness of the spatial theory is that it assumes that left–right preferences exist among the voters but does not explain where they come from. They are 'exogenous' or explained by forces that are outside of the theory. In fact, experimental evidence shows that this exogeneity assumption is wide of the mark because parties and the media can change people's preferences by campaigning.[80] But the assumption simplifies the theory and allows analysts to focus on individuals' attempts to 'maximize utility' by supporting a party closest to them in the left–right policy space.

For their part, parties are strategic actors who try to maximize electoral support in light of their knowledge of the distribution of voters across the commonly shared issue/ideological space. Parties do this by moving around on this left–right dimension in search of votes. Spatial models have been imaginatively elaborated in various ways, but they retain the core assumption that salient *position* issues drive the choices of utility-maximizing voters. The spatial model implies that the fragmentation of the British party system has occurred because of a lack of ideological distance between parties. If there are no ideological differences between the two parties of government, then there is no incentive to vote or support either of them.

One of the key predictions of the theory is the so-called 'median voter theorem' which asserts that in a two-party system where most voters are to be found close to the 'centre ground' of politics, both parties will try to occupy the position of the median voter on the left–right scale.[81] The parties do this to maximize their vote, but paradoxically it means that if this happens then no significant ideological differences will exist between them. In this situation, voters will always get the set of policies favoured by the median voter, regardless of whether they participate in an election. And, in fact, they have no incentive to participate since policy outcomes will be invariant regardless of which party wins.

Again, we will use left–right ideology as a contextual variable in our statistical analysis.[82] At the aggregate level, we include a measure of the

---

[80] Sanders, Clarke, Stewart and Whiteley (2008).
[81] See Black (1958).
[82] Note that some BES surveys contained indicators of left–right ideological scores, but these were not available in the early studies.

ideological distance between Labour and the Conservatives as a period effect using data from the Comparative Manifesto project.[83] This is a long-standing cross-national project which codes party manifestoes in each of the post-war elections into a left–right ideological scale using a technique known as content analysis. The data generated by the Manifesto Project provides the necessary contextual measure of ideological distance between the two major British parties over all general elections since 1964.[84]

Extended Modelling Results

The results of the extended modelling of turnout appear in Figure 6.7. For technical reasons we use a single variable to identify period effects while retaining different variables for the cohort effects.[85] To examine the individual-level fixed effects first, all variables in Figure 6.7 are statistically significant predictors of turnout with the sole exception of gender. Thus, older people are more likely to vote, but again the quadratic specification of age shows that the effect declines as people get even older. Occupational status and education have strong positive impacts on turnout whereas unemployment has a strong negative effect. This replicates the findings in the earlier analyses.

Turning next to the aggregate-level variables, the class-related measures, namely the proportions of professionals and workers in the workforce both influence turnout. However, the latter effect is much weaker than the former. Thus, the growth of middle-class professional occupations stimulates turnout much more than the decline in working-class occupations reduces it. Clearly, the individual level effects of occupational status described above are reinforced by these aggregate contextual effects, although it is important to remember the effect of relative status on turnout discussed earlier. The implication is that changes in the occupational structure will not have a large impact on turnout.

The valence measures are interesting in the turnout model, since there is evidence to suggest that both period inflation and period unemployment stimulate turnout, so in the latter case the contextual effect offsets the individual-level effect. This is largely because voters who are personally unemployed are likely to be demobilized by the experience, whereas

---

[83] Budge, et al. (2001).

[84] We cannot code ideological differences for cohorts using these data, since they are not available prior to the Second World War.

[85] The expanded model creates problems of multicollinearity with dummy variables for the periods, so we impose the assumption that the period effects are linear. This is a more restrictive assumption than in the earlier modelling, but it makes estimation possible.

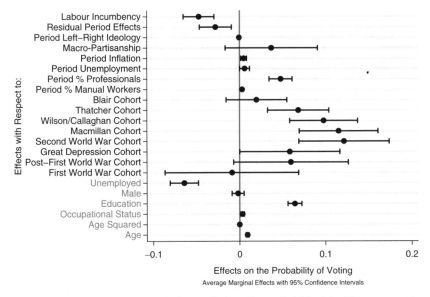

Figure 6.7 Hierarchical Age Cohort Extended Model of Turnout with Cohort and Period Controls, 1964–2019.

national rates of unemployment are a symptom of recession which mobilizes some people to vote against the government.

Once again there are striking cohort effects in the modelling as was evident in Figure 6.4. In this extended model, turnout among the Blair, First World War and post–First World War cohorts is no different from those of the Austerity cohort. But all the other cohorts record higher participation. The First World War–related effects are likely to be a product of age, with the very old being less likely to vote than their middle-aged counterparts. But the Blair cohort effect, which is the same as the Austerity cohort effect, is likely to be influenced by the growing insecurity in the labour market, which young people have experienced since the Great Recession.

Macropartisanship is not a significant predictor in the turnout model, and nor is the difference between the ideological positions of Labour and the Conservatives as measured using the Manifesto data. Of course, both are period effects, since pre–Second World War data are not available to identify cohort effects associated with these measures. But it seems likely that cohort effects might be important if they were available, in view of the decline in partisanship observed in Table 6.3.

Finally, residual period and cohort effects were included in the analysis to pick up anything missed by the modelling. In addition, a dummy variable was included identifying if Labour was in office at the time of the election to determine if party incumbencies make a difference. The results show that there are additional period effects in the data, and a Labour incumbency effect, but there are no additional cohort effects. The period effect charts a long-term decline in turn-out in successive elections, and the Labour incumbency effect denotes lower electoral participation when Labour was in power. The latter is exemplified by the turnout of 59 per cent in the 2001 election, the second election won by Tony Blair and the lowest turnout since the Second World War.

Figure 6.8 illustrates the impact of the different variables on voting for the governing party, a specification which allows us to examine valence effects on party support. To repeat an earlier point, the valence model emphasizes the performance of the governing party, with opposition parties gaining support from poor performance and losing it from good performance. This means that the incumbency status of a party is controlled in the modelling to avoid missing this distinction.

The results in Figure 6.8 indicate that in the individual-level model occupational status and unemployment are significant predictors of support for incumbent governments, but none of the other demographics are significant. This shows that, when indicators of the valence model are included, the relationship between individual demographics and support for the governing party are no longer important, with the exception of the workforce measures. The fact that age differences cease to be predictors in this extended model highlights the importance of including economic variables in the analysis. Put differently, the age effects we have observed are a lot to do with the impact of the economic circumstances and the experiences of young people.

With regard to the percentage of professionals and workers in the aggregate contextual model, the former boosts support for the incumbent party, while the latter is non-significant. This should be understood in the context of the Conservatives being in office for thirty-one of the fifty-five years between the 1964 and 2019 elections. The party has consistently been supported by middle-class professionals to a greater extent than Labour, although the gap is narrowing in recent elections. This means that class is still important in British politics, but the class divide favours the Conservatives in the long run. This is because the middle class are more likely to support them, than the working class are to support Labour.

The period inflation and period unemployment variables are both significant and negative in the analysis, which is consistent with the valence model, since economic problems reduce support for incumbent governments. In addition, the estimates show that unemployment has

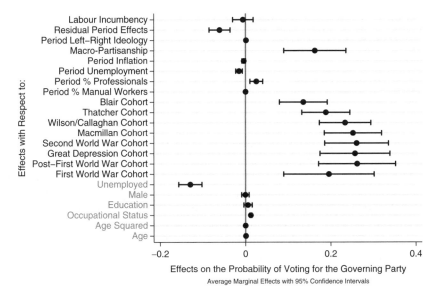

Figure 6.8 Hierarchical Age Cohort Extended Model of Voting for the Governing Party with Linear Period Controls, 1964–2019.

a bigger impact on incumbency support than does inflation.[86] British governments have more to fear from rising unemployment than they have from increased inflation. However, it should be noted that inflation was only a serious problem in the 1970s and has been at relatively low levels ever since, which reduces its salience. That has changed in the post-pandemic period, but overall in the past half century, rising unemployment is more of a problem for successive British governments than price rises.

Once again, the most striking feature of the government support model in Figure 6.8 is the very strong cohort effects. All cohorts, including the Blair cohort, were significantly more likely to support the government than the Austerity cohort. This finding is the same as earlier findings in Figure 6.6, which show how much the younger generation has deserted the Conservative Party in office since 2010. The party may have won three elections in a row after Labour left office in 2010, but it is vulnerable to generational replacement in the long run, as these large cohort effects demonstrate.

---

[86] The expanded model creates problems of multicollinearity with dummy variables for the periods, so we impose the assumption that the period effects are linear. This is a more restrictive assumption than in the earlier modelling, but it makes estimation possible.

Finally, macropartisanship clearly plays an important role in influencing support for the governing party. The finding implies that there is greater support for the governing party when macropartisanship moves in favour of the Conservatives. We observed in Table 6.3 that Conservative partisanship fell from 39.9 per cent in 1964 to 29.8 per cent in 2017. The decline for Labour is slightly greater, with 42.1 per cent identifying with the party in 1964 and only 28.4 per cent doing so in 2019.

Clearly, both parties have experienced a sizeable erosion of their partisan bases. The long-term implications of this depend on the extent to which partisanship is a largely static product of socialization in early adulthood or, alternatively, a dynamic 'running tally' of updated performance-related evaluations. Existing research suggests that in Britain the latter is more important than the former.[87] So the long-run effects of declining partisanship at any point in time are mitigated by the possibility that increases in parties' partisan shares are ongoing possibilities. That said, the weakening of early-life political socialization creates problems for both major British parties.

Conclusion: The Dynamics of Turnout and Party Support

This chapter has investigated both the short-run and long-run influences of age, period and cohort effects on turnout and party support in Britain. It is clear that the class and valence models help to explain the relationship between these different aspects of age-related voting in Britain over the fifty-five-year period between 1964 and 2019. With regard to turnout, there have always been differences in rates of electoral participation between age groups, but these became far more pronounced after the Labour landslide of 1997 when Tony Blair's New Labour became the dominant party. This resulted in lower rates of voting among members of the Blair cohort, and this has subsequently carried over to the Austerity cohort.

Another important finding is that over this long period of time the Labour and Conservative HAPC models are very different. In the case of Labour, changes in support are related to different periods or elections with little evidence of enduring cohort effects. In contrast, the Conservatives appear to have relied heavily on socialization processes which strongly influenced their support prior to the New Labour era. These have subsequently largely disappeared, such that 'socialization politics' have become very much weaker.

---

[87] Whiteley and Kölln (2019).

The fragmentation of the class system as measured by changes in the occupational structure has weakened the relationship between social status, partisanship and electoral behaviour. The decline of traditional working-class occupations and the rise of managers and professionals have weakened support for Labour more than for the Conservatives. Labour won a lot of support from middle-class voters during the Blair years and subsequently the party has done better than expected in a number of relatively middle-class constituencies, even in the most recent 2019 election.[88] At the same time, as Chapter 5 shows, the party lost a number of traditional working-class constituencies in the so-called 'Red Wall' of Labour strongholds in the North West in that election, illustrating the continuing fragmentation of the association between class and party affiliation.

Another finding is the lack of support for the spatial model of party competition. It is well established that divisive issues can play an important role in electoral politics, exemplified by the 2019 general election, which, as we have seen, was influenced by the issue of Brexit. However, that chapter revealed that the impact of Brexit on the vote was rather modest, with the possible exception of support for the Liberal Democrats. In the present context there were no significant contextual left–right ideological effects in the modelling, either in relation to turnout or support for the governing party. That said, macropartisanship is very influential in general elections, and this is clearly associated with ideology. But partisanship is much more strongly related to political identity and policy delivery than long-term support for left-wing or right-wing policies. The implication is that either the Manifesto data do not capture ideological differences very well, or more likely their influence on electoral behaviour has been exaggerated by the popularity of the spatial model.

It also bears emphasis that prosperity increases support for incumbents regardless of the party they represent, and recession reduces their support, in line with the valence model. This has important implications for future elections relating to the longer-term consequences of the protracted Brexit crisis, the ongoing Covid-19 pandemic and the cost of living crisis. This topic is discussed in more detail in Chapters 9 and 10. The responses to these shocks will vary between the parties and will be influenced by ideological differences between them over the next decade. The valence model suggests that these events will make life difficult for incumbents until prosperity returns and the economy recovers. There

---

[88] For example, the party won Putney and also Canterbury, the latter being formerly a safe Conservative seat.

is an argument that the fragmentation of party support in Britain may make government less effective in the future, but the counterargument is that valence voting which focuses tightly on performance rather than ideology can actually improve accountability, a topic to be examined in Chapter 8.

This chapter has been a story of the fragmentation of party support and the strength of the relationship between partisan attachments and demographics such as age and social class over time. However, there is a second perspective on these political changes which relates to the geography of the vote – the spatial dimension in British politics. This is examined in the next chapter.

7 Space and the Fragmenting Party System

Chapter 6 investigated the relationship between demographics, principally age, and changes in voting behaviour in the British party system since the mid-1960s. Over time, we see a more fragmented party system and a more divided electorate, reflecting a more fragmented society and a more divided politics. But does fragmentation imply greater polarization in British politics? It is clearly possible for a political system to fragment without it necessarily polarizing, i.e., there are more divisions in society, but they are not necessarily more antagonistic to each other. However, polarization and fragmentation may go together. The key question to consider in the present chapter is: has greater heterogeneity in voting behaviour and party support led to sharper divisions of opinion between groups, particularly in different areas of the country?

The protracted Brexit negotiations certainly polarized British politics between Leavers and Remainers, with relatively few people willing to accept either outcome. But arguably, this was an exception, and may not imply greater polarization in British politics overall. The aim of this chapter is to investigate if we are destined to become an ever more politically divided society in the future. This is done by examining trends in the geography of polarization in British politics which have occurred over the past half century.

Following the analysis in Chapter 6, we examine sources of change in electoral politics since 1964, when the first British Election Study (BES) was conducted. But unlike that chapter, the focus here is on aggregate analyses of constituency results rather than individual-level survey data. In effect we are looking at macro-polarization and the geography of the vote over time. We begin by examining electoral polarization, where this is defined as trends in the proportion of marginal seats to safe seats in successive elections. If the proportion of marginal seats has declined, this suggests that geographical polarization has taken place with communities becoming increasingly supportive of one party rather than switching between them. If there is no such trend, then polarization will not have occurred. Evidence relating to this issue is subsequently linked to changes in demographic and contextual variables to help explain why these developments have occurred.

We begin by considering changes in electoral behaviour at the regional level, before drilling down to the constituency level to see how things have evolved there. These analyses involve investigating the extent to which regions and constituencies within them have changed politically and demographically over a long time interval. As the discussion in Chapter 6 indicates, there were a total of sixteen general elections between 1964 and 2019, and there are reasons to think that the country might have become more polarized politically over time. One is the growth of inequality which has produced greater differences in standards of living between regions across the country.[1] Another is the decline of traditional manual working jobs, which reflects enormous changes in the labour market since the mid-twentieth century.

The growth of inequality at the individual level has been accompanied by a growing North–South geographic divide which raises important questions about the relationship between economic inequality and political polarization. After examining regions of the country, we consider developments at the constituency level, while at the same time looking at the effects of the clustering of constituencies at the subregional level. This approach enables us to investigate effects which operate between the regional and constituency levels of analysis.

Space and Electoral Choice

There is a long-standing research tradition in political geography which investigates the relationship between electoral behaviour and the geographical context in which voting takes place. As a team of leading political geographers explain: 'people are influenced in the choice of party by their environment, by the people they live among and by the economic and social conditions in their localities.'[2] An important debate among electoral geographers concerns the balance between social and spatial differences as determinants of electoral behaviour. Social differences refer to the demographic characteristics of communities such as the proportions of voters with high- or low-status occupations. Another important factor is type of housing tenure, i.e., the proportion of owner-occupiers as opposed to private or social renters in a community. Also considered are the age profiles of inhabitants in different constituencies.

[1] See, e.g., Atkinson (2015).
[2] Johnston, Pattie and Allsopp (1988), p. 41.

In contrast, spatial differences refer to the historical evolution, economic performance and political cultures of communities which give rise to different localized political traditions that affect voting behaviour. Voting patterns may be influenced by demographics but cannot be explained by population characteristics alone. The distinction is between demographics and culture. To illustrate this, if, for example, council tenants are equally likely to vote Labour, or homeowners to vote Conservative in different parts of the country, then variations in support for these parties will merely reflect differences in housing tenure across constituencies. Constituencies with a high proportion of social housing will tend to support Labour and those with a high proportion of owner-occupation will favour the Conservatives. This means that social differences based on demographics will dominate the picture.

However, if social housing tenants are much more likely to vote Labour in certain constituencies in comparison with their counterparts in other constituencies when both have similar proportions of social housing, then housing tenure cannot be the full explanation. Other factors which are related to spatial variables such as the political cultures of different communities and historical legacies that have influenced voting over a long period of time must be at work. This is what is meant by spatial differences.

For example, one possible constituency-level spatial variable is level of social deprivation. If high levels of unemployment and social deprivation exist in one constituency compared with another, then council tenants in the former constituency may well be more pro-Labour than tenants living in more affluent constituencies. This distinction is important in light of the loss of many traditional Labour 'Red Wall' constituencies to the Conservatives in the North of England and Midlands in the 2019 general election. If this change represents a significant shift in the demographics of the vote, it is likely to be much more enduring than if it is due to Britain leaving the European Union. The impact of the latter could erode rapidly in reaction to the severe economic and social shocks precipitated by the Covid pandemic and government efforts to alleviate it.

Social deprivation is a demographic variable, whereas support for Brexit is a spatial measure reflecting differing political cultures across constituencies. Of course, social and spatial factors interact with each other, such as the age profile of constituencies linking with Brexit voting to produce varying effects. Factors associated with the historical development of regions, their economic prosperity, migration patterns in the past and local political cultures all will be part of the mix in explaining the geography of voting behaviour.

As observed in Chapter 6, when the first national surveys of the British electorate were conducted in the 1960s, the focus was very much on the social class cleavage.[3] There was a debate at that time about how class should be measured although it was generally accepted that occupational status was central to its definition.[4] Miller identified two 'core' class categories: firstly, the 'employers and managers', whom he described as 'controllers', and suggested that they benefited most from the election of Conservative governments.[5] Secondly, he defined the 'anti-controllers' or manual workers and trade union members, who benefited most from Labour governments. Social class defined in this way is a socio-demographic variable, but one which might be affected by spatial considerations at the local level.

Some researchers have argued that spatial variables are only residual effects left after the demographic variables are taken into account. The implication is that they would be superfluous in models of electoral choice if all the key demographics were included in the analysis.[6] However, this argument has its critics, notably Agnew, who argues that: 'context counts in electoral geography and is not merely a residual effect after demographics have been taken into account.'[7] He stresses the importance of locales in which people live their day-to-day lives and which are linked to other communities through a variety of social, economic and cultural ties. These locales are at the base of a hierarchy of spatial groupings varying from households to workplaces, neighbourhoods, towns, regions, and nations at the macro level.[8]

In this view, places are part of an individual's identity and so are influential in creating the values, beliefs and attitudes which underpin electoral choice. Historians who have studied national identities have shown how powerful they are, not merely in influencing voting behaviour but also in producing strong emotional attachments to places which go well beyond demographics.[9] Such identities play an increasingly important role in contemporary politics, as indicated by the rise of populist parties in Europe and elsewhere.[10]

In national surveys we observe attitudes and behaviour which are products of a myriad of social processes operating at multiple levels in society, including in the family, neighbourhood, community, town, conurbation and region, as well as at the national and international

[3] Alford (1963); Butler and Stokes (1969); Miller (1977).
[4] Dunleavy and Husbands (1985); Heath, Jowell and Curtice (1985).
[5] Miller (1977).
[6] McAllister and Studlar (1992); King (1996).
[7] Agnew (1996).
[8] Johnston and Pattie (2006).
[9] Anderson (1983); Hobsbawm (1990).
[10] Eatwell and Goodwin (2018).

levels. As Johnston and Pattie put it: 'Voting patterns by class are not imposed on places by some nationally invariant process; rather they are the summation of a myriad of interacting local processes.'[11] One implication is that socio-demographic and spatial variables work together to explain differences in electoral support for parties over time and across country. Another is that we only get a limited picture of what is going on if an analysis is restricted to parliamentary constituencies alone, many of which are amalgams of several different communities rather than distinct geographical and cultural entities in their own right.

Electoral Polarization over Half a Century

We begin the analysis of polarization by examining evidence for changes in voting support between the 1964 and 2019 elections, a period of more than half a century. Figures 7.1 and 7.2 show vote shares for Labour, the Conservatives, the Liberals (subsequently the Liberal Democrats), and Nationalist parties in Britain, examined by region in these two general elections. Labour won the 1964 general election by a narrow margin, taking 44.1 per cent of the vote and 317 of the 630 seats, while the Conservatives captured 43.4 per cent of the vote and 304 seats. The Liberals obtained 11.2 per cent of the vote and 9 seats in that election and the Nationalist parties in Scotland and Wales won only 0.5 per cent of the vote and no seats at all.[12] As a result, the two major parties took 87.5 per cent of the vote and 98.6 per cent of the seats in the House of Commons.[13]

The differences in electoral support for the two major parties by regions in 1964 appear in Figure 7.1. As the figure illustrates, Labour was at its strongest in London, the North East and Wales in comparison with the Conservatives, and had modest leads over the latter in the East Midlands, the North West, Scotland and Yorkshire and Humberside. In contrast, the Conservatives were at their strongest in the South East and the South West and had small leads over Labour in the East of England, and the West Midlands. The Liberals did relatively well in the South West and the South East and to a lesser extent the East of England, so their pattern of support was similar to the Conservatives. In the 1960s the Nationalists were a mere blip on the electoral map, with Plaid Cymru taking a bigger vote share in Wales than the Scottish Nationalists did in Scotland. In Northern Ireland, the Ulster Unionists took all twelve seats.

---

[11] Johnston and Pattie (2006), p. 42.
[12] Cowley and Kavanagh (2018), pp. 496–497.
[13] Pilling and Cracknell (2021).

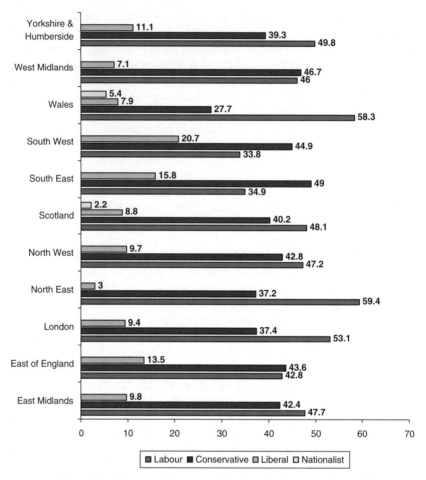

Figure 7.1 Vote by Country and Region in the 1964 General Election.
Source: House of Commons Library.

The picture in 2019 was very different. In this most recent election Labour captured 32 per cent of the popular vote and 203 seats out of a total of 650, and the Conservatives took 44 per cent and 365 seats, a majority of 80. The two major parties took 76 per cent of the vote and 87 per cent of the seats in the House of Commons.[14] The Liberal Democrats received 11.5 per cent of the vote but obtained only eleven seats. For their part the Nationalist parties, captured 4.4 per cent and

[14] House of Commons (2020).

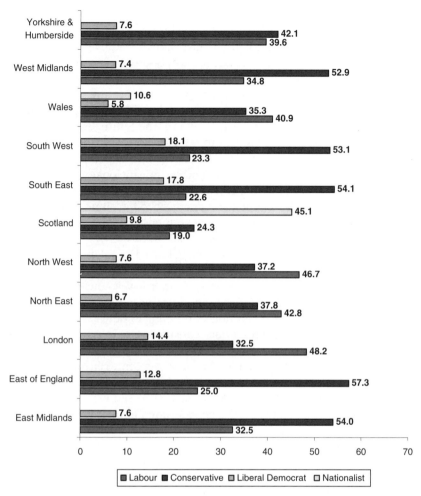

Figure 7.2 Vote by Country and Region in the 2019 General Election. Source: House of Commons Library.

a total of fifty-two seats, the SNP doing particularly well, winning forty-eight of the fifty-nine seats in Scotland. Unlike 1964, when minor parties did not capture any seats, they obtained a total of nineteen seats in 2019. In fact, similar to 2017, the 2019 election showed a reversal of the decline in the two-party system which had been going on for some time.[15]

---

[15] Cowley and Kavanagh (2018).

If we compare Figures 7.1 and 7.2, the Conservatives overtook Labour in the East Midlands, Scotland, and Yorkshire and Humberside in 2019 compared with 1964. Equally, the Conservatives lead over Labour widened in the East of England, the South East, South West and in the West Midlands. Labour continued to outperform the Conservatives in London, the North East, the North West and Wales, but the gap narrowed in each case, with the sole exception of London. The Liberal Democrat vote share rose in the North East, Scotland, the South East and in the West Midlands, and fell in all the other regions.

We can use the voting gap between the two major parties to measure the degree of polarization over time. This is done by looking at the variation in their vote shares across constituencies. If vote shares are similar across the country, with Labour marginally ahead in some seats and the Conservatives marginally ahead in others, then the variation in the vote across the country would be relatively small. In this case, many marginal seats mean that the country is not that polarized in relation to the two major parties. On the other hand, if the average gap between them is large in the great majority of seats, such that fewer constituencies are won or lost by small margins, this is an indicator of polarization.

Figure 7.3 shows the distribution of differences between the Conservative and Labour vote shares across constituencies in 1964. The average difference between the Conservative and Labour Party vote shares by constituencies in that election was −2.2 per cent, reflecting the fact that the Conservatives won fewer votes and seats than Labour. The figure is clearly dominated by marginal seats with relatively small gaps in the vote shares between the parties concentrated in the centre of the distribution. The 'tails' of the distribution, containing constituencies with large differences between the partys' votes, are relatively few in number. The standard deviation of the distribution is 28.6, which can be interpreted as the average dispersion of the vote shares across constituencies.

Figure 7.4 shows the same distribution of the differences between the Conservative and Labour vote shares in the 2019 general election, and it is very different from 1964. In this case, the average difference between the parties was 10.2 per cent because the Conservatives won a decisive victory over Labour. There are many fewer marginal seats in the centre of the distribution and the modal category is seats with a Conservative lead over Labour of 40 per cent. The standard deviation of 30.2 is higher than in 1964, indicating that not only are there fewer marginal seats, but the variation in the margin between the two parties has grown larger over time. In addition, increasing support for minor parties shows that electoral fragmentation grew significantly, implying that electoral politics in Britain has been both fragmenting and polarizing at the same time.

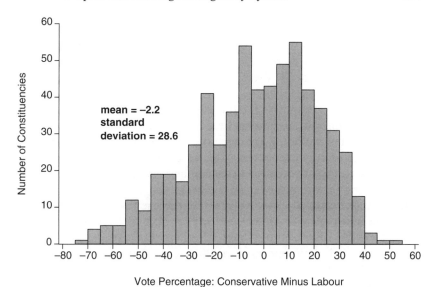

Figure 7.3 Difference between Conservative and Labour Vote Shares in the 1964 General Election, Great Britain.

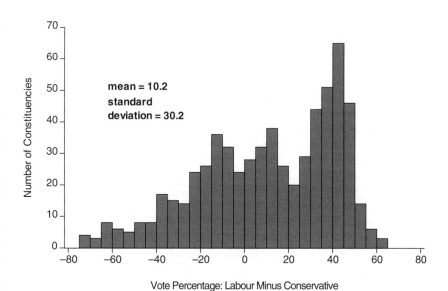

Figure 7.4 Difference between Conservative and Labour Vote Shares in the 2019 General Election, Great Britain.

Social Polarization over Time

What are the relationships between the demographic characteristics of constituencies and electoral support for the two major parties over time? In this section we explore these links using data from the 1966 Census mid-term sample survey to look at this for the 1964 election and the 2011 Census to examine it for the 2019 election. The 1966 data are much more limited than those gathered in 2011, so the comparisons are confined to a few variables. But it is possible to explore the role of social class as measured by occupational status in some detail since as Butler and Stokes and many other analysts emphasized, this was the key electoral demographic in mid-twentieth-century Britain.[16]

In addition to social class, we examine the age profile of constituencies, their housing stock and unemployment rates as a proxy measure of deprivation. As discussed in Chapter 5, there was a strong relationship between age and party support in the 2019 general election, with support

A. 1964

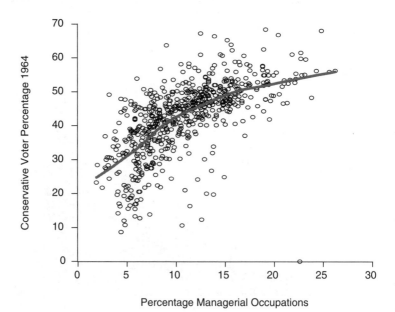

Figure 7.5 Conservative Vote Share by Social Class (Managerial Occupations) in 1964 and 2019 (A) 1964 (B) 2019.

[16] Butler and Stokes (1969).

B. 2019

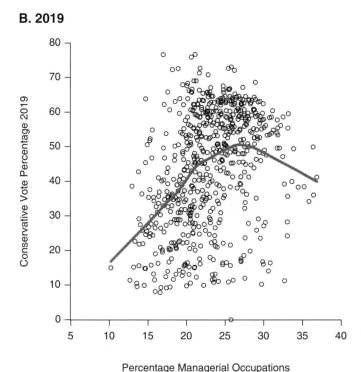

Figure 7.5 (cont.)

for Labour being particularly strong among younger voters, and support for the Conservatives being considerably stronger among older voters. Here we investigate how this has changed since the 1960s.

Figure 7.5 shows the relationship between social class and party support, where class is measured by the percentage of managers in the two elections.[17] Each dot on the graph is a constituency, and the summary line is a 'nearest neighbour' regression which means that it captures the relationship between class and party support at each point, without assuming that the relationship is linear.[18] Figure 7.5 shows that the Conservatives benefited greatly from the presence of managers in a constituency both in 1964 and 2019. However, in constituencies with high levels of these people in 2019, the relationship peaked at about 25 per cent and subsequently went into reverse. It appears that constituencies with very high

[17] Miller (1977).
[18] See Altman (1992). Here, the nearest neighbour regressions are estimated using Eviews 9.

concentrations of managers were more likely to support parties other than the Conservatives in this election, something not seen in 1964.

Another feature of Figure 7.5 is that the scatter of constituencies around the summary line was much greater in 2019 than in 1964. This means that the proportion of managers in a constituency was a much more reliable predictor of Conservative voting in the earlier election than it was in 2019. This confirms a pattern seen in the individual-level survey data that social class has weakened markedly as a determinant of party support over time.

The other side of the relationship between social class and voting is support for Labour among working-class voters. Workers classified in the census as being in routine and semi-routine occupations provide an indicator of the working-class character of a constituency. As the analysis in Chapter 5 revealed, one of the striking features of the 2019 election was that Labour lost a number of constituencies in its 'Red Wall' in the North and Midlands. Figure 7.6 compares the relationship between the proportion in working-class occupations and constituency-level Labour voting in 1964 and 2019.

In 1964 there was a clear linear relationship between the percentage of semi-skilled and unskilled workers in a constituency and Labour's share of the vote, indicating the extent to which the party was the organized political representative of working-class communities at that time. The comparison with the relationship between managers and the Conservative vote share in Figure 7.5 reveals, in Miller's terms, how at that time the Conservative Party represented 'controllers' and the Labour Party 'anti-controllers' in British politics.

Moving to 2019, Figure 7.6 illustrates that the relationship between working-class occupations and voting Labour had almost disappeared. In fact, the relationship was weakly negative in constituencies containing up to about 25 per cent of working-class occupations. Beyond that, a positive relationship between these variables emerges, indicating that the party retained support in highly working-class constituencies, but overall, the link was weak. Taken together, Figures 7.5 and 7.6 indicate that over the past half-century social class has greatly weakened as the basis of British electoral politics.

Figure 7.7 displays the correlation of age with support for Labour, a relationship which has grown much stronger over time. The figure shows that, in 1964, the relationship between the proportion of young people in a constituency and Labour support was quite weak and highly non-linear.[19] At that time, Labour's vote share increased as the percentage of

[19] Note that this is the percentage of people between the ages of 15 and 24, defined by the 1964 census data.

A. 1964

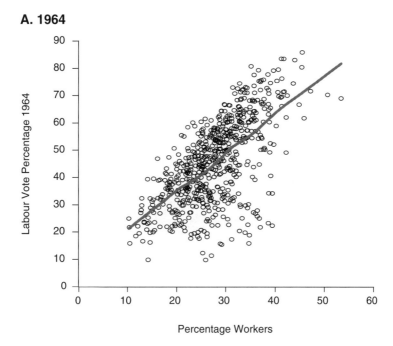

B. 2019

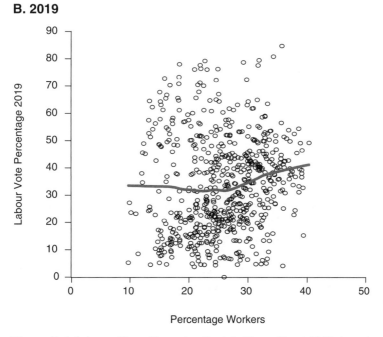

Figure 7.6 Labour Vote Share by Social Class (Semi-Skilled and Unskilled Workers) in 1964 and 2019 (A) 1964 (B) 2019.

A. 1964

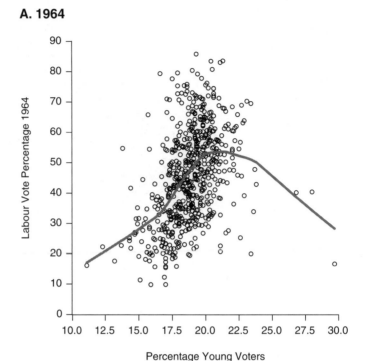

Figure 7.7 Labour Vote Share by Percentage Younger People in 1964 and 2019 (A) 1964 (B) 2019.

younger voters grew, up to the point at which 20 per cent of the voters were young. From then on it started to decline.

In sharp contrast, in 2019 there was a very strong relationship between Labour voting and the proportion of young people in constituencies up to about 10 per cent of the population. Beyond that, the relationship weakened and so the nearest neighbour regression line flattens, although it is still positive. This relationship was also apparent in the 2017 general election and at the time it was attributed in large part to Jeremy Corbyn's campaign appeal.[20] But the fact that it continued to be strong in 2019, despite Corbyn's growing political weaknesses, suggests that it is not merely a reflection of how voters reacted to a particular party leader.

The equivalent figure (Figure 7.8) showing the relationship between the number of retired people in a constituency and Conservative support is a mirror image of Figure 7.7. In 1964 the Conservatives received no extra support in constituencies where the number of retired people

[20] Whiteley, Poletti, Webb and Bale (2018).

B. 2019

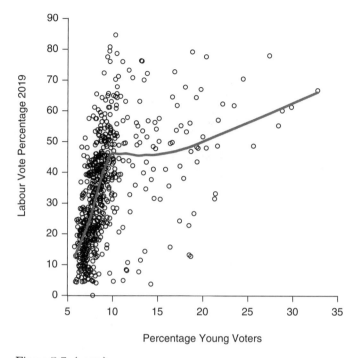

Figure 7.7 (cont.)

was less than about 15 per cent. But their support did grow in constituencies with more than that percentage of retired voters. In contrast, in
2019 the more retired people there were in a constituency, the more
likely it was to be won by the Conservatives. The latter relationship was
almost linear, but with a bit of a dip in the middle, while the overall
relationship was much stronger than in 1964. These two figures show
how age has emerged as a polarizing dimension in British electoral politics over time.

A third socio-demographic variable is housing tenure, which has
played an important role in influencing voting behaviour in the past.[21]
This is related to social class, with homeowners being more likely to vote
Conservative and social renters and council house tenants more likely to
vote Labour. Housing tenure is an indicator of the voter's relationship

[21] Dunleavy and Husbands (1985); Johnston and Pattie (2006).

A. 1964

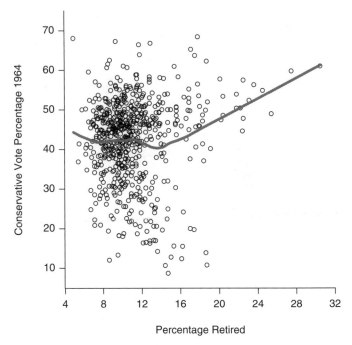

Figure 7.8 Conservative Vote Share by Percentage Retired in 1964 and 2019 (A) 1964 (B) 2019.

with the state, since local authorities provided an increasing proportion of social housing from the 1950s to the 1970s, and this helped to stimulate support for Labour.

Figure 7.9 shows that the relationship between Conservative voting and home ownership in the 1964 election was almost linear, with a greater concentration of homeowners associated with a higher Conservative vote across all constituencies. By contrast, in the 2019 election the relationship was positive, but it grew markedly stronger over a home ownership range varying from about 60 per cent to 80 per cent. In other words, very high concentrations of home ownership, reflecting higher incomes and greater wealth, correlated positively with much greater support for the Conservatives in 2019 than was true in 1964, even though the relationships were positive in both elections.

Finally, Figure 7.10 displays the relationship between Labour support and unemployment, a key indicator of economic deprivation at the constituency level. Up to this point we have examined the relationship between

B. 2019

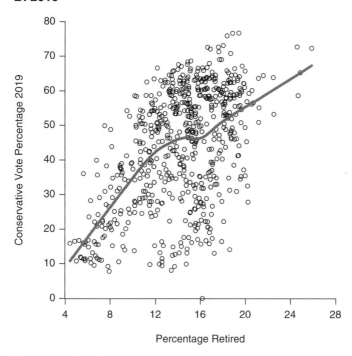

Figure 7.8 (cont.)

demographic variables and party vote shares, but arguably unemployment is a spatial rather than a demographic variable. It reflects government policies rather than just occupational status or wealth. In this case, higher rates of unemployment were associated with greater support for Labour in both elections, but the relationship appeared to be much stronger in 2019 than it was in 1964. In 1964, unemployment rates were significantly lower than they were in 2019 and again the relationship with Labour voting was linear across the whole range. However, in 2019, the correlation grew stronger for unemployment rates between about 2 per cent and 6 per cent. Thereafter it weakened, while still remaining positive, suggesting that Labour was still seen as 'owning' the unemployment issue in that election.

Table 7.1 looks at summary descriptive statistics for the demographic and spatial variables in 1964 and 2019. Unsurprisingly, there has been a significant increase in the percentage of managers in the workforce, with that number more than doubling. The other significant changes have been in the percentage of younger voters which fell from 19 per cent to 13 per cent. Finally, the percentage

A. 1964

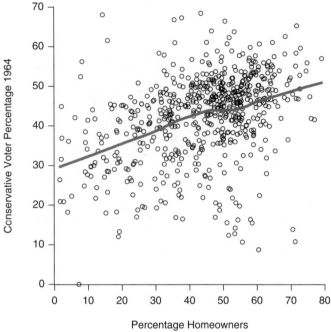

Figure 7.9 Conservative Vote Share by Home Ownership in 1964 and 2019 (A) 1964 (B) 2019.

of homeowners increased from 44 per cent in 1964 to 64 per cent in 2019 and the percentage of retired voters increased from 11 per cent to 14 per cent. The standard deviations show that variations in management and workers across constituencies have fallen slightly, whereas variations in the percentage of younger and retired people have increased. But the most striking change relates to housing tenure. Variations in home ownership across constituencies have narrowed, so that constituencies are now more like each other in housing tenure than they were in 1964.

Table 7.2 displays correlations between vote shares and demographic variables in 1964 and again in 2019, highlighting changes which have occurred over time. Correlations are based on the assumption that there is a linear relationship between the variables, and as we have seen, this is not always the case. The strength of the relationships should be interpreted with this in mind. That said, the correlations between party vote

B. 2019

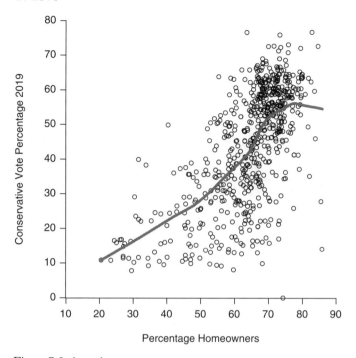

Figure 7.9 (cont.)

shares and the demographic variables have weakened in the case of the occupational status variables, but have considerably strengthened in the case of age, housing tenure, and unemployment.

Illustratively, the correlation between occupational status and Labour voting in 1964 was –0.85, showing that high-status individuals were very unlikely to support the party. But this was reduced to –0.49 in 2019, reflecting the fact that Labour had attracted many middle-class voters. On the reverse side, the correlation between Conservative voting and the percentage of unskilled workers in a constituency fell from –0.56 in 1964 to –0.01. Taken together, these relationships show how much occupation has weakened as a predictor of two-party voting between 1964 and 2019.

One of the most striking changes in Table 7.2 relates to age. In 1964, the correlation between Conservative voting and the proportion of younger voters in a constituency was –0.18, but by 2019 it was –0.48. There are fewer younger voters now, but they are much more polarized in

A. 1964

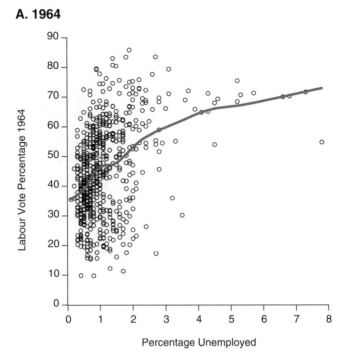

Figure 7.10 Labour Vote Share by Percentage Unemployed in 1964 and 2019 (A) 1964 (B) 2019.

their support for the two main parties. Similarly, the correlation between Labour voting and the proportion of retired voters in a constituency went from −0.29 to −0.55 in 2019, again indicating that age polarization has increased substantially.

A similar pattern exists for housing tenure, with the correlation between the proportion of homeowners and Conservative voting changing from 0.38 in 1964 to 0.64 in 2019. This is a huge change, indicating that housing tenure is associated with polarization in the electorate. It appears that the Conservatives have been rewarded by their policies of encouraging home ownership with big discounts for tenants who buy, while at the same time neglecting investment in social housing. That said, Labour did little to reverse these changes when it was in office in the 1960s and 1970s, and again in the Blair years after 1997, and this neglect of the issue was related to reduced Labour support.

The results in Table 7.2 suggest that demographic polarization has occurred over time, except for occupational status which has fragmented.

B. 2019

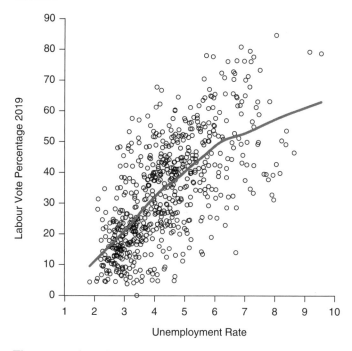

Figure 7.10 (cont.)

In 1964, age played a relatively minor role in distinguishing between Labour and the Conservatives, although the latter always benefited from relatively greater support among older cohorts. However, by 2019 age had become one of the most important demographic factors distinguishing between Labour and Conservative voters.

This analysis is based on correlations largely because of the limited data available in 1964, but the 2011 Census provides an opportunity to examine the effects of demographic and spatial variables on voting in the 2019 election in much greater detail. Constituencies are convenient units of analysis to measure relationships between social characteristics and party support, but they often do not represent meaningful communities, and this changes the relationship between spatial locations and voting.

In many places, such as large conurbations, the communities voters identify with are likely to be much larger than constituencies. For example, inner-London constituencies have a lot in common and so demographic factors associated with these neighbourhoods will spill

Table 7.1 *Descriptive Statistics for Socio-Demographic Correlates of Labour and Conservative Voting in 1964 and 2019*

Socio-Demographic Characteristics	Mean 1964 (%)	Standard Deviation 1964 (%)	Mean 2019 (%)	Standard Deviation 2019 (%)
Managers	11.0	4.7	23.0	4.6
Workers	27.8	7.0	25.8	6.5
Younger Voters	18.9	1.9	13.0	3.4
Retired Voters	11.1	3.3	14.3	3.8
Homeowners	44.0	15.7	64.1	11.4
Unemployed	1.2	0.92	4.4	1.4

Table 7.2 *Socio-Demographic Correlates of Labour and Conservative Voting in 1964 and 2019*

Socio-Demographic Characteristic	Labour Vote in 1964 (%)	Conservative Vote in 1964 (%)	Labour Vote in 2019 (%)	Conservative Vote in 2019 (%)
Managers	−0.85	0.64	−0.49	0.34
Workers	0.63	−0.56	0.11	−0.01
Young	0.41	−0.18	0.49	−0.48
Retired	−0.29	0.09	−0.55	0.51
Homeowners	−0.51	0.38	−0.63	0.64
Unemployed	0.38	−0.42	0.67	−0.55

over from one constituency to another. If these effects are ignored, then we will get only a limited picture of the impact of demographic and other variables on voting behaviour. Accordingly, in the next section we employ a modelling strategy that examines the impact of the social and economic characteristics of wider communities than constituencies alone.

Sources of Polarization in the 2019 General Election

The 2011 Census contains a wealth of information relevant for understanding demographic and societal relationships with voting behaviour. In addition to the standard occupational status and housing measures already examined, the census also included indicators of health, education and standards of living in constituencies. These are policy related outcomes which vary a lot across communities and can influence electoral participation and party support. However, one of the problems of using such data is that many of the census variables are highly correlated. This makes it

Table 7.3 *Factor Loadings from Principal Components Analysis of Income, Education and Health Defining the Human Development Index*

Census Variable	Human Development Index
Mean Income (£1000s)	0.85
Percentage with Level 4/5 Qualifications	0.95
Percentage in Very Good Health	0.79
Percentage Professionals and Senior Managers	0.95
Eigenvalue	3.13
R^2	95.94

difficult to separate their effects when analysing voting.[22] Accordingly, it is useful to construct a single broad index of the socio-economic status of constituencies which does not encounter this problem.

The Human Development Index (HDI) is one such broad measure and it has been used in the past to analyse the economic and social development of states across the globe.[23] It was originally created by the United Nations Development Programme, with the aim of identifying a more comprehensive measure of economic and social progress than Gross Domestic Product (GDP). GDP has been the standard measure in the past, but it has the weakness of focusing exclusively on economic performance. The standard version of the HDI combines three variables – income level, educational attainment and health standard – into one comprehensive indicator. We have added a fourth measure, namely occupational status as a proxy measure for social class. This is captured by the percentage of professionals and senior managers in a constituency, making the revised index a very broad measure of human welfare at the constituency level in Britain.

Table 7.3 displays the principal components analysis which created the Human Development Index, and it has an excellent fit to the data. Correlations between the four variables and the index are very strong. The revised version of the HDI provides a more comprehensive measure of human welfare across British constituencies than just income alone.[24]

---

[22] This is the problem of multicollinearity in regression analysis, which makes the estimation of individual effects difficult.

[23] See http://hdr.undp.org/en/content/human-development-index-hdi

[24] Education and health are measured with indicators taken from the 2011 Census. Income is measured using the mean income of the population in each constituency using data from the Office for National Statistics. The education variable measures the proportion of the population in each constituency with a first or higher degree, NVQ qualifications at levels 4 and 5, HNC or HND qualifications, or who are qualified teachers, doctors, dentists, nurses, midwives and health visitors. The health variable is measured with the percentage of census respondents who report that they are in very good health.

This indicator confirms the widely accepted idea that standards of living as captured by national income or economic growth are only part of the story when it comes to measuring human welfare.

The revised HDI provides a convenient summary of key demographic characteristics of constituencies that we can employ in statistical modelling. In addition, the analyses include the size of the Brexit vote in the 2016 EU referendum as an indicator of an important relatively short-run spatial variable. This approach makes it possible to identify the extent to which the 2019 election represented an enduring shift to the Conservatives in 'Red Wall' seats, as opposed to being a shorter term phenomenon.

If we use both measures to predict Conservative vote shares, then a weak positive HDI score as a predictor means that affluence and high social status are no longer the key determinant of Conservative voting that they were in the past. It means that the party can continue to win in constituencies with relatively low HDI scores in the future. When this is combined with a strong Brexit referendum effect, it means that the party's success in breeching the Red Wall may well continue in the future.

If, on the other hand, the referendum vote is a relatively weak predictor of Conservative support while at the same time the HDI is strong, it means that the collapse of the 'Red Wall' in 2019 is more likely to be a temporary phenomenon. This is because a strong relationship between the affluence of an area and Conservative voting suggests that this is likely to continue in the future. The party will struggle to retain these seats after Brexit becomes a distant memory.

A similar set of relationships applies to the Labour vote model. If the HDI is a weak negative predictor and the Brexit vote effect is strong, it suggests that the party could struggle to hold on to its remaining seats in 'Red Wall' areas well into the future. However, a strong HDI effect combined with a relatively modest Brexit effect means that the seats captured by the Conservatives could be won back by Labour in a future election as public attention to EU membership recedes.

The other side of this coin is that while Labour suffered a serious defeat in stronghold seats which it had held for decades in 2019, it nonetheless retained support in some relatively affluent constituencies in London and the South East.[25] If this pattern continues, it will mean that a negative HDI effect will weaken as class politics continues to decline. If this is combined with a relatively weak Brexit effect, it suggests that the party

---

[25] For example, Putney in West London, Canterbury in Kent and Westminster North, which includes the House of Commons, are all relatively affluent constituencies retained by Labour in 2019.

will be able to retain support in poor communities while at the same time doing well in affluent communities once the Brexit controversy fades from public consciousness.

Support for the Conservatives will be the mirror image of Labour's support in these circumstances. In this case, a weakening HDI effect alongside a relatively powerful Brexit effect suggests that some affluent constituencies were attracted to Labour on a temporary basis by the party's pro-Remain stance. The implication is that once the Brexit issue passes into history, these constituencies will have less reason to stay in the Labour camp.[26]

Modelling the Vote

We can estimate the effect of the Human Development Index on turnout and party support in 2019 to determine how much political participation and party voting reflect constituency demographic characteristics. The salience of the Brexit issue in the 2019 election reflected the deep divisions in the country over membership of the European Union. Here, the modelling assesses the extent to which Brexit influenced the election by including the constituency-level percentage voting to Leave in the 2016 EU referendum as a predictor variable.[27]

In addition to attitudes towards the EU, age differences were strongly correlated with voting in 2019. As Figures 7.7 and 7.8 illustrated, age has become a much more important predictor of electoral choice in Britain than it was in the 1960s. Figure 7.7 shows that the younger and retired voters were highly polarized in their support for the two major parties in 2019. Here, we include the percentage of individuals between the ages of 18 and 29 in constituencies in the analysis to capture this effect.

A lot of research has been done on relationships between constituency characteristics and voting in Britain, as the earlier discussion indicated.[28] However, there is a problem in interpreting these analyses. As observed, many constituencies have arbitrary boundaries which do not accurately reflect voters' perceptions of the communities in which they live. The Electoral Commission is empowered to draw constituency boundaries in a way which tries to represent traditional communities in Parliament, but this goal conflicts with a second objective of ensuring that constituencies are of a roughly similar size in population terms. The latter aim

---

[26] Clarke, Goodwin and Whiteley (2017).
[27] These data were constructed by Hanretty (2017) from the local authorities' records of voter participation in the referendum published by the Electoral Commission.
[28] Johnston, Pattie, Dorling and Rossiter (2001); Johnston and Pattie (2006).

is to ensure that the electorate is as fairly represented in Parliament as possible, but it makes the relationship between communities and constituencies problematic.

To illustrate this problem, the town of Reading is represented in Parliament by two constituencies, Reading East and Reading West. In practice, voters are much more likely to identify with the town than with one of these two constituencies. By focusing only on what is a relatively artificial community of a constituency, we may get a misleading picture. A similar point can be made about the five constituencies in Sheffield, or the seven constituencies in Glasgow. These and other distinctive communities are divided for reasons of representational fairness, but in ways which can disrupt the effects of community demographics and identities on voting behaviour.

Recent methodological advances have greatly improved the ability of researchers to incorporate spatial factors in geographical models. It is possible to take account of the influence of surrounding constituencies on voting behaviour in a particular constituency with the use of what are called spatial autoregressive models.[29] This type of analysis takes account of demographics and other predictors in nearby constituencies when modelling relationships. This means that when we are studying the effects of demographics and other variables on voting in Reading East, we can simultaneously incorporate the influence of these measures from Reading West and other nearby constituencies into the analysis.

Darmofal, one of the analysts who has written on this topic, explains why it is necessary to look at wider communities beyond constituencies when modelling electoral support. He writes:

spatial dependence may be produced by the diffusion of behaviour between neighbouring units. If so, the behaviour is likely to be highly social in nature and understanding the interactions between interdependent units is critical to understanding the behaviour in question. For example, citizens may discuss politics across adjoining neighbourhoods such that an increase in support for a candidate in one neighbourhood directly leads to an increase in support for the candidate in adjoining neighbourhoods.[30]

There are different ways of measuring the impact of neighbouring constituencies, but in the present analysis we adopt a simple measure of

---

[29] Anselin (1988); Franzese and Hays (2007); Darmofal (2015).

[30] Darmofal (2015), p. 4. Spatial autoregressive models work by including a weighting matrix in the analysis which takes into account data from surrounding constituencies, but weights are weaker the further away from the constituency in question. The weighting matrix can be defined in different ways, e.g., by taking into account data from constituencies which share a border with a given constituency. In this case we use a simple distance measure defined by the longitude and latitude of constituencies.

the geographical distance between constituencies to define how influential they are in shaping the relationships. The assumption is that nearby constituencies will have a bigger impact on relationships between voting and demographics in a given constituency than those that are more distant. Essentially, we are assuming that geographical distance proxies the social distance we are really interested in studying.

This approach has a potential weakness that social distance may not be the same as geographical distance and it may exaggerate the importance of geography when we are really interested in the sociopolitical links between communities. For example, constituencies in conurbations like London, Birmingham and Greater Manchester are often small because of population densities. However, the political interaction between voters in these constituencies may be no different from those in Reading East and Reading West, both of which are larger in size. Equally it may be that diffusion processes work quite effectively in large rural constituencies with many scattered villages and small communities over a wide area.

This could be a serious problem for the analysis if it were not for the fact that there are very distinct clusters of constituencies which vote in a rather similar way. We have mentioned the 'Red Wall' already, but there are large clusters of adjacent 'True Blue' constituencies in rural areas like the East of England, indicating that voting behaviour clearly diffuses across space. The only way to avoid the possible problem of assuming that space is a useful proxy measure for political diffusion is to have data from an extremely large-scale national survey which identifies political interactions between individuals across the entire country. If this were available and contained the right questions, we would know the actual details of political diffusion. Unfortunately, such data do not exist, although studies of that kind have been done in small communities.[31]

Social and geographical distances may not be identical, but they are likely to be strongly related to each other. For example, constituencies in central London are more likely to have extensive political links with each other than they have with constituencies in the outer-London suburbs. Residents of Bethnal Green and Bow are more likely to interact with residents of Hackney South and Shoreditch than with residents of Richmond Park.

We can test the hypothesis that political diffusion is more likely to take place between small densely populated constituencies in inner-city areas than in larger geographically dispersed constituencies by including population density as a predictor in the analysis. If this

[31] Huckfield and Sprague (1995).

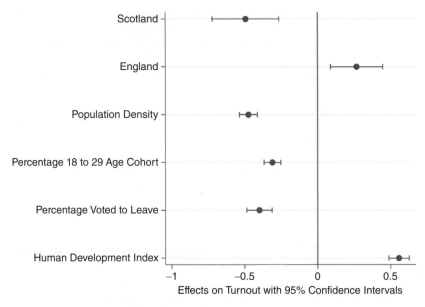

Figure 7.11 Impact of Human Development Index, Age, Brexit Vote and Population Density on Turnout in the 2019 General Election.

hypothesis is true, then density will influence both electoral participation and party support in the modelling. The effects of density will be positive if diffusion processes stimulate turnout and political support, but they could be negative if electoral hesitancy disseminates in high population areas. The intermediate case of density having a negligible effect would mean that population concentration was a poor indicator of political diffusion.

Figure 7.11 displays ordinary least squares (OLS) regression estimates of turnout in constituencies in Britain using the HDI measure, the percentage of young voters, the percentage of Leave voters in the EU referendum and population density as predictors. Country of residence (England and Scotland, with Wales as the reference category) also is included as a statistical control. This preliminary analysis ignores the effects of neighbouring constituencies and so provides a benchmark for judging the spatially autoregressive models examined subsequently.

In the turnout model summarized in Figure 7.11, the HDI measure has the strongest impact, indicating that constituencies with many high-status, affluent, healthy and educated people are significantly more likely to go to the polls than are their counterparts with the opposite characteristics. This has been known for a long time, but the strength of the

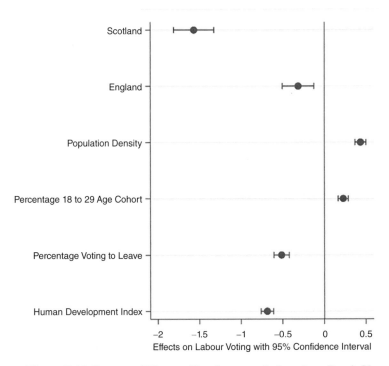

Figure 7.12 Impact of Human Development Index, Age, Brexit Vote and Population Density on Labour Voting in the 2019 General Election.

relationship at the constituency level demonstrates how important these demographics can be in practice.[32]

Other predictors in the turnout model have smaller effects and they are all negative apart from turnout in England. Densely populated urban constituencies are likely to have lower turnouts than larger and more scattered rural constituencies. The negative effect of the presence of young voters in a constituency shows how vote hesitancy among youth discussed in Chapter 5 translates into lower turnout at the constituency level. Equally, the size of the Brexit vote in the EU referendum is also associated with lower turnout at the constituency level. Finally, the country controls show that turnout in England was higher than in Wales (the reference category) and lower in Scotland once other factors are taken into account.

Figure 7.12 shows the effects of the predictor variables on Labour voting across constituencies. Once again, the HDI measure has the

[32] Miller (1977); Johnston and Pattie (2006); Clarke, Goodwin and Whiteley (2017).

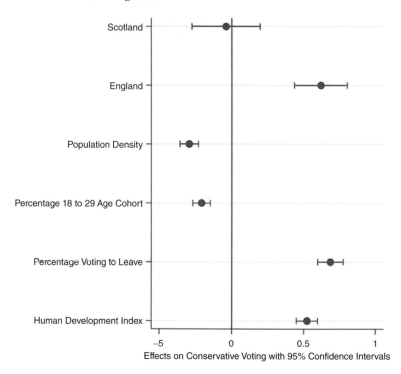

Figure 7.13 Impact of Human Development Index, Age, Brexit Vote and Population Density on Conservative Voting in the 2019 General Election.

largest impact, but in this case the effect is negative. Constituencies with many high-status, affluent, educated and healthy people are much less likely to vote Labour than those living in their poorer counterparts, a pattern which is well known. However, unlike in the turnout model, a large proportion of young voters and a densely populated urban area are both associated with an increase in Labour's vote share. Finally, voting to Leave the EU had a rather similar negative effect on support for Labour as it did on turnout, supporting the idea that Labour was damaged in its traditional heartland constituencies by the Brexit issue in 2019. That said, the effect was overshadowed by the continuing strong impact of HDI on Labour support.

Figure 7.13 shows the impact of these variables on Conservative voting at the constituency level. Strikingly, of all the predictors, Brexit had the strongest impact on the Conservative vote share. The HDI measure has a significant positive impact on support for the party, but the effect is weaker than Brexit. In addition, Brexit had a significantly stronger relationship with Conservative support than population density or the presence of young voters, both of which are related to reductions in constituency-level Conservative vote shares.

A comparison of the Conservative and the Labour models in relation to the Brexit measure is revealing. The effect of voting to Leave the EU is roughly three times as strong in a positive direction in the Conservative model as it is in a negative direction in the Labour model. Brexit thus helped the Conservatives a lot and it also harmed Labour, but to a significantly lesser extent.

Above we suggested that if the referendum vote was a powerful predictor of Conservative support while at the same time the HDI effect was weak, this implies that the capture of the 'Red Wall' seats could become a permanent feature of electoral politics in the future. However, in Figure 7.13 we observe that while Brexit was very important for increasing the Conservative vote share, so was the HDI. In other words, at the constituency level, the relationship between class, affluence and Conservative voting remains quite strong, suggesting that it is likely to continue. If the party is to maintain its gains in the Red Wall constituencies, the relationship between the HDI variable and Conservative support needs to be weaker, since these constituencies are not at all affluent communities.

This interpretation is reinforced by the very strong relationship between the HDI measure and Labour voting. If Labour strongholds are to continue to fall to the Conservatives in future elections, then the relationship between affluence and support for the party needs to be relatively weak, whereas Figure 7.12 shows that it is very strong. Taken together, both findings suggest that a 'Brexit effect' could be a temporary phenomenon and, while social class is weakening as a predictor of voting, the relationship between deprivation and Labour voting, and affluence and Conservative voting remains strong at the aggregate level. Looking to the future, long-run demographics are likely to be more important than the effects of attitudes towards Brexit.

In earlier chapters we have seen that occupational status, the standard measure of social class, is a relatively weak predictor of voting at the individual level of analysis. But we see strong HDI effects at the constituency level. There are three related explanations for these differences. Firstly, constituencies are not simply aggregations of individuals, an idea identified by Miller in the 1970s.[33] He showed that working-class voters were much more likely to be Labour supporters in constituencies with large numbers of working-class individuals, compared with constituencies lacking such numbers.

---

[33] Miller (1977).

He attributed this to local political cultures reinforced by day-to-day interactions between people. The probability of working-class voters interacting and being influenced by middle-class Conservatives is much smaller in dominant working-class constituencies than it is in communities with many middle-class individuals. If working-class 'anti-controllers' seldom if ever interact with middle-class 'controllers' then interpersonal influences will have little effect on their support and so will reinforce class politics at the constituency level.

The second reason why class politics appears to be much stronger at the constituency level relates to the HDI measure, which picks up multiple aspects of affluence and deprivation not identified by occupational status. As Table 7.3 shows, occupational status is only one indicator of human welfare which encompasses educational performance, health issues and income. This broader indicator is a much more effective measure of inequality and deprivation than occupational status alone. Class politics is still present at the constituency level in Britain, but to view it exclusively through the lens of occupational status gives a misleading picture.

Finally, the third reason is the phenomenon of geographical sorting. This refers to increased political homogeneity within communities, caused by individuals moving into areas with neighbours who are rather similar politically and demographically to themselves. If communities become more internally homogeneous and this is accompanied by greater heterogeneity between them, this can create dominant local political cultures which reinforce each other. Research in the United States attributes much of the polarization observed in contemporary US politics to geographic differences between and among the states.[34] This is consistent with Figure 7.4, which shows a similar process of political polarization at work in the UK.

Spatial Effects

As mentioned earlier, the results in Figures 7.11–7.13 do not account for the impact of the predictor variables diffusing from surrounding constituencies when these are likely to be consequential. This problem is addressed by including spatial effects in the turnout and party support models in Table 7.4, remembering that these effects decline in importance the further away a constituency is located geographically. This type of analysis produces both direct and indirect effects of the predictor variables in constituencies, the latter from surrounding areas. When these

---

[34] See, e.g., Gelman et al. (2008); but also Fiorina, Abrams and Pope (2005).

are combined, we can then observe the total effects of the predictors on turnout and party support.[35]

Table 7.4 includes the direct, indirect and total effects on the predictors on turnout and party support. Examining turnout first, the most immediate impression of the direct effects is that they are rather similar to those in Figure 7.11, which is to be expected. In the direct-effects model, the HDI variable has a strong positive impact on turnout, while Brexit voting, the proportion of young people and population density all have negative effects. At the same time the indirect effects are all quite strong, with the exception of population density, and they all reinforce the direct effects, with the exception of the HDI variable and the control for residence in England.

HDI has the effect of suppressing turnout in the indirect model, and this cancels out the combined or total effects. This is consistent with the fact that many affluent constituencies are geographically close to poorer constituencies, even though clusters of similar constituencies exist. For example, we mentioned earlier that voters in central London may have more in common with their immediate neighbours than with voters in the outer-London suburbs. Nonetheless, affluent constituencies like Westminster North are quite geographically close to much poorer constituencies in the East End of London such as West Ham.[36]

It is noteworthy that the presence of young people and voting to Leave in the referendum have both negative direct and indirect effects on turnout, making them particularly important in the total effects section of the table. These findings suggest that as far as turnout is concerned modelling which focuses purely on the direct effects, the traditional approach, is likely to provide a misleading picture. There are clearly spill-over effects from surrounding constituencies which influence electoral participation in a given constituency. As discussed earlier, many parliamentary constituencies are artificial communities and so the influence of adjacent constituencies is strong.

The Brexit issue was very much a matter of national concern and so it does not surprise that its effects cross electoral boundaries. With respect to the youth vote, one explanation of the strong indirect effects is that relationships between the young operate beyond constituency

---

[35] The estimates were obtained using spatial autoregression commands in STATA15 (particularly spregress). These take into account the effects of the predictor variables in surrounding constituencies but also the relationship with error terms in the constituency equations. These are included in the modelling in order to take into account variables which are not in the model, but which can influence relationships across constituencies. See Appendix B.

[36] Average incomes in Westminster were £54,090 compared with £27,682 in West Ham.

Table 7.4 *Spatial Autoregressive Models of Constituency-Level Turnout and Party Support in the 2019 General Election*

Predictors	Turnout	Labour Voting	Conservative Voting
Direct Effects			
Human Development Index	0.74***	−0.54***	0.36**
Percentage Aged 18–29	−0.34***	0.27***	−0.25***
Percentage Voting to Leave	−0.22***	−0.37***	0.52***
Population Density	−0.21***	0.25***	−0.19***
England	0.53***	−0.24	0.60***
Scotland	−0.40*	−1.13***	−0.37*
Indirect Effects			
Human Development Index	−1.85*	−1.58***	3.06**
Percentage Aged 18–29	−2.09*	1.14***	−3.60***
Percentage Voting to Leave	−3.24*	−2.37**	5.48*
Population Density	0.27	−0.83***	2.73*
England	−0.66**	0.95***	−0.97*
Scotland	−4.67*	−1.95**	6.1*
Total Effects			
Human Development Index	−1.11	−2.13***	3.42**
Percentage Aged 18–29	−2.43*	1.41***	−3.85**
Percentage Voting to Leave	−3.46*	−2.74***	6.00*
Population Density	0.06	−0.58**	2.53*
England	−0.13	0.71***	−0.37
Scotland	−5.07*	−3.09***	5.73*
Pseudo R^2	0.76	0.75	0.75
AIC	840.1	808.9	747.6

Note: †: $p \leq 0.10$; *: $p \leq 0.05$, **: $p \leq 0.01$; ***: $p \leq 0.001$, one-tailed test.

boundaries in a way which is less true for the middle-aged and elderly. This is because the young are more likely to use social media and the Internet more generally for political information than their older counterparts. The Internet diffuses geographically-based political effects more widely, whereas the political community for older people is more local and driven by face-to-face interactions. The implication is that as political communication on the Internet becomes ubiquitous across all age groups, then indirect effects will become stronger in the future.

The Labour voting spatial autoregression model appears in the third column of Table 7.4. Once again, the direct effects are very similar to those in Figure 7.12, but the indirect effects are also important. The HDI has a negative impact on Labour voting, as does Brexit, and concentrations of young people and a densely populated area increase support for the party. The indirect effects reinforce the direct effects except for population density and the control variable for residence in England.

In the total-effects model, the impacts of HDI and Brexit are therefore strong and rather similar in magnitude. The latter hints at the possibility that Brexit may still be important issue in an early election in the future, but the HDI effect could well cancel this out, particularly if the Government's 'levelling up' agenda turns out to be ineffective.

The Conservative voting model appears in the fourth column of Table 7.4 and it is largely a mirror image of the Labour model. The HDI effect is positive in both the direct and indirect models, producing a strong positive overall impact. A similar point can be made about the Brexit vote, where the total effect is particularly strong, indicating this variable was significant for explaining the Conservative victory in 2019. The youth vote is strongly negative in both the direct and indirect models, producing a large total effect. But the indirect positive population density measure offsets the direct negative effect, producing an overall positive effect in the analysis. Finally, the Conservatives did better in Scotland in comparison with Labour.

We have observed that the EU referendum vote played a role in explaining both turnout and party support in the 2019 general election. Both the direct and indirect effects had a significant impact on voting for Labour and the Conservatives, but with opposite signs. The results in Table 7.4 suggest that the effect was particularly important for the Conservatives and, as the earlier discussion indicated, this draws attention to the possible longevity of the Brexit effect. To probe this further, we can reverse the causal story and ask the question: did voting behaviour in the 2015 general election influence voting in the EU referendum a year later? This can help identify how long any Brexit effect might last and so we investigate this next.

Party Support and the 2016 European Union Referendum

In the 2016 EU referendum campaign, the official position of both Labour and the Conservative parties was to support Remain.[37] Prime Minister David Cameron had called the referendum and he strongly campaigned for Britain to stay in the EU. But leading Conservatives such as Boris Johnston and the former party leader Iain Duncan Smith campaigned to leave. This meant that the party was badly split on the issue, even though its official position was to stay in the EU.

On the Labour side, Jeremy Corbyn became the party leader in September 2015 after Ed Miliband stepped down. As a party, Labour was

---

[37] Clarke, Goodwin and Whiteley (2017).

much more in favour of remaining in the EU than the Conservatives, but a few Labour MPs such as Gisela Stuart and Frank Field none-theless joined the Leave campaign. Jeremy Corbyn had been a lifelong Eurosceptic, despite Labour's commitment to stay in the EU, and his contribution to the campaign was rather low-key, something criticized by many Remain supporters at the time. So Labour was also split during the referendum campaign, but not so badly as the Conservatives.

In contrast, the minor parties such as the Liberal Democrats and the Nationalists were enthusiastically in favour of remaining in the EU, while UKIP, which achieved a vote share of nearly 13 per cent in the 2015 general election, was strongly in favour of leaving. As far as the voters were concerned, Conservative supporters tended to favour leav-ing the EU, and Labour and Liberal Democrat supporters tended to support staying.[38] That said, as we observed earlier, Conservative voters have higher occupational status and incomes than Labour voters, and this demographic profile was a positive predictor of Remain voting at the time.[39] So the effects of individual voters' support for the two major parties on their referendum vote are rather ambiguous.

Table 7.5 shows relationships between the vote shares for the national parties in the 2015 general election and the percentage voting to Leave in the subsequent EU referendum.[40] There are two models, one for Labour and the second for the Conservatives, with both including support for minor parties. This is done because the correlation between Labour and the Conservative vote shares in elections at the constituency level is very strongly negative. This creates technical problems for estimating a single model which contains both variables.[41]

An interesting finding in the analysis in Table 7.5 is that while the Labour and Conservative direct effects accord with expectations with the Labour vote reducing and the Conservative vote increasing support for leaving the EU, the direct effects are much weaker than the indirect effects. It is also the case that the Labour voting effect is roughly half that of the Conservative voting effect in both the direct and indirect ver-sions. The implication is that voting in the 2015 general election was significantly associated with support for Leaving in the EU referendum, but the key statistical effects were much broader than at the constituency level alone, making diffusion very important.

---

[38] Clarke, Goodwin and Whiteley (2017), p. 83.
[39] Clarke, Goodwin and Whiteley (2017).
[40] There are not enough constituencies in Scotland or in Wales to estimate the spatial autoregressive models for the nationalist parties and so they are omitted from the analysis.
[41] The correlation between them is r = −0.76 which creates multicollinearity in the model-ling making it difficult to get accurate estimates.

Table 7.5 *Effects of Voting in the 2015 General Election on Voting to Leave in the 2016 European Union Referendum*

Predictors	Voting to Leave: Labour Model	Voting to Leave: Conservative Model
Direct Effects		
Labour Vote Share	−0.04*	----
Conservative Vote Share	----	0.09***
Liberal Democrat Vote Share	−0.09***	−0.02
Green Vote Share	−0.89***	−0.89***
UKIP Vote Share	1.08***	1.09***
Turnout	−0.20***	−0.29***
Indirect Effects		
Labour Vote Share	−0.24**	----
Conservative Vote Share	----	0.40*
Liberal Democrat Vote Share	−0.31†	1.16†
Green Vote Share	−1.81†	−2.94*
UKIP Vote Share	0.51	0.42
Turnout	0.15	−0.32†
Total Effects		
Labour Vote Share	−0.28***	----
Conservative Vote Share	---	0.49**
Liberal Democrat Vote Share	−0.41	1.15†
Green Vote Share	−2.69*	−3.82**
UKIP Vote Share	1.59***	1.51***
Turnout	−0.05	−0.61**
Pseudo R^2	0.80	0.79
AIC	3335.9	3323.3

Note: †: $p \leq 0.10$, *: $p \leq 0.05$, **: $p \leq 0.01$; ***: $p \leq 0.001$, one-tailed test.

The Liberal Democrats were an exception to this pattern with the direct effects of voting for the party reducing the Leave vote in the referendum as expected, but the indirect effects were negligible. Overall, although high levels of support for the party in 2015 were associated with a reduced Leave vote in the referendum, something which was also true for the Greens. Interestingly the strongest total effect for any party was for the Greens, with a bigger effect on Leave voting than Labour or the Liberal Democrats. That said, their relatively small vote shares across constituencies meant that this did not have a big impact on the outcome of the referendum.

Not surprisingly, the UKIP vote share was associated with enhanced support for Leave in the referendum, with the direct effect being stronger than the indirect effect. With an average vote share approaching 13 per cent in the 2015 general election, the party played a key role in swinging the referendum towards the Leave victory. In the total Conservative model, the Leave effect was about three times smaller than in the UKIP total model, which is not surprising given that the latter party was identified with one single issue in the minds of the voters.

These differences between direct and indirect effects for the political parties suggest that diffusion which was likely to be strong in the EU referendum campaign was much more important for the two major parties than for the minor parties. The implication is that the Liberal Democrats, Greens and UKIP relied more on constituency-based campaigns than the two major parties. The 'ground war' involving local campaigning was more important for these parties than for Labour and the Conservatives, who could rely more on the 'air war' or the national campaign in the EU referendum.

Conclusion: Fragmentation and Polarization

Analyses of the geography of the vote in Britain presented in this chapter testify that electoral politics in Britain have become more fragmented and more polarized over time. The impact of occupational status as a proxy measure for social class has greatly weakened at the individual level during this period, but a more broadly defined measure of community social and economic characteristics captured by the Human Development Index is still a very strong predictor of both Labour and Conservative voting. If we go beyond narrowly defined versions of social class and look at broader aspects of human welfare, then the Human Development index is an important factor in constituency electoral politics.

Spatial modelling does not fundamentally change this picture, although it does establish that constituency-level party support is significantly influenced by the demographic and spatial characteristics of surrounding constituencies. Geographical distance is only an imperfect measure of political communities that we are seeking to identify. But the measure is clearly important, making any statistical exercise based on individual constituencies alone inaccurate.

The analyses in Chapter 6 and in the present chapter point in the direction of a more polarized society and greater fragmentation of the party system over both time and space. The important question is what these developments do to the quality of British democracy. Arguably, they imply a weakening of the effectiveness of democratic representation and also a reduction in the effectiveness and quality of governance. We take up these questions in the next chapter.

8   Who is Responsible?
The Dynamics of Accountability

Are UK governments accountable to the electorate, or is there now a deep gulf between what the voters want and what governments deliver? If so, this denotes a considerable weakening of the quality of democracy in Britain. This is perhaps the most important question facing British politics at the present time, particularly in the aftermath of the Brexit negotiations and the Covid-19 crisis. Governmental accountability in modern democracies crucially depends on elections.[1] Theories of representative democracy support the idea that elections are the most important mechanism for citizens to incentivize governments and politicians to deliver on the promises they make.[2] The question is: does this accountability mechanism work effectively in Britain today?

This issue has been highlighted by the gap between public opinion and Parliament over the issue of Britain's membership of the European Union following the referendum vote in 2016. As mentioned in Chapter 1, a large majority (75.2 per cent) of MPs (479 of 637) who declared their views sided with Remain during the early part of the referendum campaign,[3] whereas Leave supporters in the electorate won the referendum vote by 51.9 per cent to 48.1 per cent. This huge difference between elite and mass opinion turned out to be a key driver of the subsequent turmoil over Brexit and brought frequent accusations from the Leave camp that Parliament was trying to subvert the expressed will of the people. This was after Theresa May's Conservative government had promised to accept and implement the voters' decision when the Bill which gave legal force to the referendum was passed. In Prime Minister May's enigmatic phraseology: 'Brexit means Brexit.'

More than a generation ago, political scientist Robert Dahl's influential writing on modern representative democracy emphasized the importance of 'the ongoing responsiveness of the government to the preferences of

---

[1] See Bernard, Przerworski and Stokes (1999).
[2] See, e.g., Urbinati (2005) and Urbinati and Warren (2008).
[3] Clarke, Goodwin and Whiteley (2017), p. 30.

its citizens, considered as political equals'.[4] Dahl proposed an elaborate set of requirements for democracy to work properly including 'effective participation', 'enlightened understanding', and 'control of the agenda'.[5] It was a formidable checklist, but in an optimistic era when the world's democracies were growing in number and influence, it set out a normative blueprint of what an ideal-type democracy would look like. Real-world political systems could aspire to meet these conditions even if on occasions they fell short.

In a recent book, two widely cited American political scientists, Christopher Achen and Larry Bartels[6], reached rather pessimistic conclusions about the state of representative democracy in the United States, which sharply contradict the standards proposed by Dahl. Their analysis of the role of elections reaches the following conclusion: 'Election outcomes turn out to be largely random events from the viewpoint of contemporary democratic theory. That is, elections are well determined by powerful forces, but these forces are not the ones that current theories of democracy believe should determine how elections come out.'[7] They suggest that: '[o]ur view is that conventional thinking about democracy has collapsed in the face of modern social scientific research.'[8] According to Achen and Bartels, none of Dahl's stringent requirements for democracy to function effectively actually operate in the United States. Crucially, they believe that American voters are too ignorant and disinterested to make effective government accountability possible.

The 2016 UK referendum did not settle the question of Britain's membership in the European Union, as the subsequent protracted and rancorous controversies surrounding the Brexit negotiations made clear. The fact that the result was so close made these debates all the more contentious. Claims that Leavers did not know what they were voting for were repeatedly used to justify the call for a second referendum – designated as a 'People's Vote' by its proponents – and assertions that both campaigns misled the public suggest that the 'enlightened understanding' called for by Dahl was far removed from reality. Both major parties were split on the Brexit issue, prompting many to conclude that they had failed to provide the clear-cut choices that the voters wanted.

The aim of this chapter is to evaluate the claim that political accountability is failing in modern Britain and that elections do not properly fulfil the task assigned to them by Dahl and other democratic theorists

---

[4] Dahl (1971).
[5] Dahl (1998), pp. 37–38.
[6] Achen and Bartels (2016).
[7] Achen and Bartels (2016), p. 2.
[8] Achen and Bartels (2016), p. 12.

of keeping governments responsive to the voters. To address this large topic, we narrow the focus and examine economic voting, which studies the relationship between economic performance and government support. As discussed in earlier chapters, the performance of the economy is typically a key issue that does much to drive voters' decisions in successive national elections in Britain and elsewhere. Research on the impact of economic conditions on electoral choice extends back more than fifty years and has produced a huge assortment of academic books and articles.[9] The central question posed is: do voters hold governments accountable for their performance in managing the economy? The answer to this question can do much to help us understand the wider issue of government accountability in modern Britain.

How Does Economic Accountability Work?

We start by introducing two distinctions drawn from the literature on economic voting. The first is between retrospective and prospective economic performance – do voters look backwards or forwards when they make judgements about the state of the economy?[10] A second is between egocentric and sociotropic evaluations. Egocentric evaluations involve voters prioritizing their personal financial circumstances whereas sociotropic evaluations emphasize the state of the national economy as a whole.[11]

There are many important findings about the nature of economic voting, and it is beyond the scope of this chapter to review the whole field. But to consider just a few, we know that retrospective and sociotropic indicators of economic voting appear to outperform prospective and egocentric measures when it comes to influencing voting decisions.[12] We also know that the weakening of partisanship discussed in Chapter 6 has strengthened economic voting in many countries.[13] Similarly, while early studies suggested that voters are relatively ignorant about the state of the economy and, by implication, cannot be expected to make informed decisions about government economic management,[14] recent research indicates that this argument has been overstated. As we shall see, voters can acquire a lot of information about the economy in their everyday lives.[15]

---

[9] Nannestad and Paldam (1994); Lewis-Beck and Stegmaier (2013).
[10] Lewis Beck (1988).
[11] Kinder and Kiewiet (1981); Lewis-Beck (1988).
[12] Anderson (2000); Lewis-Beck, Nadeau and Foucault (2013).
[13] Kayser and Wlezien (2011).
[14] See, e.g., Converse (1964); Delli Carpini and Keeter (1996);Lupia and McCubbins (1998); Lupia (2016).
[15] Clarke, Goodwin and Whiteley (2017).

Not surprisingly, media coverage is an important factor influencing how voters react to the economy.[16] But there is a question about whether such coverage is accurate and understandable enough for the public to make sound judgements.[17] Equally, an important finding from comparative analyses of accountability shows that the clarity of the responsibility of the incumbent government for economic decision-making makes a difference.[18] In countries where coalition governments are the norm, accountability is obscured by the fact that it is shared between several parties. But in the Westminster system where one-party government is the norm, clarity of responsibility is brought into much sharper focus. These are just a few examples of the findings in this field.

Research on economic voting is characterized by a number of long-lived controversies. One debate concerns the relationship between perceptions of the economy and partisanship. It has been suggested that economic voting largely reflects the voters' partisan predispositions rather than the actual state of the economy.[19] The argument is that voters are likely to think that the economy is performing better when their preferred party is in power and worse when it is in opposition. In statistical terms, economic evaluations are strongly endogenous and their apparent effects in models of the vote are largely spurious. Such evaluations reflect the effects of other explanatory variables instead of making sizeable independent contributions to understanding why voters choose one party rather than another.

This controversy has produced a lively debate among researchers with evidence being produced on both sides of the argument. Van der Brug and his collaborators have gone so far as to suggest that subjective judgements about the economy based on questions in surveys should not be used in the modelling since they: 'are strongly contaminated and subject to severe endogeneity problems'.[20] For this reason they focus exclusively on objective measures of economic performance such as rates of unemployment and inflation. In contrast, Duch and Stevenson take the opposite view and focus entirely on subjective economic evaluations.[21] Recent research suggests that the endogeneity problem has been exaggerated, a topic we will discuss more fully below.

A typical example of a survey question used to elicit subjective judgements of the economy is: 'How do you think the general economic

---

[16] See, e.g., Hetherington (1996) and Sanders (2000).
[17] See, e.g., Iyengar (1991) and Soroka (2006).
[18] Powell and Whitten (1993).
[19] Wlezien, Franklin and Twiggs (1997); Evans and Andersen (2006).
[20] van der Brug, van der Eijk and Franklin (2007).
[21] Duch and Stevenson (2008).

situation in this country has changed over the last 12 months? Has it: got a lot better, got a little better, stayed the same, got a little worse, got a lot worse?' This question aims to identify retrospective-sociotropic evaluations of the economy and is used in conjunction with other indicators to provide information about the state of the 'subjective' economy in voters' minds.

Another controversy concerns the relationship between the objective and subjective economies, a topic which has been relatively neglected in the literature. This is very important for deciding whether subjective judgements are real or merely reflect people's partisan predispositions. If subjective judgements closely track objective measures like unemployment and inflation, this weakens the argument that they are merely a reflection of voters' partisan predispositions.

In fact, there is no shortage of evidence to show that subjective economic evaluations do closely track objective measures if responses are aggregated to the national level and compared with statistics such as unemployment or growth rates.[22] In addition, while partisanship may influence people's subjective judgements about the economy, it also appears to be influenced in turn by objective economic conditions. Relationships among these measures appear to be quite complicated and need to be untangled if they are to be properly understood.[23]

The latter point raises the important issue of causal relationships between the subjective and objective economies over time. As we shall see, they appear to track each other, but this does not identify which is the cause and which is the effect. Is economic growth making people more optimistic about the economy, or is economic optimism driving up economic growth? The almost universal assumption in the economic voting literature is that the objective economy drives the subjective economy, a view encouraged by early findings that the latter have a stronger effect on voting behaviour than the former.[24]

This is a convenient assumption to make, since it justifies omitting objective variables like the growth rate from models if their only effect on voting works via the subjective variables. The relationships can be captured entirely by what individuals think about the state of the economy if it is true. Another advantage of this assumption is that the relationship between the economy and voting can be modelled using cross-sectional survey data at one point of time. However, if objective economic variables

[22] Lewis-Beck, Nadeau and Foucault (2013); Whiteley, Clarke, Sanders and Stewart (2016); Curtin (2019).
[23] Whiteley and Kölln (2018).
[24] Lewis-Beck (1988).

are driven in part by the subjective measures then longitudinal data is required to identify effects, since at any one point of time variables like the unemployment rate or growth are constants.

Another important debate concerns the nature of voter decision-making when individuals are using information about the economy to make voting choices, an issue which raises broader questions in the social sciences. The problem is that much of this research makes unrealistic assumptions about the way voters make up their minds. This is a legacy of the use of rational choice models of decision-making exemplified by the popularity in political science of the work of Anthony Downs. His much-cited book on economic models of democracy influenced decades of subsequent research.[25] He adopted the expected-utility model of decision-making adopted from neoclassical economics to describe how voters cast their ballots. According to this model, voters should calculate their 'party differential' when deciding how to vote, i.e., the utility or satisfaction arising from one party being elected compared with another. He writes:

> In order to find his current party differential, a voter in a two-party system must do the following: (1) examine all phases of government action to find out where the two parties would behave differently, (2) discover how each difference would affect his utility income, and (3) aggregate the difference in utility and arrive at a net figure which shows by how much one party would be better than the other. This is how a rational voter would behave in a world of complete and costless information – the same world in which dwell the rational consumer and the rational producer of traditional economic theory.[26]

Expected utility theory provides a *normative* account of decision-making, purporting to describe how individuals should make decisions, as opposed to understanding how they actually do make them. Two leading economists have recently described this approach as 'axiomatic rationality'.[27] In fact, the model bears little relationship to the way people actually do decide when they vote, or for that matter make decisions in general.[28] Downs recognizes that the expected-utility model is a simplification of reality, but it is nonetheless fundamental to his analysis and continues to dominate much of the work on spatial theories of electoral politics.[29]

The polymath social scientist, Herbert Simon, first challenged this model a half-century ago when he introduced the concept of 'bounded

[25] Downs (1957).
[26] Downs (1957), pp. 45–46.
[27] Kay and King (2020).
[28] See Whiteley (2022).
[29] See, e.g., Merrill and Grofman (1999).

rationality' into the analysis of choice in general.[30] In his approach, decision-makers seek solutions which they find satisfactory rather than those which are optimal, and for this reason it is described as 'satisficing'. More recently a great deal of work has been done on the psychology of decision-making under uncertainty, which has identified many shortcomings in the expected utility model.[31]

The main rival to expected-utility theory is the theory of heuristics. As the discussion in earlier chapters indicates, heuristics are 'cues' – rules of thumb or shortcuts in reasoning which enable decisions to be made in real-world situations of ignorance and uncertainty. In the context of voting behaviour, the idea of heuristics was first introduced by Samuel Popkin who investigated their role in presidential voting in the United States. He wrote: 'The term low information rationality – popularly known as "gut reasoning" – best describes the kind of practical thinking about government and politics in which people actually engage.'[32] He cites the *partisanship* heuristic as an example of a shortcut in which voters draw on feelings of loyalty and attachment to political parties to help them decide how to cast their ballots, a topic we discussed earlier in the book.

Another example, also discussed earlier, is the *leader* heuristic whereby electors use their reactions to party leaders in terms of likeability and perceptions of their competence and responsiveness. If voters like a leader then they are likely to voter for the leader's party. The leader heuristic plays an important role in economic voting since economic conditions have a direct effect on leadership evaluations, and these in turn affect voting behaviour.[33] Other policies linked to the economy such as public spending and taxation are also relevant. These ideas are linked to the *valence model* of electoral choice discussed in previous chapters, since valence judgements are grounded in the heuristics approach to understanding voter decision-making.[34] The key heuristic underlying the valence model is governmental performance. It focuses on the question: is the incumbent government delivering what voters want in key policy areas such as the economy, healthcare and personal and national security?

A leading advocate of the heuristics approach to decision-making is the psychologist Gerd Gigerenzer who introduced the idea of 'fast and frugal' heuristics. He describes this in the following terms: 'A heuristic is fast if it can solve a problem in little time and frugal if it can solve it

---

[30] Simon (1957); Conlisk (1996).
[31] Kahneman (2011).
[32] Popkin (1991).
[33] Clarke, Sanders, Stewart and Whiteley (2004), p. 119.
[34] Clarke, Sanders, Stewart and Whiteley (2009), pp. 30–52.

with little information .... Heuristics work in real world environments of natural complexity, where an optimal strategy is often unknown or computationally intractable.'[35] In the world of electoral politics, 'fast and frugal' heuristics involve voters using readily available information to help them evaluate government performance. For example, when they see prices rising when they are shopping or purchasing petrol for their cars, they get a sense of the rate of inflation. Similarly, their pay packets tell them about their own financial situation, which is one of the elements driving the subjective economy. Equally, the state of the local job market illuminates national unemployment rates.

Other unobtrusive measures which help to provide information about the economy are the number of empty premises on the high street as a guide to a possible recession, the condition of local roads as an indicator of public spending on transport, and the time it takes to get a doctor's appointment in the NHS which provides information about health spending. There is also the experience of unemployment in one's family and friendship groups as an indicator of an economic slowdown. Equally, interest rates directly affect voters' mortgage payments or any bank loans they might hold and so provide a measure of the state of monetary policy and the housing market. Finally, media reporting on the local economy helps them to gauge the state of the economy nationally.

Achen and Bartels take issue with the idea that economic voting provides effective government accountability.[36] They make two arguments: first, they question whether the US electorate has any sense of what presidents can do to influence the economy, citing evidence that this is widely misunderstood. Americans tend to think that the president has more power over the economy than is the case. Second, Achen and Bartels point out that voters are myopic and inclined to judge the economy in the short term rather than over an entire presidential term. A related aspect of this myopia is that voters appear to focus on retrospective evaluations rather than prospective evaluations of economic performance. The former face the 'sunk costs' fallacy, which is that the past cannot be changed and so a rational actor should focus entirely on the future where improvements might be possible.

It is clear that Achen and Bartels' criticisms are based on an implicit acceptance of the expected – utility model of decision-making. Many researchers continue to see this as the 'gold standard' model and some are actively hostile to the idea of heuristics.[37] Others recognize the

---

[35] Gigerenzer (2008), p. 7.
[36] Achen and Bartels (2016), pp. 146–176.
[37] Kuklinski and Quirk (2000).

expected-utility model's limitations but nonetheless see decision-making in the real world as a failure to follow the ideal which is distorted by various considerations.[38] However, as Gigerenzer notes, there are numerous psychological experiments in which the heuristic model outperforms optimization strategies. His comprehensive critique shows how the expected-utility model is intractable in most natural situations, will not work with multiple goals or imprecise subjective criteria, is not feasible when problems are unfamiliar or time is short, and does not guarantee that an optimal outcome is actually achieved.[39] The growth of behavioural economics based on experimental studies of decision-making has added to growing scepticism about the usefulness of the classical expected-utility model despite its continuing dominance in economic theory.[40]

An additional problem for the expected-utility model is that the key assumption that voters have well-defined preferences for policies which parties then try to deliver is misleading. In a series of case studies of policymaking in the United States, Canada, Britain and the Netherlands, Gabriel Lenz demonstrates that this is not the case.[41] Rather, the process appears to work in reverse, with voters choosing parties and leaders largely as a result of their past performance in delivering desirable outcomes in highly prioritized policy areas. Once voters have done this, they then tend to adopt the policy positions advocated by these leaders and parties. In other words, voters follow leaders rather than leaders following voters. This is consistent with a heuristics model of decision-making but is wholly inconsistent with the expected-utility model.

It should be noted that rational choice advocates often assert that the theory is not intended to provide a realistic account of decision-making. In an influential book, the Nobel Prize–winning economist Milton Friedman advocated the 'as if' assumption in models of economic decision-making.[42] His argument is that assumptions are irrelevant in economic theory and can be completely unrealistic providing that the model accurately predicts outcomes in the real world. This implies that we can assume that people will behave according to the tenets of expected-utility theory even if they fail to provide a realistic depiction of how people actually make decisions. The 'as if' view is now widely criticized, but it nonetheless justifies axiomatic rationality.[43] While rational

[38] Shiller (2019) argues that rational behaviour is distorted by narratives or stories of various kinds which distort the judgements of investors.
[39] Gigerenzer (2008), pp. 80–91.
[40] Baddley (2013).
[41] Lenz (2012).
[42] Friedman (1953).
[43] Maki (2009).

choice models have been dominant for decades in economics, they were late coming to political science. When they gained prominence in the latter field, a rancorous debate took place between advocates of this approach and their opponents.[44]

A recurring theme in support of rational choice accounts is that the 'as if' assumption is justified by a Darwinian process of natural selection. The idea here is that anything less than an optimal utility-maximizing strategy will be eliminated by evolutionary processes, so we end up with optimization even if the mechanisms involved are obscure. However, recent work in neuroscience suggests that this argument is incorrect. This is because there is a clear difference between optimization strategies and evolutionary decision-making.

In a cleverly designed study, psychologists Mark, Marion and Hoffman use simulations to estimate the extent to which 'truth strategies' defeat 'survival strategies' in an evolutionary game.[45] The former require that actors see the world as it is, an obviously crucial requirement in rational choice accounts. In contrast, survival strategies only require limited attention to objective reality just so long as it ensures survival. The latter, for example, give rise to the well-known phenomenon that humans are more likely to pay attention to negative news which might be a potential threat to their survival than positive news which does not put survival at stake.[46] This analysis shows clearly that human decision-making ignores objective reality if it does not have survival value.

The criticisms by Achen and Bartels lose their relevance once the expected utility model is replaced by heuristics as a theoretical approach to voter decision-making. If political leaders influence the state of the economy even if they do not directly steer it, then it is reasonable for voters to hold them responsible. This is analogous to football fans calling for the manager to be sacked when their team repeatedly loses. They do not need to know the details of the manager's strategy and tactics or his relationship with the players and the club owners to reach this conclusion. A fast and frugal heuristic is to replace the manager who they hold responsible for the losing streak. There is no elaborate expected-utility calculation which can give any sensible guidance to decision-making in this situation, so they opt for a simple strategy, which often proves accurate in practice.

Economist Richard Curtin has incorporated subjective measures of the economy into mainstream macroeconomic theory. He demonstrates

---

[44] Hindess (1988); Tsebelis (1990).
[45] Mark, Marion and Hoffman (2010).
[46] Soroka and McAdams (2015).

that ordinary US citizens do as good a job at forecasting the performance of the economy as experts.[47] He writes: 'The new paradigm holds that most economic expectations are formed by nonconscious cognitive activity. Conscious deliberation, however, is likely to dominate when people initially learn to form a specific expectation, or when there is a sudden change in the underlying economic circumstances and in other unusual situations.'[48] This argument is that reasoning based on people's everyday experience, much of it subliminal, provides individuals with the ability to forecast future economic conditions, and this works equally well as expert models based on economic theory.[49]

This interpretation is consistent with recent work on the psychology of decision-making. For example, Nobel Prize–winner Daniel Kahneman argues that there are two modes of thinking: 'Fast and Slow', the first being largely unconscious and rapid, dealing with routine problems, the second being more conscious and deliberative, which takes over in situations of uncertainty and threat.[50] Axiomatic rationality has nothing to say about unconscious reasoning since it operates entirely in the 'slow' mode of conscious cognitive calculations and logical inference.

One of the key problems of 'slow' thinking is that it prevents people from reacting to new information and considering alternative approaches to a problem because they are heavily preoccupied with a complex task. This was vividly illustrated in an experiment by psychologists Chabris and Simons.[51] They asked various subjects to view a video recording of a basketball game and count the number of passes made by one of the teams during the game. This is a demanding task requiring close attention to detail and extensive use of slow thinking. When asked to report on what they had observed, more than half of the subjects did not notice a woman wearing a gorilla suit crossing the court during the game, even though she was on camera for a total of nine seconds. In effect, slow thinking blinded them.

We can judge the success of axiomatic reasoning by examining the performance of macroeconomic forecasting models in Britain, since

---

[47] Curtin (2019).
[48] Curtin (2019), pp. 310–311.
[49] Curtin tries to retain the rational expectations version of the expected utility model in his analysis by arguing that aggregate expectations are a good guide to outcomes when it comes to public forecasts of inflation and unemployment and so individuals must be rational maximizers. However, his analysis suffers from the ecological fallacy, the assumption that collective outcomes are an accurate guide to individual behaviour. Individual behaviour cannot be inferred from aggregate correlations without additional assumptions. See, e.g., Robinson (1940) and King (1997).
[50] Kahneman (2011).
[51] Chabris and Simons (2010).

they are all based on expected-utility theory. In fact, the popular NiGem model is based on rational expectations, an extreme version of the theory which assumes that all actors abide by a neoclassical economic model in the long run, even though they might make mistakes in the short run.[52] In fact, the evidence suggests that these models have a very poor record in predicting economic performance.[53] This is true for both the Treasury as well as the Office for Budget Responsibility, which is now largely responsible for government forecasting.

In the next section we turn to the task of understanding relationships between the economy and public opinion, as a means of understanding how government accountability in Britain actually works viewed through the lens of heuristic reasoning.

Modelling Economic Accountability

We have reviewed important controversies in the literature on economic voting and now consider how accountability works in practice. We focus on the relationship between the objective and subjective economies and public support for governments in Britain over the forty-six-year period from 1974 to 2020. This long-running time series provides insight into enduring relationships between these variables, something which is much less easy to identify with data gathered over a limited period.[54]

We introduce an important distinction at this point which is relevant for understanding the heuristics which drive economic voting. This is the *visibility* of economic variables to the public, a key issue in heuristic reasoning. Visible variables are those which play a prominent role in the day-to-day lives of ordinary people and which are reported widely in the media. Note that visibility does not mean that individuals know the precise rate of economic growth, the numbers of unemployed in Britain or the exact rate of inflation at a given point of time. Precise knowledge is not required to identify if the economy is buoyant or stagnant or improving or deteriorating. Voters will pick up reasonably accurate impressions using the various 'fast and frugal' heuristics discussed earlier. This will then translate into optimistic or pessimistic expectations about the future and help to shape judgements about the performance of the incumbent government.

---

[52] Lucas and Sargent (1981). For the NiGEM econometric model of the British economy see: https://nimodel.niesr.ac.uk

[53] Whiteley and Clarke (2020).

[54] Details of the sources and measures, together with other technical information about the modelling, appear in Appendices A and B.

Visibility means that the public may have a biased sense of what drives economic performance since, if a variable is not visible, it will not be considered when judging the state of the economy. An example of this is economic openness or the amount of trade between Britain and the rest of the world. This is an important variable in models of economic growth,[55] but it is unlikely to attract much attention from the public. A similar point can be made about labour productivity, which also has an important influence on growth but is not at all obvious to the average voter. However, the extent to which this distortion matters depends on the relevance of the visible measures for identifying how the economy is doing.

One simple way of assessing visibility is to look at the extent to which the economy figures as an important issue in the minds of voters during election campaigns. As we observed in Chapter 3, in the 2017 general election, 40 per cent of respondents thought that the economy was one of the top three most important issues facing the country at that time (see Figure 3.7). Moreover, as Figure 5.4 in Chapter 5 shows, this did not change two years later, even though the 2019 general election campaign was dominated by the Brexit issue.

A further test of visibility is the extent to which the subjective and objective economic variables are correlated with each other. Low correlations denote weak perceptions on the part of the public of the actual state of the economy, whereas strong correlations have the opposite interpretation. Here, we employ economic growth, inflation and unemployment as indicators of the objective economy, using quarterly data.[56] This yields a total of 185 observations altogether from the first quarter of 1974 to the first quarter of 2020. The subjective economy is captured by the index of consumer confidence which is derived from surveys conducted by the OECD and represents a composite measure of retrospective and prospective evaluations of the state of the economy.[57]

The first task is to examine the dynamics of these variables over this long period before making comparisons between them. Figure 8.1 shows trends in voting intentions for Labour and the Conservatives. There are some striking fluctuations in support for the two parties reflecting events we have discussed in previous chapters. Labour was in office at the start and suffered from the inflationary surge caused by the rise in oil prices

---

[55] Acemoglu (2009).

[56] Economic growth has been reported quarterly in the Office for National Statistics databases until very recently, which explains the use of quarterly data over this long period. Inflation and unemployment are reported monthly and so they are averaged by quarters in the analysis.

[57] https://data.oecd.org/leadind/consumer-confidence-index-cci.htm

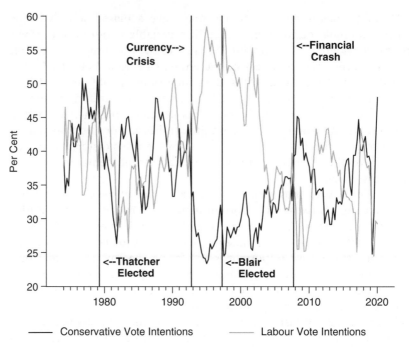

Figure 8.1 Conservative and Labour Vote Intentions, 1974Q1–2020Q1.
Source: See Appendix A.

after the Arab–Israeli war of 1973. Following the Conservative victory in the 1979 general election, Mrs Thatcher's government imposed severe austerity policies on the economy which made her government very unpopular. However, she was rescued by the split in Labour which led to the creation of the Social Democratic Party in 1981 and by victory in the Falklands War in the spring of 1982.[58] These events helped her party achieve a resounding victory in the 1983 general election.

Perhaps the most striking feature of Figure 8.1 is the strength of Labour in the polls following the September 1992 'Black Wednesday' currency crisis. The currency crisis triggered a rapid rise in Labour's popularity in the polls, and together with Tony Blair's victory in the 1994 leadership contest, the party achieved a landslide victory in the 1997 general election. Labour's dominance in the polls then persisted for most of the subsequent decade. However, Labour support rapidly declined after Gordon Brown took over from Tony Blair in June 2007

---

[58] Clarke, Mishler and Whiteley (1990).

and the financial crisis hit later that year. The financial crisis signalled the start of the Great Recession and the effects of this were felt up to the 2010 general election. Labour's defeat in that contest was effectively the end of the New Labour era in British politics. Subsequently, support for the newly elected Conservative–Liberal Democrat coalition government eroded after it embarked on a policy of austerity.[59]

By the time of the 2015 election, the economy had recovered sufficiently to deliver a modest victory for the Conservatives. The hapless Liberal Democrats largely took the blame for the austerity policies and lost the great majority of their MPs in the House of Commons in that election. The EU referendum vote then took place in June 2016 and subsequently British politics was dominated by the Brexit issue. And, as discussed in Chapter 5, Labour subsequently lost ground after it chose Jeremy Corbyn as party leader in 2015 following the 2017 general election.[60]

As the earlier discussion in Chapter 1 showed, Remain's defeat in the referendum triggered a leadership contest in the Conservative Party and Theresa May emerged as the new leader. Negotiations with the European Union followed, and this produced a period of acrimony and turmoil in the relationship between the EU and Mrs May's government. As observed in Chapter 3, May's problems were made worse by her opportunistic decision to call an early election in 2017 that resulted in the Conservatives losing their majority in Parliament. However, as Chapter 4 shows, May soldiered on and only stepped down in June 2019 after the Conservatives' disastrous performance in the EU Parliament elections. Boris Johnson then took over as party leader and delivered a decisive victory for the Conservatives in the December 2019 general election.

Figure 8.2 shows trends in economic growth, inflation and unemployment – the three related measures of the objective economy. It is apparent that inflation was a serious problem in the 1970s and early 1980s. However, it subsequently receded and was at a low level since the Great Recession, which began in 2009 up until the recovery from the Covid-19 pandemic starting in 2022. For its part, economic growth has varied over time, but it appears to be relatively stable in the long run, apart from a few years following the financial crisis. In contrast, the unemployment rate has fluctuated much more than economic growth, and upturns and downturns have occurred periodically. These were apparent in the late 1970s, the early 1980s and the mid-1990s, with a clear spike occurring between 2008 and 2010.

[59] Whiteley, Clarke, Sanders and Stewart (2013).
[60] Whiteley, Seyd and Clarke (2020).

A. Economic Growth

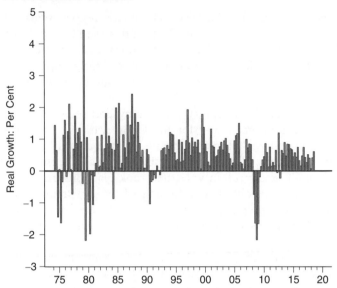

B. Inflation and Unemployment Rates

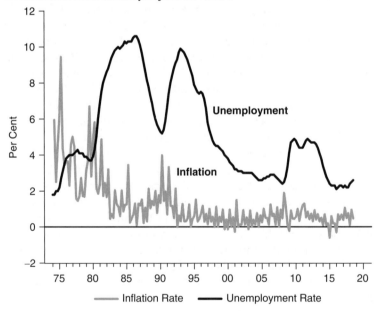

Figure 8.2 Economic Growth, Inflation Rate and Unemployment Rate, 1974Q1–2020Q1 (A) Economic Growth (B) Inflation and Unemployment Rates.
Source: ONS.

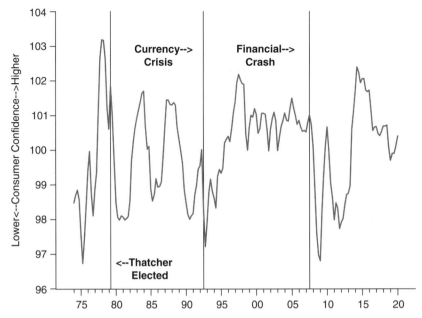

Figure 8.3 Consumer Confidence Index, 1974Q1–2020Q1.
Source: OECD.

Figure 8.3 maps trends in consumer confidence, our key indicator of the subjective economy. The figure shows that consumer confidence tends to fluctuate following prosperity and recession and appears to be quite volatile in comparison with the objective economic variables illustrated in Figure 8.2. A downturn in confidence is often followed by a rapid recovery, such as occurred in the mid-1970s. Again, in the first term of the Thatcher government, which first came to power in 1979, confidence slumped rapidly, as her austerity measures took effect. Based on the theories of the economist Milton Friedman, this 'monetarist experiment' subsequently failed.[61]

The 1997 Labour landslide was accompanied by a significant increase in consumer confidence, which remained high until the 2008 financial crash. Thereafter, confidence became very volatile. It rose after the 2015 general election but then declined, reflecting ongoing economic uncertainty and strident warnings by leading economists and prominent 'Remainers' about the deleterious effects that would ensue if the UK left the EU. The downward trend continued, albeit irregularly, up to the start of 2020.[62]

[61] Desai (1981).
[62] Note that the series ends just before the impact of the coronavirus when the economy was locked down and consumer confidence collapsed.

In the next section, we consider relationships between the measures of the objective and subjective economy.

Relationships Between the Objective and Subjective Economy

One of the problems of dynamic modelling is identifying causal relationship between variables or, in technical terms, identifying which variables are endogenous (being caused) and which are exogenous (causing). As mentioned earlier, the dominant assumption in previous studies is that the objective economy drives the subjective economy. However, this is quite at odds with many years of macroeconomic theory in which economic expectations play a fundamental role in influencing outcomes. This literature suggests that economic expectations defined in the present context by consumer confidence drives the objective economy.

Following the pioneering work of John Maynard Keynes and others, economic expectations have played a central role in explaining macroeconomic performance.[63] In Keynes' view, uncertainty about the future of the economy was the central problem facing policymakers attempting to control the business cycle and avoid damaging recessions of the type which occurred in the 1930s.[64] In 1936 he wrote:

If we speak frankly, we havè to admit that our basis of knowledge for estimating the yield ten years hence of a railway, a copper mine, a textile factory, the goodwill of a patent medicine, an Atlantic liner, a building in the City of London, amounts to little and sometimes to nothing.[65]

Despite this uncertainty, actors are obliged to form expectations to make decisions about investment, consumption, savings and other economic variables. Keynes showed that the failure of these expectations creates coordination problems in the economy that in turn produce instability, business cycles and recessions. One key element in his analysis was identifying a failure of coordination between savings and investment which can seriously destabilize the macroeconomy.[66] At the time, Keynes had no access to reliable data on investor and consumer expectations, so he had to make assumptions about how these worked in practice. For example, he conjectured that rising interest rates would increase investor expectations that rates would subsequently fall in the future.[67]

---

[63] Knight (1921); Keynes (1936); Sims (1980).
[64] Skidelsy (2009).
[65] Keynes (1936), pp. 149–150.
[66] Skidelsky (2009), pp. 83–85.
[67] Keynes (1936), pp. 147–164.

This tradition of making assumptions about economic expectations instead of measuring them in the real world persists to this day in macroeconomic modelling. In the 1970s the so-called rational expectations revolution, sought to solve the coordination problem by assuming that expectations were formed from an optimal neoclassical economic model which all participants shared and fully understood.[68] In effect, this approach ruled out the possibility of persistent systematic errors in expectations by assuming away the problem. More recently, 'New Keynesian' theorists have challenged the neoclassical assumptions underlying the rational expectations analysis by identifying market failures of various kinds that can occur in the economy. These arise from a variety of sources such as imperfect competition, asymmetric information between actors, rigidities in price and in wage adjustments, among other factors.[69]

Perhaps the biggest problem for contemporary macroeconomic modelling is the distinction between risk and uncertainty. The economist Frank Knight first introduced this distinction in 1921.[70] Risk means that a probability distribution of outcomes is known, but specific events are not. For example, we can attach a probability to motorists of a certain age and gender with a given number of years' driving experience being involved in a road accident. However, we cannot know if a particular driver is going to have an accident on a given day. Risks of this type can be incorporated into statistical modelling by averaging large numbers of outcomes over time and are the basis of the insurance industry.

In contrast, uncertainty is a very different concept. In this case, there is no probability distribution of possible outcomes available to model effects. We simply do not know what is going to happen in the future. Despite this, the practice has grown up of defining such uncertainties as risks in financial markets, in the belief that both can be measured by the volatility of indices such as stock prices. However, as the economist John Kay and the former Governor of the Bank of England Mervyn King explained in their recent book:

The erroneous belief that the absence of current volatility demonstrates the absence of risk was at the heart of the financial crisis ... The world is inherently uncertain and to pretend otherwise is to create risk, not to minimise it.[71]

---

[68] Muth (1981) triggered the rational expectations revolution in economics by referring to subjective measures of economic expectations which, as the earlier discussion indicates, do as good a job as experts in forecasting the economy. However, he made the same mistake as Curtin (2019) in inferring from aggregate results that individuals must be highly rational, which is an ecological fallacy.

[69] Mankiw and Romer (1991); Carlin and Soskice (2005).

[70] Knight (1921); Taleb (2007).

[71] Kay and King (2020), p. 422.

Robert Bookstaber, a financial risk management advisor, puts it like this: 'Our unanticipated future experiences, on the one hand, and the complexity of our social interactions, on the other, lead to uncertainty which cannot be expressed or anticipated.'[72] If uncertainty is assumed to be the same as risk in order to make calculations tractable then the resulting models are likely to give misleading answers. Given these considerations, we turn next to the task of modelling the relationship between economic performance and support for governing parties.

Modelling the Political Economy of Party Support

We have suggested that the basis of most human decision-making, particularly in the context of voting, involves the use of heuristics. These can be surprisingly accurate when they are aggregated to the level of society. In fact, research on the 'wisdom of crowds' suggests that voter expectations about which party is likely to win an election are a better predictor of the result than average vote intentions for parties.[73] The 'law of large numbers' can be invoked to explain this – the idea that large numbers of people making different individual judgements will on average get close to the true outcome. The implication is that a few heuristics have a good chance of producing a reliable forecast of an uncertain event even if people use different heuristics at different points of time.

In a landmark article published forty years ago called 'Macroeconomics and Reality', the economist Christopher Sims challenged the orthodox approach to modelling at that time, arguing that it involved making 'incredible' assumptions to estimate effects. He wrote: 'Whether or not one agrees that economic models ought always to assume rational behaviour under uncertainty, i.e., "rational expectations," one must agree that any sensible treatment of expectations is likely to undermine many of the exclusion restrictions econometricians had been used to thinking of as most reliable.'[74]

Sims introduced the statistical technique of Vector Autoregression (VAR) to macroeconomic modellers. This approach allows relationships in a dynamic system of equations to be estimated without having to make restrictive and unrealistic assumptions about the causal relationships in the system.[75] VAR focuses on identifying relationships in the data by analysing the effects of the history of one variable on the

---

[72] Bookstaber (2017).
[73] Murr (2011).
[74] Sims (1980), p. 6.
[75] For the definition of the VAR model, see Appendix B.

current value of another one. This simple insight is closely associated with the concept of 'Granger causality', named after the Nobel Prize–winning economist Clive Granger, who first introduced it in the late 1960s.[76] It is defined as follows: 'X is said to Granger-cause Y if Y can be better predicted using the histories of both X and Y than it can be by using the history of Y alone.'[77]

There are as many equations as there are variables in a VAR analysis, since each variable in the system is modelled as a function of the histories of all the others. This avoids the problem highlighted earlier of making arbitrary assumptions about what causes what. However, this technique is very demanding of the data, since it involves estimating many parameters, and so it is not suitable for modelling relationships in short-run time series data. There are four possibilities in a Granger causal analysis: X can cause Y, Y can cause X, neither causes each other, or they both cause each other. As we see below when analysing the relationship between the economic variables and government support, all these possibilities can occur.

Most VAR modellers assume that all variables of interest should be stationary, i.e., they should fluctuate around a constant mean and have a constant (co)variance, rather than increase or decrease over time. Clearly, a variable which is stationary is unlikely to cause one which is non-stationary, since that would mean something which is not changing systematically but merely fluctuating, causing something else to grow or decline indefinitely over time. This may be possible, but it is highly unlikely.

To summarize the discussion up to this point, the present analysis of government accountability focuses on the relationship between voting for a governing party and economic performance. The latter is divided into subjective and objective variables, and we need to examine relationships without making questionable assumptions about causation or using unrealistic models of human decision-making. Instead, we examine relationships in the data using a VAR estimation strategy to see what it reveals about causation between the different measures over this period of forty-six years.

What Causes What?

Figure 8.4 depicts the relationships between growth, consumer confidence, unemployment, inflation and voting intentions for the governing

[76] Granger (1988).
[77] Giles (2011).

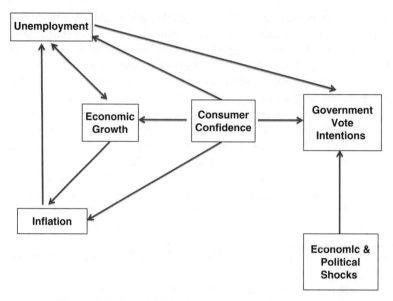

Figure 8.4 Causal Links between Government Voting Support, Consumer Confidence, Inflation, Unemployment and Economic Growth.

party over this period. There is a different equation for each variable in the VAR and a preliminary analysis suggests that two lags are required in the modelling to identify effects. This means, for example, that consumer confidence in the previous quarter and the quarter before that – a total of six months – has a causal impact on current voting intentions for the governing party. This exercise takes into account the past history of voting intentions, which is driven by other factors, and so captures the inertia in government support. All variables are subject to this type of analysis, and the diagram in Figure 8.4 shows the causal links.[78]

In Figure 8.4 we observe one-way causation such as the relationship between consumer confidence and government voting intentions. We also observe two-way causation such as the interaction between unemployment and economic growth. Not surprisingly, when economic growth declines, it has the effect of increasing unemployment, but this also works in reverse and produces a feedback effect. There is also an absence of direct causation in the figure between inflation, economic growth and voting intentions. That said, while there are no direct links between these measures, there are indirect links at work. Both economic growth and inflation influence unemployment, and this in turn has a

---

[78] The technical details of the analysis appear in Appendix B.

causal impact on voting intentions. There are more extended interactions in the model as well, such as the relationship between consumer confidences and voting intentions. This works both directly but also through indirect links with economic growth, inflation and unemployment.

The most striking finding in Figure 8.4 is the centrality of consumer confidence in the modelling. Confidence or expectations have a causal influence on all three objective economic measures but themselves are not *directly* influenced by them. The importance of expectations, which is emphasized in macroeconomic analyses, is strongly confirmed in this analysis. It reveals that subjective perceptions of the economy drive the objective measures rather than the other way around. Consumer expectations are central to the political economy of government accountability and they drive the performance of the objective economy.

The modelling also includes controls for various political and economic shocks which can distort relationships. Each of these shocks are regarded as exogenous, i.e., they cause changes in voting intentions but are not themselves influenced by them. They are unexpected events and are captured with dummy variables scored one during the period when the shock occurred and zero otherwise. Specifically, the shocks considered include the effects of the oil price rises in the 1970s, 'Black Wednesday' in the 1990s and the financial crash in 2008. As expected, these shocks all had negative impacts on voting intentions for the governing party.

In addition to economic shocks, the model also takes account of various important political shocks. The first was the British victory in the Falklands War in June 1982, which had a significant positive effect on support for Mrs Thatcher's government. A second took place when Gordon Brown replaced Tony Blair as prime minister in June 2007. Brown had been pressing Blair to step down for some time, and his arrival in Number 10 gave a temporary boost to Labour's standing in the polls. However, this impact was rapidly overtaken by events, as the imminent financial crash was signalled by a run on the Northern Rock bank in the autumn of 2007. A third political shock occurred when Theresa May stepped down as prime minister after her party's disastrous performance in the May 2019 EU Parliament elections. As the discussion in Chapter 2 revealed, she stayed on despite her poor performance in the 2017 election, but was finally forced to resign after the European Parliament elections in 2019, and this had a temporary negative impact on voting intentions for the Conservative government.

Figure 8.1 also illustrates that elections can have a big impact on support for governments, particularly when the parties switch from opposition to government and vice versa. This was abundantly evident when Labour won its 1997 landslide victory, giving a huge boost to its popularity. It was also important in the 1979 election when Mrs Thatcher won a decisive victory over Labour. Finally, the 2019 general election had a big positive impact on government support, although in this case it did not involve a change of government.

Up to this point we have seen that the objective and subjective economies have strong effects on government popularity, particularly when political and economic shocks to the system are taken into account. But these results present a puzzle, namely if the objective economic variables do not drive consumer confidence then what does? We turn to this question in the next section.

What Drives Consumer Confidence?

We have suggested that consumer confidence provides a strong fast and frugal heuristic that drives government popularity. If confidence is depressed the governing party will suffer in the polls. In addition, unemployment has an independent effect on support for governing parties, which makes it also a visible and important heuristic. At the same time growth, inflation and unemployment do not directly drive consumer confidence. So how do we account for changes in consumer confidence?

Our argument is that a number of financial variables and shocks drive consumer confidence, but the links between these variables and confidence is not simple. This is because they are all, by and large, not visible to the public. Instead, the link depends on the impact of experts who do follow these measures. To illustrate how this works, the performance of the stock market influences the incomes of millions of people even if they do not invest directly in stocks and shares. The mechanism works via pension funds, investments and savings, and these are closely monitored by experts. These 'smart money' investors are a small minority of the population, but they pay close attention to the behaviour of financial markets and so are likely to pick up signals of a change in economic circumstances before the general public.[79]

---

[79] Shiller (1989) introduced a model of the social dynamics of stock market investing which makes this distinction between 'smart money' investors and 'ordinary' investors. In his analysis the former rely on the efficient markets hypothesis, which postulates that stock prices reflect optimal forecasts of company future earnings, whereas the latter ignored this model. In fact, the efficient markets hypothesis faces the same problems as the rational expectations hypothesis discussed earlier. It assumes individual rationality of the axiomatic type. In addition, no one has ever been able to make an optimal forecast of future earnings which accurately predicts how they behave, making it impractical as a guide to the behaviour of investors. But the argument that 'smart money' investors will react more quickly than the ordinary investor is sound.

These experts can move consumer confidence because they are responding rapidly to a change in the economy at a time when the public is ignoring the signals. The signals the experts provide drive consumer confidence because they dominate the 'noise' coming from everyone else.[80] The signal is driving the change even though it is subject to a lot of noise. Experts' actions trigger reactions in the market which can produce investment 'bubbles' and 'herding' behaviour that influence consumer confidence as the general public joins in.[81]

One key variable is interest rates, which determine returns on savings and investment for millions of people. Interest rates also play a key role in influencing the cost of mortgage repayments for homeowners. High interest rates are welcomed by savers but disliked by borrowers, so their overall effect on economic expectations depends on the balance between the two groups in the population. A recent survey showed that 40 per cent of households Britain had savings of less than £100 and would therefore receive no benefits at all from rising interest rates.[82] Equally, since credit card debt is based on multiples of prevailing interest rates, card holders are penalized if they use them to borrow beyond repayment periods in the face of rising rates. Moreover, the 2011 UK Census showed that 64 per cent of households in Britain are owner-occupiers, most of them with mortgages that are closely tied to the level of interest rates.[83] They are clearly worse off financially when interest rates rise. Overall, this means that borrowers outnumber lenders by a significant margin, so on average economic expectations are likely to become more pessimistic when interest rates rise.

A relatively unknown financial indicator called the 'yield curve' is closely related to interest rates but is likely to be visible only to the experts. This is an indicator of expectations about the behaviour of interest rates in the future and identifies the yields on bonds, i.e., loans to the public and private sectors, made over varying periods of time.[84] In normal times the rate of return or yield on short-term bonds will be lower than they are for longer-term bonds because investors will demand compensation for the greater uncertainty associated with investing for longer periods of time. But if investors think that the economy is likely to slow down in the near future this yield gap will narrow, and it can even

---

[80] Silver (2012).
[81] Shiller (2000); Kahneman, Sibony and Sunstein (2021).
[82] www.moneyadviceservice.org.uk/en/corporate/press-release-low-savings-levels-put-millions-at-financial-risk
[83] census/2011-census-analysis/a-century-of-home-ownership-and-renting-in-england-and-wales/short-story-on-housing.html?format=print
[84] Cairns (2004).

go into reverse. This works because 'smart money' investors anticipate a recession, slower growth, rising unemployment and poorer returns on investments in the future.

This process then creates a 'bear' or declining stock market as investors switch their assets from stocks to long-term bonds. The latter provide a fixed return over a specific period and therefore represent a safe haven in the face of an impending recession.[85] But an increased demand for long-term bonds will bring down their returns and so narrow the yield curve. This dynamic is likely to reduce consumer confidence through contagion effects affecting the wider public once the process starts.[86] This is a good example of the signal from smart money investors moving markets because the message from ordinary investors is largely random noise until the contagion effects kick in.

The stock market is also likely to have a direct influence on consumer confidence. Again, only a small minority of the UK population invest directly in the stock market, but equities have a big impact on the returns from savings and investments and also on the value of pension funds. By the same token, people invest in unit trusts which provide an indirect way of trading in stocks. The state of the stock market is regularly reported in the media which focuses heavily on movements of the FTSE (or 'Footsie') All Share index. Again, smart money investors can trigger shifts in economic expectations which influence consumer confidence. This analysis does not mean that smart money investors use 'rational expectations'; they are just as likely to use heuristics as everyone else, but they are more sophisticated and attentive to forces that will change economic expectations and subsequently influence the state of the objective economy.

Research shows that stock prices are driven by a combination of economic fundamentals and market psychology.[87] But a key difference between equity prices and interest rates is that rising stock prices generally make investors better off, something which is not true for borrowers when interest rates increase.[88] Accordingly, we might expect that a 'bull' market will generate optimistic economic expectations and a 'bear' market is likely to produce pessimism. The stock market performance is a good barometer of subjective economic evaluations.

The stock price index would be described as an objective rather than a subjective economic variable by those who continue to support the efficient markets hypothesis. According to this view, stock prices accurately

---

[85] Estrella and Mishkin (1996), pp. 1–5.
[86] Chamley (2004).
[87] Shiller (1989); Akerlof and Shiller (2009).
[88] The exception to this is traders who short stocks and related financial instruments in anticipation of a bear market.

reflect discounted future expected returns from the companies which make up the index.[89] This idea is justified by the argument that stock prices are a 'random walk', i.e., an inherently unpredictable time series.[90] The reasoning is that if markets systematically underprice or overprice stocks in relation to future returns, this would make the market predictable, and the smart money investors could then profit from this. As a result, the inference is drawn that markets must be efficient.

However, there is a much simpler explanation for the randomness, namely the fact that future stock prices are uncertain and inherently unpredictable. Ignorance rather than omniscience on the part of investors produces this state of affairs. Research shows that the stock market is driven to a large extent by irrational attitudes and so subject to 'boom and bust' bubbles.[91] It is far too volatile to reflect future earnings from firms so that the efficient markets hypothesis, a variant of expected-utility theory, is clearly at odds with reality. That said, some financial experts do forecast developments accurately in the long run and make serious money in the stock market.[92]

A fourth variable that is relevant for understanding the behaviour of consumer confidence is the currency exchange rate. If the pound falls in value relative to the euro, the US dollar or other currencies, this will directly affect trade, financial transactions and industries like tourism. Importers will get fewer euros, dollars or other currencies in exchange for their pounds. A weakening pound also has an indirect effect on the economy by increasing the price of imports, something which is reflected by higher prices in the shops. Given that almost half of the food consumed in Britain is imported, this essential component of every household budget is directly affected by currency fluctuations.[93] Exchange rates are widely reported in the media, and the many tourists who travel abroad will be aware of them, so we should expect that a weakening pound will have a negative impact on consumer confidence.

Figure 8.5 shows the Granger causality estimates of the relationships between these variables and consumer confidence over the period from 1974 to 2020. The links are complex and they show that all four variables have statistically significant impacts on consumer confidence, either directly as in the cases of stock prices and exchange rates, or indirectly via other variables. The figure shows the centrality of the bank rate, the standard measure of interest rates in the economy, in influencing the

---

[89] Fama (1965).
[90] Malkiel (1973).
[91] Shiller (2000).
[92] Lowenstein (2008).
[93] See www.foodsecurity.ac.uk/challenge/your-food-is-global/

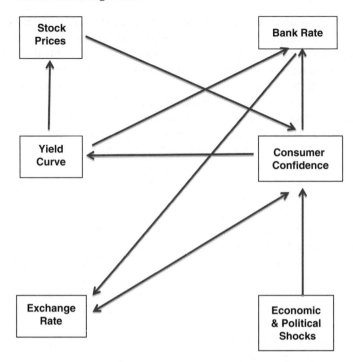

Figure 8.5 Causal Links between Consumer Confidence, Stock Prices, the Bank Rate, the Exchange Rate and the Yield Curve.

other variables. It is directly influenced by consumer confidence, interacts with stock prices and influences the exchange rate, and the latter in turn helps to drive consumer confidence. A similar point can be made about the yield curve, which is influenced by consumer confidence and which helps to drive stock prices and bank rate. Finally, the exchange rate is influenced directly by the bank rate.

Consumer confidence is also influenced by exogenous economic and political shocks, but fewer in number than was true of voting intentions. Confidence was affected by the oil prices crisis of the 1970s, the 1979 election and the Falklands War in 1982, but the other shocks were not statistically significant predictors in the analysis. It is no surprise that these financial variables all interact directly or indirectly with consumer confidence and it suggests that they are primarily responsible for driving subjective judgements about the state of the economy rather than the real economy of growth and employment. These judgements then subsequently influence unemployment, economic growth and inflation, which, as we saw in Figure 8.4, have direct or indirect influences on voting intentions.

It also seems likely that other variables such as subjective well-being, social capital, poverty and deprivation, health pandemics, terrorism and wars, and widely publicized events like successes in international sporting events or even a royal wedding might influence consumer confidence, at least in the short run. Unfortunately, data limitations prevent larger and even more complex models from being estimated to examine these hypotheses.

Conclusion: Governments Held Accountable

In this chapter we have examined government accountability over a long period by looking closely at the topic of economic voting. The conclusions signalled by the statistical analyses are clear, namely that government accountability for the performance of the economy is alive and well in Britain. There are strong links between the performance of both the subjective and objective economies and support for incumbent parties. As previous studies often have argued, when governments are perceived to be managing things poorly, they are punished in the polls and when they do a good job they are rewarded.

A few illustrative examples round off this chapter. The 'Black Wednesday' crisis which occurred in September 1992 had an immediate, strong impact on John Major's newly elected government. Trust in the Conservatives' ability to manage the economy was lost overnight and did not recover for years. The party went on to lose the 1997 election to Tony Blair and 'New Labour' in a massive landslide. Similarly, Gordon Brown's Labour government suffered from the financial crash which occurred in late 2007 and early 2008 and produced the Great Recession. Labour never recovered from this crisis and subsequently lost the 2010 general election.

The other side of the coin is the effect of a buoyant economy on support for governing parties. When the monetarist experiment was abandoned by the Thatcher government after the 1983 general election, economic expectations rebounded. This helped the Conservative win re-election in 1987. A similar situation occurred after Labour's victory in 1997, when the economy was buoyant and consumer confidence was high. This felicitous combination helped produce Labour's electoral victories in 2001 and 2005.

A major argument of this chapter is that contemporary theorists who are pessimistic about the state of democracy and the apparent inability of elections to hold governments to account have an unrealistic theory of how voters make decisions and an inaccurate perception of what is required to make democracy work. The expected-utility theory misreads public evaluations of the effectiveness of electoral accountability because it sets up an unrealistic model of voter decision-making as the standard for judging their behaviour. This misleading model of how people make decisions when they vote subsequently prompts analysts to discount the ability of voters to hold governments to account for their performance in office.

This argument does not gainsay the fact that governments are often blown off course by unexpected events and indeed by 'politics' more generally as they attempt to manage the economy. The financial crash and subsequent Great Recession are prime examples. Prior to the recession, many decision-makers suffered from a Panglossian view of the effectiveness of markets and failed to institute adequate regulatory safeguards. That said, British governments were not primarily responsible for the crisis, which started in the US real estate market and rapidly spread throughout the world's financial system.[94] But government actions, both Conservative and Labour, in the run-up to the crisis contributed to it and Labour subsequently paid the price in the 2010 general election.

Finally, there is a pessimistic conclusion about government accountability which can be drawn from this analysis. Governments are beholden to financial markets and limited in what they can do, particularly if they favour redistribution and higher taxes. As James Carville, a political advisor to President Clinton once said, he would like to be reincarnated as the Bond market, for the following reason: 'You can intimidate everyone.'[95]

In the next chapter and the third section of the book we look to the future by examining the likely consequences of Brexit on the performance of the British economy. This task is greatly complicated by the economic effects of the Covid-19 pandemic, which started to have a major impact in early 2020. Nonetheless we attempt to separate out these effects. The long-term consequences of leaving the EU on the British economy are largely unknown, but it is safe to say that, at least in the short term, downside effects have been significantly reinforced by the pandemic. So the chapter addresses the question of whether the economic effects of Brexit were larger or smaller than those of the pandemic.

[94] Tett (2009).
[95] https://en.wikipedia.org/wiki/Bond_vigilante

Part III

The Future

9   A Disaster or a Damp Squib?
The Economic Effects of Brexit

It has proved quite difficult to identify the effects of membership of the European Union on the UK economy in the past, even before the Covid-19 pandemic. One recent study looked at the gains from membership of the EU in a number of member states and concluded that:

> In spite of a large literature on the benefits from trade liberalization associated to the EU, from the Single Market, and from the Euro, there is a relative dearth of econometric estimates of the benefits from EU membership. Not only studies about the benefits of EU membership are few, but also the majority of these (few) studies openly warn against the lack of robustness of their estimates.[1]

Despite this, in a White Paper published in June 2016 just prior to the vote in the referendum on UK membership, the UK Treasury was bold enough to forecast what would happen to the economy by the year 2030 if Britain left the European Union.[2] The forecasts examined three different Brexit scenarios and they were uniformly pessimistic about the outcomes. In our book on the EU Referendum vote we criticized these forecasts in some detail.[3] The main points were that uncertainty about the future, problems with the underlying methodology and weaknesses in the theory make it impossible to credibly forecast the performance of the UK economy fifteen years into the future.[4] We simply cannot know outcomes that far ahead using current econometric practice. This means that pessimistic (or optimistic) predictions about the long-run effects of Brexit are little more than guesswork.

Shortly after the publication of this long-term analysis, the Treasury produced a second report, this time on the short-term effects of the UK leaving the EU over a two-year period assuming that there was a Brexit vote.[5] Short-term forecasting is potentially much more accurate than

---

[1] Campos, Coricell and Moretti (2019, p. 90).
[2] HM Government (2016a).
[3] Clarke, Goodwin and Whiteley (2017).
[4] Clarke, Goodwin and Whiteley (2017), pp. 175–180.
[5] HM Government (2016b).

long-term forecasting because the closer the forecasts are to the behaviour of the actual economy the more likely they are to hit the targets. In the event, these short-term forecasts were equally as gloomy as the long-term ones about Britain's economic prospects under Brexit.

The aim of this chapter is to try and evaluate the effects of Brexit on the UK economy in the future. To do this we begin by looking at the short-term Treasury forecasts and find them to be as unreliable as predictors of what happened as their long-term counterparts. Accordingly, we try a different approach by undertaking an exercise in 'backcasting', which involves looking at past data to estimate how much of a difference joining the EU made to the economy after Britain's accession in 1973. Needless to say, joining and leaving the European Union are not the same thing, but we should nonetheless gain insight into what is likely to happen in the future from this exercise. If joining provided a big stimulus to economic growth and innovation, then it is reasonable to infer that leaving the EU could seriously damage the economy. However, if the effects of joining on growth were negligible it would be hard to draw the same conclusion.

A further reason for not relying on forecasts is that any effects of Brexit on the economy might easily be overshadowed by the Covid-19 pandemic. As is well known, Britain has suffered considerably both in relation to cases and deaths from this disease, and it is likely to have significant economic consequences in the future. We investigate this issue later in the chapter by looking at the long-term effects of past pandemics on economic performance. This involves trying to learn from history about the effects of earlier large-scale pandemics on the economy. The overall aim is to gain insights into what might happen, without being overambitious about what can be inferred from forecasting. We start by looking closely at the short-term Treasury forecasts.

Short-Term Treasury Forecasts of the Economic Effects of Brexit

The Treasury report on the short-term consequences of a Brexit vote did not mince words about what it thought were likely to be the consequences:

A vote to leave would cause an immediate and profound economic shock creating instability and uncertainty which would be compounded by the complex and interdependent negotiations that would follow. The central conclusion of the analysis is that the effect of this profound shock would be to push the UK into recession and lead to a sharp rise in unemployment.[6]

[6] Treasury (2016b), p. 5.

The approach taken in the modelling was to estimate a vector autoregressive model (VAR) of the economy focusing on measures thought likely to be affected by Brexit. This forecasting technique introduced in Chapter 8 was pioneered by the Nobel Prize–winning economist Christopher Sims. In a very influential article, he argued that the large-scale forecasting models were very unreliable because they made too many implausible assumptions about the way the economy works.[7] These assumptions were necessary to make forecasting possible. He advocated a different approach which focuses only on a few key variables and makes as few assumptions as possible about causal relationships. This approach has subsequently been extended and has become very popular in econometric work.[8]

The Treasury used this type of modelling to make forecasts, but unfortunately it combined this technique with a more traditional approach by feeding the forecasts into a large-scale econometric model of the type Sims had criticized. This model is known as NiGEM and was developed at the National Institute for Economic and Social Research. It is widely used by governments and other forecasting agencies.[9] The results of this exercise suggested that there would be three different economic effects of Brexit in the short run:

1. A *'transition effect'* arising from the assumption by individuals that the UK would become less open to trade and investment after leaving the European Union.
2. An *'uncertainty effect'* arising from the effects of the referendum on decisions made by business corporations and other actors.
3. A *'financial conditions effect'* created by the uncertainty in financial markets arising from a Brexit vote in the referendum.

The transition effect assumed that 'Businesses would start to reduce investment spending and cut jobs in the short term, consistent with lower external demand and investment in the future.'[10] The uncertainty effect was thought to be due to the expectation that: 'Businesses and households would respond to this by putting off spending decisions until the nature of new arrangements with the EU became clearer.'[11] Finally, the financial conditions effect related largely to the impact of the vote on financial markets. It argued that in the event of a leave vote: 'The UK

---

[7] Christopher (1980).
[8] Kennedy (2008).
[9] See https://nimodel.niesr.ac.uk/
[10] Treasury (2016b), p. 6.
[11] Treasury (2016b), p. 6.

Table 9.1 *Treasury Forecasts of the Economic Consequences of Brexit and Actual Outcomes, 2016/2017–2017/2018*

	Shock Scenario	Severe Shock Scenario	Actual Outcomes
Gross Domestic Product (%)	−3.6	−6.0	+3.4
Consumer Price Index Inflation Rate	+2.3	+2.7	+2.0
Unemployment Rate	+1.6	+2.4	−0.9
Unemployment Level	+520,000	+820,000	−280,000
Average Real Wages (%)	−2.8	−4.0	+4.8
House Prices (%)	−10	−18	+4.9
Sterling Exchange Rate Index (%)	−12	−15	−6.3
Public Sector Net Borrowing (£ Billion)	+24	+39	−7.2

Source: HM Treasury (2016b) and Office for National Statistics.

would be viewed as a bigger risk to overseas investors, which would immediately lead to an increase in the premium for lending to UK businesses and household.'[12]

The modelling produced specific predictions two years into the future about the economic effects of a vote to leave the EU. Two scenarios were examined, one of which was described as a 'shock scenario' and the second a 'severe shock scenario'. The first assumed that the shock would be rather similar in magnitude to the effects of the recession of 1990–1991 and the 'severe shock scenario' was assumed to be 50 per cent worse than that.

The predictions arising from the two scenarios appear in Table 9.1, and it can be seen that the forecasts were uniformly negative, anticipating a reduction in GDP of 3.6 per cent in the 'shock scenario' and 6.0 per cent in the 'severe shock scenario'. The modelling also predicted significant increases in inflation and a rise in unemployment of just over half a million in the first scenario and over three-quarters of a million in the second. Similarly, the predicted reductions in real wages, house prices and in the sterling exchange rate were equally pessimistic. Finally, it forecast that the Public Sector Borrowing Requirement, or the difference between government income and expenditure, would increase by at least £25 billion over the two-year period.

The actual outcomes appear in the last column of Table 9.1 using data up to the third quarter of 2018. In every case, the forecasts were wrong by significant margins, with GDP increasing by 3.4 per cent rather than declining, and inflation growing at a significantly lower rate

[12] Treasury (2016b), p. 7.

than predicted. In addition, unemployment fell by more than a quarter of a million rather than increased during this period. Equally, average wages and house prices rose rather than declined and the sterling exchange rate fell, but by much less than was predicted. Finally, the Public Sector Borrowing Requirement ended up being less than a third of the size predicted in the 'shock' scenario and lower still for the 'severe shock' scenario. To summarize, the forecasts in this pre-referendum White Paper turned out to be seriously misleading in light of what subsequently happened.

To be fair, radical uncertainty about the future makes it very difficult to forecast economic trends with any hope of identifying an accurate picture. This is particularly true in the context of the turmoil created by Brexit and the Covid-19 pandemic. In their recent book, two leading economists, John Kay and Mervyn King, make the following point about forecasting models which spectacularly failed to predict the financial crises and subsequent Great Recession starting in 2008: 'The inability of experts to anticipate the crisis was not simply the result of incompetence, or wilful blindness, but reflected much deeper problems in understanding risk and uncertainty.'[13] In other words, the present state of modelling is not up to the task of providing accurate forecasts, because we cannot deal with uncertainty.

Since the referendum, a serious attempt has been made to estimate the economic effects of EU membership in a number of member states including Britain. One approach is to use methods that have been developed in the counterfactual causation literature to predict outcomes.[14] This methodological approach tries to estimate what would have happened to the economy of a member state if it had not joined the EU in the first place. The latter is referred to as the counter-factual case and, in effect, the technique tries to re-run history to see what would have happened. When this is done the effects of membership are obtained by comparing the results of this hypothetical exercise with actual outcomes.[15] In the case of Britain, an analysis by Compos, Corricelli and Moretto suggested that growth rates would have been significantly lower than were achieved, if the country had failed to join the EU in 1973.[16]

Needless to say, since the counterfactual scenario cannot be directly observed, the methodology relies on accurately identifying what would have happened by looking at the experience of countries that have similar

---

[13] Kay and King (2020), p. 7.

[14] See Morgan and Winship (2015) for an extensive discussion of this methodological approach.

[15] See, e.g., Abadie, Diamond and Hainmueller (2015).

[16] Compos, Corricelli and Moretto (2019), p. 94.

economies to Britain, but which are not member states. This unknown counterfactual outcome is created by estimating a 'synthetic' country, from economic trends in several countries. Unfortunately, a major problem with this exercise is that 92.5 per cent of the 'synthetic' version of Britain was derived from New Zealand, with the remaining 7.5 per cent from Argentina. While New Zealand and Britain have a common history, language, similar cultures and are both developed economies, there are major differences between them.

In 1973 when Britain joined the Common Market, New Zealand had a population of just under 3 million people compared with Britain's 54 million. The New Zealand economy was (and still is) heavily dependent on agriculture, but this is a relatively minor sector of Britain's economy. The UK economy is much more dependent on industrial production and services, particularly financial services, than New Zealand. These rather large differences raise the strong possibility that the synthetic version of Britain is a poor substitute for the actual version. If the exercise had utilized a more extensive set of matching variables in a variety of different countries to create a more convincing synthetic Britain it might be more persuasive. Counterfactual modelling can be very useful, but it is hard to make the case for it in this instance.

This conclusion is reinforced by another exercise in counterfactual modelling by Saia, who attempted to estimate the effects on trade if the UK had joined the Eurozone in 1999.[17] He claimed that aggregate trade flows between Britain and the other Eurozone countries would have been 16.8 per cent higher if the UK had adopted the euro. The analysis also suggests that trade flows with non-EU countries such as the US, Japan and Switzerland would have been higher as well. One of the estimates goes so far as to suggest that UK trade with the US would have been about 12 per cent higher if Britain had been a member of the Eurozone. This analysis faces the same problem of not being able to define a convincing counterfactual case when creating the synthetic country alternative making these predictions rather dubious.

It seems clear that the existing approaches to forecasting the economic effects of UK membership are not up to the task of predicting what is likely to happen to the economy as a result of Brexit. We have previously argued that researchers need to be much more modest about what can be said about the effects of Britain leaving the EU in our earlier book. This is where the exercise in 'backcasting' rather than forecasting comes into play. Essentially, this involves learning from the past, rather than trying to forecast a very uncertain future.

[17] Saia (2017).

In our earlier analysis of economic growth in Britain, we found that joining the common market made no difference to the long-term rate of growth in the country.[18] In addition, a further analysis showed that this was also true for the great majority of the other member states who joined at various different times over the years. That said, this earlier modelling used a relatively simple specification to analyse economic growth, and so it is worth repeating this exercise, but this time with a more refined measure. This alternative measure focuses specifically on innovation rather than on economic growth, and we discuss it in the next section.

The Effects of EU Membership on Technological Innovation in Britain

Since the time of Adam Smith, economic growth has been an important focus of study for economists.[19] In 1987, MIT economist Robert Solow won the Nobel Prize for Economics largely as a result of his pioneering work on economic growth.[20] He showed that over 80 per cent of economic growth could be attributed to improvements in technology rather than increased capital investment or higher rates of employment.[21] Investment and employment are relatively easy to measure, whereas technological innovation is much harder. This creates a problem for researchers trying to identify how innovation actually works in a modern economy.

More recently, endogenous growth theory has emerged as a very influential approach, pioneered by Paul Romer.[22] This places new ideas and technological innovation at centre stage. The key insight is to identify innovative ideas as non-rival goods. In standard theory most goods and services are rivals, that is, consumers and producers are bidding against each other for products. If demand increases for a particular good or service, their immediate availability will start to decline, and their price will rise. Supply will eventually respond to this after prices have risen, although this does not always happen.

Ideas and innovation are quite different from this since they are non-rival goods. This means that if someone comes up with a new idea, say, for designing computer chips, this innovation can potentially spread rapidly through the economy without having any effect on the supply of such ideas. Equally, it is possible for anyone to make use of innovative

---

[18] Clarke, Goodwin and Whiteley (2017), p. 185.
[19] Acemoglu (2009).
[20] Solow (1970).
[21] Solow (1957).
[22] Romer (1990).

ideas, subject to limitations imposed by patents and copyrights, and subsequently apply them to other technologies. In this view, the creation and dissemination of new ideas is the key to explaining economic growth. One contemporary problem is that it appears that large IT companies like Microsoft, Amazon and Google are slowing innovation with a dual policy of absorbing competition via takeover bids as well as by creating legal barriers to small start-up competitors.[23]

There is an alternative measure of economic growth, originally known as the Total Factor Productivity of an economy, which focuses directly on innovation.[24] This is a measure of growth with the effects of labour and capital inputs controlled for in the analysis, thereby making innovation the focus of attention. With this measure, if a country increases its GDP by employing more workers or increasing capital investment, this will not directly improve Total Factor Productivity unless it is also accompanied by innovation. A measure of this is included in the Penn World Dataset, a high-quality database that compares the economic performance of countries across the world over a long period of time.[25]

Figure 9.1 shows the growth in Total Factor Productivity, or innovation as we will describe it, in the three largest founder member states of the EU, namely Germany, France and Italy alongside Britain over the period 1950–2019. Compared with standard comparative growth charts, Figure 9.1 shows that Germany has been the laggard country in innovation despite its rates of growth. This is partly due to the country being very open to immigration, which allows it to increase growth by expanding employment rather than by technological innovation.[26]

The three founder EU member states enjoyed a significant increase in innovation during the early 1950s compared with Britain. Italy experienced the most rapid growth during these years, followed by France and then Germany. This was related to the recovery from the devastation of the Second World War, so that these countries experienced a rapid increase in innovation and in effect caught up with Britain. As a result, their standards of living were comparable to those in Britain by the early 1950s.

Figure 9.1 also shows that Britain experienced a brief but relatively sharp decline in innovation immediately after joining the common market in 1973. However, this had very little to do with newly acquired membership but was rather the result of a quadrupling of oil prices by the Organization

[23] Aghion, Antonin and Bunel (2021), ch. 6.
[24] This has been renamed Multi-Factor Productivity by the Office for National Statistics.
[25] Feenstra, Inklaar and Timmer (2015).
[26] Constant and Tien (2011).

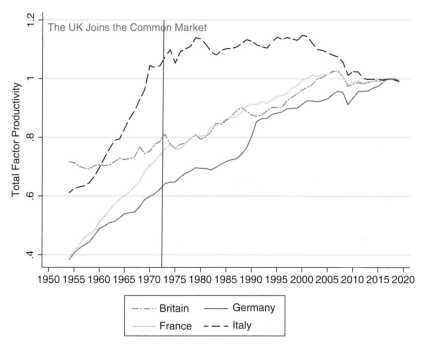

Figure 9.1 Total Factor Productivity Growth in Real Terms in Britain, France, Germany and Italy, 1950–2019.
Source: Penn World Data for Britain, Version 10.

of Petroleum Exporting Countries (OPEC) cartel during that period. This had a massive impact across the world economy by boosting inflation. This and other economic shocks are discussed more fully below.

Despite this blip, the trend growth in innovation in Britain had returned to normal by 1975, but the oil shock suggests that innovation is quite sensitive to economic and political events of various kinds. Figure 9.1 shows the oil shock and rising inflation put an end to the rapid growth in innovation in the three original member states, so that after that they all grew at rather similar rates to Britain.

When looking at Figure 9.1 it is easy to see why a key theme in the referendum campaign for Britain to remain a member of the common market in 1975 was the rapid growth in the prosperity of existing member states. Their stellar performance was frequently referred to by remain campaigners at that time.[27] In the event, two-thirds of the voters in that referendum supported remain, ensuring that the issue was settled for a long period of time.

[27] Butler and Kitzinger (1999).

A common theme used in the election campaign of 1979 by the Conservative Party was that Britain was the 'sick man of Europe' and that radical changes in the economy were needed to deal with the problem. But the evidence in Figure 9.1 shows that Britain's performance in technological innovation at the time was well above that of Germany and rather similar to that of France. It was not until the 1990s and the advent of John Major's government that innovation started to fall behind that of France. After that, the arrival of Tony Blair's government in 1997 provided a modest boost, so that Britain caught up with France by 2005.

By the end of the millennium, Figure 9.1 shows that Italy began to experience significant problems as its rate of innovation started to decline, and all four countries were severely affected by the financial crash and subsequent recession which started in 2008. The 'Great Recession' produced a lasting legacy by reducing innovation in all of these major European economies, since it appears to have basically stalled during the post-crash period.

In the next section we model the determinants of innovation in Britain with the aim of examining the links between Britain and the rest of the European community. The interesting question is whether growing economic integration and trade links between the EU and Britain imply that Brexit has serious consequences for innovation in the future if it leads to a weakening of these ties. The model will look closely at the impact of key economic shocks which Britain has experienced over this period.

Modelling the Determinants of Innovation

We begin by examining innovation in Britain before looking at relationships between Total (or Multi-) Factor Productivity in the UK and in the European Union. We have already mentioned that two key drivers of economic growth, capital investment and increased employment, are controlled for in estimating Total Factor Productivity, but the rate of depreciation of capital assets in the economy is not taken into account. This is likely to have an important impact on innovation since if depreciation is slow, something which is related to low levels of investment in the economy, we are likely to observe innovation slowing down as well. So it is important to take this into account in the modelling, since rapid depreciation should stimulate productivity and innovation.[28]

---

[28] This variable is called 'delta' in the dataset.

A second variable which is of considerable importance in the relationship between Britain and the EU is trade. We might expect growing trade relationships with other countries to stimulate technological progress and innovation in Britain. In the Penn Database, this is measured by the share of exports less imports as a percentage of overall economic output.[29] Since the EU is Britain's largest trading partner, this measure should be strongly influenced by economic ties to Europe. However, it can also be stimulated by trading relationships with the rest of the world, so the analysis looks at total levels of trade.

Figure 9.1 suggests that technological innovation is sensitive to economic shocks of various kinds given the marked fluctuations in the series at different points of time. Accordingly, we create a number of dummy variables designed to identify the possible effects of economic and political shocks on technological progress, and these are summarized in Table 9.1. Each variable identifies a major crisis which either might be expected to affect the economy directly such as the devaluation of the pound in 1967, or indirectly such as the poll tax riots in 1988. In each case, the assumption is that technological innovation will be influenced by these events after a lag of usually a year following the event, depending on when it took place.

To capture the effects of joining the EU on innovation we use two dummy variables. The first measures short-term influences which might have occurred in the immediate period after Britain joined on the first of January 1973. This measure scores 1 in 1973 and 0 otherwise. The second looks at the longer-term effects, scoring 0 before 1973 and 1 in every year thereafter. In this way we can identify both the short-run and long-run effects of joining on innovation in the UK.

There is a variety of political and economic shocks defined in Table 9.2. The first is the Suez crisis of October 1956 which involved Britain conspiring with France and Israel to take over the Suez Canal, which had been nationalized by the Egyptian President Gamal Nasser. The invasion faced considerable opposition around the world. US President Eisenhower privately threatened sanctions against the pound unless these countries withdrew their forces. They promptly did so, and historian Keith Kyle describes this debacle as the end of the British Empire in the Middle East.[30] Suez was primarily a political crisis, but it had the potential for economic consequences that could have influenced innovation.

---

[29] This is the share of merchandise imports of GDP at current Purchasing Power Parities (csh_m) minus the share of merchandise exports of GDP at current Purchasing Power Parities (csh_x). Exports are coded positively and imports negatively in the database, thus the net measure captures total trade as a percentage of GDP.

[30] Kyle (2011).

Table 9.2 *Economic Shock Variables Included in the Total Factor Productivity Models,*
1950–2019

Description of Economic Shock Variable	Coding in the Model
Suez crisis of October 1956	1957 = 1, else = 0
Devaluation of the pound in October 1967	1968 = 1, else = 0
Major cuts in public expenditure in the March 1968 budget	1969 = 1, else = 0
Britain joined the common market, January 1973 – short-term impact	1973 = 1, else = 0
Britain joined the common market, January 1973 – long-term impact	1973 to 2019 = 1, else = 0
Quadrupling of oil prices by the OPEC cartel, October 1973	1974 = 1, else = 0
Inflation reaches post-war record high of 27 per cent, August 1975	1975 = 1, else = 0
UK requests stand-by credits from the IMF, September 1976	1977 = 1, else = 0
The Thatcher government's monetarist experiment	1980 = 1, else = 0
Miners' year-long strike starts in March 1984	1984 = 1, else = 0
The poll tax introduced in the Local Government Finance Act of July 1988, subsequently leading to protests and riots	1989, 1990 = 1, else = 0
Pound ejected from the European Monetary System on 'Black Wednesday', September 1992	1993 = 1, else = 0
Great Recession starts with the run on the Northern Rock Bank, September 2007	2008 to 2010 = 1, else = 0
Austerity policies imposed by the newly elected coalition government in the emergency budget of June 2010	2011 to 2013 = 1, else = 0

The second major crisis was purely an economic shock, the devaluation of the pound by Harold Wilson's Labour government in 1967. This arose because Britain was still a member of the fixed exchange currency regime, put in place by the Bretton Woods Agreement of 1944. This landmark conference created the post-war framework for managing international trade, and it survived until the 1970s.[31] Prime Minister Wilson tenaciously held on to what was an uncompetitive exchange rate for the pound after his government was elected in 1964, but finally was forced to devalue following pressure from international financial markets.[32] The devaluation created a

[31] Steil (2013).
[32] Pimlott (1992).

political crisis for the government, but it had the potential to stimulate growth and technical progress, because the pound was no longer held at an uncompetitive rate.

The Wilson government subsequently followed up devaluation with major cuts in public expenditure in the budget of 1968, which had the effect of choking off any longer-term stimulus to growth and innovation created by the currency devaluation. The effects of this deflationary policy started to be felt in late 1968 and 1969 and it laid the ground for Labour's defeat in the general election of 1970. The policy of deflating the economy to reduce the demand for imports and improve the balance of payments deficit had been a feature of economic policy in Britain since the Bretton Woods Agreement. Unfortunately, it had the longer-term effect of slowing growth and technological innovation.[33] A dummy variable is designed to estimate the size of this effect.

The quadrupling of oil prices following the Arab–Israeli War of 1973 was a huge shock to economies around the world because they were so reliant on oil for energy supplies. The Organization of Petroleum Exporting Countries (OPEC) cartel imposed the price increases in retaliation for Western support for Israel, and it hit Western economies hard.[34] It produced 'stagflation', or a combination of stagnation and inflation, which was a particular problem for Britain for the rest of the 1970s. The effects are captured by a dummy variable indexing the oil price shock and a second associated with the high point of inflation which occurred in August 1975.[35]

Harold Wilson stepped down as prime minister in 1976 and was replaced by the former Chancellor of the Exchequer, James Callaghan. Shortly after this happened, Britain faced another currency crisis and had to approach the International Monetary Fund in September 1976 for a loan of $3.9 billion to shore up the pound.[36] This was caused by another run on the pound, since currency traders expected it to fall in value against other currencies given rampant inflation. The IMF loan crisis was regarded as a serious policy failure which damaged the Labour government's reputation for economic competence at the time.

When Mrs Thatcher's Conservative Party won the general election in 1979 it was in the context of an unemployment rate of over 5 per cent and an inflation rate of over 10 per cent. The new government

---

[33] Pollard (1982).
[34] Ikenberry (1988).
[35] Inflation reached 27 per cent in that month.
[36] Harmon (1997).

broke with the Keynesian consensus on economic policy and embarked on an experiment designed to squeeze inflation out of the system. This was known as 'monetarism', a doctrine advocated by economist Milton Friedman which asserted that inflation could be controlled only by restricting the supply of money in the economy.[37] This meant that the economy was deflated at a time of high unemployment, and as a result it rose to a post-war record of 12 per cent by the end of 1983. The policy was eventually abandoned as a failure;[38] however, it is likely to have had a strong effect on economic growth and innovation at the time.

The other major event in the early years of the Thatcher government was the miners' strike which started in March 1984 and lasted for a year. When Edward Heath's government faced industrial action by the miners in 1974 it had to impose a three-day working week because power stations started to run out of coal. The Thatcher government prepared for a showdown with the miners by building up coal stocks to record levels after taking office. It won the strike after a bitter struggle, but this had the potential to impact economic growth and innovation while it lasted.

In July 1988, during the Thatcher government's third term of office, the Local Government Finance Act was passed. This abolished the property tax which had funded local government for many years and adopted a poll tax instead. As is well known, a poll tax means that every householder pays the same amount regardless of their income or the value of their property. Many MPs in the Parliamentary Conservative Party had serious reservations about this tax, and these were borne out by subsequent events. Its introduction was followed by a widespread refusal to pay, extensive protests and some riots across Britain.[39] The policy damaged Conservative support to such an extent that the parliamentary party subsequently removed Mrs Thatcher from office and replaced her with Chancellor of the Exchequer, John Major.

John Major faced a serious economic crisis shortly after winning the general election of 1992. His government introduced a policy of shadowing the European Monetary System, the predecessor of the Eurozone. The aim was to align the pound with the system as a first step towards joining the Eurozone when it finally came into existence. However, financial markets did not believe that the exchange rate chosen for the pound could be sustained, and they began to short it in currency trading.[40]

---

[37] Friedman and Schwartz (1963).
[38] Desai (1981).
[39] Hannah (2020).
[40] This involved selling the pound at a fixed price for delivery at a later date, in the expectation that it would fall in value by the time that date arrived. If this happened, it could be bought more cheaply on spot markets and so delivered for a profit.

Despite frantic attempts to support the pound by raising interest rates to unprecedented levels, it was forced out of the European Monetary System, delivering a considerable political blow to the government.[41]

The financial crash of 2008, and the subsequent 'Great Recession', was clearly one of the most significant economic crises since the Second World War. As such, it was very likely to have a negative effect on innovation, not just in Britain but also in other EU member states. The crisis initially arose from problems in the US real estate market produced by reckless lending practices, but its arrival in Britain was signalled by a run on the Northern Rock bank in September 2007.[42] The effects lasted for a number of years and contributed to the loss of the 2010 election by the Labour government.

The final shock variable to be examined in the modelling relates to the policies of the Conservative–Liberal Democrat coalition government which emerged from the 2010 election. Much as its predecessor had done after the Conservative victory in the 1979 election, the government opted for austerity by introducing extensive cuts to public spending. The aim was to deal with the rapid increase in the budget deficit caused the Great Recession, starting with an emergency budget in June 2010. In the end, the policy failed to reduce the budget deficit, but it did delay recovery from the crisis and so had the potential to slow technical innovation.

Modelling Innovation in Britain

Figure 9.2 shows the effects of modelling trends in innovation from 1950 to 2019 using the variables described earlier. The chart consists of standardized coefficients which measure the impact of each of the predictor variables on innovation. We can identify their relative importance as predictors of innovation. Overall, the model has an excellent fit, as measured by the R-square statistic (0.84), indicating that a very high proportion of the variation in innovation is explained by the model.

The analysis reveals that the oil shock which occurred in 1973 had the largest negative effect on innovation in Britain over this sixty-nine-year period. The impact of the crisis was even larger than the effects of the Great Recession. There were in fact three related effects associated with it. The first was the negative effect of the oil price increases themselves, followed by the very high rates of inflation which reached a post-war peak in the middle of 1975. Both of these had the effect of slowing innovation. The third effect occurred in 1976 when the Labour government

[41] Keegan, Marsh and Roberts (2017).
[42] Tett (2009).

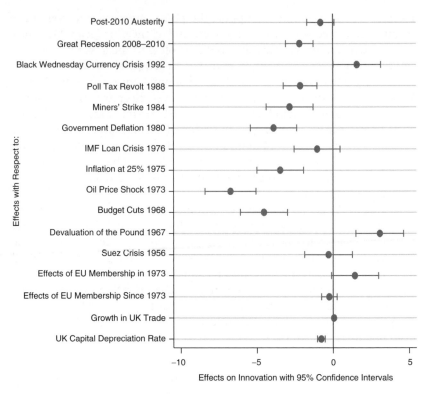

Figure 9.2 The Effects of Predictor Variables on Total Factor Productivity in Britain, 1950–2019.
Source: Penn World Data for Britain, Version 10 (Standardized Coefficients).

was forced to appeal to the IMF for a loan to deal with the balance of payments crisis. This was a significant political shock, but as Figure 9.2 shows, it did not have a statistically significant impact on innovation.

Three of the predictor variables in Figure 9.2 relate to the pursuit of austerity policies by different governments. The first occurred when the Labour government of Harold Wilson introduced the cuts in public expenditure in 1968 mentioned earlier. This had a serious negative impact on innovation at the time. The second was the monetarist experiment conducted by the Thatcher government in 1980–1981 mentioned earlier, which also had a deflationary impact on innovation. Finally, the third was the cuts imposed by the Conservative–Liberal Democrat coalition government after the 2010 election which had a smaller but significant negative impact. These events all contributed to slowing growth and innovation, which illustrates the dangers of governments attempting to cut spending as a way out of recessions.[43]

Three of the variables in Figure 9.2 related to major political events. Of these the poll tax riots in 1988 had a marginally larger negative impact on innovation than the miners' strike of 1984. These were predominantly political rather than economic shocks, but they nonetheless slowed innovation. Finally, the Suez crisis of 1956 also had a negative impact, but it was not statistically significant. This major political crisis nonetheless ended the career of the then Prime Minister Anthony Eden.

The rate of depreciation of the capital stock had a large negative impact on innovation, but with a much narrower confidence interval than some of the other shocks, making it hard to see in Figure 9.2. This means that low levels of investment in the economy are associated with slower rates of depreciation of capital stocks, and this in turn has the effect of reducing innovation. This is an indirect impact, but it shows the importance of the low rates of capital investment which Britain has been experiencing in recent years, particularly since the financial crisis and Great Recession. It is hard to grow fast if the capital stock is old and in need of replacement.

Turning to the positive effects on innovation, expanding trade clearly stimulates technological innovation, although again the narrow confidence intervals make it hard to identify this in Figure 9.2. This is something which is of course very relevant for identifying the effects of Brexit if it leads to reduced trade levels between Britain and the European Union. A second effect was associated with the devaluation of the pound in 1967. This worked by making exports cheaper and imports more expensive, thereby providing a stimulus to domestic production. This illustrates the point that if the exchange rate is fixed and too high then this creates balance of payments problems with deflating the economy becoming the default option. This in turn has the effect of slowing technological innovation. Unfortunately, the benefits of the 1967 devaluation were short-lived because budget cuts were imposed on the economy in the following year, and the resulting austerity slowed innovation.

Given the effects of devaluation in 1967, it is perhaps not surprising that the Black Wednesday crisis of 1992 had a positive impact on innovation. This crisis was a repeat of the mistake made by the Wilson government in trying to maintain a fixed exchange rate for the pound. John Major's government sought to control the exchange rate by manipulating interest rates, but financial markets did not believe this was possible and so the pound was forced to devalue. However, once it had happened

---

[43] Blyth (2013).

it produced a short-term recovery in innovation. The political fallout from this destroyed the Conservatives' reputation for economic competence and undoubtedly influenced the later decision by Gordon Brown not to join the Eurozone when he was Chancellor of the Exchequer in the Labour government.

Recent work in monetary theory suggests that countries which control their own currencies have a distinct advantage over those that do not when it comes to their ability to deal with economic problems. 'New Monetary Theory' suggests that the only constraint on an expansive monetary policy which really matters is the threat of inflation.[44] This means that if a country is part of a currency system like the Eurozone, it will lose the ability to stimulate growth using monetary policy, and so will have to resort to deflation instead. As we have seen, imposing austerity for reasons to do with balancing the budget or reducing a balance of payments deficit is likely to be self-defeating. In addition, such policies carry significant political costs for incumbent governments.

The two variables in the modelling which are central to our concerns in this chapter are the measures of the short-term and long-term effects of Britain joining the common market in 1973. The long-term effects variable had no statistically significant impact on innovation, as Figure 9.2 shows. However, there was a weak significant positive short-term effect when Britain joined the EU in 1973, but one which only lasted for a year. This result is consistent with our previous analysis which showed that joining the EU had no long-term effect on economic growth in Britain.[45] This does not of course imply that Brexit will have no longer-term effects on the UK economy, but it does cast doubts on predictions that leaving the EU will create a long-term crisis for the British economy.

That said, the findings in Figure 9.2 show that a variety of economic and political shocks had a considerable impact on innovation in Britain, creating the possibility that the economy will be damaged in the future if Brexit reduces trade and other links with the EU. Consequently, in the next section we will focus more closely on the impact of the European Union on innovation in Britain.

Modelling the Impact of Trade with the EU on Innovation in Britain

In this section, we look at the relationship between technological innovation in Britain and in the European Union. The key question is whether

---

[44] Kelton (2020).
[45] Clarke, Goodwin and Whiteley (2017).

innovations which originated in the EU helped to stimulate innovation in Britain. If so, it follows that technical progress in Britain will be reduced by leaving the EU. There is likely to be reciprocal relationships between innovation in the EU and in Britain, but this is still a threat to the future performance of the UK economy if these relationships are strong.

That said, there is a theoretical reason for expecting Brexit not to undermine the relationship between innovation in the EU and in Britain mentioned earlier. This is the idea that technological innovation is a non-rival good. This means that a country does not have to be an EU member state to benefit from innovations which originate in the EU. Any country in the world can use innovations created in any other country to boost their productivity and growth. This is the essence of the so-called 'catch-up' process, a well-known phenomenon in which developing countries can copy innovations introduced in developed countries in order to help close the gap between them.[46]

This theoretical argument must be qualified by the fact that countries with close trading relationships as well as extensive political, geographical and cultural ties are more likely to adopt innovations from each other, than they are from countries with fewer ties. We can therefore examine innovation in the EU as a predictor of innovation in Britain, while at the same time taking into account such ties. An important proxy measure of these ties is the trading links between the EU and Britain.

Figure 9.3 has the same specification as the model in Figure 9.2 except it contains three additional variables. Firstly, there is total factor productivity in the six founder member states of the European Union, so we are examining the same set of countries over the entire period.[47] These are Belgium, Germany, France, Luxembourg, Italy and the Netherlands. These economies vary a lot in their size and rates of growth and innovation. In order to compare them with Britain we have constructed an aggregate index of their total factor productivity weighted by their population size. Germany has the highest weighting in the index and Luxembourg has the lowest. Figure 9.3 shows that this innovation index has a significant positive impact on productivity in Britain, indicating that innovation in Europe does influence innovation in Britain. Again, the confidence interval on this effect is very narrow, making it difficult to discern in the figure.

The second extra variable in Figure 9.3 is an aggregate index of the growth of trade in the six original member states, again weighted by their population sizes. This is designed to take into account the economic,

---

[46] Popov and Jomo (2018).
[47] Note the time period is 1954–2019 due to missing data.

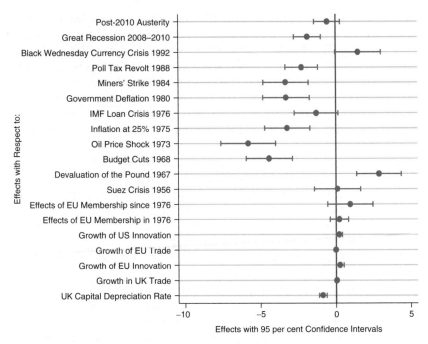

Figure 9.3 The Effects of Predictor Variables on Total Factor Productivity in Britain Including Innovation in the EU and the US, 1950–2019.
Source: Penn World Data for Britain, Version 10.

geographical, cultural and other ties between Britain and the European Union which might be expected to boost the impact of innovation. In the event, this variable was not a statistically significant predictor of innovation in Britain, implying that the UK trade variable in the model fully captures this effect.

The third extra variable designed to test the 'non-rival good' hypothesis is the innovation rate in the United States. It turns out that the growth of total factor productivity in the US has a rather similar positive impact on innovation in Britain comparable to that of the six founder EU member states. This confirms the point that a country does not have to be a member of the EU to benefit from technological innovations created in Europe since these are non-rival goods. In other words, Britain can continue to take advantage of innovations in the EU even though it is no longer a member state.

The overall conclusion of this discussion is that innovation in Britain was not influenced by joining the common market in 1973, except for a rather weak short-term blip which occurred in that year. That is not to say that innovations in Europe have not influenced Britain, but this influence would have existed even if Britain had not joined the EU in the first place. The implication is that innovation will not be significantly affected by Britain leaving the EU once short-term adjustments are taken into account.

One event that overshadows this discussion of innovation and growth is the impact of the Covid-19 pandemic which began to seriously affect the world economy from the start of 2020. Many countries shut down a lot of their economic activity and quarantined their populations, and this seriously affected all European countries including Britain in a way which might well overshadow any impacts of Brexit. We investigate this possibility in the next section.

Has the Covid-19 Pandemic Damaged Innovation in Britain?

We have seen how difficult it was to accurately forecast the performance of the economy in the immediate period after the referendum on EU membership in 2016. It will come as no surprise to say that forecasting the consequences of the Covid-19 pandemic, which has ravaged economies around the world since 2020, is likely to be even more difficult. That said, significant economic shocks in the past have been caused by epidemics such as the Spanish flu, which broke out after the First World War and rapidly spread around the world.

Recent research suggests that such epidemics can be quite disruptive. One view is that they follow a V-shaped trajectory in their impact. In other words, they have a severe negative impact in the short run, but this is then followed by a fairly rapid recovery.[48] However, there is an alternative view which argues the opposite case, namely that Britain's poor record of investment in recent years is likely to be responsible for a slow recovery from the pandemic. This is even more likely to be true if it brings about permanent changes in consumer behaviour such as increased savings, which have the effect of reducing consumer demand and slowing growth.[49]

The latter reasoning is reinforced by research which reaches a very pessimistic conclusion about the effects of major economic and political shocks on economic growth across the world. Two IMF economists, Cerra and Saxena, have shown that such shocks can produce enduring

[48] Carlsson-Szlezak, Reeves and Swartz (2020).
[49] Romei and Strauss (2021).

losses of economic output. They use panel data from 190 countries over a forty-year period from 1960 to 2001 and conclude that: 'the magnitude of persistent output losses ranges from around 4 per cent to 16 per cent for various shocks.'[50] They also found that significant rebound in the economy tends to occur only in the case of wars, but not for economic or political shocks, which can have enduring effects lasting over a decade or more. A recent update of their research in light of the Covid-19 pandemic suggests that the economic effects are going to be felt for a long period of time.[51]

Another perspective on this issue relates to research on the effects of major pandemics on rates of return from investments over very long periods of time. One study of the return on assets since the fourteenth century concluded that major pandemics had the effect of depressing rates of return for decades.[52] This in turn reduced investment and slowed innovation and growth. The same study also looked at major wars and found that these had a different impact from pandemics. In this case, the effect tended to follow the V-shaped pattern of a sharp recession followed by a fairly rapid recovery mentioned earlier. The authors attribute the difference to the fact that pandemics produced labour scarcity which in turn lowers demand and inhibits growth. In contrast, wars produced a significant destruction of capital assets, which can be replaced fairly rapidly after peace returns.

To estimate the effect of the Covid-19 pandemic we adopt the same strategy as earlier and try to estimate the impact of pandemics in the past on economic performance at the time rather than attempting to forecast the future. The aim is to get a broad sense of the likely consequences of the Covid-19 pandemic on innovation in Britain. To do this requires an even longer-run time series than is available in the Penn Data, since major epidemics are relatively few and far between. In addition, there are considerable difficulties in identifying when these occurred, how long they lasted and in estimating the magnitude of their impact on the economy.

A very long-run time series on economic performance in Britain is available from the Bank of England Millennium Macroeconomic dataset.[53] Some of the variables in this dataset go back to the year 1270 and were compiled from the work of economic historians, geographers and demographers. The earliest data in the database are limited in scope

---

[50] Cerras and Saxena (2008).
[51] Cerras, Fatas and Saxena (2020).
[52] Jordà, Singh and Taylor (2020).
[53] See www.bankofengland.co.uk/statistics/research-datasets

and accuracy, but additional measures were added as they became available. In the event, the Bank of England was able to estimate the growth of total factor productivity in Britain from the year 1761 to 2016 in the data.

With regard to data on pandemics, Cirrillo and Taleb have compiled a dataset of major pandemics that have occurred from the year 429 BC up to the present Covid-19 crisis.[54] This database includes approximate estimates of the numbers who died and the duration of each of the pandemics. For example, they estimated that the 'Black Death' plague, which started in 1331 and continued for some 22 years, killed 137.5 million people worldwide. That pandemic had major effects which changed both the economies and the politics of the countries affected. That said, the authors make clear these estimates are subject to wide margins of error.

By combining these datasets we can examine the impact of major pandemics on technological innovation in Britain since 1761, a period of more than 250 years. At the time of writing, the Covid-19 pandemic has caused over 5 million deaths worldwide,[55] so we need to focus on comparable pandemics in the past. To make this exercise manageable we include only those pandemics that were estimated to have killed at least 2 million people worldwide, and these are summarized in Table 9.3. It is readily apparent in this table that the Spanish flu epidemic which followed the First World War is a very large outlier. It was estimated to have killed nearly 59 million people and did so in a relatively short period of time. The deaths from the Great Plague which occurred in the middle of the nineteenth century were also on a much larger scale than the Covid-19 pandemic. That said, Table 9.3 suggests that the Covid-19 pandemic is the third worst in terms of deaths over this period of more than 250 years.

Since the duration of the various pandemics is subject to wide uncertainty, we estimate their impact using dummy variables identifying a year at the end of the period. The idea is to take into account any lags in their impact on the economy, assuming that things get worse as the pandemic continues.[56] The dates of the dummy variables are identified in the third column of Table 9.3. In addition, the modelling incorporates controls for economic shocks, which are separate from the effects of pandemics,

---

[54] Cirrillo and Taleb (2020).
[55] https://covid19.who.int/?adgroupsurvey={adgroupsurvey}&gclid=CjwKCAjwndCKBh
AkEiwAgSDKQXRgDPaVaD1mPXlCwDzZWC2CN1ZVdlBPxkjncYNmh70jEY35x
9H7qhoCZSQQAvD_BwE
[56] Note that this may underestimate their total economic impact, so the estimates are conservative.

Table 9.3 *Major Worldwide Pandemics and Major Economic Shocks, 1761–2016*

Pandemics	Duration	Estimates of Deaths in Millions	Dummy Variables
Persian Plague	1772–1772	2.0	1772 = 1, else = 0
Great Plague and Cholera	1855–1860	18.5	1860 = 1, else = 0
Spanish Flu	1918–1920	58.5	1920 = 1, else = 0
Asian Flu	1957–1958	2.0	1958 = 1, else = 0
Economic Shocks			
Post–Napoleonic War Recession	1811–1812	---	1812 = 1, else = 0
1930s Great Depression	1930–1931	---	1931 = 1, else = 0
Second World War Disruption	1944–1945	---	1944 = 1, else = 0
1970s Oil Shock	1974–1975	---	1974 = 1, else = 0
2000s Great Recession	2008–2009	---	2009 = 1, else = 0

Source: Bank of England and Cirrillo and Taleb (2020).

such as the depression which followed the Napoleonic Wars. These are also listed in Table 9.3.[57]

Figure 9.4 identifies the effects of these pandemics and economic shocks on innovation in Britain over the period 1761–2016. Unsurprisingly, Spanish flu had the largest impact since it was the deadliest pandemic in the list. The loss of lives resulting from Spanish flu had a major impact on productivity in Britain, and the additional deaths and disruption from the First World War undoubtedly added to this effect. Apart from Spanish flu, two other pandemics had a significant negative impact on innovation. These were the 'Persian Plague' of 1772 and the 'Great Plague' of 1855–1860. The fourth pandemic, 'Asian flu', occurred in the post-war period and was estimated to have killed 2 million people worldwide. However, it had no statistically significant impact on innovation in Britain, probably because the epicentre of the outbreak was in Asia.

The remaining effects in the modelling were all related to economic shocks of different kinds. They were the recession following the Napoleonic Wars, the Great Depression of the 1930s, the disruptive effect of the Second World War, the Oil Shock of the 1970s and the Great Recession of 2008–2010. These all had negative statistically significant impacts on innovation, with the exception of the Great Depression, whose effect was captured by two additional control variables that are included in the modelling. These are the rate of inflation and the level of unemployment, both

---

[57] Additional controls for wars were included in an expanded version of the model but none of these variables were statistically significant, suggesting that wars do not have a long-term effect on productivity. The exception to this was the Second World War, when mobilization and lack of investment in non-war-related production appeared to have damaged productivity by 1944.

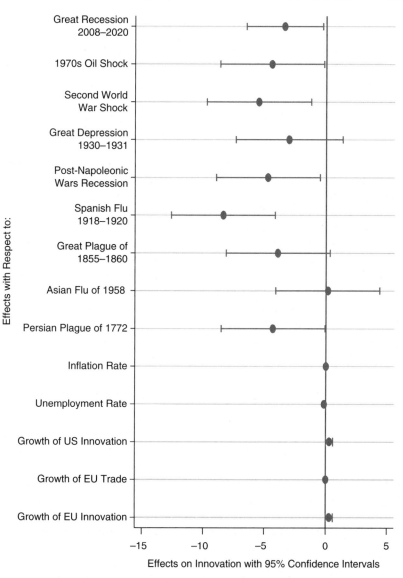

Figure 9.4 The Effects of Pandemics and Economic Shocks on Total Factor Productivity in Britain, 1761–2016.
Source: Bank of England and Cirrillo and Taleb (2020).

of which effects are hard to see in Figure 9.4 because of the tight confidence intervals. These measures capture any disruption to innovation caused by recurring peaks and troughs in the business cycle over this long period of time. In the upsurge of the cycle, inflation can be a problem, although before 1931, Britain adopted the gold standard, which naturally inhibits inflation since the Bank of England could not easily increase the money supply and credit when the supply of gold was restricted. In contrast in the post–gold standard era, the Bank can easily create credit, making inflation more likely if monetary policy is very loose.

In contrast, unemployment captures downturns in the cycle which have occurred on numerous occasions. In the event, the modelling in Figure 9.4 shows that rising unemployment had a significant negative impact on innovation, whereas increased inflation had no impact at all. These control variables indicate that innovation tends to slow down during regular recessions but does not necessarily speed up during subsequent periods of recovery.

These estimates are of course approximations, since they are based on data which are subject to a lot of uncertainty. Notwithstanding this point, they suggest that the economic effects of the Covid-19 pandemic are likely to be serious and enduring in Britain. Despite a labour shortage and falling unemployment in the immediate aftermath of opening up the economy, there are likely to be more serious long-term effects from such a large-scale shock. Admittedly, it will be some years before the full effects can be identified, but since our focus in this chapter is on trying to distinguish between the economic impacts of Brexit and Covid-19, this issue is examined in more detail in the next section.

The Effects of Brexit and Covid on Innovation in Britain

Having established that the Covid-19 pandemic is likely to have a large negative effect on innovation in Britain using long-run historical data, we turn to the task of separating out the effects of Covid-19 and Brexit. Given that the Bank of England Millennium data ends in 2016, there is a need to bring things up to date. To do this we look closely at recent quarterly data on Total or Multi-Factor Productivity in Britain. The series runs from the first quarter of 1995 to the first quarter of 2021 and is published by the Office for National Statistics. Figure 9.5 shows trends in these data over this period.

The ONS makes the point that multi-factor productivity has recently fallen more than in any period since records began, which reinforces the point that the UK economy is likely to be affected by the pandemic for many years to come.[58] Figure 9.5 illustrates the huge magnitude of the Covid-19 shock on innovation, which is not surprising given that large parts of the economy shut down during 2020. That said, it also shows a

---

[58] www.ons.gov.uk/economy/economicoutputandproductivity/productivitymeasures/articles/labourandmultifactorproductivitymeasuresuk/apriltojune2020

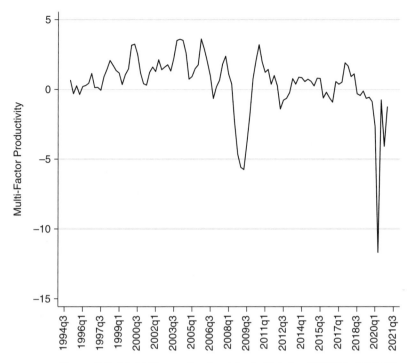

Figure 9.5 Multi-Factor Productivity in Britain, 1995Q1–2021Q1.
Source: Office for National Statistics.

fairly rapid recovery in 2021, so the question about the long-term effects remains open.

To focus specifically on the effects of the pandemic compared with those of Brexit we use a regression model estimated from the quarterly data in Figure 9.6. The model contains a lagged version of the multi-factor productivity variable as a predictor which takes into account inertia in the series. This means that we are identifying the impact of three shocks on changes in innovation over this period. The first such shock measures the impact of the Great Recession referred to earlier. The second estimates the impact of the Brexit negotiations which started after the referendum and formally ended in December 2019, when Britain finally left the European Union in January 2020. The third variable measures the impact of Covid-19, which starts in January 2020 and continues until the end of the series in the first quarter of 2021.

These variables provide rough-and-ready estimates of the impact of the three major shocks on innovation in Britain which have occurred since the start of the new Millennium. Figure 9.6 shows that all three variables had a negative impact on innovation, but while the Covid-19

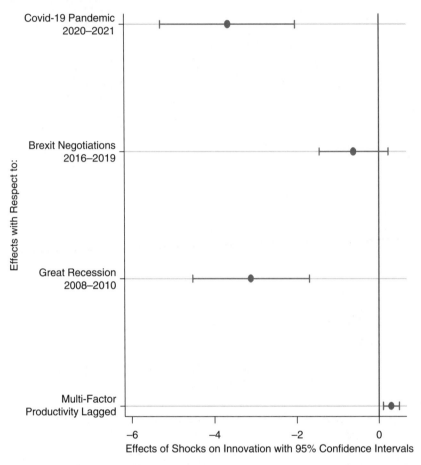

Figure 9.6 Predictions of the Impact of the Great Recession, Brexit and Covid-19 on Multi-Factor Productivity in Britain, 1995Q1–2021Q1. Source: Office for National Statistics.

and Great Recession effects were statistically significant, the Brexit effect was not. The Covid-19 effect had a slightly larger negative impact on innovation than the Great Recession, but the difference between them is relatively small. The conclusion is that up to the start of 2021 the Brexit negotiations had no significant effect on innovation, whereas the Great Recession and the Covid-19 pandemic both had large effects.

This picture may well change in the future as the long run impacts of the pandemic and Brexit are subsequently felt in the economic data. So these estimates are clearly provisional. However, it appears unlikely that future estimates will overturn the finding that the effect of the pandemic was a lot more serious than the effect of Brexit when it comes to identifying the impact of major shocks on growth and prosperity in Britain.

Discussion and Conclusion

This completes our examination of the likely effects of Brexit on the British economy. The general conclusion is that official forecasting models, particularly those which claim to be accurate many years into the future, are of little value when it comes to judging the effects of Britain leaving the European Union. In contrast, the backcasting exercise conducted in this chapter suggests that the negative effects of Brexit have been exaggerated, and they have been overshadowed by the effects of the Covid-19 pandemic.

In the most recent International Monetary Fund report on world economic performance available at the time of writing, the IMF showed that world output fell by 3.3 per cent in 2020, with a larger reduction of 4.4 per cent taking place in the advanced industrial countries.[59] According to the report, the decline in output in the UK in 2020 was 9.9 per cent, a figure considerably larger than in any other advanced industrial country apart from Spain. Despite this, the IMF puts an optimistic spin on the prospects for recovery in the world economy in the future, arguing that: 'Multispeed recoveries are under way in all regions and across income groups, linked to stark differences in the pace of vaccine rollout, the extent of economic policy support, and structural factors such as reliance on tourism.'[60] The report makes predictions that world output will recover by 6 per cent in 2021, with the UK projected to recover by 5.3 per cent. We have seen that such forecasts are highly uncertain and imply a V-shaped pattern to the recovery, a view which is questionable in light of the previous discussion.[61] In fact, if we compare economic growth in Britain up to the third quarter of 2022 with pre-pandemic growth up to the fourth quarter of 2019, it fell by 0.8 per cent. This decline was unique among leading economies, all of which had positive growth over this period.[62]

Having closely examined the economic consequences of Brexit in the next chapter, we go on to look at some of the likely effects on UK politics and the British political system more generally, thus widening the scope of the investigation of post-Brexit Britain.

---

[59] *IMF World Economic Outlook Report* (2021), p. 8.
[60] *IMF World Economic Outlook Report* (2021), p. xiii.
[61] For example, the projected recovery in GDP for India is forecast to be 12.5 per cent, which seems highly optimistic when the Johns Hopkins database shows that it has the second highest number of Covid-19 cases in the world and the country's healthcare system is currently in crisis. (https://coronavirus.jhu.edu/map.html).
[62] See https://commonslibrary.parliament.uk/research-briefings/sn02784/

10 Brexit Britain, Covid Britain
The Political Fallout

The vote for Brexit heralded the beginning of a new and tumultuous era in British politics. This book has chronicled major events in this period including the Conservative Party's landslide victory in the 2019 general election. But what happened after Boris Johnson and the Conservatives began their fourth term in office? In this chapter, we employ data from a 2021 national survey to investigate British public attitudes towards the country's EU membership after Brexit was formally achieved. Next, we use the 2021 survey data to examine the effect of another major shock to British party politics – the Covid-19 pandemic.

We compare the impact of public reactions to Brexit and the pandemic on support for the governing Conservative Party and Prime Minister Boris Johnson. We also consider the possibility that the effects of Brexit and Covid on public attitudes extended to the 'regime level' of British politics, i.e., attitudes to the political system itself rather than just parties, issues and leaders. Our analyses indicate that the impact of these two major shocks to the political system affected trust in major governmental institutions and levels of satisfaction with how democracy works in Britain. We conclude the chapter with a discussion of the effects of Brexit and the pandemic on the likelihood of Scotland voting for independence, thereby initiating the break-up of the United Kingdom.

We begin by investigating levels of stability in public attitudes towards the consequences of Brexit and factors that account for variation in these attitudes now that Britain has departed from the European Union.

Brexit Britain

The Brexit vote was highly consequential for the future of the United Kingdom, and it initiated a protracted, oftentimes bitter, battle between Leave and Remain supporters. The latter were desperate to reverse what they saw as a catastrophic mistake while the former were convinced that their hard-fought win represented the legitimate, democratically expressed preference of the British people. As discussed in earlier chapters, the conflict continued unabated for three-and-a-half years, with Remain supporters in Parliament repeatedly thwarting attempts by Theresa May's Conservative government to secure passage of a Brexit deal with the EU.

The turning point only came when May resigned after her party's disastrous performance in the May 2019 EU Parliament elections and new Conservative leader Boris Johnson led his party to a convincing victory in the subsequent December 2019 general election. Johnson's campaign slogan 'Get Brexit Done' strongly appealed to frustrated Leavers, as well as resonating positively with many voters who were fed up with the seemingly never-ending battle between the irreconcilable Remain and Leave forces.

That struggle was fuelled in part by the narrowness of the Leave majority. Leave had won in 2016, but if only one person in fifty had voted differently, Remain would have won the referendum. Moreover, more than one-quarter of those eligible to vote had failed to cast a ballot, a fact Remainers seized on to claim that the referendum was not a genuine expression of the will of the people.[1] These considerations encouraged Remainers to believe that a majority of the UK public had really favoured EU membership. That, in turn, provided them with a basis for rejecting the 2016 result and demanding another referendum which they claimed would be a genuine 'People's vote'.[2]

A close divide about the desirability of EU membership was repeatedly documented in post-2016 soundings of public opinion.[3] A number of polls detected a pro-EU shift in opinion, although this was evident in only one of our 2017–2021 Essex–UTD national surveys. When respondents who participated in the 2017 survey were asked how they would vote in another EU referendum, 44 per cent said they would opt to remain and almost as many (43 per cent) favoured leaving (see Figure 10.1). Subsequently, Leave supporters constituted slim pluralities ranging from 2 per cent to 4 per cent in our 2018, 2019 and 2021 surveys. In 2021, 44 per cent said they would vote to stay out of the EU and 40 per cent said they would vote to rejoin. These surveys also revealed that there were groups ranging in size from 9 per cent to 16 per cent who said that they were not sure how they would vote or declared they would not cast a ballot.

---

[1] Simulations of the likely behaviour of non-voters in the referendum suggest that if everyone had cast a ballot, the average result would have been 50.3 per cent Remain and 49.7 per cent Leave, with a 95 per cent confidence interval varying from 48 per cent to 52 per cent. See Clarke. Goodwin and Whiteley (2017), ch. 9.

[2] https://en.wikipedia.org/wiki/People per cent27s_Vote

[3] https://whatukthinks.org/eu/opinion-polls/uk-poll-results/

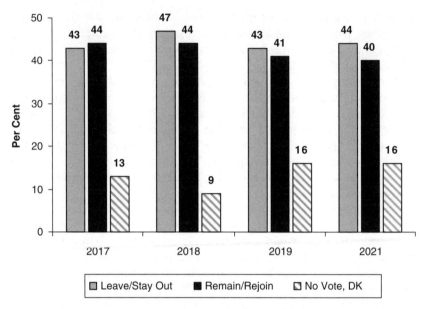

Figure 10.1 Vote If Another Referendum on European Union Membership, 2017–2021.
Source: 2017–2021 Essex–UTD surveys.

The persistently close division between Leavers and Remainers testifies to substantial aggregate stability in public attitudes towards Brexit. This stability was also evident at the *individual* level. Data from our 2021 survey reveal that 86 per cent of people who voted Remain in 2016 reported five years later that they would vote to rejoin the EU. Similarly, 90 per cent of those who had voted to leave in 2016 said they would opt to stay out (see Figure 10.2). The almost equal size of the opposing groups of Leave and Remain supporters coupled with impressive stability in their attitudes towards Brexit helped to keep the issue at the forefront of UK politics in the years after the 2016 referendum.

This impression is reinforced when we consider public opinion about the likely consequences of leaving the EU. In *Brexit: Why Britain Voted to Leave the European Union*, we presented survey evidence gathered at the time of the referendum concerning how people perceived the consequences of leaving the EU or staying in it.[4] Our statistical analyses indicated that public opinion was structured along two strongly correlated dimensions. One of them concerned the economic consequences of Brexit and its perceived effects on the UK's international influence,

---

[4] See Clarke, Goodwin and Whiteley (2017).

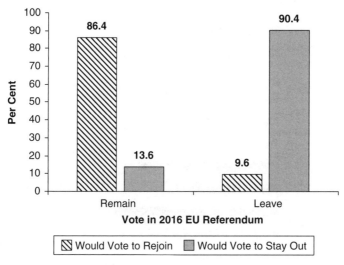

Figure 10.2 Vote Intention if Another Referendum on European Union Membership by Vote in 2016 European Union Referendum. Source: 2021 Essex–UTD survey.

whereas the second tapped into fears about high levels of immigration and the threat of terrorism. These two dimensions mirrored prominent themes in the referendum campaign, with Remain champions focusing almost exclusively on the adverse economic consequences that they insisted would ensue should the UK exit the EU. In contrast, Leave campaigners emphasized the need to 'Take Back Control', arguing that reclaiming the country's national sovereignty was crucial for rejuvenating British democracy and stemming what they characterized as an unceasing tide of migrants, many coming from central and Eastern European Union member states.

Our 2021 survey shows that public opinion about the consequences of leaving the EU did not change much over the five years following the referendum. As Figure 10.3 illustrates, in both 2016 and 2021, sizeable pluralities endorsed the core Remain argument that exiting the EU would have serious negative economic effects at both the national and personal level. In 2021, 41 per cent thought the national economy would suffer because of Brexit, whereas considerably fewer (29 per cent) thought it would improve (Figure 10.3a). In 2016, the comparable percentages had been 39 per cent and 24 per cent (Figure 10.3b). Many people also anticipated negative consequences for their own personal finances; in both 2016 and 2021 a clear plurality feared that Brexit would have negative effects on their own financial position. This story is replicated for

A. March 2021

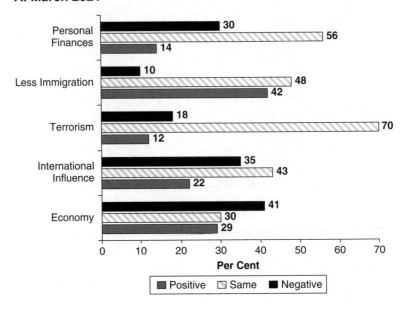

B. June 2016

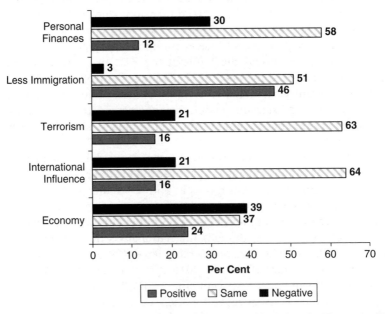

Figure 10.3 Perceived Consequences of Leaving the European Union, 2016 and 2021 (A) March 2021 (B) June 2016.
Source: 2021 Essex–UTD survey; ECMS Pre-Referendum Survey.

forecasts about the UK's international influence, although the margin by which people anticipated negative as opposed to positive effects had receded by 2021.

Expectations about Brexit's impact on immigration were also similar in both 2016 and 2021. At the time of the referendum, 46 per cent believed that immigration would be reduced if the UK left the EU and only 3 per cent thought otherwise. Five years later, 42 per cent believed that immigration would decrease with the UK being out the EU and 10 per cent thought otherwise. Predictions about terrorism were different – in both years' large majorities (63 per cent in 2016 and 70 per cent in 2021) said the risk of terrorist attacks would be the same regardless of whether the UK was an EU member state. Of the remainder, the percentage who thought the UK would be safer if it stayed in the EU was slightly greater (by 5 per cent in 2016 and 6 per cent in 2021) than the number thinking the threat of terrorism would grow after Brexit. Overall, comparisons of the 2016 and 2021 data emphasize there was substantial aggregate stability in public opinion about the likely consequences of Brexit.

Although observers unfamiliar with British politics might have been tempted to conclude that Brexit 'came out of nowhere', in fact 'Europe' had been a topic of growing controversy for many years. Early on, much of this controversy involved sporadic internecine conflicts between 'Europhiles' and 'Eurosceptics' in the Conservative Party.[5] However, in the decade preceding the referendum, UKIP leader Nigel Farage had raised the salience of the issue among the public by making EU membership the core theme of his populist political rhetoric and linking it to immigration. Demonstrating his skill at attracting media coverage, Farage did much to bring what he argued was Britain's profoundly unsatisfactory relationship with the EU to the attention of an increasingly large number of voters.[6] Some people strongly agreed with Farage, others vehemently disagreed and public opinion on the issue was deeply polarized. As discussed, comparisons of 2016 and 2021 survey data show that levels of support for leaving or remaining in the EU was quite even and largely unchanged in the years after the referendum.

To facilitate a more detailed analysis of the 2021 data, we construct a summary index of the perceived consequences of leaving the EU.[7] We use this measure to conduct a multivariate statistical analysis of these perceptions. Predictor variables in the models include evaluations of national and personal economic conditions, a sense of being

---

[5] www.theguardian.com/politics/2018/dec/09/tories-europe-eternal-battleground
[6] Clarke, Goodwin and Whiteley (2017), ch. 6.
[7] See Appendix A for descriptions of the measurement of variables used in various analyses.

left behind economically, attitudes towards immigration, ethnic/racial attitudes, partisanship, left–right ideology, value orientations and socio-demographic characteristics (age, education, gender, income, country of residence). This analysis reveals that collectively the several predictors are quite strongly related to perceptions of the consequences of exiting the EU – the goodness-of-fit statistic (R^2) equals 0.52.

The effects of various predictors are summarized in Figure.10.4. Consistent with the importance of the economy and immigration, which both heavily influence people's attitudes toward their country's EU membership, positive economic evaluations and anti-immigration sentiments are the two strongest predictors of whether someone will feel positively about the consequences of exiting the EU. Other strong predictors include Conservative partisanship, racial attitudes and values. As expected, Conservative identifiers, individuals who have conservative racial attitudes and those espousing pro-establishment or conformist values were more likely to view the consequences of leaving the EU favourably. Three other predictors have weaker positive effects – people further to the right on the left–right ideological spectrum, those supporting 'traditional British values' and older persons were all more likely to be relatively sanguine about the consequences of Brexit.

Figure 10.4 also catalogues that several predictors have negative effects. Labour and Liberal Democrat identifiers were less likely to think Brexit would produce favourable consequences. In addition, better educated individuals and those with higher incomes were less likely to have positive views of ending EU membership, as were residents of Wales and Scotland compared with people living in England.

Viewed generally, these relationships are consistent with our own and other research. The result of the 2016 referendum ensured that Brexit would be the pre-eminent issue in British politics as the government at Westminster attempted to negotiate the terms under which the UK would leave the EU. As observed, the sharp divisions in opinion about EU membership had been exacerbated by repeated rounds of bitter post-referendum wrangling.

Although it dominated the agenda, the Brexit cleavage was not independent of existing ideological and partisan divisions. As reported in Chapter 5, pro-Leave sentiments lined up closely with Conservative partisanship and a variety of supportive attitudes, beliefs and opinions at the time of the 2019 general election. This helped to produce the Conservative landslide victory in that contest, as Remain enthusiasts divided their votes between Labour and several minor opposition parties.

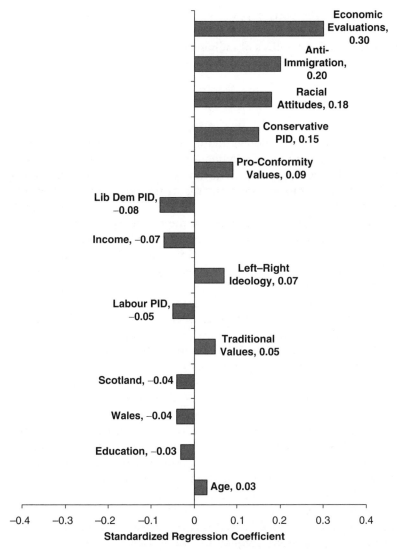

Figure 10.4 Predictors of Perceived Positive Consequences of Leaving the European Union, March 2021 National Survey.
Note: OLS regression, R^2 =.52.

Correlations between attitudes towards Brexit, partisanship and other political beliefs were not unique to the forces that drove voting in this election. Rather, as the analysis summarized in Figure 10.4 emphasizes, these relationships remained in place in the spring of 2021, and they worked to shape the party support and the contours of political conflict after Brexit became a reality. However, an unexpected and hugely important shock affecting the lives of millions of people around the world was about to push Brexit aside.

Covid Britain

Accompanied by a muted chorus of Big Ben chimes, the UK formally departed the European Union at midnight 31 January 2020. As it did so, attention continued to be heavily focused on what the consequences of this historic decision would be. Unbeknown to virtually everyone, however, Brexit was about to lose its status as the dominant issue on the public stage. Just a day earlier, on 30 January 2020, the World Health Organization (WHO) had declared that the rapidly spreading Covid-19 virus constituted 'a public health emergency of international concern'.[8] The novel coronavirus had first claimed victims in Wuhan China some months earlier and soon afterwards cases began to be reported around the globe. Britain was not spared. The virus was highly contagious and caused serious illness in many of its victims. Hospital wards soon began filling and deaths caused by the virus escalated rapidly. NHS resources were stretched thin, and fears were expressed that the health service would be overwhelmed. On 11 March 2020, the WHO underlined the seriousness of the situation by declaring Covid-19 had become a worldwide pandemic.[9] Over the following year, over 4 million UK citizens contracted the disease and over 120,000 died from it.[10] Brexit Britain has been transformed into Covid Britain.

Like many other countries, Britain was ill-prepared to deal with the pandemic. Boris Johnson's government adopted two basic strategies to cope with the crisis. The first involved adopting measures that would encourage or force people to minimize their exposure to the virus in the form of a lockdown. This approach to serious threats to public health had been used for centuries.[11]

People were encouraged to self-isolate by 'social distancing'. This involved refraining from frequenting pubs, restaurants, workplaces and other public gatherings large and small. Lending force to these

---

[8] www.npr.org/sections/7ygoatsandsoda/2020/01/30/798894428/who-declares-coronavirus-outbreak-a-global-health-emergency

[9] www.npr.org/sections/goatsandsoda/2020/03/11/814474930/coronavirus-covid-19-is-now-officially-a-pandemic-who-says

[10] www.statista.com/statistics/1101947/coronavirus-cases-development-uk/

[11] Perhaps the most famous example is Sir Isaac Newton, who decamped to Cambridge twice in the 1660s, returning to his family home in Woolsthorpe Lincolnshire to escape the ravages of the Great Plague.

recommendations, the Johnson government imposed an extensive series of legally mandated 'lockdowns'. Hospitality venues were closed, sporting events and theatre productions were cancelled and millions of people were laid off or forced to work from home using their computers. Schools and universities soon began to hold classes remotely. Social events including extended family gatherings were forbidden and strict domestic and foreign travel restrictions were imposed.

'Hiding' from Covid was not the only strategy. The Johnson government strongly promoted the development of vaccines that would provide a measure of protection from the virus. Although historically it had taken several years to create vaccines that could effectively counter viral pathogens, major pharmaceutical companies worked at what former US president, Donald Trump, called 'warp speed' to produce anti-Covid-19 vaccines.[12] These efforts were successful and this allowed the UK to begin a large-scale vaccination programme in December 2020, only nine months after the WHO's pandemic declaration. Avoiding clumsy bureaucratic procedures that bedevilled similar efforts in several EU countries and Canada, the UK's vaccine roll-out proceeded rapidly.

Also, unlike countries such as the United States and France, a very large majority of Britons (87 per cent in our 2021 survey) were willing to be vaccinated. Starting with the elderly and other vulnerable groups, a large proportion of the adult population was administered at least one 'jab' over the following months.[13] Although the pandemic continued to pose a serious threat as new variants of the virus emerged and the incidence of cases repeatedly surged when lockdowns were relaxed, highly visible and at least partially effective steps to combat Covid-19 were being taken.

Although these measures helped contain the spread of the deadly disease, they engendered many painful economic, social and psychological side effects. Our 2021 survey inquired about how people assessed the damage caused by the pandemic and the draconian efforts the Johnson government had instituted to reduce its impact. As Figure 10.5 shows, more than one-third (38 per cent) of our survey respondents indicated that they had encountered financial difficulties, and sizeable groups reported child care (15 per cent) or elder-care (17 per cent) problems. Moreover, over half (52 per cent) reported that they had suffered psychologically. The latter number is impressive, but not surprising given that the pandemic and measures taken in response to it caused large-scale disruptions well outside the realm of experience for people in all

---

[12] https://en.wikipedia.org/wiki/Operation_Warp_Speed
[13] www.england.nhs.uk/statistics/statistical-work-areas/covid-19-vaccinations/covid-19-vaccinations-archive/

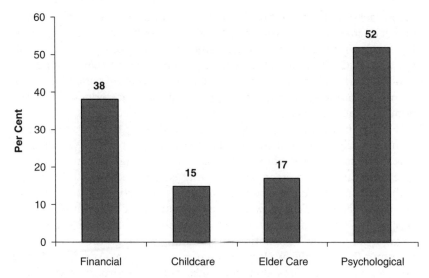

Figure 10.5 Reported Personal Problems Caused by Covid-19 Pandemic, March 2021 National Survey.
Source: 2021 Essex–UTD survey.

walks of life. Although a large majority (75 per cent) of those participating in the 2021 survey supported the government's lockdowns, many people had suffered adverse effects from the anti-Covid protocols that the government had put in place.

Also, not unexpectedly given the massive disruptions it occasioned, Covid-19 soon stimulated significant political fallout. It quickly became the pre-eminent issue on the public's mind. Our March 2021 national survey shows that nearly four respondents in five (77 per cent) designated the pandemic as one of their 'top three' most important issues and nearly three in five (59 per cent) chose it as the single most important one (see Figure 10.6). Although clearly a topic of great concern, the pandemic did not drive all other issues completely off the agenda. Typically salient issues in British politics such as the state of the economy and the NHS continued to attract widespread attention, with 61 per cent mentioning the former and 45 per cent, the latter as a top three issue. However, relatively few people thought either the economy or the NHS was most important. Concern with Brexit, meanwhile, receded. As Figure 10.6 shows, just over a quarter of those participating in our 2021 survey chose Brexit as one of their top three issues, but fewer than one person in twenty identified it as the most important. Similarly, although immigration and climate change continued to attract attention, they were much less salient than before the pandemic began.

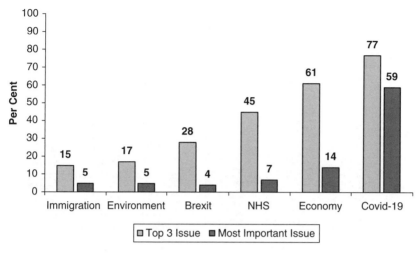

Figure 10.6 Most Important Issues, March 2021 National Survey.
Source: 2021 Essex–UTD survey.

Figure 10.7 displays data on public judgements about the ability of the two major parties to deal with Covid-19 and various other issues. These data document that a sizeable plurality (39 per cent) of those choosing Covid-19 as their single most important issue believed that the governing Conservatives were the party best able to cope with it. Substantial levels of approval of the government's efforts to deal with the Covid-19 crisis accords well with other evidence in our 2021 survey showing that a large majority (67 per cent) believed that the pandemic likely would be brought under control in 2021.

Respondents were less bullish about Labour's ability to deal with the pandemic – only slightly over one person in five selected it as the party best able to handle the situation. The Conservatives had a large lead (44 per cent to 21 per cent) over Labour on the economy (see Figure 10.7). However, Labour was viewed favourably on some issues. On Brexit, the party had a wide lead (37 per cent to 13 per cent) over the Conservatives and its lead on the NHS was even larger (43 per cent to 14 per cent). Labour's problem was that these two issues were deemed most important by only small minorities. Building on their lead on Covid-19, the Conservatives were chosen as best across all most important issues by a comfortable 10-point margin (35 per cent to 25 per cent). When asked directly to judge how the government was dealing with the pandemic, 41 per cent approved and 37 per cent disapproved of its performance.

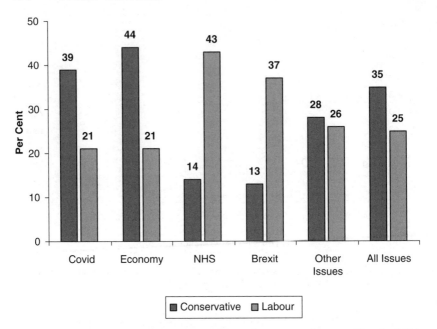

Figure 10.7 Party Best on Most Important Issues, March 2021 National Survey.
Source: 2021 Essex–UTD survey.

Trends in party support in opinion polls conducted in December 2021 after the Conservatives came to power suggest that the party's handling of the crisis and, more specifically, the rapid and successful administration of the Covid-19 vaccination programme, paid dividends. Polls tracking vote intention dynamics[14] show that the selection of Keir Starmer to be Jeremy Corbyn's replacement as Labour leader in April 2020 was accompanied by an immediate increase in that party's support and a corresponding decrease in Conservative support (see Figure 10.8). These opposing trends continued and the two parties were level-pegging circa December 2020. Then, the government began its Covid-19 vaccination programme and trends in the polls quickly reversed, with the Conservatives moving upwards and Labour downwards. Although the size of the gap between the two parties fluctuated, the Conservatives were clearly in the lead throughout the first half of 2021.

But their lead did not last. As 2021 wore on, the Conservatives were buffeted by two widely publicized scandals – one involving one of their

[14] https://en.wikipedia.org/wiki/Opinion_polling_for_the_next_United_Kingdom_ general_election

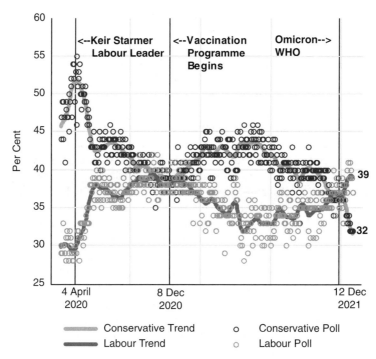

Figure 10.8 Conservative and Labour Vote Intentions in 416 National Polls, January 8, 2020–December 12, 2021.
Source: https://wikipedia.org/wiki/Opinion_polling_for_the_next_United_Kingdom_general_election

MPs, Owen Patterson, engaging in improper lobbying activity and a second concerning a 2020 Christmas party at Number 10 when the country was supposed to be in lockdown to combat a surge in Covid cases. In addition, the pandemic was not over; rather in late autumn came news that a new variant, Omicron, had been discovered in South Africa. It quickly made its way to the UK, and by mid-December 2021, thousands of cases had been reported and the government was once again considering locking down the country over the Christmas holidays. Scores of Conservative MPs were exercised about the proposed anti-Covid measures, and ninety-nine of them rebelled by voting against a government bill to introduce health passes for admission to large public gatherings.

The public reaction to these events was predictably negative, and Conservative support in the polls fell markedly. As Figure 10.8 shows, circa mid-December 2021, Conservative support had dropped to a meagre

32 per cent on trend. Boris Johnson's job approval rating was even more dismal – falling to 28 per cent. Indicative of the negative public mood, the Conservatives were routed in the 16 December North Shropshire by-election, in a massive swing to the Liberal Democrats. Criticism of Johnson's leadership was increasingly harsh, and even normally Conservative friendly media outlets like *The Daily Telegraph* speculated that he might be ousted as party leader.

While it is difficult to untangle which of several closely spaced events had the greatest impact on the Conservatives' slide in the polls, it is likely that the continuing Covid-19 crisis was especially significant. In this regard, our individual-level survey data reveal that the government's successful roll-out of the coronavirus vaccine had positive effects for the prime minister and his party in the spring of 2021. The Conservatives led Labour in vote intentions by a 42 per cent to 38 per cent margin in our March 2021 survey, and favourable judgements about the government's handling of the pandemic were an important reason for this. Most obviously, the percentage of survey respondents supporting the Conservatives ranged from 80 per cent among those who strongly approved of the party's performance on Covid-19 to merely 3 per cent among those who strongly disapproved. In a mirror image, Labour's vote intention share climbed from 15 per cent in the former group to 61 per cent in the latter one.

Multivariate statistical analyses reinforce the conclusion that voters' judgements about the government's performance on Covid-19 mattered. First, a binomial probit model[15] was employed to assess the impact of these judgements on Conservative vote intentions. This analysis includes several other predictor variables including feelings about party leaders, partisanship, left–right ideology, economic evaluations, a sense of being left behind economically, judgements about the government's handling of the NHS and immigration, racial attitudes, value orientations and socio-demographic characteristics (age, education, gender, income, country of residence). Controlling for all of these variables, the analysis indicates that judgements about the government's performance on Covid-19 were influential (see Table 10.1). Although perennially important considerations such as party leader images and partisanship were clearly at work, the impact of perceptions of how Prime Minister Johnson and his colleagues were handling the pandemic was highly statistically significant and positive ($p \leq 0.001$).

---

[15] See Long and Freese (2014).

Table 10.1 *Predictors of Conservative Vote Intentions, March 2021 National Survey*

Predictor	b	s.e.
Government Performance Covid-19	.377***	.066
Vote Leave if 2nd EU Referendum	.247***	.068
Party Leaders;		
Johnson	.245***	.031
Starmer	−0.116**	.028
Davey	−0.001	.036
Party Identification:		
Conservative	1.347***	.152
Labour	−1.758***	.176
Liberal Democrat	−1.103***	.216
Other	−2.118***	.255
Left–right Ideology	−0.003	.034
Positive Economic Evaluations	−0.122	.075
Left behind Economically	−0.142*	.070
Negative NHS Evaluations	−0.188*	.088
Anti-Immigration Attitudes	.077	.085
Racial Attitudes	.026	.095
Traditional Values	−0.004	.081
Pro-Conformity Values	.058	.084
Age	.007*	.004
Education	−0.089	.118
Gender	.081	.117
Income	−0.006	.019
Country:		
Wales	−0.492*	.261
Scotland	−2.462***	.484

McKelvey R^2 = 0.89
Per cent Classified Correctly = 95.0
N = 2,335
*** – $p \leq 0.001$; ** – $p \leq 0.01$; * – $p < 0.05$, one-tailed test.
Note: binomial probit model.

The role of leader images in the model suggests that judgements about how Johnson was dealing with the Covid-19 crisis likely had indirect effects on support for his party. The OLS regression model[16] summarized in Table 10.2 accords well with this idea. Results of this analysis of feelings about Johnson using judgements about his party's Covid-19 performance and all of the other predictors listed above make the case.

[16] See Kennedy (2008).

Table 10.2 *Predictors of Feelings about Boris Johnson, March 2021 National Survey*

Predictor	b	s.e.
Government Performance Covid-19	1.383***	.036
Vote Leave if 2nd EU Referendum	.349***	.068
Party Identification:		
Conservative	.877***	.110
Labour	−0.156	.106
Liberal Democrat	−0.130	.160
Other	−0.331**	.137
Left–right Ideology	.214***	.021
Positive Economic Evaluations	.328***	.050
Left behind Economically	.154*	.082
Negative NHS Evaluations	−0.108*	.051
Anti-Immigration Attitudes	.069	.053
Racial Attitudes	−0.031	.055
Traditional Values	.124**	.052
Pro-Conformity Values	.204***	.052
Age	−0.007**	.002
Education	−0.014	.075
Gender	−0.182**	.075
Income	−0.000	.012
Country:		
Wales	.109	.159
Scotland	−0.116	.130
Constant	.029	.217

$R^2 = 0.67$
$N = 3,002$
*** – $p \leq 0.001$; ** – $p \leq 0.01$; * – $p < 0.05$, one-tailed test.
Note: OLS regression model.

Controlling for all of the other predictors, judgements about how the government was addressing the pandemic exerted a highly significant effect ($p \leq 0.001$) on feelings about the prime minister. Voters' perceptions of how the government was reacting to the crisis mattered.

Additional analyses underscore the strength of the influence of these judgements on support for Johnson and his party. This point is illustrated in Figure 10.9, which displays how changes in approval of the government's performance on Covid-19 affect the probability of supporting the Conservatives and feelings about the prime minister. To investigate these effects, we vary judgements about the government's Covid performance from 'strongly disapprove' to 'strongly approve' while holding all other predictors in the models of Conservative vote intentions and the feelings about the prime minister at their average values. As Figure 10.9 illustrates, changing evaluations of how the government was handling

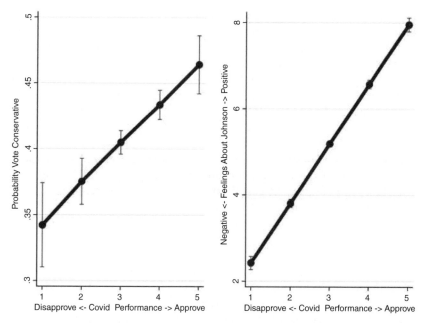

Figure 10.9 Effects of Evaluations of Government's Handling of Covid-19 Pandemic on Probability of Voting Conservative and Feelings About Boris Johnson.

Note: binomial probit analysis of Conservative vote intentions; OLS regression analysis of feelings about Boris Johnson.

the pandemic had a sizeable effect on the probability of supporting the Conservatives, with that probability increasing from 0.34 to 0.47 for an average person. And, impressively, feelings about Prime Minister Johnson climb sharply upward from slightly over 2 points to just over 8 points on a 0–10 'dislike–like' scale as Covid-19 performance judgements move from negative to positive. The pandemic topped the issue agenda and public perceptions of how the government was handling the crisis had substantial direct and indirect effects on party support.

System-Level Attitudes

Although Covid-19 and measures taken to deal with the spread of the virus dominated political discourse, the pandemic and efforts to combat it were occurring in a context where the 'Battle for Brexit' had raged for over five years. Thus far in this book we have focused on the party-political effects of attitudes towards Brexit. However, given the intense, protracted conflict the issue stimulated, its impact may well have extended to attitudes towards the wider political system, influencing trust in political institutions and judgements about the functioning of British democracy itself. As political scientists long have emphasized, levels of institutional trust and (dis)satisfaction with how the system is operating are important components of political psychology that underpin democratic regimes.[17] The prolonged battle over Brexit is precisely the kind of abrasive, high-profile conflict that could alter that psychology by corroding public support for the existing institutions and processes of British democracy. If so, Brexit would have had important consequences over and above those arising directly from the decision to sever ties with the EU. Here, we entertain this possibility by examining political trust and democracy satisfaction measured in our 2019 and 2021 national surveys.

Trust

We begin by looking at trust in 'government in general' and trust in the Parliament at Westminster. Both of these variables are measured using 0–10 scales where 0 indicates 'no trust' and 10 indicates a 'great deal of trust'. Figure 10.10 shows that average levels of trust in government in general were very similar among Leave and Remain proponents in 2019, with an average score of 4.4 for both groups. Trust in Parliament scores for the two groups also were very similar, with the averages being 4.0 and 4.3, respectively. After three-and-one-half years of acrimonious wrangling over Britain's future relationship with the EU, neither Leavers nor Remainers were minded to accord high levels of trust to major political institutions.

Figure 10.10 also indicates that the situation had changed in 2021. In the wake of the UK actually leaving the EU, levels of institutional trust shifted upward among Leavers while remaining largely unchanged among Remainers. Thus, average trust in government among the former group moved upward from 4.4 to 5.7 while falling just slightly to 4.0 among the latter. As for trust in Parliament, Leavers recorded an average score of 5.4 in 2021 as compared to 4.4 in 2019. The comparable scores for Remainers were 4.4 in both years. These numbers indicate that the Johnson Government's success in leaving the EU worked to restore Leave supporters' confidence in UK political institutions, at least to a limited degree. Although neither Leavers nor Remainers exhibited high levels of institutional trust, after Brexit there were clear differences between them.

---

[17] See, e.g., Easton (1965), Dahl (1971), Kornberg and Clarke (1992); Anderson, Blais, Bowler, Donovan and Listhaug (1997); Uslaner (2018).

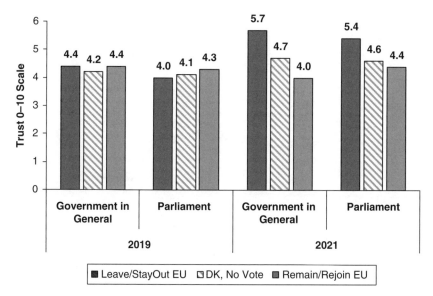

Figure 10.10 Average Levels of Trust in Government and Parliament by Vote if Another European Union Referendum, 2019 Pre-General Election and March 2021 National Surveys.
Source: 2019 Essex–UTD pre-general election survey and 2021 Essex–UTD survey.

Democracy (Dis)satisfaction

Data on levels of (dis)satisfaction with the working of British democracy gathered in several national Essex–UTD surveys conducted since 2015 strongly suggest that support for major political institutions has dynamic properties. As Figure 10.11 documents, levels of satisfaction/dissatisfaction with British democracy were quite similar from 2016 through 2018, with the percentage stating they were dissatisfied always being slightly greater than the percentage saying they were satisfied. For example, circa 2018, nearly half (49 per cent) of those surveyed were dissatisfied and slightly fewer (46 per cent) were satisfied.[18] Then, as the Brexit conflict remained stubbornly unresolved, the size of the dissatisfied group ramped up to 58 per cent at the time of the May 2019 EU Parliament elections. It was almost as large seven months later when the December

[18] Widespread dissatisfaction with how democracy is performing in one's country is not unique to Britain. Studies conducted in 2019 and 2020 by the Pew Research Foundation report that democracy dissatisfaction has reached high levels in many countries. See www.pewresearch.org/global/2020/02/27/satisfaction-with-democracy and www.pewresearchorg/global/2019/04/29/many-across-the-globe-are-dissatisfied-with-how-democracy-is-working/

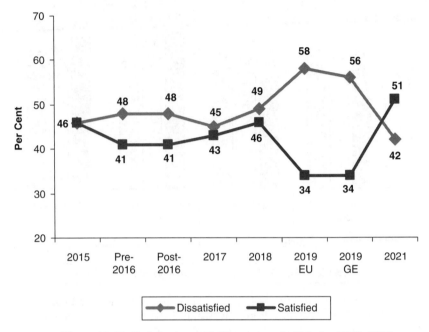

Figure 10.11 Satisfaction with Democracy in Britain, 2015–2021.
Source: 2015–2021 Essex–UTD surveys.

2019 general election was held. In contrast, only just over one-third of the participants in our two 2019 surveys declared that they were satisfied with how British democracy was performing.

The substantial increase in democracy dissatisfaction circa 2019 is consistent with the proposition that a large segment of the British electorate was increasingly frustrated by the continuing stalemate between Leavers and Remainers. When that stand-off was finally broken by the election of a Conservative government with a strong parliamentary majority, dissatisfaction with how democracy was working subsequently dropped by 14 per cent and satisfaction increased by 17 per cent. This change and the more general pattern over time in these survey data suggest that the struggle over Brexit had exerted substantial effects on how the public evaluated the operation of British democracy.

As is the case for institutional trust, major differences in public satisfaction with democracy among Leavers and Remainers emerged once Brexit had been achieved. Figure 10.12 tells the tale. As Panel A of this figure indicates, in 2019 both Leavers and Remainers were about equally likely to say that they were dissatisfied with British democracy, with 59 per cent of the former group and 55 per cent of the latter one expressing

A. 2019 Pre-General Election Survey

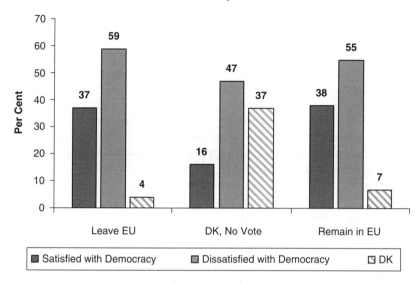

B. 2021 Survey

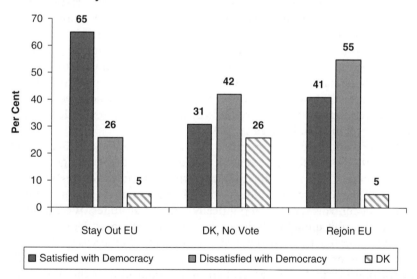

Figure 10.12 Satisfaction with Democracy in Britain by Vote if Another European Union Referendum, 2019 and 2021 (A) 2019 Pre-General Election Survey (B) 2021 Survey.
Source: 2019 Essex–UTD pre-general election survey, 2021 Essex–UTD survey.

their displeasure. In contrast, just over one-third of both groups indicated they were satisfied. Panel B shows that the pattern had changed markedly two years later. In the wake of the UK's departure from the EU, nearly two-thirds of Leave supporters said they were satisfied with how British democracy worked and only one-quarter said they were dissatisfied. In sharp contrast, just two-fifths of Remainers were satisfied and over half were dissatisfied.

Earlier in this chapter we emphasized that once the pandemic struck it quickly replaced Brexit as the pre-eminent issue on the issue agenda. And as we have seen, evaluations of the Government's handling of the situation had a strong impact on support for the governing Conservative Party and Boris Johnson. Similar to Brexit, it is possible that reactions to the pandemic also had regime-level effects, influencing levels of satisfaction with the working of British democracy. Data summarized in Figure 10.13 strongly support this idea.

This figure illustrates how evaluations of democracy varied as expectations about the future course of the pandemic move from pessimistic to optimistic. Among those who believed that Covid-19 was very unlikely to be brought under control over the next year, fully 69 per cent were dissatisfied with the working of British democracy. The percentage dissatisfied then declined steadily among survey respondents who were more optimistic about the likelihood of controlling Covid-19. Among those who thought controlling the pandemic was very likely, only 25 per cent were dissatisfied. Levels of democracy satisfaction were a mirror image, growing from 24 per cent among those who were very pessimistic about the future course of the crisis to fully 71 per cent among those who were very optimistic. These large percentage differences suggest that the politics of the pandemic extended to the regime level in Covid Britain.

The preceding analyses indicate that these two shocks – Brexit and Covid-19 – both influenced how people evaluated the workings of British democracy. To study the impact of these attitudes on (dis)satisfaction with democracy we conduct a multivariate analysis which includes statistical controls for several politically relevant attitudes. We employ a binomial probit model with democracy dissatisfaction as the dependent variable – scored 1 if someone is dissatisfied and 0 otherwise. The principal predictor variables are attitudes towards Brexit and level of confidence that Covid-19 will be brought under control over the next year. Other predictors include Conservative partisanship, economic evaluations, feeling being left behind economically, left–right ideology, political efficacy, social trust, life satisfaction and socio-demographics (age, education, ethnicity, gender, income, country of residence).

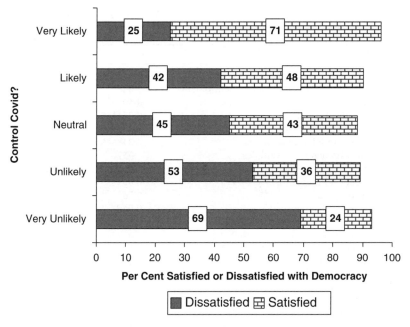

Figure 10.13 Satisfaction with Democracy in Britain by Likelihood Covid-19 Pandemic Will Be Brought Under Control Over Next Year. Source: 2021 Essex–UTD survey.

Table 10.3 shows that several of these predictor variables have statistically significant effects. Most important in the present context, attitudes towards Brexit and expectations regarding the future course of the pandemic both affect dissatisfaction with democracy in expected ways. People who support Brexit and those who anticipate that Covid-19 will be brought under control over the next year were less likely to express dissatisfaction with British democracy than were those who oppose Brexit and those who were pessimistic about circumscribing the pandemic's predations.

To gauge the strength of these effects, we compute the probability of being dissatisfied with democracy as attitudes towards Brexit and expectations of controlling Covid vary while all other predictor variables set at their average values. Figure 10.14 illustrates that the probability of being dissatisfied with democracy falls from 0.45 among people who wish to rejoin the EU to 0.37 among those who wish to stay out. The effect of expectations about controlling Covid is stronger. Among those who believe the likelihood of curtailing the pandemic's effects is low, the

Table 10.3 Predictors of Dissatisfaction with Democracy in Britain, March 2021 National Survey

Predictors	b	s.e.
Vote Leave if 2nd EU Referendum	−0.125***	.034
Likelihood Covid-19 Under Control	−0.048***	.011
Conservative Party Identification	−0.505***	.068
Positive Economic Evaluations	−0.271***	.039
Left behind Economically	.124***	.033
Negative NHS Evaluations	.238***	.038
Anti-Immigration Attitudes	.057	.036
Left–right Ideology	−0.061***	.015
Political Efficacy	−0.031***	.010
Social Trust	−0.049***	.012
Life Satisfaction	−0.040***	.015
Age	.004**	.002
Education	.027	.056
British/English Ethnicity	.164	.085
Gender-Male	.155***	.052
Income	.164	.009
Country:		
Wales	.144	.113
Scotland	.132	.089
Constant	.630***	.190

McKelvey R^2 = 0.38
Per cent Classified Correctly = 72.5
N = 3002
*** − p ≤ 0.001; ** − p ≤ 0.01; * − p < 0.05, one-tailed test.
Note: binomial probit model.

probability of being dissatisfied with democracy is 0.50. This recedes to 0.35 among persons who are very optimistic that the virus will be contained. The greater strength of attitudes towards Covid-19 compared to Brexit accords well with the pandemic's dominance of the issue agenda and fits in with the findings in Chapter 9. In the spring of 2021 Brexit remained a contentious topic in British politics but Covid had become the major driver of how voters were evaluating the political system's performance

It also is noteworthy that several other predictors had significant effects on dissatisfaction with democracy. Consistent with expectations, compared to supporters of other parties or those who failed to identify with any party, people who identified with the governing Conservatives were less likely to be dissatisfied as were respondents who placed themselves on the right of the ideological spectrum. In addition, people who evaluated economic conditions positively were less likely to

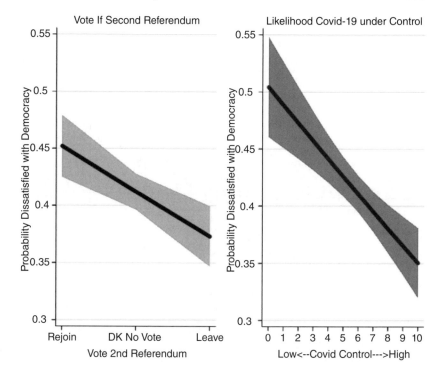

Figure 10.14 Probability Dissatisfied with Democracy in Britain by Vote if Another European Union Referendum, and Likelihood Covid-19 Pandemic Under Control in Next Year.

be dissatisfied, whereas those who felt left behind economically were more likely be dissatisfied. Similarly, negative judgements about the performance of the NHS worked to increase democracy dissatisfaction, while higher levels of political efficacy, social trust and life satisfaction all worked to decrease it. Controlling for these several effects, the impact of socio-demographic variables was muted. Two exceptions were that older people and men were more likely to be dissatisfied than younger people and women. The weakness of socio-demographic characteristics is understandable given that these variables stand well back in the list of causal forces affecting political attitudes and behaviour.

Brexit, Covid and Support for Scotland's Independence

The most salient regime-level issue in the contemporary UK politics concerns the possible independence of Scotland. In a September

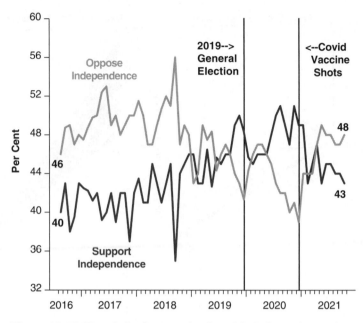

Figure 10.15 Trends in Support for Scottish Independence, August 2016–October 2021.
Source: 'What the UK Thinks' and Wikipedia.

2014 referendum the Scottish electorate voted by a 55.3 per cent to 44.7 per cent margin to remain in the United Kingdom. However, in the subsequent 2016 Brexit referendum Scottish voters opted strongly (67.2 per cent to 32.8 per cent) to remain in the EU, thereby suggesting the possibility that favourable attitudes towards EU membership might encourage Scots to opt for independence from the UK if another independence referendum were held. In this regard, Figure 10.15 shows trends in support for independence in polls conducted between August 2016 to October 2021. It is apparent that the EU referendum had no immediate effect on support for Scottish independence. Opponents of independence outnumbered supporters, albeit by a relatively narrow margin, and this continued until the Conservatives won the 2019 general election.

After Boris Johnson led his party to victory in that contest support for Scotland's independence surged in the polls, but this was a short-run reaction and by January 2020 opposition to independence was level-pegging with support for it. Soon afterwards the onset of the pandemic rapidly changed the picture with pro-independence sentiment again

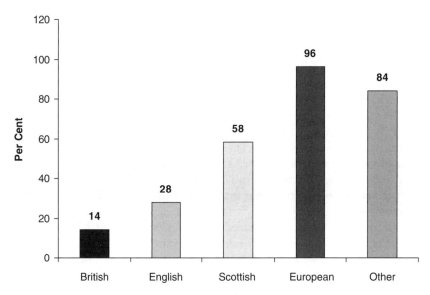

Figure 10.16 Support for Scottish Independence Among National Identity Groups.
Source: 2021 Essex–UTD survey.

surging and remaining high for the rest of the year. This development encouraged the SNP to vigorously reaffirm its desire for another independence referendum when the party campaigned in the May 2021 Scottish parliamentary elections. However, as Figure 10.15 illustrates, 2021 brought yet another change, with support for independence waning and opposition to it again becoming the majority view.

What could explain this pattern? A plausible answer is that attitudes towards independence are driven largely by two factors – identity politics and valence politics. Regarding the first, Figure 10.16 displays responses to survey questions asking respondents in Scotland about their national identities and support for Scottish independence. The figure documents that a majority (58 per cent) of those identifying as Scots favoured independence when the survey was conducted in March 2021. This survey also showed that just over three-fifths of the respondents in Scotland thought of themselves as Scots, with a large majority of the remainder identifying as British or, English. Only 19 per cent of the former group and 28 per cent of the latter one favoured independence. Although those identifying themselves as European or 'Other' strongly favoured independence, they constituted slightly less than 2 per cent of the survey respondents.

These numbers, in part, explain why support for independence has been a minority view for most of the time since the vote on Scottish independence in 2014. Scots identifiers are a majority in Scotland but a large minority of them oppose independence. In doing so, they are joined by overwhelming majorities of those who think of themselves as British or English.

The valence dimension of attitudes towards independence was made clear by the effects of the pandemic reported by people participating in the survey. Some 44 per cent of the respondents in Scotland who indicated that they encountered serious financial difficulties as a result of the pandemic favoured Scottish independence compared with only 21 per cent who said they had no financial problems. Similarly, 41 per cent who stated that they experienced significant mental health problems favoured independence compared with only 21 per cent who reported no psychological problems. The explanation of this pattern is simple – if an individual had a rough time coping with the pandemic they wanted a change, and this desire extended to the constitutional order in Britain. It is clear that valence politics which at their core are about government performance play a big role in explaining whether Scots favour or oppose another referendum and independence. If an incumbent government is judged to perform well on a pressing issue like the pandemic this helps to build support for the extant political regime. Negative judgements have the opposite effect.

The revival of opposition to independence in 2021 is explained by this process. In early December 2020 when the UK was beginning the Covid vaccine rollout, 48.5 per cent stated that they would vote yes in another independence referendum and 41.5 per cent said they would vote no. Five months later, in early May, when the vaccine distribution programme was well under way, these numbers were reversed with 42.9 per cent indicating they would vote yes and 47.1 per cent saying they would vote no. It seems that the Government's successful vaccination programme combined with the European Union's difficulties implementing a similar programme along with its heavy-handed threats to cut off vaccine supplies to the UK took a toll on the EU's reputation. It encouraged Scots to see the advantages of a UK-wide response to the pandemic and changed some minds about the advantages of independence.

To summarize, it appears unlikely that differences in support for Brexit in Scotland and the rest of the UK are large enough to assure a pro-independence majority in a second independence referendum. Equally, the pandemic created real problems for many people across the UK, but the government's successful vaccine rollout and its financial assistance programmes for those rendered jobless by measures taken to combat the pandemic changed minds north of the border. Some Scots were rethinking the advantages of going it alone in a world where a rampaging virus emphasized that serious threats to personal well-being could quickly become a dangerous reality.

Conclusion: Pandemic Politics Joins Brexit Politics

On January 31, 2020, Britain formally left the European Union. At the time it seemed that conflict over Brexit might continue largely unabated with Remainers – now 'Rejoiners' – fighting an 'I told you so' rearguard action, hoping against hope to propel the UK back into the EU. It was not to be. Although the division of opinion regarding the desirability of Brexit and its consequences remained essentially unchanged, the issue's salience was soon diminished as the surging Covid-19 pandemic engulfed the country. The pandemic posed serious health risks and governmental efforts to limit them by having people 'hide' from the virus caused major economic, social and psychological damage. Almost overnight, Brexit Britain was transformed into Covid Britain.

There were political consequences. Unlike people in countries like France and the United States, a large majority of Britons accepted the necessity of the Johnson Government's lockdowns, and its successful implementation of an anti-Covid vaccination programme paid dividends for the prime minister and his party. Efforts by new Labour leader Keir Starmer to restore his party's fortunes after its disastrous performance in the 2019 general election were thwarted as the Conservatives dominated vote intention polls after the vaccination programme got underway.

However, the Conservatives' lead in the polls did not last. Rather than fading away, the Covid crisis persisted, and Omicron, a new variant of the virus, began to wreak havoc in the UK as 2021 drew to a close. Government attempts to deal with the situation appeared to many observers to be a hesitant, disorganized rehash of what been done a year earlier. Criticism by press and public quickly mounted. Adding to the Government's woes, the economy showed increasing signs of stress, with inflation climbing to its highest level in a decade. In concert with widely publicized scandals, a by-election defeat in a historically safe Conservative seat, a near-loss in another such locale, the renewed Covid crisis and Government reactions to it caused public support for Prime Minister Boris Johnson and his party to plummet. The revelation that civil servants and ministers in Whitehall and 10 Downing Street exempted themselves from the lockdown restrictions by organizing frequent parties was particularly damaging. It created the impression that there was one law for political elites and another law for the rest of the population

There were regime-level consequences as well. Our March 2021 survey testifies that Brexit and Covid-19 both influenced levels of people's trust in political institutions and their evaluations of the performance of British democracy. Institutional trust and democracy satisfaction increased substantially among Leave proponents but not among Rejoiners once the UK had departed the EU. The effects of attitudes towards Covid were stronger. People who were optimistic about controlling the disease exhibited significantly lower levels of democracy dissatisfaction than did those who were pessimistic about the prospects of curtailing the virus's predations. It also appears that favourable public reactions to the Westminster Government's efforts to combat the pandemic eroded support for Scotland's independence. The durability of this important regime-level effect remains to be seen.

In the Postscript which follows we summarize major arguments and key findings in the book as a whole and consider their possible implications for the future of UK politics.

Postscript
Brexit Britain: Retrospect and Prospect

The narrow Leave majority in Britain's 2016 referendum on continued European Union membership was widely unexpected and hugely consequential. The referendum campaign had been hotly contested and the temperature of political rhetoric did not subside when the result was known. Rather, the controversy over Brexit escalated and continued to dominate Britain's political life over the next several years and, in many respects, remains with us today.

The continuing 'Battle of Brexit' shaped the decisions to hold two general elections which in turn powerfully influenced the results of the negotiations with the EU and also reshaped electoral support for the left and right. This battle may well again become a major fault line in the country's political culture at both the elite and mass levels, dividing those who want a closer relationship between Britain and the EU, and those who want to keep the two sides firmly apart. Since 2016, our regular national surveys have shown how the British people's attitudes toward Brexit have also been very stable at both the aggregate and individual levels. Also, although the UK has now left the EU, no consensus has emerged on the wisdom of that decision.

As indicated by the percentages of people who say they would either vote to leave or rejoin the EU if another referendum were held, the country remains very evenly divided on the issue. It is highly uncertain what the outcome of such a referendum would be or whether such a vote would even be held. At the time of finishing this book, in the summer of 2022, one regular poll by YouGov found that while 49 per cent of people felt that the country had been 'wrong' to vote to Leave the European Union, 37 per cent felt that the country had been right. Yet Remainers and Leavers remained highly polarized; while 87 per cent of Remainers still felt Brexit had been the wrong decision, 75 per cent of Leavers felt it had been the right one.[1]

---

[1] https://docs.cdn.yougov.com/m5m97b82y6/TheTimes_VI_220525_W.pdf

At the time of the 2016 referendum, public opinion on the likely consequences of Brexit was organized along two dimensions. One of these dimensions concerned the economy. Substantial pluralities accepted the argument of many economists and Remain proponents that Brexit would seriously damage both the economy and their own finances. A second dimension was political-cultural, and involved a mix of concerns about the erosion of national sovereignty and, more specifically, the need to curtail what was characterized as a continuing flood of immigrants into Britain. 'Take Back Control' became a highly effective rallying cry for the Leave campaign because it tapped into both dimensions. Our more recent 2021 national survey shows that these dimensions continue to structure public opinion about the consequences of Brexit. Opinion on both dimensions is very similar to what it had been five years earlier. What most people believed about the pros and cons of EU membership in 2016 is still what they believe now.

As powerful as the effects of the Brexit controversy have been, it would be a mistake to conclude that the issue is all that mattered for voting in the 2017 and 2019 general elections. Research on British voting behaviour has repeatedly shown that party leader images, partisan identifications, and judgements about party performance on issues such as the economy and healthcare also do much to shape voters' decisions. Our analyses of the impact of economic conditions on governing party vote shares since the mid-1960s in Chapter 6 confirms this point.

Valence politics forces were not 'cancelled' by the Brexit controversy, but rather continued to be influential in both 2017 and 2019, as well as in the 2019 elections to the European Parliament. Voters' images of former Labour leader, Jeremy Corbyn, were especially important on both occasions. Although many people viewed Corbyn negatively before the 2017 election campaign began, this changed in the run-up to polling day, especially among younger voters, many of whom flocked to the Labour banner. Almost overnight Corbyn became a political rock star for young people and videos of crowds chanting 'Oh Jeremy Corbyn!' went viral on social media. Statistical analyses show that feelings about Corbyn had very strong effects on voting in 2017 and did much to propel Labour's surge in the polls as the campaign progressed.

Two years later, voters' feelings about Corbyn again were very influential, but the impact was quite the opposite of what had happened in 2017. There was no upward trend in pro-Corbyn sentiment; rather his image in 2019 remained profoundly negative throughout much of the campaign. In the end Labour paid a heavy price for this on election day, with the party slumping to their lowest number of seats won since 1935 and losing much of their northern Red Wall.

The public's image of Boris Johnson was also very important. Johnson had played a key role in the successful Leave campaign in 2016 and when he became leader of the Conservative Party in July 2019, feelings about him helped to boost his party's support. To be sure, the Conservatives' 2019 campaign slogan 'Get Brexit Done!' and Johnson's claim to have an 'Oven Ready Brexit' deal to offer the EU did much to attract Leavers and voters who were increasingly frustrated with the stalemate over Brexit in Parliament. But over and above attitudes towards Brexit, statistical analyses document that feelings about Johnson were a major positive driver of Conservative voting. Although highly salient, Brexit did not negate the strong impact of voters' images of party leaders on electoral choice in recent general elections.

Jeremy Corbyn's positive image among young people was, in part, a reflection of broader age differences in political attitudes and behaviour. Our survey data presented in Chapters 3, 4 and 5 reveal large age divides in party support in the 2017 and 2019 general elections as well as the 2019 European election. The surveys that we conducted in 2018 and then 2021 echo these findings – young people consistently tend to be strongly pro-Labour. Substantial age differences are also apparent in attitudes towards Brexit. Young people, particularly those with higher education, are much more likely to express pro-Remain attitudes than are older Britons. These persistent differences signify the presence of a strong age and educational divide in the British electorate and one that will likely remain with us for years ahead, reshaping and driving politics through the 2020s and beyond.

Other studies also have detected this age cleavage and two explanations have been offered for it. One concerns the differential impacts of the Great Recession and the austerity policies that were pursued by Conservative governments over the past decade on the young. Seen through this lens, major increases in university tuition fees, difficulties in finding stable employment in well-paying jobs and an 'out-of-reach' housing market have combined to make many young people unhappy with the incumbent government. At the same time this increased the attractiveness of the redistributive policies offered by a Corbyn-led Labour Party.

The second explanation focuses on values and a deep cultural divide between different age groups. Some observers argue that this cultural chasm has developed as a result of an increasingly large number of young people experiencing higher education where they are exposed to radical, cosmopolitan ideas. These draw attention to issues like the oppression of ethnic, gender and racial minorities and prompt young people to seek more radical political alternatives that better reflect their values. In the Corbyn era, Labour could be seen as providing that option.

If this explanation has validity, age differences may diminish in strength if Labour becomes more ideologically moderate under Keir Starmer. Although this is possible, our survey data indicate that the age cleavage remains very much in evidence in British politics and, so, many of these younger voters will continue to search out more radical political options.

The Brexit divide and these sharp age differences stand in sharp contrast to the weakness of traditional social class divisions in party support. Although the correlation between class and voting behaviour was never as strong or stable as some observers assumed, it was a defining feature of British politics throughout the last century, and also structured competition between the Conservative and Labour parties. But, as we have seen, today, at the level of individual voting behaviour, this cleavage has now virtually disappeared. That said, analyses in Chapter 7 reveal that at the constituency level broader differences in class captured by the Human Development Index are strongly related to party support. Britain's geographical divisions have a variety of economic, educational and health consequences which remain strong.

Those effects notwithstanding, in 2019 the Conservatives were able to breach Labour's Red Wall and capture a sizeable number of seats. These Red Wall constituencies were characterized by a combination of relatively low scores on the Human Development Index coupled with relatively strong anti-EU sentiment. Testifying to the importance of the latter, Boris Johnson's 'Get Brexit Done' campaign slogan helped to move a sizeable share of these constituencies into the Conservative column in 2019. However, the findings in Chapter 7 indicate that these results were strongly influenced by Brexit, implying that these constituencies may not stay Conservative if the Brexit cleavage recedes and their human development deficit continues into the future. If the Johnson Government's efforts to 'level up' these constituencies are judged by voters to be unsuccessful, many of these seats are likely to return to Labour in the years ahead.

Assessing the impact of Brexit on Britain's economy, society and politics is hugely complicated by the onset of the Covid-19 pandemic. Starting in the winter of 2020, shortly after the country exited from the EU, the Covid crisis and government efforts to mitigate it have had a variety of negative effects that are likely to persist long after the immediate dangers to public health have receded. As this is written, the economy is increasingly beset by a worrisome combination of sluggish growth and rising inflation which readers of a certain age might characterize as 'stagflation' – an echo of the 1970s and which helped set the stage for the far more radical Thatcher experiment.

Many Remain, now Rejoin, proponents are likely to attribute these economic maladies to Brexit as well as to Covid-19. Their thinking is that if only the electorate had heeded the many gloomy economic predictions made in advance of the 2016 referendum, they would have rejected Brexit and all would be well. However, our analyses in Chapter 9 show that many of these pessimistic forecasts have been very wide of the mark. Stated simply, many prominent economists got it wrong. Moving forward, any assessment of Brexit's impact on the economy faces the huge challenge of taking into account the downside effects of the Covid-19 crisis and the Ukraine war. Available data shows that the impact of historical pandemics on the economy and society can be severe and long-lived, or even permanent.

This is not to say that the economic effects of Brexit will be positive in the short – or long run. Rather, as Kay and King[2] recently observed, when it comes to economic forecasting, we are often dealing with a world where deep uncertainty rather than calculable risk is the order of the day. This prescient observation echoes arguments advanced by American economist Frank Knight[3] a century ago and it is very relevant to present circumstances. Our analyses suggest that the negative impacts of the pandemic are likely to exceed those associated with Brexit. However, this should not give Leave supporters a reason to celebrate. Leavers as well as Rejoiners will likely suffer from the negative economic and social effects that follow the Covid-19 pandemic.

Covid has had political effects as well. Analyses in Chapter 10 demonstrate that the speedy and successful implementation of an anti-Covid vaccine programme in the first quarter of 2021 gave Boris Johnson's government a substantial boost in the polls while undercutting a revival of Labour support invigorated by the party's new leader, Keir Starmer. Like healthcare more generally, the pandemic is a quintessential valence issue and a government that is seen to handle it effectively can expect to be rewarded at the polls. However, administering a vaccine has not proven to eradicate Covid; new variants of the virus have appeared, and they continue to pose substantial public health risks to Britain and to the wider world.

The longer-term effects of the pandemic and other problems have ensured that the Johnson government subsequently suffered a loss of support from an increasingly restive and impatient electorate. In summer 2022, the Johnson government has also come under fire from allegations of Conservative Party cronyism, Covid-19 rule-breaking in Number 10

---

[2] Kay and King (2020).
[3] Knight (1921).

Downing Street associated with the 'Partygate' scandal, and growing exasperation with how the prime minister is handling these ongoing crises, especially on his 'anti-Lockdown' and 'tax-cutting' right-wing flank. The criticism is that with taxation at its highest level since the immediate post-war period and very ambitious public spending plans, he is not behaving like a traditional Conservative prime minister. In addition, rising rates of inflation are creating difficulties for both the government and the wider electorate.

In December 2021, Johnson suffered a major rebellion (of 100 Conservative MPs) over his plans to introduce further Covid-19 restrictions – a larger rebellion than the 81 Conservative MPs who rebelled against David Cameron in the EU referendum debate in 2011. Subsequently, the discontent culminated in a vote of no confidence in his leadership by Conservative MPs in early June 2022. The prime minister won this vote by 211 votes to 148, but the fact that 41 per cent of the Parliamentary Conservative Party expressed no confidence in his leadership significantly weakened his authority, and it points to ongoing intra-party difficulties. The party stopped soon thereafter. Amid growing reports of scandals involving him, increasing worries about his competence and his honesty, and rising numbers of resignations of cabinet members and aides, Boris Johnson announced his resignation outside of No. 10 on 7 July 2022, effective when a new Conservative Party leader was selected. This turned out to be Liz Truss, whose short-lived premiership resulting from catastrophic economic policy announcements has made the Conservatives' prospects for a future election win remote.

Meanwhile, Labour took a lead in voting intentions in the polls. The extent to which a Starmer-led Labour Party can profit from growing discontent with the Conservative government over these various issues in the next general election has been made much clearer by the turmoil in Conservative ranks. We have observed that the political attitudes of young people are considerably more progressive than those of their elders and more supportive of the party. They are more supportive of the identity politics of ethnicity, gender and race than are older, less well-educated, less well-off traditional Labour voters. Many of the latter, who live in historic Labour strongholds in the Midlands and North, are much less supportive of these concerns. Appealing simultaneously to both groups is a major challenge for Labour and its leader. What will win back the 'Red Wall' may not be what the progressives want to hear, and what appeals to them may well prove disconcerting to Labour's traditional base.

Analyses also show that the effects of the bitter Brexit controversy have extended beyond party politics to influence public attitudes towards important governmental institutions and processes. These 'regime-level' effects are evident in low levels of trust in the Westminster Parliament and government more generally, as well as negative assessments of the functioning British democracy. As the struggle between Leavers and Remainers continued, substantial numbers of people in both camps indicated that they were dissatisfied not just with their leaders in Westminster but with the operation of British democracy.

Then, when the Johnson-led Conservatives won the December 2019 general election and proceeded to take the country out of the EU, the mood among Leavers changed. Predictably, they became considerably more positive about how democracy worked in Britain – they had elected a government that delivered on a key issue. In contrast, Remainers had seen Brexit enacted and many of them expressed their lack of trust in major national political institutions and feelings of unhappiness with the state of British democracy. The system had failed to give them what they wanted. This reflects how Brexit has had broader systemic effects.

Efforts to secure Scotland's independence constitute the most immediate regime-level problem facing the UK. Although attitudes to the independence question are driven in part by deep-seated ethnic identities, these attitudes have a dynamic that indicates that public judgements about government performance are significant to them as well. In this regard, analyses of poll data show that support for independence became the majority position in the wake of the Conservative victory in the 2019 general election. However, more recent polls suggest that perceptions that the UK government was handling the Covid crisis effectively while some EU governments were ensnared in webs of bureaucratic inertia and mismanagement convinced some Scots to reconsider their position on independence. As a result, pro-independence sentiment receded. Of course, if judgements about the Westminster government's performance should turn negative again, another reversal in the balance of opinion about Scottish independence is possible. More generally, voters' judgements about government performance on major valence issues such as the pandemic and the economy will do much to determine the success or failure of the Scottish independence movement and, by implication, the future of the United Kingdom.

Writing in the dark days of the Great Depression of the 1930s, Winston Churchill expressed reservations about the operation of modern Western democracies: 'Democratic governments drift along the line of least resistance, taking short views, paving their way with sops and doles, and smoothing their path with pleasant-sounding platitudes.'[4] Although

---

[4] Churchill (1931).

this characterization has a ring of truth as a description of their politics, sometimes democratic governments find themselves confronting major, even historically significant, challenges.

The Leave victory in the 2016 EU referendum is a case in point. Almost overnight, it transformed British politics in ways few would have imagined beforehand. Some four and a half years later, the ensuing Battle of Brexit ultimately led to the UK's departure from the EU. But decamping Brussels did not terminate the Brexit controversy, and it did little to bridge the chasm between Leave and Remain. Heighted fragmentation and polarization continue to characterize party politics, and support of major political institutions varies significantly by attitudes towards European Union membership. Furthermore, as just observed, the possibility that Brexit will be followed by Scoxit – with Scotland potentially voting to leave the UK – remains very real.

Overlaid by the multifaceted threats posed by the worldwide Covid-19 pandemic, the Ukraine war and Brexit continue to challenge the UK political system and its leaders. Although the 2016 referendum was called to debate the specific question of Europe, the result of that debate has since gone on to have much broader and profound effects on the political system, the effects of which will remain with us for years to come. But to reiterate an earlier point, Britain's future lies in the hands of its own people, and in 2016 these people spoke. They sought to reverse the growing internationalism, cosmopolitanism and globalization advocated by elites in Britain and across the Western world, whose members have often been insulated from the consequences of such policies in the past. It is no surprise that as these developments have largely concentrated the gains from these policies in the hands of these elites, many of those who have been excluded have demanded a change of direction.

Appendix A: Survey Methodology

This appendix describes the survey data and the key variables that are used in the analyses presented in various chapters of this book.

Survey Data

The Essex Continuous Monitoring Survey (ESCM) and the Essex University–University of Texas at Dallas (Essex–UTD) project includes the 2016 EU referendum survey as well as the following surveys.

The fieldwork for the 2015 and 2017 general election surveys was conducted by YouGov under the direction of Joe Twyman. Sample sizes for the 2015 pre- and post-election surveys are N = 3033 and N = 3035, respectively. The sample size for the 2015 pre-/post-election panel is N = 2505. Sample sizes for the 2017 pre- and post-election surveys are N = 4014 and N = 5134, respectively. The sample size for the pre-/post- panel is N = 4014.

The 2019 European Parliament election surveys include a pre-election survey carried out during the four days preceding the 23 May 2019 election (N = 2525) and a post-election survey (N = 2506) conducted following the election. A pre-/post-election panel (N = 1584) completed both the pre- and post-election waves.

The fieldwork for the 2019 general election surveys and for the 2021 survey was done by Deltapoll again under the direction of Joe Twyman. A representative national panel survey of the British electorate was conducted in the two weeks before the 12 December 2019 election. The post-election survey was conducted immediately after the election. The sample sizes are: pre-election wave, N = 2515; post-election wave, N = 2688; and pre-/post-election panel, N = 1940. The 2021 survey was done in March, approximately fifteen months after the formal departure of the UK from the European Union on 31 January 2020. The survey N is 3002.

The survey data and accompanying questionnaires are soon to be archived on Harvard Dataverse (https://dataverse.harvard.edu).

For additional information, please contact Paul Whiteley (whiteley@ essex.ac.uk).

Key Measures

Benefits and Costs of Leaving the European Union, 2017 and 2019 Surveys

a) 'Do you think that the British economy would be better or worse off if we left the European Union, or would it make no difference?' The response categories are 'better off' = 1 'worse off' = −1, 'would make no real difference to the British economy' = 0, and 'don't know' = 9.

b) 'Do you think Britain would have more or less influence in the world if we left the European Union, or would it make no difference?' The response categories are 'more influence' = 1, 'less influence' = −1, 'would make no real difference to British influence' = 0, and 'don't know' = 9.

c) 'Do you think Britain would be more or less at risk from terrorism if we left the European Union, or would it make no difference?' The response categories are 'Britain would be more at risk from terrorism if we left the EU' = −1, 'Britain would be less at risk from terrorism if we left the EU' = 1, 'would make no real difference to the risk from terrorism' = 0, and 'don't know' = 9.

d) 'Do you think there would be more or less immigration into Britain if we left the European Union, or would it make no difference?' The response categories are 'more immigration into Britain' = −1, 'less immigration into Britain' = 1, 'would make no real difference to the amount of immigration' = 0, and 'don't know' = 9.

e) 'Do you think you personally would be financially better or worse off if Britain left the European Union, or would it make no difference?' The response categories are 'better off' = 1, 'worse off' = 2, 'no real difference' = 3, and 'don't know' = 9.

The structure of the 5 items (a)–(e) is analysed using confirmatory factor analysis (CFA).[1] A two-factor model, with inter-correlated economy-international influence and immigration-terrorism benefit–cost factors, has a satisfactory fit (RMSEA = 0.05). Factor scores from the two-factor model are created to measure the two types of perceived benefits and costs of leaving the EU.

---

[1] For more discussion of confirmatory factor analysis, see Acock (2013).

Benefits and Costs of Leaving the European Union,
2021 Survey

a) 'Do you think that the economy will be better or worse off now that Britain has left the European Union, or will it make no difference?' The response categories are 'better off' = 1, 'worse off' = 2, <3> 'will make no difference to the British economy' = 3, and 'don't know' = 9.
b) 'Do you think Britain will have more or less influence in the world now that it has left the European Union, or will it make no difference?' The response categories are 'more influence' = 1, 'less influence' = 2, 'will make no difference to British influence' = 3, and 'don't know' = 9.
c) 'Do you think Britain will be more or less at risk from terrorism now that it has left the European Union, or will it make no difference?' The response categories are 'Britain will be more at risk from terrorism', = 1, 'Britain will be less at risk from terrorism' = 2, 'will make no difference to risk from terrorism' = 3, and 'don't know' = 9.
d) 'Do you think there will be more or less immigration into Britain now that it has left the European Union, or will it make no difference?' The response categories are 'more immigration into Britain' = 1, 'less immigration into Britain' = 2, 'will make no real difference to the level of immigration' = 3, and 'don't know' = 9.
e) 'Do you think you personally will be financially better or worse off now that Britain has left the European Union, or will it make no difference?' The response categories are 'better off' = 1, 'worse off' = 2, 'will make no difference' = 3, and 'don't know' = 9.

The structure of the five items (a)–(e) is analysed using confirmatory factor analysis (CFA). A two-factor model, with inter-correlated economy-international influence and immigration-terrorism benefit–cost factors, has a satisfactory fit (RMSEA = 0.05). Factor scores from the two-factor model are created to measure the two types of perceived benefits and costs of leaving the EU. For the analyses in Chapter 10, the two sets of factor scores are added to produce an overall index of perceived benefits and costs of leaving the European Union.

Best Prime Minister: 'Who would make the best prime minister?' The response categories are Labour leader = 1, Conservative leader = 2, Liberal Democrat leader = 3, and 'don't know' = 9. The aggregate analysis uses the percentage choosing the Conservative leader minus the percentage choosing the Labour leader.

Covid-19 Pandemic Brought Under Control: 'Using a scale where 0 means "very unlikely" and 10 means "very likely", how likely do you think it is that the Covid-19 pandemic will be brought under control in Britain this year?' 'Don't know' responses are recoded to the mean.

Covid-19 Pandemic Personal Problems: Respondents were asked four questions regarding whether they had experienced any financial, childcare, elder-care, or emotional problems because of the Covid-19 pandemic. The response categories are 'serious problems' = 1, 'minor problems' = 2, 'no problem' = 3, and 'don't know' = 9.

Democracy Satisfaction: 'Thinking about how well democracy works in this country, on the whole, are you very satisfied, fairly satisfied, a little dissatisfied, or very dissatisfied with the way that democracy works in this country?' The response categories are 'very dissatisfied' = 1, 'a little dissatisfied' = 2, 'fairly satisfied' = 3, 'very satisfied' = 4, and 'don't know' = 9. For the multivariate analyses of democracy dissatisfaction presented in Chapter 10, 'very dissatisfied' and 'a little dissatisfied' responses are scored 1 and other responses are scored 0.

Emotional Reactions to Economic Conditions: 'Which, if any, of the following words describe your feelings about the country's general economic situation? (Please tick up to FOUR.)' The words are: angry, happy, disgusted, hopeful, uneasy, confident, afraid and proud. A word is scored 1 if mentioned and 0 if not mentioned. Overall national emotional reactions to economic condition variables are constructed by subtracting the number of negative words (angry, disgusted, uneasy, afraid) mentioned from the number of positive words (happy, hopeful, confident, proud) mentioned.

European Union Membership – Emotional Reactions: Respondents were presented with a list of eight words and asked which ones described their feelings about European Union membership. The words are: angry, happy, disgusted, hopeful, uneasy, confident, afraid and proud. A summary variable was created by subtracting the number of negative words (angry, disgusted, uneasy, afraid) mentioned from the number of positive words (happy, hopeful, confident, proud) mentioned.

European Union Membership-Favour/Oppose: 'Overall, do you strongly approve, approve, disapprove, or strongly disapprove of Britain's membership in the European Union?' The response categories are 'strongly approve', 'approve', 'neither approve nor disapprove', 'disapprove', 'strongly disapprove', and 'don't know'.

European Union–Government Handling of Negotiations: Thinking about the government's negotiations with the European Union over Brexit, do you think they have been handled well or badly?' The response categories are 'very well' = 1, 'fairly well' = 2, 'neither well nor badly' = 3, 'fairly badly' = 4, 'very badly' = 5, and 'don't know' = 9.

European Union-Risks of Leaving: 'On a scale from 0 to 10 where 0 means "not at all risky" and 10 means "very risky", how risky do you think it would be for Britain to leave the European Union?' 'Don't know' responses were coded to the mean.

Feelings of Being Left Behind Economically: Respondents were asked about their evaluations of national and personal economic conditions using five-point Likert scales ranging from 'a lot better' = 5 to 'a lot worse' = 1. The 'Left Behind' variable is the difference between the national and personal evaluation variables.

Government Performance on Covid-19 Pandemic: 'Overall, do you approve or disapprove of the government's handling of the Covid-19 pandemic?' The response categories are 'strongly approve' = 1, 'approve' = 2, 'neither approve nor disapprove' = 3, 'disapprove' = 4, 'strongly disapprove' = 5, and 'don't know' = 9.

Immigration Attitudes: The following questions are used to measure negative attitudes towards immigration:

a) 'What do you think are the three most important problems facing the country at the present time?' Respondents choosing immigration are scored 1 and other respondents are scored 0.

b) 'Which of the following statements comes closest to your view?' The response categories are 'Britain should increase the number of immigrants coming to the country' = 1, 'The current number of immigrants coming to Britain is about right' = 2, 'Britain should reduce the number of immigrants coming to the country' = 3, and 'don't know' = 9.

c) 'Using the 0–10 scale, how important a problem is the number of immigrants coming to Britain these days?'

d) 'Do you think the number of immigrants coming to Britain these days is "a lot better" = 1, "a little better" = 2, "the same" = 3, "a little worse" = 4 "a lot worse" = 5, or "don't know" = 9?'

e) 'Which, if any, of the following words describe your feelings about the number of immigrants coming to Britain? (Please tick up to FOUR.)' The words are: angry, happy, disgusted, hopeful, uneasy, confident, afraid, and proud. A word is scored 1 if mentioned and 0 if not mentioned. Overall emotional reactions to immigration are measured by subtracting the number of negative words (angry, disgusted, uneasy, afraid) mentioned from the number of positive words (happy, hopeful, confident, proud) mentioned.

A single-factor confirmatory factor analysis of the resulting five variables has a satisfactory fit (RMSEA = 0.07). The results of this analysis are used to construct a factor score variable.

Left–right Ideology: 'People sometimes use the labels "left" or "left-wing" and "right" or "right-wing" to describe political parties, party leaders and political ideas. Using the 0 to 10 scale below, where the end marked 0 means left and the end marked 10 means right, where would you place yourself on this scale?' Missing data are recoded to the mean score.

Life Satisfaction: 'Here is a ladder scale where 0 is the "worst possible life" and 10 is the "best possible life". On which step of the ladder do you feel you stand at the present time?' Missing data are recoded to the mean score.

Most Important Issues: Respondents were presented with a list of several issues and asked to designate the three most important issues facing the country at the present time. For example, the 2021 issue list included crime, the economy, education, the environment, Brexit/Europe, NHS/care, housing, immigration, Covid-19/pandemic, tax, inflation and unemployment. The order of issues was randomized. Respondents then were asked which issue was the single most important. For the single most important issue, respondents were asked which party could handle it best.

National Health Service: The following questions are used to measure negative attitudes towards the National Health Service:

a) 'NHS/Health Service' chosen as the most important issue facing the country: 'Do you think the National Health Service these days is "a lot better", = 1, "a little better" = 2, "the same" = 3, "a little worse" = 4, "a lot worse" = 5, "don't know"= 9?'
b) 'Using the 0–10 scale, where the end marked 0 means not at all important, and the end marked 10 means very important, how important a problem is the National Health Service these days?'
c) 'Which, if any, of the following words describe your feelings about the National Health Service?' Negative words include: angry, disgusted, uneasy and afraid. An index ranging from 0 to 4 is constructed by counting the number of negative words mentioned.

The responses to these four questions are used in a confirmatory factor analysis to construct a factor-score variable measuring negative attitudes towards the NHS.

National Identities: 'Generally speaking, do you think of yourself as British, English, European, Scottish, Welsh or something else?' Answers were used to create a series of 0–1 dummy variables with 'British' as the reference category.

Party Best on the Economy: 'With Britain in economic difficulties, which party do you think could handle the problem best – the

Conservative Party, the Labour Party or the Liberal Democrats?' The response categories are 'Conservatives', 'Labour', 'Liberal Democrats', 'None of them', and 'don't know'.

Party Identification: 'Generally speaking, do you think of yourself as Conservative, Labour, Liberal Democrat or what?' The response categories are 'Conservative', 'Labour', 'Liberal Democrat', 'Plaid Cymru', 'Scottish Nationalist', 'Greens', 'United Kingdom Independence Party', 'British National Party', and 'Other Party'. This question is followed by the standard 'how strongly' question.

Party Leaders-Feelings: 'Using a scale that runs from 0 to 10, where 0 means "strongly dislike" and 10 means "strongly like", how do you feel about the "Conservative leader"; "Labour leader"; "Liberal Democrat leader"?' Respondents saying 'don't know' were assigned the mean score.

Party Leaders-Images: Respondents were asked how well the words 'strong leader', 'competent', 'caring', and 'trustworthy' describe various party leaders. The response categories are 'not very well', 'not too well', 'quite well', and 'extremely well'.

Personal and National Economic Evaluations: 'How does the financial situation of your household now compare with what it was 12 months ago?' and 'How do you think the general economic situation in this country has changed over the last 12 months?' The response categories for each question are 'got a lot better' = 1, 'got a little better' = 2, 'stayed the same' = 3, 'got a little worse' = 4, 'got a lot worse' = 5, and 'don't know' = 9.

Political Efficacy: 'On a scale from 0 to 10, where 10 means "a great deal of influence" and 0 means "no influence", how much influence do you have on politics and public affairs?' 'Don't know' responses were recoded to the mean score.

Pro-Anti-Establishment Attitudes: Respondents were asked whether they 'strongly agree', 'agree', 'neither agree nor disagree', 'disagree' or 'strongly disagree' with the following four statements:

a) 'Economic inequality is a major problem in Britain';
b) 'Social injustice is a major problem in Britain';
c) 'Corporate greed is a major problem in Britain';
d) 'British banks are making excessive profits at the expense of ordinary people'.

A single-factor model is fit to the data.

Racial/Ethnic Attitudes: Respondents were asked whether they 'strongly agree', 'agree', 'neither agree nor disagree', 'disagree', 'strongly disagree', or 'don't know' for each of the following four questions:

a) 'Over the past few years, racial and ethnic minorities have got less than they deserve.'
b) 'Some ethnic and racial communities and many other minorities overcame prejudice and worked their way up. Racial and ethnic minorities should do the same today without any special favours.'
c) 'It's really a matter of some people not trying hard enough; if racial and ethnic minorities would only try harder they could be just as well off as white people.'
d) 'Generations of slavery and discrimination have created conditions that make it difficult for racial and ethnic minorities to work their way out of the lower class.'

'Don't know' responses are recoded to the mid-point of the scale ('neither agree nor disagree'). A confirmatory factor analysis is used to fit a one-factor model to the data.

Social Trust: 'Think for a moment about whether people with whom you have contact can be trusted. Use the 0 to 10 scale again, where 10 means "definitely can be trusted" and 0 means "definitely cannot be trusted". "Don't know" responses are recoded to the mean.'

Tactical Voting: Respondents were asked 'People give different reasons for why they vote for one party rather than another. Which of the following BEST describes your reasons?' The response categories are 'The party had the best policies' = 1, 'The party had the best leader' = 2, 'I really preferred another party but it stood no chance of winning in my constituency' = 3, 'I voted tactically' = 4, and 'Other reasons' = 5.

Respondents choosing 3 or 4 were classified as tactical voters and scored 1; other respondents were scored 0.

Trust in Political Institutions: Respondents were asked to indicate their level of trust in 'government in general' and 'the Parliament at Westminster' on 0–10 scales where 0 indicated 'no trust' and 10 indicated a 'great deal of trust'. 'Don't know' responses were coded to the mean.

Socio-Demographic Characteristics

a) Age: age in years, collapsed into a set of ordinal categories for some analyses;
b) Country of residence: two 0–1 dummy variables are created for residents of Scotland and Wales with England as the reference category;
c) Education: respondents who had attended university are scored 1 and other respondents are scored 0;
d) Gender: men are scored 1 and women are scored 0;

e) Income: an ordinal scale with several categories. Categories vary across surveys;
f) Social class: A/B = 4, C1 = 3, C2 = 2, D/E = 1.

***Value Orientations, 2019 Survey*:** Respondents were asked whether they 'agree' or 'disagree' with each of the following statements:

a) 'Young people today don't have enough respect for traditional British values.'
b) 'Censorship of films and magazines is necessary to uphold moral standards.'
c) 'People in Britain should be more tolerant of those who lead unconventional lifestyles.'
d) 'Marijuana should be legalized.'
e) 'The death penalty, even for very serious crimes, is never justified.'
f) 'Convicted criminals should be given longer prison sentences.'

A confirmatory factor analysis, with items (a), (b) and (e) and (f) loading on factor 1 and items (c), (d) and (e) loading on factor 2, fits the data well (RMSEA = 0.04). For multivariate analyses, factor scores for these two factors are added to produce an overall 'social values' index.

***Value Orientations, 2021 Survey*:** Respondents were asked whether they 'strongly agree' = 1, 'agree' = 2, 'neither agree nor disagree' = 3, 'disagree' = 4, 'strongly disagree' = 5, or 'don't know' = 6 with each of the following eight statements:

a) 'Young people today don't have enough respect for traditional British values.'
b) 'Censorship of films and magazines is necessary to uphold moral standards.'
c) 'People in Britain should be more tolerant of those who lead unconventional lifestyles.'
d) 'The death penalty is never justified even for very serious crimes like murder.'
e) 'Convicted criminals should be given longer prison sentences.'
f) 'Freedom of speech must be upheld even for people we strongly disagree with.'
g) 'There is a real danger that love of country – patriotism – is being forgotten in modern Britain.'
h) 'There is a major problem of racism in contemporary Britain.'

Responses to statements (a), (b), (c), (f) and (g) are recoded: 'strongly agree' = 5, 'agree' = 4, 'neither agree nor disagree' = 3, 'disagree' = 2, and 'strongly disagree' = 1. 'Don't know' responses to all items are recoded to 3.

A confirmatory factor analysis is used to estimate a model with 'traditional' and 'conformity' values factors. Items (a), (b), (e), (f) and (g) load on the traditional values factor and items (c), (d), (f) and (h) load on the conformity values factor. The model fits the data well (RMSEA = 0.05).

***Vote in 2016 European Union Referendum*:** Respondents stating they voted to Leave are scored 1 and respondents saying they voted to Remain are scored 0. Respondents who said 'don't know' or indicated that they did not vote are not included in the analyses.

***Vote if Another European Referendum*:** Respondents stating they would vote to stay out of the European Union are scored 1 and respondents saying they would vote to rejoin are scored 0. Respondents who said 'don't know' or indicated that they did not vote are not included in the analyses.

***Vote in 2017 and 2019 General Elections, and Vote in 2019 European Parliament Elections*:** Respondents were asked if they voted and, if so, which party they voted for. A series of 0–1 dummy variables was created for the multivariate analyses of voting, e.g., vote Conservative = 1, vote for another party = 0. Non-voters and 'don't knows' are not included in the analyses.

***Voting Intentions in Next General Election*:** Respondents were asked, 'If there were a general election tomorrow, which party would you vote for?' Those saying they 'don't know' are asked: 'Which party would you be most inclined to vote for?' Respondents who said that they 'would not vote' or that they 'don't know' which party they would vote for are removed before these percentages are computed.

Appendix B: Statistical Methodology

This book uses a variety of statistical methodologies and models which are presented in the form of figures and simple tables for ease of interpretation by a general reader. The book uses statistical software, including Eviews 9 and Stata 15 for the statistical analyses of the survey data, and these programs together with Excel, for preparation and presentation of the graphs in the various chapters. For additional information, please contact Paul Whiteley (whiteley@essex.ac.uk).

1. The Multivariate Regression Model (used in various chapters): As in most social science applications, the workhorse model in this book is ordinary least squares (OLS) multivariate regression. Given q equations and p independent variables (including the constant), the parameter estimates in an OLS regression are given by the **p x q** matrix:

$$\mathbf{B} = (\mathbf{X'WX})^{-1}\mathbf{X'WY}$$

where $\mathbf{Y}$ is an **n x q** matrix of dependent variables and $\mathbf{X}$ is a **n x p** matrix of independent variables. This model is used extensively in the various chapters. It is implemented in STATA using the **regress** command. As an example, actual turnout (actual) is used as a predictor of reported turnout (reportpct) in Figure 6.1. The STATA commands (in bold) and output are:

.regress reportpct actual

				Number of obs = 16
Source	SS	df	MS	F(1, 14) = 93.63
Model	375.32	1	375.31973	Prob > F = 0.0000
Residual	56.12	14	4.00841214	R-squared = 0.8699
				Adj R-squared = 0.8606
Total	431.4375	15	28.7625	Root MSE = 2.0021

Reportpct	Coef.	Std. Err.	t	P>|t|	[95% Conf. Interval]	
Actual	0.84	.087233	9.68	0.000	0.66	1.03
_cons	21.68	6.221343	3.49	0.004	8.33	35.03

. predict resids, residual
. estat durbinalt
Durbin's alternative test for autocorrelation

lags(p)	chi2	df	Prob > chi2
1	0.928	1	0.3353

Ho: no serial correlation

.estat ovtest
Ramsey RESET test using powers of the fitted values of reportpct
   Ho: model has no omitted variables
       $F(3, 11) = 0.48$
       Prob > F = 0.7016

. estat ic
Akaike's information criterion and Bayesian information criterion

Model	Obs	ll(null)	ll(model)	df	AIC	BIC
	16	−49.05929	−32.74193	2	69.48	71.03

The model is an excellent fit with no problems of autocorrelation in the residuals, and the RESET specification test indicates that it is fully specified with no missing variables.

2. The Hierarchical Age-Period-Cohort Model (HAPC): The HAPC Model used in Chapter 6 is a cross-level multilevel model with the respondent's age and related demographic variables appearing at the (fixed effects) individual level, and the period and cohort (random) effects at the aggregate level.[1] The version used in the chapter significantly restricts period effects associated with elections. It only refers to elections producing a change of government, rather than all elections, over the period 1964–2019. This helps to solve the problem of

---

[1] The HAPC model was developed by Yang and Land (2013), but it has been criticized particularly by Bell and Jones (2013) for not solving the collinearity problem associated with these models.

collinearity with the use of a theoretically driven version of the period variable, rather than all elections. The specification of the model in its simplest form is given by the following equations:

$$y_{i(j1j2)} = \beta_{0j1j2} + \beta_1 Age_{i(j1j2)} + \beta_2 Age^2_{i(j1j2)} + e_{i(j1j2)} \; (\textbf{level 1})$$

$$\beta_{0j1j2} = \beta_0 + u_{1j1} + u_{2j2} \; (\textbf{level 2})$$

$$e_{i(j1j2)} \sim N(0, \sigma^2_e), u_{1j1} \sim N(0, \sigma^2_{u1}), u_{2j2} \sim N(0, \sigma^2_{u2})$$

Where the dependent variable, $y_{i(j1j2)}$ measures the turnout or party choice of individual i in period j_1 and cohort j_2. The individual level model has a quadratic age term, and a constant β_{0j1j2} that varies across both periods and cohorts. The dependent variable in the second level model is the constant term in the level one model, and itself has a non-varying constant β_0, and a residual term for each period and cohort which by assumption follows a Normal distribution. The second level random model in the chapter includes various covariates not included above. An example of this is Figure 6.4 which shows the HAPC model of turnout using the **xtlogit** command:

. **xtlogit turnout age agesq occupation education male ww1 postww1 depression ww2 /// macmillan wilson thatcher blair /// period64 period70 period741 period79 period97 period10 period15, intpoints (50)**

Fitting comparison model:

Iteration 0:   log likelihood = –21769.8
Iteration 1:   log likelihood = –20584.934
Iteration 2:   log likelihood = –20512.038
Iteration 3:   log likelihood = –20511.967
Iteration 4:   log likelihood = –20511.967

Fitting full model:

tau = 0.0   log likelihood = –20511.967
tau = 0.1   log likelihood = –20317.779
tau = 0.2   log likelihood = –20333.039

Iteration 0:   log likelihood = –20317.742
Iteration 1:   log likelihood = –20306.824
Iteration 2:   log likelihood = –20306.268
Iteration 3:   log likelihood = –20306.266

Random-effects logistic regression   Number of obs = 45,285
Group variable: pcohort   Number of groups = 100

Random effects u_i ~ Gaussian   Obs per group:
                                        min = 5
                                        avg = 452.9
                                        max = 1,553

Integration method: mvaghermite   Integration pts. = 50

Wald chi2(20) = 904.43

Log likelihood = −20306.266   Prob > chi2 = 0.0000

Turnout	Coef.	Std. Err.	z	P>|z|	[95% Conf. Interval]	
age	.0610672	.0069556	8.78	0.000	.0474345	.0746998
agesq	−0.0004813	.0000668	−7.21	0.000	−0.0006122	−0.0003504
occupation	.1126286	.0076012	14.82	0.000	.0977306	.1275266
education	.3778059	.0293404	12.88	0.000	.3202997	.4353121
male	−0.0196669	.0252662	−0.78	0.436	−0.0691879	.029854
ww1	.7413371	.2856177	2.60	0.009	.1815366	1.301138
postww1	1.183875	.2473267	4.79	0.000	.6991237	1.668627
depression	1.116863	.2185601	5.11	0.000	.6884933	1.545233
ww2	1.425969	.2017989	7.07	0.000	1.030451	1.821488
macmillan	1.279622	.1843584	6.94	0.000	.9182857	1.640957
wilson	1.06784	.1713422	6.23	0.000	.7320154	1.403664
thatcher	.7498671	.1670358	4.49	0.000	.4224829	1.077251
blair	.2659658	.1757935	1.51	0.130	−0.0785832	.6105148
period64	.4030958	.1640309	2.46	0.014	.0816012	.7245905
period70	−0.2057511	.1546921	−1.33	0.183	−0.5089421	.0974399
period741	.3131483	.1466135	2.14	0.033	.0257912	.6005055
period79	.1215859	.1472663	0.83	0.409	−0.1670507	.4102225
period97	−0.0876494	.1384749	−0.63	0.527	−0.3590552	.1837564
period10	−0.1118991	.1455581	−0.77	0.442	−0.3971878	.1733895
period15	−0.3158872	.1503614	−2.10	0.036	−0.61059	−0.0211844
_cons	−1.524301	.1936595	−7.87	0.000	−1.903867	−1.144736
/lnsig2u	−2.49008	.1909331			−2.864302	−2.115857
sigma_u	.2879295	.0274876			.2387948	.3471742
rho	.0245802	.0045778			.0170376	.0353419

LR test of rho=0: chibar2(01) = 411.40   Prob >= chibar2 = 0.000

. estat ic
Akaike's information criterion and Bayesian information criterion

Model	Obs	ll (model)	df	AIC	BIC
	45,285	−20306.27	22	40656.53	40848.39

Unlike the OLS regression model, the HAPC model has no analytical solution, so the estimation proceeds iteratively with the aim of finding the maximum likelihood solution. The individual-level variables (age to male) appear first and the cohort effects second (ww1 to blair). Finally, the period effects or specific elections involving a change of government appear last (period64 to period15). This order is reversed in the figures to emphasize the random effects in the modelling.

3. The Spatial Autoregression Model: This model is directly analogous to the time series autoregression model, except the autoregressive errors correspond to spatial rather than temporal effects. In this case, we are estimating the effects as described in Table 7.4. The simplest version of the model is written as follows:

$$\mathbf{y}_t = \mu + (\mathbf{W})\mathbf{B}\mathbf{x}_{t-i} + \varepsilon_t$$

$\mathbf{y}_t$ is a vector of jointly endogenous variables
$(\mathbf{W})$ is a spatial weighting matrix
$\mathbf{x}_{t-i}$ is a vector of exogenous variables
$\mathbf{B}$ is a matrix of exogenous coefficients
μ is a vector of constants
ε_t is a vector of random disturbance

The values in the spatial weighting matrix $(\mathbf{W})$ identify the impact of the characteristics of adjacent constituencies on voting behaviour in a constituency. The analysis first has to define the spatial coordinates, which in this case are the longitudes and latitudes of constituency centroids, which creates the weighting matrix. This weights nearby constituencies to be more important than remote constituencies in the modelling. Again in STATA the commands are:

. spset, modify coordsys(latlong, miles)

Sp dataset Constituency Spatial & Census GB 2019.dta
   data: cross sectional
   spatial-unit id: _ID (equal to objectid)
       coordinates: _CY, _CX (latitude-and-longitude, miles)
   linked shapefile: none

. spmatrix create idistance W
It then proceeds to estimate the spatially weighted regression using
spregress where the Human Development Index (hdis), the percentage voting to Leave in the EU referendum (euleaves) the percentage of
young voters (age18_29), population density (densitys) and the dummy
variables for English and Scottish constituencies are included as predictors of turnout in the 2019 election (turn19s) in the modelling. All
the variables are expressed in standardized form and are estimated with
robust standard errors.

**. spregress turn19s hdis euleaves age18_29s densitys england scot-
land, ///
ml vce(robust) dvarlag(W) ivarlag(W: hdis euleaves age18_29s
densitys england /// Scotland) errorlag(W)**

(weighting matrix defines 632 places)Performing grid search ... finished
Optimizing concentrated log pseudolikelihood:

Iteration 0:   log pseudolikelihood = −418.34076
Iteration 1:   log pseudolikelihood = −406.08807
Iteration 2:   log pseudolikelihood = −405.09739
Iteration 3:   log pseudolikelihood = −404.07353
Iteration 4:   log pseudolikelihood = −404.05421
Iteration 5:   log pseudolikelihood = −404.05411
Iteration 6:   log pseudolikelihood = −404.05411

Optimizing unconcentrated log pseudolikelihood:

Iteration 0:   log pseudolikelihood = −404.05411
Iteration 1:   log pseudolikelihood = −404.05 (backed up)

Spatial autoregressive model   Number of obs = 632
Maximum likelihood estimates   Wald chi2(13) = 1741.85
Prob > chi2 = 0.0000
Log pseudolikelihood = −404.05411   Pseudo R2 = 0.7613

. estat impact

Progress: 17%   33%   50%   67%   83%   100%

Average impacts   Number of obs = 632

| | Delta-Method | | | | | |
	dy/dx	Std. Err.	z	P>|z|	[95% Conf. Interval]	
direct						
hdis	.741297	.0397191	18.66	0.000	.6634491	.819145
euleaves	−0.2189495	.0452591	−4.84	0.000	−0.3076557	−0.1302433
age18_29s	−0.3382124	.0309157	−10.94	0.000	−0.398806	−0.2776188
densitys	−0.2078042	.051841	−4.01	0.000	−0.3094107	−0.1061976
England	.5340273	.106351	5.02	0.000	.3255831	.7424715
Scotland	−0.4023137	.174949	−2.30	0.021	−0.7452074	−0.05942
indirect						
hdis	−1.85323	.924483	−2.00	0.045	−3.665183	−0.0412764
euleaves	−3.244128	1.523435	−2.13	0.033	−6.230006	−0.2582501
age18_29s	−2.092553	1.223888	−1.71	0.087	−4.49133	.3062247
densitys	.2713185	.5499135	0.49	0.622	−0.8064922	1.349129
England	−0.6646587	.2702372	−2.46	0.014	−1.194314	−0.1350035
Scotland	−4.672542	2.363666	−1.98	0.048	−9.305243	−0.0398411
total						
hdis	−1.111933	.9237305	−1.20	0.229	−2.922411	.6985457
euleaves	−3.463078	1.522187	−2.28	0.023	−6.446509	−0.4796461
age18_29s	−2.430765	1.236084	−1.97	0.049	−4.853445	−0.0080843
densitys	.0635143	.5608722	0.11	0.910	−1.035775	1.162804
England	−0.1306314	.2880165	−0.45	0.650	−0.6951334	.4338707
Scotland	−5.074856	2.319857	−2.19	0.029	−9.621692	−0.5280188

. estat ic

Akaike's information criterion and Bayesian information criterion

Model	Obs	ll(null)	ll(model)	df	AIC	BIC
	632	.	−404.0541	16	840.1082	911.2905

4. The Vector Autoregression Model and Granger Causality Tests: The Vector Autoregression (VAR) model[2] is defined as follows:

$$\Phi(\mathbf{L})\mathbf{y}_t = \mu + \mathbf{B}\mathbf{x}_{t-i} + \varepsilon_t$$

---

[2] This model was first developed by Sims (1980).

where

y_t is a vector of jointly endogenous variables (see Figures 8.4 and 8.5 for specific variables) (L) is the lag operator

x_{t-i} is a vector of exogenous variables

B is a matrix of exogenous coefficients

μ is a vector of constants

ϕ are matrices of endogenous coefficients

ε_t is a vector of random disturbance

Granger causality tests rely on temporal sequence to identify causality. A time series variable is described as a 'Granger cause' of another time series if at least one element of x_{t-i} has a statistically significant coefficient in B, while controlling for values of $\phi(L)y_t$. It is implemented in STATA using the **var** and **vargranger** commands. An example of this relates to Figure 8.4 which models the causal links between government voting support (govote) consumer confidence (consumer), inflation, unemployment and real economic growth (rgrowth). The commands are:

. **quiet var govote consumer rgrowth unemploy inflation, lags(1/2)**
. **vargranger**

Granger causality		Wald		tests
Equation	Excluded	chi2	df	Prob > chi2
govote	**consumer**	**19.555**	**2**	**0.000**
govote	rgrowth	1.7614	2	0.414
govote	**unemploy**	**9.5745**	**2**	**0.008**
govote	inflation	3.6415	2	0.162
govote	ALL	30.962	8	0.000
consumer	govote	2.8908	2	0.236
consumer	rgrowth	.01881	2	0.991
consumer	unemploy	.54586	2	0.761
consumer	inflation	2.2136	2	0.331
consumer	ALL	5.924	8	0.656
rgrowth	govote	1.386	2	0.500
rgrowth	**consumer**	**4.6038**	**2**	**0.100**
rgrowth	**unemploy**	**5.5539**	**2**	**0.062**
rgrowth	inflation	2.3546	2	0.308
rgrowth	ALL	19.834	8	0.011
unemploy	govote	4.3484	2	0.114
unemploy	**consumer**	**16.727**	**2**	**0.000**
unemploy	**rgrowth**	**25.411**	**2**	**0.000**
unemploy	**inflation**	**10.099**	**2**	**0.006**
unemploy	ALL	71.947	8	0.000

Granger causality		Wald		tests
inflation	govote	.31705	2	0.853
inflation	**consumer**	**9.796**	**2**	**0.007**
inflation	**rgrowth**	**13.344**	**2**	**0.001**
inflation	unemploy	2.2115	2	0.331
inflation	ALL	23.429	8	0.003

The test proceeds by estimating each variable as a function of all the others with all the predictors lagged for one and two periods (the individual equations are not shown). Note that if there is a significant reduction in the fit as measured by the Wald statistic when a variable is excluded from the equation, then that is evidence of Granger causality. These effects are in bold.

References

Abadie, A., A. Diamond and J. Hainmueller. 2015. 'Comparative Politics and the Synthetic Control Method'. *American Journal of Political Science* 59: 495–510.

Abrams, Mark and Richard Rose. 1960. *Must Labour Lose?* Baltimore: Penguin Books.

Acemoglu, Daron. 2009. *Introduction to Modern Economic Growth*. Princeton, NJ: Princeton University Press.

Achen, Christopher H. and Larry Bartels. 2016. *Democracy for Realists: Why Elections Do Not Produce Responsive Governments*. Princeton, NJ: Princeton University Press.

Acock, Alan. 2013. *Discovering Structural Equation Modeling Using Stata*. College Station, TX: Stata Press.

Adams, James, Samuel Merrill and Bernard Grofman. 2005. *A Unified Theory of Party Competition*. Cambridge: Cambridge University Press.

Aghion, Philippe, Celine Antonin and Simon Bunel. 2021. *The Power of Creative Destruction: Economic Upheaval and the Wealth of Nations*. Cambridge MA: The Belknap Press of Harvard University Press.

Agnew, J. A. 1996. 'Mapping Politics: How Context Counts in Electoral Geography'. *Political Geography* 15: 129–146.

Akerlof, George A. and Robert J. Shiller. 2009. *Animal Spirits*. Princeton, NJ: Princeton University Press.

Alford, Robert R. 1963. *Party and Society*. Chicago: Rand McNally.

Allen, Nicholas. 2018. 'Gambling with the Electorate: The Conservatives in Government'. In Nicholas Allen and John Bartle, eds., *None Past the Post. Britain at the Polls 2017*. Manchester: Manchester University Press, Chapter 2.

Allen, Nicholas and John Bartle, eds. 2018. *None Past the Post: Britain at the Polls, 2017*. Manchester: Manchester University Press.

Allen, Nicholas and John Bartle, eds. 2021. *Breaking the Deadlock: Britain at the Polls 2019*. Manchester: Manchester University Press.

Altman, N. S. 1992. 'An Introduction to Kernel and Nearest-Neighbor Nonparametric Regression'. *The American Statistician* 46: 175–185.

Alwin, Duane and Jon A. Krosnick. 1991. 'Aging, Cohorts and the Stability of Socio-Political Orientations Over the Life Span'. *American Journal of Sociology* 97: 169–195.

Anderson, Benedict. 1983. *Imagined Communities: Reflections on the Origins and Spread of Nationalism*. London: Verso.

Anderson, Christopher. 2000. 'Economic Voting and Political Context: A Comparative Perspective'. *Electoral Studies* 19: 151–170.

Anderson, Christopher J., André Blais, Shaun Bowler, Todd Donovan and Ola Listhaug. 1997. *Losers' Consent: Elections and Democratic Legitimacy.* New York: Oxford University Press.

Anselin, Luc, 1988. *Spatial Econometrics: Methods and Models.* Dordrecht: Kluwer Academic Publishers.

Arzheimer, Kai. 2018. 'Explaining Electoral Support for the Radical Right'. In Jens Rydgren, ed., *The Oxford Handbook of the Radical Right.* Oxford: Oxford University Press.

Atkinson, A. B. 2015. *Inequality: What Can be Done?* Cambridge, MA: Harvard University Press.

Baddley, Michelle. 2013. *Behavioural Economics and Finance.* London: Routledge.

Barwell, Gavin. 2021. *Chief of Staff: Notes from Downing Street.* Atlantic.

Becker, H. A. 1990. *Life Histories and Generations.* Utrecht: ISOR.

Bell, Andrew and Kelvyn Jones. 2014. 'Another "Futile Quest"? A Simulation Study of Yang and Land's Hierarchical Age-Period-Cohort Model'. *Demographic Research* 30: 333–368.

Bell, Andrew and Kelvyn Jones. 2018. 'The Hierarchical Age-Period-Cohort Model: Why Does It Find the Results That It Finds?' *Quality and Quantity* 52: 783–799.

Bernstein, Robert, Anita Chadha and Robert Montjoy. 2001. 'Overreporting Voting: Why It Happens and Why It Matters'. *Public Opinion Quarterly* 65: 22–44.

Black, Duncan. 1958. *The Theory of Committees and Elections.* Cambridge: Cambridge University Press.

Blyth, Mark. 2013. *Austerity: The History of a Dangerous Idea.* Oxford: Oxford University Press.

Bookstaber, Richard. 2017. *The End of Theory: Financial Crises, the Failure of Economics and the Sweep of Human Interaction.* Princeton, NJ: Princeton University Press.

Budge, Ian, Hans-Dieter Klingemann, Andrea Volkens, Judith Bara and Eric Tanenbaum. 2001. *Mapping Policy Preferences: Estimates for Parties, Electors, and Governments, 1945–1998.* Oxford: Oxford University Press. https://manifesto-project.wzb.eu/

Burnham Kenneth P. and David R. Anderson. 2011. *Model Selection Criteria and Multi-Model Inference: A Practical Information Theoretic Approach,* 2nd edn. New York: Springer-Verlag.

Butler, David and Gareth Butler. 1994. *British Political Facts, 1900–1994,* 7th edn. Basingstoke: Palgrave Macmillan.

Butler, David and Uwe W. Kitzinger. 1996. *The 1975 Referendum,* 2nd edn. London: Macmillan.

Butler, David and Donald E. Stokes. 1969. *Political Change in Britain: Forces Shaping Electoral Choice.* New York: St Martin's Press.

Cairns, Andrew. 2004. *Interest Rate Models – An Introduction.* Princeton, NJ: Princeton University Press.

Campbell, Angus, Philip Converse, Warren Miller and Donald Stokes. 1960. *The American Voter.* New York: John Wiley & Sons.

Campos, Nauro F., Fabrizio Coricelli and Luigi Moretti. 2019. 'Institutional Integration and Economic Growth in Europe'. *Journal of Monetary Economics* 103: 88–104.

Carl, Noah. 2017. *What Sort of Brexit Deal does the British Public Want? A Review of the Evidence So Far.* Centre for Social Investigation, Nuffield College, Oxford/UK In a Changing Europe.

Carl, Noah, James Dennison and Geoffrey Evans. 2019. 'European but Not European Enough: An Explanation for Brexit'. *European Union Politics* 20: 282–304.

Carlin, Wendy and David Soskice. 2005. *Macroeconomics: Imperfections, Institutions and Policies.* Oxford: Oxford University Press.

Carlsson-Szlezak, P., M. Reeves and Swartz, P. 2020. 'What Coronavirus Could Mean for the Global Economy'. *Harvard Business Review*, March 3.

Cerras, Valerie, Antonio Fatas and Sweta C. Saxena. 2020. *'Hysteresis and Business Cycles'. IMF Working Paper, 20/73.* Washington DC: International Monetary Fund.

Cerras, Valerie and Sweta Chaman Saxena. 2008. 'Growth Dynamics: The Myth of Economic Recovery'. *American Economic Review* 98: 439–457.

Chabris, Christopher and Daniel Simons. 2010. *The Invisible Gorilla: How Our Intuitions Deceive Us.* London: Harper-Collins.

Chamley, Christopher. 2004. *Rational Herds: Economic Models of Social Learning.* Cambridge: Cambridge University Press.

Churchill, Winston. 1931. 'Fifty Years Hence'. Magazine. December. www .nationalchurchillmuseum.org/fifty-years-hence.html

Cirrillo, Pasquale and Nassim N. Taleb. 2020. 'Tail Risk of Contagious Diseases'. *Nature Physics*, June: 606–613.

Clarke, Harold D., Mathew Goodwin and Paul Whiteley. 2017. *Brexit: Why Britain Voted to Leave the European Union.* Cambridge: Cambridge University Press.

Clarke, Harold D., Mathew Goodwin and Paul Whiteley. 2019. 'Why Britain Voted for Brexit: An Individual-Level Analysis of the 2016 Referendum Vote'. *Parliamentary Affairs* 70: 439–464.

Clarke, Harold D., Allan Kornberg and Thomas J. Scotto. 2009. *Making Political Choices: Canada and the United States.* Toronto: University of Toronto Press.

Clarke, Harold D. and Allan McCutcheon. 2009. 'The Dynamics of Party Identification Reconsidered'. *Public Opinion Quarterly* 73: 704–728.

Clarke, Harold D., William Mishler and Paul Whiteley. 1990. 'Recapturing the Falklands – Models of Conservative Popularity, 1979–1983'. *British Journal of Political Science* 20: 63–81.

Clarke, Harold D., David Sanders, Marianne C. Stewart and Paul Whiteley. 2004. *Political Choice in Britain.* Oxford: Oxford University Press.

Clarke, Harold D., David Sanders, Marianne C. Stewart and Paul Whiteley. 2009. *Performance Politics and the British Voter.* Cambridge: Cambridge University Press.

Clausen, Aage R. 1968–69. 'Response Validity: Vote Report'. *Public Opinion Quarterly* 32: 588–606.

Conlisk, John. 1996. 'Why Bounded rationality?' *Journal of Economic Literature* 34: 669–700.

Constant, Amelia F. and Bienvenue N. Tien. 2011. 'Germany's Immigration Policy and Labour Shortages'. *IZA Research Report No. 41.*

Converse, Philip E. 1964. 'The Nature of Belief Systems in Mass Publics'. In David E. Apter, ed., *Ideology and Discontent.* Glencoe, Il: The Free Press.

Cowley, Philip and Dennis Kavanagh. 2016. *The British General Election of 2015.* London: Palgrave Macmillan.

Cowley, Philip and Dennis Kavanagh. 2018. *The British General Election of 2017.* London: Palgrave Macmillan.

Curtice, John. 2017. 'Why Leave Won the UK's EU Referendum', *Journal of Common Market Studies Supplement* 1. 55: 19–37.

Curtice, John. 2018. 'Why Chequers Has Gone Wrong for Theresa May', *What UK Thinks: EU*, 17 July. Available online: https://whatukthinks.org/eu/why-chequers-has-gone-wrong-for-theresa-may/ (accessed 2 April 2020).

Curtice, John. 2019. 'What Do the Public Think?' In *Parliament and Brexit* report. UK in a Changing Europe. Available online: https://ukandeu.ac.uk/wp-content/uploads/2020/03/Parliament-and-Brexit-report.pdf (accessed 1 April 2020).

Curtin, Richard. 2019. *Consumer Expectations: Micro Foundations and Macro Impact.* New York: Cambridge University Press.

Cutts, David, Matthew Goodwin, Oliver Heath and Caitlin Milazzo. 2019. 'Resurgent Remain and a Rebooted Revolt on the Right: Exploring the 2019 European Parliament Elections in the United Kingdom'. *Political Quarterly* 90: 496–514.

Dahl, Robert. 1971. *Polyarchy: Participation and Opposition.* New Haven, CT: Yale University Press.

Dahl, Robert. 1998. *On Democracy.* New Haven: Yale University Press.

Dalton, Russell, David Farrell and Ian McAllister. 2011. *Political Parties and Democratic Linkage: How Parties Organize Democracy.* Oxford: Oxford University Press.

Darmofal, David. 2015. *Spatial Analysis for the Social Sciences.* Cambridge: Cambridge University Press.

Dassonville, Ruth. 2013. 'Questioning Generational Replacement: An Age, Period and Cohort Analysis of Electoral Volatility in The Netherlands, 1971–2010'. *Electoral Studies* 32: 37–47.

DeBell, Matthew et al. 2018. 'The Turnout Gap in Surveys: Explanations and Solutions'. *Sociological Methods and Research* 50: 1–30.

Delli Carpini, Michael X. and Scott Keeter. 1996. *What Americans Know About Politics and Why It Matters.* New Haven: Yale University Press.

Desai, Meghnad. 1981. *Testing Monetarism.* London: Frances Pinter.

DeVries, Catherine. 2018. *Euroscepticism and the Future of European Integration.* Oxford: Oxford University Press.

Downs, Anthony. 1957. *An Economic Theory of Democracy.* New York: Harper & Row.

Duch, Raymond and Randolph T. Stevenson. 2008. *The Economic Vote: How Political and Economic Institutions Condition Election Results.* Cambridge: Cambridge University Press.

Dunleavy, Parick and Christopher T. Husbands. 1985. *British Democracy at the Crossroads: Voting and Party Competition in the 1980s.* London: Allen and Unwin.

Easton, David. 1965. *A Systems Analysis of Political Life.* New York: John Wiley & Sons.

Eatwell, Roger and Matthew Goodwin. 2018. *National Populism: The Revolt Against Liberal Democracy.* London: Penguin.

Erikson, Robert S., Michael B. Mackuen, James A. Stimson. 2002. *The Macro-Polity.* Cambridge: Cambridge University Press.

Estrella, Arturo and Frederic S. Mishkin. 1996. 'The Yield Curve as a Predictor of U.S. Recessions'. *Federal Reserve Bank of New York Current Issues in Economics and Finance* 2: 1–5.

Evans, Geoffrey and Robert Andersen. 2006. 'The Political Conditioning of Economic Perceptions'. *Journal of Politics* 68: 194–207.

Evans, Geoffrey and James Tilley. 2017. *The New Politics of Class: The Political Exclusion of the British Working Class.* Oxford: Oxford University Press.

Fama, Eugene. 1965. 'The Behavior of Stock Market Prices'. *Journal of Business* 38: 34–105.

Feenstra, R. C., R. Inklaar and M. P. Timmer. 2015. 'The Next Generation of the Penn World Table'. *American Economic Review* 105: 3150–3182.

Fieldhouse, Edward, Jane Green, Geoffrey Evans, Jonathan Mellon, Christopher Prosser, Hermann Schmitt and Cees Van der Eijk. 2021. *Electoral Shocks: The Volatile Voter in a Turbulent World.* Oxford: Oxford University Press.

Finnis, John. 2019. *The Unconstitutionality of the Supreme Court's Prorogation Judgment.* London: Policy Exchange.

Fiorina, Morris P. 1981. *Retrospective Voting in American National Elections.* New Haven, CT: Yale University Press.

Fiorina, Morris P. with Samuel J. Abrams and Jeremy C. Pope. 2005. *Culture War? The Myth of a Polarized America.* New York: Pearson Education, Inc.

Ford, Robert, and Matthew Goodwin. 2014. *Revolt on the Right: Explaining Support for the Radical Right in Britain.* London: Routledge.

Franklin, Mark N. 2004. *Voter Turnout and the Dynamics of Electoral Competition in Established Democracies Since 1945.* Cambridge: Cambridge University Press.

Franzese, Robert and Jude Hays. 2007. 'Spatial Econometric Models of Cross-Sectional Interdependence in Political Science Panel and Time Series-Cross Section Data'. *Political Analysis* 15: 140–164.

Friedman, Milton. 1953. *Essays in Positive Economics.* Chicago: University of Chicago Press.

Friedman, Milton and Anna Schwartz. 1963. *A Monetary History of the United States 1867 to 1960.* Princeton, NJ: Princeton University Press.

Gamble, Andrew. 1994. *The Free Economy and the Strong State,* 2nd edn. New York: New York University Press.

Gelman, Andrew, David Park, Boris Shor, Joseph Bafumi and Jeronimo Cortina. 2008. *Red State, Blue state, Rich State, Poor state: Why Americans Vote the Way They Do.* Princeton, NJ: Princeton University Press.

Gigerenzer, Gerd. 2008. *Rationality for Mortals: How People Cope With Uncertainty.* Oxford: Oxford University Press.

Gigerenzer, Gerd, Ralph Hertwig and Thorsten Pachur. 2015. *Heuristics: The Foundations of Adaptive Behavior*. Oxford: Oxford University Press.

Giles, David. 2011. 'Testing for Granger Causality'. http://davidgiles.blogspot .co.uk/2011 04/testing_for_granger_causality.html

Glenn, Norval D. 1976. 'Cohort Analysts' Futile Quest – Statistical Attempts of Separate Age, Period and Cohort Effects'. *American Sociological Review* 41: 900–904.

Goldstein, Harvey. 1979. 'Age, Period and Cohort Effects – A Confounded Confusion'. *Journal of Applied Statistics* 6: 19–24.

Goldthorpe, John H., David Lockwood, Frank Bechhofer and Jennifer Platt. 1968. *The Affluent Worker: Industrial Attitudes and Behaviour*. Cambridge: Cambridge University Press.

Goodwin, Matthew and Caitlin Milazzo. 2016. *UKIP: Inside the Campaign to Redraw the Map of British Politics*. Oxford: Oxford University Press.

Goodwin, Matthew and Caitlin Milazzo. 2017. 'Taking Back Control? Investigating the Role of Immigration in the 2016 Vote for Brexit'. *British Journal of Politics and International Relations* 19: 450–464.

Gould, Philip. 1998. *The Unfinished Revolution: How the Modernizers Saved the Labour Party*. London: Little Brown.

Granger, Clive W. 1988. 'Some Recent Developments in the Concept of Causality'. *Journal of Econometrics* 2: 111–120.

Grasso, Maria T. 2016. *Generations, Political Participation and Social Change in Western Europe*. London: Routledge.

Hannah, Simon. 2020. *Can't Pay, Won't Pay: The Fight to Stop the Poll Tax*. London: Pluto Press.

Hanretty, Christopher. 2017. 'Areal Interpolation and the UK's Referendum on EU Membership'. *Journal of Elections, Public Opinion and Parties* 27: 466–483.

Harmon, Mark D. 1997. *The British Labour Government and the 1976 IMF Crisis*. London: Macmillan.

Harris, Kenneth. 1982. *Atlee*. London: Weidenfeld and Nicolson.

Heath, Anthony, Roger Jowell and John Curtice. 1985. *How Britain Votes*. Oxford: Pergamon Press.

Heath, Oliver and Matthew J. Goodwin. 2016. 'The 2016 Referendum, Brexit and the Left Behind: An Aggregate-Level Analysis of the Result'. *Political Quarterly* 87: 323–332.

Heath, Oliver and Matthew J. Goodwin. 2017. 'The 2017 General Election, Brexit and the Return to Two-Party Politics: An Aggregate-Level Analysis of the Result'. *Political Quarterly* 88: 345–358.

HM Government. 2016a. *HM Treasury Analysis: The Long-Term Economic Impact of EU Membership and the Alternatives*. CMND 9250, April.

HM Government. 2016b. *HM Treasury Analysis: The Immediate Economic Impact of Leaving the EU*. CMND 9292, May.

Hetherington, Marc J. 1996. 'The Media's Role in Forming Voters' National Economic Evaluations in 1992'. *American Journal of Political Science* 40: 372–395.

Hindess, Barry. 1988. *Choice, Rationality, and Social Theory*. London: Unwin Hyman.

Hobolt, Sara and Thomas Leeper. 2017. 'The British Are Indifferent about Many Aspects of Brexit, but Leave and Remain Voters are Divided on Several Key Issues'. LSE Blogs, 13 August. Available at: https://blogs.lse.ac.uk/brexit/2017/08/13/the-british-are-indifferent-about-many-aspects-of-brexit-but-leave-and-remain-voters-are-divided-on-several-key-issues/

Hobolt, Sara, Thomas Leeper and James Tilley. 2018. 'Emerging Brexit Identities'. UK In a Changing Europe Blog, 3 February. Available at: ukandeu.ac.uk/emerging-brexit-identities/

Hobolt, Sara, Thomas Leeper and James Tilley. 2020. 'Divided by the vote: Affective Polarization in the Wake of the Brexit Referendum'. British Journal of Political Science 50: 1–18.

Hobolt, Sara and James Tilley. 2014 Blaming Europe? Responsibility without Accountability in the European Union. Oxford: Oxford University Press.

Hobsbawm, Eric. 1990. Nations and Nationalism Since 1780. Cambridge: Cambridge University Press.

Hodrick, Robert and Edward C. Prescott. 1997. 'Postwar U.S. Business Cycles: An Empirical Investigation'. Journal of Money, Credit and Banking 29: 1–26.

Horne, Alistair. 1989. Harold Macmillan, Volume 1: 1894–1956. London: Penguin Books.

Hotelling, Harold. 1929. 'Stability in Competition'. The Economic Journal 39: 41–57.

House of Commons. 2017. Briefing Paper Number CBP 7979, 8 September. London: House of Commons Library.

House of Commons. 2020. 'General Election 2019: Results and Analysis'. Briefing Paper Number CPB8749. London: House of Commons Library.

Hox, Joop J., Mirjam Moerbeek and Rens Van de Schoot. 2018. Multilevel Analysis: Techniques and Applications. London: Routledge.

Huckfield, Robert and John Sprague, 1995. Citizens, Politics and Social Communication. Cambridge: Cambridge University Press.

Ikenberry, G. John. 1988. Reasons of State: Oil Politics and the Capacities of American Government. Ithaca, NY: Cornell University Press.

Inglehart, Ronald. 1977. The Silent Revolution: Changing Values and Political Styles Among Western Publics, Princeton, NJ: Princeton University Press.

Inglehart, Ronald. 1990. Culture Shift in Advanced Industrial Society. Princeton: Princeton University Press.

Inglehart, Ronald. 2018. Cultural Evolution: People's Motivations Are Changing, and Reshaping the World. Cambridge: Cambridge University Press.

Institute for Fiscal Government. 2019. The Brexit Effect: How Government Has Changed since the EU Referendum. London: Institute for Government.

Iyengar, Shanto. 1991. Is Anyone Responsible? How Television Frames Political Issues. Chicago: University of Chicago Press.

Jensen, M. D. and J. D. Kelstrup. 2019. 'House United, House Divided: Explaining the EU's Unity in the Brexit Negotiations'. Journal of Common Market Studies 57: 28–39.

Johnston, Ron and Charles Pattie. 2006. Putting Voters in Their Place. Oxford: Oxford University Press.

Johnston, Ron, Charles Pattie and J. G. Allsopp. 1988. *A Nation Dividing? The Electoral Map of Great Britain 1979–1987*. London: Longman.

Johnston, Ron, Charles Pattie, Danny Dorling and David Rossiter. 2001. *From Votes to Seats*. Manchester: Manchester University Press.

Jordà, Òscar, Sanjay R. Singh and Alan M. Taylor. 2020. 'Longer-Run Economic Consequences of Pandemics'. *Federal Reserve Bank of San Francisco Working Paper 2020–09*.

Kahneman, Daniel. 2011. *Thinking Fast and Slow*. London: Penguin Books.

Kahneman, Daniel, Oliver Sibony and Cass R. Sunstein. 2021. *Noise: A Flaw in Human Judgement*. London: Harper-Collins.

Kay, John and Mervyn King. 2020. *Radical Uncertainty: Decision-Making Beyond the Numbers*. London: The Bridge Street Press.

Kayser, Mark Andreas and Christopher Wlezien. 2011. 'Performance Pressure: Patterns of Partisanship and the Economic Vote'. *European Journal of Political Research* 50: 365–394.

Keegan, William, David Marsh and Richard Roberts. 2017. *Six Days in September: Black Wednesday, Brexit and the Making of Europe*. London: OMFIF Press.

Kelton, Stephanie. 2020. *The Deficit Myth: Modern Monetary Theory and How to Build a Better Economy*. London: John Murray Publishers.

Kennedy, Peter. 2008. *A Guide to Econometrics*, 6th edn. New York: Wiley-Blackwell.

Kettell, Steven and Peter Kerr. 2020. 'From Eating Cake to Crashing Out: Constructing the Myth of a No-Deal Brexit'. *Comparative European Politics* 18: 590–608.

Keynes, John Maynard. 1936. *The General Theory of Employment, Interest and Money*. London: Macmillan.

Kinder, Donald and Roderick D. Kiewiet. 1981. 'Sociotropic Politics: The American Case'. *British Journal of Political Science* 11: 129–161.

King, Gary. 1996. 'Why Context Should Not Count'. *Political Geography* 15: 159–164.

King, Gary. 1997. *A Solution to the Ecological Inference Problem: Reconstructing Individual Behavior from Aggregate Data*. Princeton, NJ: Princeton University Press.

Knight, Frank. 1921. *Risk, Uncertainty and Profit*. Boston: Houghton Mifflin.

Kornberg, Allan and Harold D. Clarke. 1992. *Citizens and Community: Political Support in a Representative Democracy*. New York: Cambridge University Press.

Kuklinski, James H. and Paul J. Quirk. 2000. 'Reconsidering the Rational Public: Cognition Heuristics and Mass Opinion'. In Arthur Lupia, Mathew D. McCubbins and Samuel L. Popkins, eds., *Elements of Reason: Cognition, Choice and the Bounds of Rationality*. New York: Cambridge University Press.

Kyle, Keith. 2011. *Suez: Britain's End of Empire in the Middle East*. London: I.B.Taurus.

Lenz, Gabriel. 2012. *Follow the Leader? How Voters Respond to Politicians' Policies and Performance*. Chicago: University of Chicago Press.

Lewis-Beck, Colin and Michael S. Lewis-Beck. 2015. *Applied Regression: An Introduction*. Thousand Oaks, CA: Sage Publications.

Lewis-Beck, Michael S. 1988. *Economics and Elections: The Major Western Democracies*. Ann Arbor, MI: University of Michigan Press.

Lewis-Beck, Michael S., Richard Nadeau and Martial Foucault. 2013. 'The Complete Economic Voter: New Theory and British Evidence'. *British Journal of Political Science* 43: 241–261.

Lewis-Beck, Michael S. and Mary Stegmaier. 2013. 'The V-P Function Revisited: A Survey of the Literature on Vote and Popularity Functions After Over 40 Years'. *Public Choice* 157: 367–385.

Long, J. Scott and Jeremy Freese. 2014. *Regression Models for Categorical Dependent Variables Using Stata*, 3rd edn. College Station, TX: Stata Press.

Lord Ashcroft. 2016. 'The New Blueprint. The Conservative Agenda in Post-Brexit Britain'. 5 September. Available online: lordashcroftpolls.com/2016/09/the-new-blueprint/

Lowenstein, Roger. 2008. *Buffett: The Making of an American Capitalist*. New York: Random House.

Lucas, Robert E. and Thomas J. Sargent. 1981. *Rational Expectations and Econometric Practice*. Minneapolis, MN: The University of Minnesota Press.

Lupia, Arthur. 2016. *Uninformed: Why People Know So Little about Politics and What We Can Do about It*. Oxford: Oxford University Press.

Lupia, Arthur and Mathew D. McCubbins. 1998. *The Democratic Dilemma: Can Citizens Learn What They Really Need to Know?* Cambridge: Cambridge University Press.

Lynch, Philip. 2019. 'The Conservative Party'. In *Parliament and Brexit*. The UK In a Changing Europe.

Mackuen, Michael D., Robert Erikson and James A. Stimson. 1989. 'Macropartisanship'. *American Political Science Review* 83: 1125–1142.

Maki, Uskali. 2009. *The Methodology of Positive Economics*. Cambridge: Cambridge University Press.

Malkiel, Burton. 1973. *A Random Walk Down Wall Street*. New York: W.W. Norton.

Manin, Bernard, Adam Przeworski and Susan C. Stokes. 1999. 'Elections and Representation'. In Adam Przeworski, Susan C. Stokes and Bernard Manin, eds., *Democracy, Accountability and Representation*. Cambridge: Cambridge University Press.

Mankiw, Gregory N. and David Romer, eds. 1991. *New Keynesian Economics, Volume 2: Coordination Failures and Real Rigidities*. Cambridge, MA: The MIT Press.

Mannheim, Karl. 1928. *The Problem of Generations: Essays on the Sociology of Knowledge*. London: Routledge.

Mark, Justin T., Brian B. Marion and Donald D. Hoffman. 2010. 'Natural Selection and Veridical Perceptions'. *Journal of Theoretical Biology* 66: 504–515.

Marquand, David. 1997. *Ramsey MacDonald*. London: Richard Cohen Books.

Mattinson, Deborah. 2020. *Beyond the Red Wall: Why Labour Lost, How the Conservatives Won and What Will Happen Next?* London: Biteback Publishing.

McAllister, Ian and Donley Studlar. 1992. 'Region and Voting in Britain 1979–1987: Territorial Polarization or Artifact?' *American Journal of Political Science* 36: 168–199.

McLachlan, Geoffrey J., Sharon X. Lee and Suren I. Rathnayake. 2019. 'Finite Mixture Models'. *Annual Review of Statistics and Its Application* 6: 355–378.

Menon, Anand and Alan Wager. 2021. '"The Long Goodbye": Brexit'. In Robert Ford, Tim Bale and Will Jennings, eds., *The British General Election of 2019*. London: Palgrave Macmillan.

Merrill, Samuel and Bernard Grofman. 1999. *A Unified Theory of Voting: Directional and Proximity Spatial Models*. Cambridge: Cambridge University Press.

Miller, William L. 1977. *Electoral Dynamics*. London: Macmillan.

Moore, Charles. 2020. *Margaret Thatcher Authorized Biography, Volume 3*. London: Penguin Books.

Morgan, Stephen L. and Christopher Winship. 2015. *Counterfactuals and Causal Inference*. Cambridge: Cambridge University Press.

Mudde, Cas and Cristóbal Rovira Kaltwasser. 2017. *Populism: A Very Short Introduction*. Oxford: Oxford University Press.

Murr, Andreas. 2011. 'Wisdom of Crowds? A Decentralised Election Forecasting Model That Uses Citizens' Local Expectations'. *Electoral Studies* 30: 771–783.

Muth, John A. 1961. 'Rational Expectations and the Theory of Price Movements'. *Econometrica* 19: 315–335.

Nannestad, Peter and Martin Paldam. 1994. 'The V-P Function: A Survey of the Literature on Vote and Popularity Functions After 25 Years'. *Public Choice* 79: 213–245.

National Centre for Social Research. 2016. 'What Do Voters Want from Brexit?' https://whatukthinks.org/eu/wp-content/uploads/2016/11/Analysis-paper-9-What-do-voters-want-from-Brexit.pdf

Neundorf, Anja and Richard Niemi. 2014. 'Beyond Political Socialization: New Approaches in Age, Period and Cohort Analysis'. *Electoral Studies* 33: 1–6.

Nie, Norman H., Jane Junn and Kenneth Stehlik-Barry. 1996. *Education and Democratic Citizenship in America*. Chicago: University of Chicago Press.

Norris, Pippa and Ronald Inglehart. 2019. *Cultural backlash: Trump, Brexit, and Authoritarian Populism*. Cambridge: Cambridge University Press.

Petrocik, John R. 1996. 'Issue Ownership in Presidential Elections, with a 1980 Case Study'. *American Journal of Political Science* 40: 825–850.

Pilling, S. and R. Cracknell. 2021. *UK Election Statistics 1918–2021: A Century of Elections*. London: House of Commons Library CBP7529.

Pimlott, Ben. 1992. *Harold Wilson*. London: Harper-Collins.

Pogrund, Gabriel and Patrick Maguire. 2020. *Left Out: The Inside Story of Labour Under Corbyn*. London: Penguin Random House

Pollard, Sidney. 1982. *The Wasting of the British Economy*. London: Croom Helm.

Popkin, Samuel L. 1991. *The Reasoning Voter: Communication and Persuasion in Presidential Campaigns*. Chicago: University of Chicago Press.

Popov, Vladimir and K. S. Jomo. 2018. 'Are Developing Countries Caching Up?' *Cambridge Journal of Economics* 43: 33–46.

Powell, G. Bingham and Guy D. Whitten. 1993. 'A Cross-National Analysis of Economic Voting: Taking Account of the Political Context'. *American Journal of Political Science* 37: 391–414.

Pulzer, Peter. 1967. *Political Representation and Elections in Britain*, London: Allen & Unwin.

Rayson, Steve. 2020. *The Fall of the Wall: 'The Labour Party No Longer Represents People Like Us'*. London: self-published.

Reif, Karlheinz and Hermann Schmidt. 1980. 'Nine Second-Order National Elections – A Conceptual Framework for the Analysis of European Election Results'. *European Journal of Political Research* 8: 3–44.

Reither, Eric A., Ryan K. Masters, Yang Claire Yang, Daniel A. Powers, Hui Zheng and Kenneth C. Land. 2015. 'Should age–period–cohort studies return to the methodologies of the 1970s?' *Social Science and Medicine* 128: 356–365.

Robinson, William. 1940. 'Ecological Correlations and the Behavior of Individuals'. *American Sociological Review* 3: 351–357.

Romei, V. and Strauss, D. 2021. 'UK Economists' Survey: Recovery Will Be Slower than in Peer Countries'. *Financial Times*, 3 January.

Romer, Paul. M. 1990. 'Endogenous Technological Change'. *Journal of Political Economy* 98: S71–S102.

Saia, A. 2017. 'Choosing the Open Sea: The Cost to the UK of Staying Out of the Euro'. *Journal of International Economics* 108: 82–98.

Sanders, David. 2000. 'The Real Economy and the Perceived Economy in Popularity Functions: How Much Do Voters Need to Know? A Study of British Data 1974–1997'. *Electoral Studies* 19: 275–294.

Sanders, David. 2017. 'The UK's Changing Party System: The Prospects for a Party Realignment at Westminster'. *Journal of the British Academy* 5: 91–124.

Sanders, David, Harold D. Clarke, Marianne C. Stewart and Paul Whiteley. 2008. 'The Endogeneity of Preferences in Spatial Models: Evidence from the 2005 British Election Study'. *Journal of Elections, Public Opinion and Parties* 18: 413–431.

Sarlvik, Bo and Ivor Crewe. 1983. *Decade of Dealignment: The Conservative Victory of 1979 and Electoral Trends in the 1970s*. New York: Cambridge University Press.

Shiller, Robert. 1989. *Market Volatility*. Cambridge, MA: The MIT Press.

Shiller, Robert. 2019. *Narrative Economics: How Stories Go Viral and Drive Major Economic Events*. Princeton, NJ: Princeton University Press.

Shiller, Robert. 2000. *Irrational Exuberance*. Princeton, NJ: Princeton University Press.

Shipman, T. 2017. *Fall Out: A Year of Political Mayhem*. London: William Collins.

Silver, Nate. 2012. *The Signal and the Noise: Why So Many Predictions Fail – but Some Don't*. New York: Penguin Books.

Simon, Herbert. 1957. 'A Behavioral Model of Rational Choice'. In Herbert Simon, *Models of Man, Social and Rational: Mathematical Essays on Rational Human Behavior in a Social Setting*. New York: Wiley.

Sims, Christopher. 1980. 'Macroeconomics and Reality'. *Econometrica* 48: 1–48.

Sivathasan, Chujan. 2021. 'How Strong Are Brexit Identities Now?' What UK Thinks Blog Post, 15 December. Available online: whatukthinks.org/eu/how-strong-are-brexit-identities-now/

Skidelsky, Robert. 2009. *Keynes: The Return of the Master*. London: Penguin Books.

Solobewska, Maria and Robert Ford. 2021. *Brexitland: Identity, Diversity and the Reshaping of British Politics*. Cambridge: Cambridge University Press.

Solow, Robert. 1957. 'Technical Change and the Aggregate Production Function'. *Review of Economics and Statistics* 39: 312–320.

Solow, Robert. 1970. *Growth Theory: An Exposition*. Oxford: Oxford University Press.

Soroka, Stuart. 2006. 'Good News and Bad News: Asymmetric Responses to Economic Information'. *Journal of Politics* 68: 372–385.

Soroka, Stuart and Stephen McAdams. 2015. 'News, Politics and Negativity'. *Political Communication* 32: 1–22.

Steil, Benn. 2013. *The Battle of Bretton Woods: John Maynard Keynes and Harry Dexter White and the Making of a New World Order*. Princeton NJ: Princeton University Press.

Stokes, Donald E. 1963. 'Spatial Models of Party Competition'. *American Political Science Review* 57: 368–377.

Stokes, Donald E. 1992. 'Valence Politics'. In Dennis Kavanagh, ed., *Electoral Politics*. Oxford: Clarendon Press.

Taleb, Nicholas. 2007. *The Black Swan: The Impact of the Highly Improbable*. London: Penguin.

Tett, Gillian. 2009. *Fool's Gold – How Unrestrained Greed Corrupted a Dream, Shattered Global Markets and Unleashed a Catastrophe*. London: Little Brown.

Tilley, James. 2002. 'Political Generations and Partisanship in the UK, 1964–1997'. *Journal of the Royal Statistical Society – Series A. Statistics in Society* 165: 121–135.

Timothy, Nick. 2020. *Remaking one nation: The future of conservatism*. John Wiley & Sons.

Traugott, Michael W. and John P. Katosh. 1979. 'Response Validity in Surveys of Voting Behavior'. *Public Opinion Quarterly* 43: 359–377.

Tsebelis, George. 1990. *Nested Games: Rational Choice in Comparative Politics*. Berkeley and Los Angeles: University of California Press.

Tsebelis, George. 2002. *Veto Players: How Political Institutions Work*. Princeton, NJ: Princeton University Press.

Urbinati, Nadia. 2005. 'Continuity and Rupture: The Power of Judgment in Democratic Representation'. *Constellations* 12: 194–222.

Urbinati, Nadia and Mark E. Warren. 2008. 'The Concept of Representation in Contemporary Democratic Theory'. *Annual Review of Political Science* 11: 387–412.

Uslaner, Eric, ed. 2018. *The Oxford Handbook of Social and Political Trust*. Oxford: Oxford University Press.

van der Brug, Wouter, Cees van der Eijk and Mark N. Franklin. 2007. *The Economy and the Vote: Economic Conditions and Elections in Fifteen Countries*. Cambridge: Cambridge University Press.

Verba, Sidney and Norman H. Nie. 1972. *Participation in America: Political Democracy and Social Equality*. New York: Harper & Row.

Verba, Sidney, Kay Schlozman and Henry E. Brady. 1995. *Voice and Equality: Civic Voluntarism in American Politics*. Cambridge: Harvard University Press.

Whitaker, Richard. 2019. 'The Labour Party'. In *Brexit and Parliament*. UK in a Changing Europe.

Whiteley, Paul. 2022. 'Rational Choice Theory and Political Participation', in Marco Guigni and Maria Grasso, eds., *The Oxford Handbook of Political Participation*. Oxford: Oxford University Press.

Whiteley, Paul and Harold D. Clarke. 2020. 'Forecasting the Economic Consequences of Brexit'. In Richard Rose, ed., *How Referendums Challenge European Democracy: Brexit and Beyond*. London: Palgrave Macmillan.

Whiteley, Paul, Harold D. Clarke, David Sanders and Marianne C. Stewart. 2013. *Affluence, Austerity and Electoral Change in Britain*. Cambridge: Cambridge University Press.

Whiteley, Paul, Harold D. Clarke, David Sanders and Marianne C. Stewart. 2016. 'Hunting the Snark: A Reply to "Re-Evaluating Valence Models of Political Choice"'. *Political Science Research and Methods* 4: 221–240.

Whiteley, Paul and Ann-Kristin Kölln. 2019. 'How Do Different Sources of Partisanship Influence Government Accountability in Europe?' *International Political Science Review* 40: 502–517.

Whiteley, Paul, Monica Poletti, Paul Webb and Tim Bale. 2019. 'Oh Jeremy Corbyn! Why Did Labour Membership Soar after the 2017 General Election?' *British Journal of Politics and International Relations* 21: 80–98.

Whiteley, Paul, Patrick Seyd and Harold D. Clarke. 2021. 'Labour Party: Leadership Lacking'. In Nicholas Allen and John Bartle, eds., *Breaking the Deadlock: Britain at the Polls 2019*. Manchester: Manchester University Press.

Wlezien, Christopher, Mark N. Franklin and Daniel Twiggs. 1997. 'Economic Perceptions and Vote Choice: Disentangling the Endogeneity'. *Political Behavior* 19: 7–17.

Yang, Claire and Kenneth Land. 2013. *Age-Period-Cohort Analysis*. New York: Chapman and Hall.

Index